UNAPOLOGETIC

A Guide for Defending Your Christian Convictions

Brian D. Seagraves

Published by Acacia Books LLC
874 Piney Village Loop,
Tallahassee, FL 32311

Printed in the United States of America

First Edition: October 2015

10 9 8 7 6 5 4 3 2 1

CONTENTS

ACKNOWLEDGMENTS

Thank you to my wife, Patricia, for her support and understanding on this long project; my mother, Betty, for her encouragement and proofreading; Marvin "AJ" Rhodes for a detailed critique of both content and character that went well beyond what was requested; and to Vicki Rhodes, for the off-handed comment one night that led to the creation of this book.

Thank you to Hampton Keathley for his friendship, mentorship, and encouragement to learn and teach apologetics.

Thank you to Thomasville Road Baptist Church in Tallahassee, Florida for the honor and opportunity of teaching this material in both high school and adult ministries.

INTRODUCTION

Let's see if this sounds like you: You're a Christian with all of the traditional convictions that accompany that, but nonetheless, you don't feel totally comfortable or equipped to enter into conversations with non-believers when topics of faith arise. Well, you're not alone. I have been there too, and so many of your fellow churchgoers find themselves in the same situation. It's not that they don't have a desire to stand up for the gospel, it's simply that they do not have the necessary tools to aid in their efforts.

This book is for such people. It will take you through a range of topics, and by the end, you will have learned how to handle the popular and difficult topics that arise in our increasingly secular culture — questions like "Does God exist?" "Is the Bible true?" "Does truth exist?" "Is it hateful to oppose same-sex marriage and homosexuality?"

If you haven't known how to respond when you've been called "intolerant" for your Bible-based convictions, this book is for you. If you've felt trapped when asked if you "take the Bible literally," this book is for you.

Sometimes Christians are portrayed as being dull or unintelligent by the world today. And, some are! However, the Christian position — our view of the world — is intelligent and intelligible. It is capable of being defended. Christians have the strong position, and my goal is to give you the confidence and tools to act from this position of strength.

This book is not written for the academic, nor is it intended to exhaustively cover the topics it discusses. There are many other books dedicated exclusively to each of the many topics that this book will cover, and I will include references for these so that you can learn more about the topics you find interesting.

Perhaps you're not a Christian. Maybe you're an atheist, or simply a Christian with many doubts. I can empathize with your position, for I have been there, too. Even though I was raised in the church, by the time I got into my early twenties, I had amassed a long list of weighty questions. I doubted that God was good. I doubted that the Bible was accurate. I doubted that God even existed.

I was drowning under the pressure of seeing my entire worldview fall apart. Yet, I still taught a small group Bible study and told no one of my doubts. I didn't think others would understand, and I was scared to harm their faith. Maybe this sounds like you or someone you know. If so, I can empathize.

Well, I finally realized that I couldn't live with the tension, with the doubts. So, I went searching for answers. I read book after book — some by atheists and some by Christians — all while trying to find the Truth, whatever it was.

You're probably guessing that I arrived back at the Christian position (since I wrote this book), and you'd be right! However, I tell this account of my past so that you will understand that the position I currently hold did not come easily to me — there was a time when I didn't see how it could possibly be true. Only after a careful examination of the evidence did I arrive back at Christianity — this time with much more *conviction* than before.

Sadly, doubt is usually taboo in the church today. When it's time to go around the circle and share prayer requests or what's "on your heart", no one feels comfortable telling their small group that they're doubting that God exists or they're doubting that God is good. If you're such a person, I hope this book provides some answers and calms some of your doubts. We are often the hardest critics we will encounter.

If you know a person who struggles with doubt, I pray that, after reading this book, you will be more equipped to help nurture them back to a healthy life of truth and trust in Christ.

1

WHY "UNAPOLOGETIC?"

Being unapologetic generally has a bad connotation. People do not think highly of others who can't bring themselves to apologize when they're wrong. In fact, there are those who refuse to apologize because they think that it's a sign of weakness. Obviously, this type of being "unapologetic" is not befitting of a Christian, who should be the first to admit when he/she is wrong.

However, there are many Christians today who almost feel like they need to apologize for their beliefs when they're confronted or questioned. They lack confidence and have little strength of conviction, and consequently, they rarely enter into conversations about their faith or values. However, we should all desire to continually grown in our ability to represent Christ well.

IN WHAT WAY SHOULD CHRISTIANS BE "UNAPOLOGETIC"?

Christians need to live with confidence that the core claims of Christianity are true. Nothing bogs a person down more than a lack of conviction, and far too many Christians today don't know the bedrock truths of the faith or how to defend or explain them to others.

Being unapologetic as a Christian means living out your convictions with confidence because you have examined the evidence and found it compelling. You have surveyed the criticisms and found them wanting. You believe that Jesus of Nazareth saw the world as it really is.

UNAPOLOGETICALLY APOLOGETIC

It's ironic to say that Christians should be unapologetic because the area of Christian study that gives answers and defenses for the Christian position is called "Apologetics." In that regard, this is a book about apologetics, and after you've read it, you will be ready to be "Unapologetically Apologetic."

2

HOW DO PEOPLE VIEW THE WORLD?

In order to better understand the people you speak with, it's helpful to have a way of categorizing their beliefs. This will allow you to quickly recall some conversation starters and questions. We actually do this all the time. For instance, when I'm around a friend who likes football, I know to ask, "How did your team play yesterday?" and not "How about that new art exhibit downtown?" The same idea applies to the topics we're concerned with here. As an example, if a coworker mentions that he doesn't think there is a god, you wouldn't want to reply with a comment that assumes the existence of God such as, "God actually became a man and died for you." This is true, but unhelpful in your situation. Instead, you need to be able to meet him where he is. We'll get to this a little later.

Christian professor and philosopher Ronald Nash says, "A worldview is a set of beliefs about the most important issues in life." These issues include truth, God, morality, evil, where we came from, and what happens when we die. A worldview is like the pair of glasses through which we view everything around us.

THE MAJOR WORLDVIEWS

The following statements of each worldview describe the average person who holds each view. You should not assume all atheists view everything the same way, just as not all Christians hold the same views. These descriptions are only intended to give you a starting place for identifying a person's worldview. However, the best way to understand what a specific person believes is by having a friendly conversation with them. Remember, everyone is unique!

Theism is the view that there is one God who created everything and is personally involved with his creation; there is objective morality; evil exists, and is the result of rebellion against God; life began when God created it; and, after death, there is some form of afterlife. *Examples*: Christianity, Judaism, and Islam.

The theist makes the claim, "God exists," and he should be prepared to defend that claim using evidence just as the New Testament writers did.

Atheism is the view that God does not exist. It is *not* the view that one is not sure about God's existence, as this would be *agnosticism*. The atheistic worldview doesn't just deny the existence of God, but of anything that is spiritual/non-material. This is also known as naturalism (only natural/material things exist). Morality is totally subjective; evil is also subjectively defined; the universe came to be, uncaused, and out of nothing. Life developed through Darwinian evolution; there is no life after death.

Like the theist, the atheist also makes a claim to know something; he claims to know that "God does not exist." He too should prove his case and supply evidence to support this bold claim. Whoever makes a claim must support it. Initially, it isn't your job to defend your position when someone makes a contrary claim; it is *their* responsibility to support their argument with evidence, not just more claims, and you must hold them to that.

Pantheism is the view that everything is god. Good and evil are just illusions; since everything is actually one thing, you can't have opposites like good and evil. Man is also god, and his goal is enlightenment. Reincarnation follows death. This is the worldview category of many eastern religions (Hinduism and Buddhism), modern "New Age" teaching, and Christian Science.

VIEWS ON TRUTH AND MORALITY

A person's worldview will affect how they understand and act in all areas of their life -- whether they are more likely to cheat on their taxes, help their neighbor, or answer damning questions honestly. The conclusion about whether morality and truth are objective or subjective will affect every type of person from the scientist, to the school teacher, to the criminal.

Objective morality says that, if an action is wrong for an individual in a certain set of circumstances, then it is wrong for anyone in those circumstances. In other words, the moral quality of an action (whether it's "good or bad") is dependent on what the action is, not who's doing it. Moral statements don't just reflect how a person feels about an action. For example, if it's wrong for me to take the life of an innocent human being without proper justification, then it's wrong for anyone to do it, whether a person agrees or not.

If it's wrong for me to lie for selfish gain, then it's wrong for everyone to do it. And, if it's *right* to lie to protect the lives of others — think Nazis at the door when you're hiding Jews upstairs — then it's *right* for everyone to do it in those same circumstances.

A second and popular view in secular culture is that morality is **subjective**. In other words, the moral quality of an action depends solely on who is doing the action (the *"subject"*) and how they feel about it. This view is also called *moral relativism* because morality is *relative* to the person making the claim. In this way, an action could be right for me, in a certain set of circumstances, but wrong for you in those same circumstances. This is the "everyone decides what is right and wrong for themselves" view. On relativism, the following is a perfectly acceptable point of view: "It may be wrong for you to steal my computer, but it isn't wrong for me to steal yours." If everyone is allowed to decide for themselves, then we can't tell someone they're wrong. This is covered in more detail later, but hopefully, you can see that this view actually self-destructs and isn't able to be consistently put into practice.

You can pick up on a person's worldview by simply paying attention when they talk; you'll be surprised at what you can learn! For instance, you may overhear an elementary school teacher lamenting about her underprivileged students who get into trouble — trouble she blames on their low socioeconomic status. What is this teacher's worldview? Well, she may believe that children are basically good, and that society and rough physical and socio-economic surroundings "make" them misbehave. However, such a view doesn't account for why privileged children also misbehave, or how anyone became "bad" in the first place.

7

On this view, people are basically good and society is a bad, corrupting influence. However, it doesn't make any sense to say that when you get enough good people together they become bad. It has been my experience that this view is prevalent today, though most people never realize that this doesn't make sense.

VIEWS ON IMMATERIAL THINGS

One of the major distinguishing marks of a worldview is its beliefs about immaterial realities (things that you can't experience or examine with the five senses; things that are non-physical). In fact, almost all of the differences between atheism and theism are rooted in how each worldview considers the immaterial.

Earlier, I mentioned that most atheists are also naturalists — as a rule, they don't believe anything supernatural exists. Such a deeply held commitment will affect all areas of a person's life. A naturalist has no reason to see intrinsic worth and dignity in people, since there is no soul and no creator — man is just slightly more evolved than other animals and is actually an animal himself. Thankfully, many naturalists do value human life, though they act inconsistently in doing so.

The glasses of naturalism will also color how such a person evaluates the evidence for the Bible. New Testament documents must be discarded as erroneous, since they describe events such as miracles, the soul, resurrections from the dead, angels, and other non-material beings. However, the evidence for these claims has usually not been evaluated on its merits. No, it has been summarily dismissed because of the *bias* of the naturalist.

These events don't fit in the world as naturalists see it and understand it. They believe that no supernatural things exist. So, anyone claiming to have witnessed a supernatural event must automatically be mistaken. I hope you see that this is actually an intellectually dishonest way of evaluating data. We should never dismiss data simply because it doesn't fit with our preconceptions. Yet, this is what atheists frequently do.

There is nothing logically contradictory about there being a *supernatural realm and a natural realm. Now, a naturalist might say that science has "shown there is no God." This phrase has a close cousin: "Science has found no evidence of the supernatural." These are claims that I dissect in the Truth chapter. But for now it should suffice to say that, as most science textbooks point out, science is a process that tells us about the *natural* world. It makes no sense to expect this naturalistic, empirical process to also tell us about the supernatural — it's simply not equipped to do so.

Let's look at some examples of immaterial things to help make this concept clearer.

The Mind

The mind — also called the soul or "self" — isn't made of material; you can't touch, taste, feel, see, or hear a soul. The mind is separate from the brain. Your brain is a physical organ in your head that works seamlessly with your mind (barring injury) to provide *you* with powerful reasoning abilities (among others things). But, just who is that italicized "you" in the previous sentence? Is it simply an organ, like the atheist would say, since they deny the existence of the mind? Or is there more to *you* than your physical parts?

If humans are just physical and don't have a mind or soul, then they are not more valuable — have no more intrinsic worth — than any other animal. This is why some people have no problem with abortion. When your worldview says that immaterial things (like souls) don't exist, it's hard to find any intrinsic worth in an undeveloped fetus. So, why not just get rid of that "inconvenience?"

Morality

While we looked at this in detail above, it's worth noting that morality isn't physical, which is why the atheist is being consistent when he says that objective morality doesn't exist.

The Laws of Logic

The laws of logic[1] are not material. When an atheist says that "God does not exist," he is using the 2nd law of logic (the Law of Non-Contradiction) because he thinks that it is impossible for God to both *exist* and *not exist* at the same time. He is also using the Law of Excluded middle, which says that there are only two options: God *exists*, or God *does not exist.*

So, when atheists try to use logic and reason to attempt to prove how immaterial things can't exist, they're using one of the very immaterial realities that they're trying to disprove!

9

Mathematics

While math can accurately express and predict the physical world, math itself isn't material. Yet, atheists have no trouble using math.

A Summary of Immaterial Things

What we've seen here should be pretty enlightening: A *consistent* atheist/materialist must say that the mind/soul, morality, the laws of logic, and math do not exist. The atheistic worldview is a jagged pill to swallow, once you understand what it really entails. However, what you will likely find is that many atheists (and indeed holders of many different worldviews) are quite *inconsistent*. They want to say that morality doesn't exist, but logic does; the soul is an illusion, but math is real, for example.

HOW SHOULD WE CHOOSE A WORLDVIEW?

A worldview *should* accurately describe reality. Therefore, we should choose a worldview because it makes the most sense of the evidence — of reality itself — when viewed with an unbiased eye. *We should not choose a worldview simply because we like it.* This seems foreign in a 21st century U.S. culture where, "If it feels good, do it" is the prevailing philosophy of the day. When you're talking with people of different worldviews, encourage them to choose the view that best fits the evidence, not just the one they like. Wouldn't you want to view reality as it actually exists?

There are things about Christianity that I don't like. I don't like the idea of people being punished in hell forever (Matthew 25:31-46). I don't like that Jesus, who was guilty of no sin, had to be punished for what I justly deserved — that isn't fair at all. However, not liking something doesn't make it not true.

Strength of character demands that we don't pretend that unpleasant things don't exist. Instead, we should address them head on. The world, accurately viewed, is full of unpleasant realities like suffering and death, but they are realities we must grapple with, nonetheless.

Christianity involves making comprehensive changes to how I would otherwise live. I constantly fight the instinct I have to be selfish and put myself first. It strikes me that it would make some things much easier if I were to hold a worldview where *I* defined good and evil. However, I am not a Christian because I like everything about Christianity. I am a Christian in part because the Christian view of the world — of reality — makes the most sense, and in the following chapters, I will build the case for the Christian worldview.

I've heard it said that worldviews are like puzzles. Some people are trying to put their puzzle together with pieces that are from different puzzles, and they just don't fit. If you can't live in your own worldview, or you have to keep making exceptions and allowances for things that just don't fit, maybe you're holding the *wrong* worldview.

WHAT WE LEARNED

- ❖ Everyone has their own unique collection of beliefs.
- ❖ The best way to know exactly what someone believes is simply to ask them, since most people like to talk about themselves.
- ❖ The main worldviews are:
  - Atheism: the belief that god does not exist.
  - Theism: the belief that one God does exist.
  - Pantheism: the belief that everything is god.
- ❖ The main views on morality, by example:
  - Objective: The unjustified taking of innocent life is always wrong. Note that this allows for killing in some situations. This would condemn murder and abortion, and allow for self-defense.
  - Subjective: Killing is wrong for me, but it might be acceptable for you.

3

DOES TRUTH EXIST?

In recent years our culture has moved from primarily valuing facts to valuing experience and emotion, especially with regards to moral and religious considerations. This is evident in the commercials that are aired on TV and on the Web. In the 1950s, it was very common to see people in white lab coats giving you facts about why one product was better than another. White lab coats were a sign of honesty and accuracy, and in fact, they still are today. I have attended the "coating" ceremonies for a few doctors and physician assistants, and when they get "coated", they are told that people will respect them, in part, because of their white coat.

However, more and more of today's marketing is not based on fact, at least not primarily; it's based on emotional and experiential appeal. We see less of, *"It cleans 72% better than its closest competitor"* and more of *"His reputation is expanding faster than the universe. He is... the most interesting man in the world."* Dos Equis made humorous and entertaining commercials about "the most interesting man" who doesn't always drink beer, but when he does, he prefers Dos Equis. However, these commercials tell us nothing about the quality of the product; they only give us a positive experience and memory to associate with it.

So, what does all of this have to do with truth? Well, this noticeable shift in advertising technique parallels a change in how the majority of Western culture views truth. Some popular claims about truth today are:

❖ "Truth doesn't exist."

- ❖ *"You can't know truth."*
- ❖ *"Only science can give us truth."*
- ❖ *"You shouldn't judge."* or "You shouldn't force your morality on others."

I'm sure that you've heard at least some of those before, and you may have even said one or two yourself, though hopefully not!

THE LAW OF NON-CONTRADICTION

Before we examine each of the aforementioned claims, we need to formalize something that many seem to know and take for granted - The Law of Non-Contradiction. This fundamental law of logic states:

A thing cannot be what it is, and what it is not, at the same time, and in the same way.

In the novel *A Tale of Two Cities*, Charles Dickens says:

It was the best of times, it was the worst of times, it was the age of wisdom, it was the age of foolishness, it was the epoch of belief, it was the epoch of incredulity, it was the season of Light, it was the season of Darkness, it was the spring of hope, it was the winter of despair, we had everything before us, we had nothing before us, we were all going direct to Heaven, we were all going direct the other way.[1]

One way to understand this is that Dickens has gone to the trouble of writing a paragraph full of nonsense, because every couplet is a contradiction. However, this view seems unlikely. We know that it can't be the *best of times* at the same time it is *the worst of times*. At least, it can't be those two things at the same time *and in the same way*. Our innate knowledge of the Law of Non-Contradiction makes this clear to us. It could be the best of times in one way and the worst of times in another way. For instance, war time could be the worst of times, but the close friendships formed while fighting could make it the best of times.

Let's look at how the law applies to the four popular claims listed above.

"Truth Doesn't Exist"

This is a very simple assertion. Like *all* assertions, it can either be true or false. So, is it true that truth doesn't exist? If it is true, then the statement is wrong; it contradicts itself, because a statement can't be both true and false at the same time. On the other hand, if it's false that "truth doesn't exist," then we shouldn't believe this statement because it's wrong.

This isn't a play on words. The person saying this statement thinks that it's true, or they wouldn't believe it. But, their belief in its truthfulness refutes the claim itself! They believe that it's true, but they're saying truth doesn't exist. *Truth has to exist in order for that person to be correct.*

This type of claim is called a self-refuting claim — the claim applies to itself, and the claim contradicts itself. Let's look at some additional examples: "I can't speak a word of English" is self-refuting, as is "There are no English sentences longer than three words." Both of these claims apply to themselves and also contradict themselves.

Here's another interesting point: Some people have written books that say truth doesn't exist. But, if truth doesn't exist, then their books can't be true either. So, why would anyone read them and take them seriously, much less give the author their money for pages full of nonsense?

All of this might be difficult to grasp, and it is somewhat dry. However, this chapter is *extremely* important. If we can't show that actual objective truth exists, then we don't have a hope of proving the truthfulness of the Bible when we're talking to a non-Christian who says, "Truth doesn't exist." So, if the concept in this section is foreign to you, please try reading it again — it's important!

"You Can't Know Truth"

This claim is even more popular than the first. Many people say that we can't know what is actually right and wrong or that we can't know if religious/spiritual statements are true. Before we address that, I want to point out that this assertion is a law-breaker, just like the first one. Let's look at how it violates the Law of Non-Contradiction.

This claim can either be true of false. For something to be true, it simply needs to accurately describe "the state of being the case."[2] So, is it true that you can't know truth? If it is true that you can't know truth, then this statement is false; it contradicts itself! If it is false that we can't know truth, then we should disregard it, as we do all falsehoods.

The belief that we can't know truth is one of the contributing factors to the *new tolerance* that says: all beliefs, behaviors, cultural practices, and religions are equally valid and correct — none is better than another. This belief is also behind comments like "everyone needs to decide for themselves what is right and wrong" and "something can be wrong in our culture but right in another one" and "Christianity is just one of many spiritual truths."

Everyone can and does know moral truth, though. In Romans 2:15 Paul says, "...the work of the law is written in their hearts, as their conscience bears witness...." Here, he is referring to the Gentiles, who did not have the Mosaic law that the Jews did. Nonetheless, these Gentiles knew right from wrong because of their conscience and the innate moral knowledge that we all have as a result of being created in the image of God (Genesis 1:26-27).

This is evident in the way people talk. For instance, if someone's iPhone gets stolen, that person will speak as though something *objectively* wrong was done to them. They won't just say, "I don't like it" or "It's wrong for me to steal, but it might be okay for someone else to do it." No, that person will feel wronged and will most likely report the crime to the police.

But how should we expect an atheist to react, based on their worldview? Well, atheists believe that only material or natural things exist — nothing supernatural exists. Additionally, the naturalists' world view is rooted in evolution, and they believe it explains how we came to be in our current state of development and society. Humans are just more evolved animals. So, is it wrong when one stronger animal kills a weaker animal? No. That is survival of the fittest. Following that worldview, should it be wrong for a more fit homo sapiens to take a less fit homo sapiens' iPhone? No. If any naturalist complains otherwise, he or she is borrowing from the Christian worldview, which says that there is objective right and wrong, and might does not make right.

Most non-Christians cannot actually live with the consequences of their own worldview. They end up borrowing from ours. Ideals such as justice, morality, human dignity, and human rights make no sense in and cannot be explained by a naturalistic world view. Only a theistic worldview makes sense of these concepts.

"Only Science Can Give Us Truth"

The shift toward experience that I talked about at the beginning of this chapter shouldn't be understood to mean that people don't care about facts; they do. But, more and more people think that science is the only source of fact, and we can't know anything in an area that science doesn't speak to. There are two major problems with this view.

First, the claim "Only science can give us truth" isn't a scientific claim. There is no laboratory experiment that could be done to determine this. Science, as a process, can never confirm this claim. So, this is another example of a self-refuting claim.

Second, science is a process consisting of observation, hypothesis, prediction, experimentation, analysis, conclusion, and report of results. So, when you hear, "Science says that the fetus isn't a person" you need to call foul. Science can't *say* anything; only people say things. Scientists – people like you and me – can construct flawed definitions based on biases and agendas. Science, as a process, creates data, but this data is only as good as its premises, interpretation, and application. In order for science to generate truth, it needs to start with some initial non-scientific truths such as the laws of logic. Science is also based on integrity, a moral principle. It requires data to be reported honestly and accurately. So, you can't do science well if the only tools and truths at your disposal are scientific ones.

"You Shouldn't Judge"

This statement and the related statement *"You shouldn't force your morality on others"* are extremely popular in the church and in the secular world. After all, Jesus said, *"Do not judge"*, right? He did say that, but he and Paul also said much more on the topic. Most of the time people cite the above fragment of one verse, without also reading the paragraph that gives context to it.

> Do not judge so that you will not be judged. For by the standard you judge you will be judged, and the measure you use will be the measure you receive. Why do you see the speck in your brother's eye, but fail to see the beam of wood in your own? Or how can you say to your brother, 'Let me remove the

speck from your eye,' while there is a beam in your own? You hypocrite! First remove the beam from your own eye, and then you can see clearly to remove the speck from your brother's eye. (Matthew 7:1–4)

The thrust of this passage speaks to avoiding hypocritical judgments. You know, the "do as I say, not as I do" types of judgments. Jesus doesn't tell us not to judge, quite the contrary! In verse 5, he says, *"First remove the beam from your own eye, and then you can see clearly to remove the speck from your brother's eye."* We're to take care of our issue, the beam, that is similar to our brother's issue, the speck. If your friend is living in sin, it's not loving to him (or to God) not to speak up and point out how it's wrong. If you had fallen in a pit, you'd want your friends to help you out. Our sin is much worse than a physical pit, yet, all too often, our pride keeps us from letting others help us out of our spiritual pit.

Just a few verses later in Matthew 7:15, Jesus also encouraged us to be on the lookout for false teachers. That involves making a judgment. You can't call someone a "false teacher" without making a moral judgment. Hopefully, this clears up the confusion and incorrect usage of one of the most quoted verses in the Bible (Matthew 7:1).

What you may, and hopefully did, notice was that the telling someone *"you shouldn't judge"* is itself a judgment. When someone tells you that you shouldn't judge, they have just judged you. The same is true for *"You shouldn't force your morality on others."* This is someone's moral view, and they're trying to force it on you – the very thing they're telling you not to do.

HOW AND WHY

The process used on each of the above statements is quite simple! We just apply the claim to itself, and see what happens. Try and think of some other self-refuting statements. The hard part about all of this is remembering to think critically about commonplace claims. Since so much of our educational system is built around remembering, not understanding or analyzing, it can be difficult to retrain yourself to question what's told to you, but you must make the effort.

Be careful not to allow anyone to captivate you through an empty, deceitful philosophy that is according to human traditions and the elemental spirits of the world, and not according to Christ. (Colossians 2:8)

Here, Paul warns us to be careful. How many of us would say that we are careful when listening to others? All too many times we simply absorb what a speaker, pastor, scientist, or news anchor is saying. We are not careful. This is also a problem in the church. Have you noticed that many sermons today seem to be teaching human traditions, pop psychology, and simple morality instead of Christ-centered messages? We *must* practice integrating caution into our learning process.

This doesn't mean we should be afraid of new ideas. Quite the contrary. We need to be open to listening to and evaluating new ideas, even ones that challenge our current ones. One of two things will happen. The first is that we will learn that we have held an incorrect view. False views need to be pruned for our good, just like a gardener prunes flowers to keep them looking their best. The second thing that can happen is that we identify this new view as wrong, and then we determine the best defense against it.

If you don't take one of these two paths and you simply leave a new view unaddressed when confronted with it, you have done yourself a grave disservice. You have potentially missed out on an opportunity to correct your current misunderstanding of something, or you have failed to learn how to defend against such an idea in the future. We shouldn't find either of these options to be acceptable.

LACK OF CONVICTION

Conviction is one of the casualties of viewing truth as subjective. You may have heard people say something like, "I think abortion is wrong — I wouldn't do it. But, I think each person needs to decide for themselves." Such a person just admitted that they think murder is happening every day, and they are fine with other people deciding that it's okay! Such a person is most likely a *moral relativist* (someone who thinks the morality of a decision is decided by the person doing the action).

Relativists characteristically lack conviction because it's hard for them to act with the assurance of belief, since they don't think anyone can know things for certain. People don't fight for ideals when they aren't convinced, when they're not convicted. Sadly, this mindset has infected the church too, and some Christians are saying things such as, "We shouldn't try to impose our views on others." They lack conviction. For some reason, they have lost touch with the grounding of Christianity — the Bible.

As God's inspired revelation to us, the Bible is the best source of truth we have. It accurately describes reality and the human condition. It is a book of history in that it describes events that either happened or did not. Those events can't just be true for me and not for you — they're either true for everyone or for no one. For instance, it's just absurd for a U.S. citizen to say, "It isn't true for me that Barack Obama is the President." Obama is either the President for all of us or for none of us. In the same way, if the events in the Bible are accurate, then Jesus *is* God, and as God, his instructions about morality are binding on all of us, whether we like them and agree with them or not. If someone really believes that, conviction is sure to follow.

Even as a Bible-believing conservative, I struggled to connect my Christian convictions with my actions on a very important issue. I thought abortion was wrong, but I didn't think it was the government's job to control it. However, I wasn't of the opinion that, "A person needs to decide for themselves." I wasn't a relativist, but I did lack conviction on this issue. My political ideologies were put ahead of God's heart for the defenseless, unborn children that bear his image. The Bible wasn't my foundation for truth on this issue, and my incorrect action flowed from that.

If you find yourself lacking conviction on issues of morality, take a long and hard introspective look at how you view truth. Does the rightness or wrongness of an action depend on how you feel about it, or does it flow from the truth of Scripture?

WHAT WE LEARNED

In this chapter we learned that:
- ❖ Western Culture has shifted to primarily valuing experience over truth in areas of mortality and religion.
- ❖ Four of today's most popular claims are all self-refuting — they apply to themselves and also contradict themselves:
  - ▪ "Truth doesn't exist."
  - ▪ "We can't know truth."
  - ▪ "Science is the only source of truth."
  - ▪ "It's wrong to make moral judgments."

- ❖ The concept of truth is foundational to being able to talk about the truthfulness of the gospel.
- ❖ We must be careful in how we think.
- ❖ The Bible is the best source of truth.

4

IS THERE A GOD?

This question has haunted many a man for centuries. It has led some like Pascal to say it is better to bet on God existing rather than not existing. No one wants to waste their life living for and because of someone who isn't there. But, on the other hand, if God exists and you aren't on his side, you're probably going to be in the hot seat. In this chapter, we're going to look at some proofs for God's existence.

Let's start by considering the Holy Spirit. Can the Holy Spirit be used as proof of the existence of God? The hymn "He Lives" says, "You ask me how I know He lives: He lives within my heart." Many Christians will say they just "know" that there's a God because of a feeling they have. I don't think such people are being untruthful. In fact, I'm convinced that people do have strong feelings and experiences as a result of their belief in God.

But, non-Christians also can have moving experiences as a result of believing in their god(s). If you're a Christian, and a Muslim co-worker shares with you that Allah appeared to her in a dream, and she is now totally convinced that Islam is true, are you going to be persuaded that Islam is the one true religion? No, you aren't. Likewise, we Christians should not expect non-believers to be convinced by our testimonies or experiences.

This example illustrates that experience and feelings might help us *know* things, but they cannot help us *show* other people. You can't connect your mind with someone else's and let them share your experiences. You need to reply with something objective — something that can be as easily accessed by the other person as it can be by you.

That brings us to the Bible. Many Christians will say that God exists because the Bible says he does. Then, when asked why they believe the Bible, they'll reply that God wrote it. How do they know God wrote it, the Bible tells them, etc. This is a circular argument, and I'll address it in the next chapter. For now, it will suffice to say that the Bible can be helpful in learning about God, but it can also introduce a fair amount of baggage into conversations. If you're talking to an atheist, you need to convince them *that a god exists*, before you can convince them of *who that God is*.

In order to do that, we can't rely on feeling or emotion. We also can't rely on the Bible. We need to find the lowest common denominator of our shared beliefs — a shared foundation — which is often logic and science. You generally can't go wrong, when you're talking with an atheist, if you're putting credence in what science reveals about the world.

We're going to use logic and science in our arguments for the existence of God. I'm using the term "argument" in the way that philosophers use it: to refer to a series of statements (or premises) which lead to some conclusion. A good argument meets three criteria:
1. It must obey the rules of logic.
2. Its premises must be true.
3. Its premises must be more plausible than their opposites.

Disclaimer: I have tried to keep the content of this book as simple as it can be, while still being true and helpful. However, to some, this will be the most complicated chapter of the book. If you really struggle here, you can skip it. I would hate for you to miss out on the rest of the helpful chapters by getting discouraged here. That being said, what follows is the *best* argument for God's existence, and would be well worth your time and effort.

THE KALĀM COSMOLOGICAL ARGUMENT

The first argument we will look at is the Kalām Cosmological Argument that was developed by Islamic scholars between the 9th and 12th centuries as a positive empirical proof of the existence of God. You may be wondering why we're learning an Islamic argument. Remember, Islam, like Christianity, is a Theistic (belief in one personal God) religion, and as such, any philosophical argument for the existence of Allah is an argument for the existence of the Christian God, too.

You should find this easy to follow and remember. Here's how it goes:

1. Whatever begins to exist has a cause.
2. The universe began to exist.
3. Therefore, the universe had a cause.

I recommend that you stop here for a minute, and just repeat that a few times; try to commit it to memory.

This is a logical argument, and as long as the logic is valid and the premises are true, the conclusion *must* follow. One can't just disagree with the conclusion without showing how one or more of the premises are false or how the logic is invalid.

This is the same type of argument as the following:

1. All men are mortal.
2. Socrates is a man.
3. Therefore, Socrates is not mortal.

Would you agree with the above conclusion? I hope you see that it is *incorrect*. If all men are mortal, and Socrates is one of those men, then Socrates *must* be mortal too. That's how an argument like this works.

In the same way, since everything that begins to exist has a cause, and the universe began to exist, the universe must have had a cause. It is commonly agreed on by scientists that time itself and all matter came into existence at the big bang. Therefore, the cause of time and matter must be something *timeless* and *immaterial*. Since time started at the big bang, the cause must be timeless, and since no material existed before the big bang, material cannot have caused it.

But there's more. Whatever caused our universe to come into existence must be *intelligent* because the universe is extremely well-suited for sustaining life. The cause must be *personal*, because it chose to bring the universe into existence, and it must be very *powerful* in order to be able to accomplish the creation of the universe.

Now, what do most people call a timeless, immaterial, intelligent, personal, and powerful being? They call it "god." This is the reasonable conclusion that the Kalām Cosmological Argument demonstrates — that some god-like being created the universe.

It is also important to understand what this argument does and does not prove. It *doesn't* prove that god is good, and it doesn't prove

25

that this god is the God of the Bible. But it *does* prove that an all-powerful god exists.

Now that we understand where we're going to end up, let's start with the first premise, and look at how we can support it and give evidence for it.

Premise 1: Whatever Begins to Exist Has a Cause

There are a few ways of supporting this premise.

Something Does Not Come from Nothing

The typical atheist's position is that the universe came into existence uncaused and from nothing. But surely such an event is worse than magic! At least when a magician pulls a beautiful woman out of an empty box, you've got the magician and the box. This isn't the case with the universe. Before the universe existed, no other physical thing existed. I don't think anyone *truly* believes that objects can pop into existence uncaused and from nothing. No one I've ever met has been afraid that, while they were away from home, a gorilla would pop into their living room, uncaused and from nothing, and ransack their house.

We have never experienced something coming from nothing. When we hear a knock at the door, we don't say, "Maybe the knock knocked itself." We intrinsically know that events have causes. Now sometimes, skeptics will point out that, in physics, certain particles come into existence from nothing. But, on these theories, "nothing" is actually the quantum vacuum. And by vacuum, they don't mean "absence of everything." The vacuum they are referring to is actually a sea of fluctuating energy governed by physical laws and having a physical structure. That's hardly "nothing." One could rightly ask, "Where did this energy come from?" Just be aware of the "alternate" definitions at play here.

Christians are often criticized as having "blind faith" — believing crazy things without evidence. But the atheist's belief is worse than this; indeed, it is worse than magic — a belief that all matter and time just popped into existence "from nothing, by nothing, and for nothing," as atheist Quentin Smith has said[1]. People who hold such a belief can never accuse Christians of the greater irrationality, for what could be more irrational than this!

If Something Can Come from Nothing, Why Don't Things Pop into Existence All of the Time?

Why don't ponies and pastries and Pavarotti pop into existence from nothing? Why do only universes get to come into existence without causes? And, what makes "nothingness" choose universes over pastries? Nothingness can't choose one thing over another because nothingness has no properties and is a total absence of everything.

Often, at this point, atheists will [often smugly] ask, "Well then, who created God?" There are a few ways to handle this. The first is by pointing out that the first premise of the argument does not say "everything has a cause." It says, "Everything *that begins to exist* has a cause." Second, you can point out that neither of you think that God was created, so there's little use in discussing it. The atheist doesn't think God was created because he doesn't think God exists, and the Christian doesn't think God was created because he believes that God is eternal.

Since God is eternal, he has no cause. The atheist may try to criticize this, but it's worth noting that the traditional atheistic perspective was that the universe was also eternal and uncaused. However, we now have excellent scientific evidence that the universe is not eternal and did, in fact, have a cause. We'll look at that evidence in the very next section.

The first premise is constantly confirmed by our observation and experience, and it is never contradicted. It's difficult to understand how a rational person would find it plausible to believe that universes can pop into existence uncaused and from nothing. Both reason and the evidence are stacked against such a view.

Premise 2: The Universe Began to Exist

We will look at several proofs for premise two — scientific ones first and then philosophical ones. This premise used to be the most debated of the two, but in recent years it seems to be more accepted than premise one.

The Universe Is Expanding

For the majority of human history, people have believed that the universe was fixed in size, not growing or shrinking. In 1917, when

Albert Einstein began to apply his General Theory of Relativity to the universe, he believed the universe to be fixed too. However, his equations pointed to a universe that was expanding or contracting — not one that was fixed.

In order to "solve" this problem, Einstein added a "fudge" factor to his equations — a constant to make it so that, on paper, the universe wasn't getting bigger or smaller; it was just staying the same size.

Only twelve years later, in 1929 at the Mt. Wilson Observatory Edwin Hubble was looking through his telescope, and he made a remarkable discovery: He saw that the light from distant, starry objects was more red than it should have been. This "red shift", as it is called, is due to the light waves stretching as distant objects move away from us.

We don't see this phenomenon with only a few far-away objects; we see it with *all* of them. At first blush, this might make it seem as if we're the center of the universe, since everything appears to be moving away from us. However, we are not the center, but it is actually space itself that is expanding. So, from a certain point of view, the galaxies in the universe are not actually moving away from each other, though they are getting farther apart. The space between them is simply expanding.

To help better understand this concept, picture a balloon with colored dots on it. As air is added to the balloon, the dots get further apart, though they haven't actually moved from their initial locations. There is just more space between them now.

When we consider that the universe is expanding, that means that the further we look back in time, the closer things are together. And, if we go back far enough, the distance between everything would reach zero. All space and matter would exist at a single point — what scientists call the "singularity."

Now, when matter came into existence, time came into existence, and time and space are integrally linked. There was no time before the singularity. In fact, it's incorrect to say "before" in that sentence because the word "before" implies time and its passage, of which there was none.

The standard "Big Bang" model of the universe is what we have just looked at (albeit very briefly). This model predicts an absolute start to the universe. While the last 100 years have resulted in large advances in scientific knowledge and many failed theories, the standard model — that the universe had an absolute beginning — has stood the test of time, and it remains the prevailing model to this day.

This is excellent news for the Christian. Since the Big Bang Theory proves that the universe began to exist, it supports the second premise of the Kalām Cosmological Argument.

The Universe Hasn't Suffered Heat Death

No, this isn't like some sort of cosmic heat stroke. *Heat Death* describes a state in which there is no movement and everything in the universe is the same temperature. This is also called equilibrium. In other words, energy would be universally distributed throughout all space.

According to the Second Law of Thermodynamics, systems continually move toward disorder unless acted on from the outside. If we were to inject air into an empty and closed container, it would expand to uniformly fill the container — it would reach equilibrium.

If you took a carton of ice cream out of the freezer and left it on the kitchen counter for long enough, the room and the ice cream would become the same temperature. The room would become a little cooler, due to giving some of its heat (energy) to the ice cream, and the ice cream would become a lot warmer due to gaining heat (energy) from the room. Energy would become evenly distributed. (**Warning**: Do not try this at home. Wasting ice cream is a sin!)

The kitchen and ice cream situation is a simplified example of what will happen to the universe: given enough time, it will reach equilibrium.

Since the universe hasn't suffered heat death and isn't at equilibrium, we can be confident that the universe *hasn't* existed forever — it isn't eternal, and the past isn't infinite. It must have had a beginning, because if it were infinitely old, equilibrium would have been reached and there would be no you and no me — you wouldn't be around to read this.

You Can't Have an Infinite Series of Events

We have looked at two scientific supports for the second premise. Now, we will look at philosophical evidence in favor of this premise.

1. If the universe never began to exist, then the number of past events must be infinite.
2. An infinite number of things cannot exist.

3. Therefore, the number of past events cannot be infinite. (The universe had a beginning.)

This is another straightforward logical argument, but I can just hear those of you who have had a calculus class starting to protest when I say, "An infinite number of things cannot exist." Calculus and physics use the concept of "infinity" regularly, but they are almost always referring to a *potential* infinite, not an *actual* infinite.

Potential infinities refer to something having a limit of infinity. To make this clearer, let's consider an example. Imagine that you're sitting on the couch reading this right now. How many steps will it take you to get to your front door? Well, in order to get to the door, you will have to walk half of the distance. Then, from there, you will have to walk another half, then another, and another, and so on. There is an infinite number of divisions on your way to the door. There is an infinite number of tasks you have to complete before you get to the door. That is to say, the number of divisions is a *potential* infinite.

Of course, you can actually walk to the door without an infinite amount of time passing, but this serves to illustrate the difference between an actual and a potential infinite. If you're interested in reading more about this example, it's called Zeno's paradox.

Husbands, next time your wife is wanting to leave the house, and it appears that you're just standing there, explain to her that there are an infinite number of divisions between you and the door... so she might be waiting there for a while!

Often, a *potential* infinite refers to a case where there can be an infinite number of *divisions*, whereas an *actual* infinite refers to there being an infinite number of *items* (or distance or time) and not just an infinite number of *divisions*.

An *actual* infinite would be something that actually exists and is larger than any natural number (Natural numbers are 1, 2, 3, etc.).

To help illustrate why you can't have an actual infinite number of things, let's consider "Hilbert's Hotel," which is the brainchild of the German mathematician David Hilbert.

Before talking about this "special" hotel, let's review how a normal hotel works. Normal hotels have a finite number of rooms, and when they're all booked and someone wants a room, the manager will say "all of the rooms are full," and the story ends there.

Now, consider Hilbert's hotel. It has an [*actually*] infinite number of rooms. Let's say that all of the rooms are full. Yes, an infinite number of rooms have been filled, which would take an infinite number of people. Then, suppose a guest shows up and asks for a room [in this full hotel]. The manager replies, "Just one moment!"

He moves the person who was staying in room #1 into room #2, the person who was staying in room #2 into room #3, and so on, all the way out to infinity. Because of this, room #1 is now vacant, and the new guest happily checks in, even though prior to this, *all of the rooms were full.*

The wackiness doesn't end there, though. Now, let's picture an *infinite* number of people showing up to the *full* hotel and wanting rooms. Once again, the manager says, "No problem. Just one moment!" He then proceeds to move every guest into a room with a room number twice that of the guest's original room.

So, #1 moves to #2, #2 moved to #4, #3 moves to #6, etc., all the way out to infinity. All of the existing guests now occupy an infinite number of just even-numbered rooms, and the infinite number of new guests are free to check into the infinite number of odd-numbered rooms.

The manager could even repeat this process an infinite number of times, so he could always accept infinitely more guests! If such a hotel could exist, it would have to have a sign which would read "NO VACANCY (Guests Welcome!)."

However, what happens if people want to check out? There are an infinite number of odd rooms in the full hotel, and if all of the people in the odd-numbered rooms check out, there are still an infinite number of people left in the hotel. This is why subtraction is simply prohibited when dealing with actual infinities: subtracting an actual infinite from another actual infinite can still leave you with an actual infinite, which is absurd.

This goes to show that you can't have an actual infinite in reality, so the past can't be actually infinite either. We have disproven premise one above — "If the universe never began to exist, then the number of past events must be infinite."

There's another philosophical argument for the past being finite, and it's easier to understand.

1. The series of past events was formed by adding events one after another.

2. No series which was formed by adding one thing after another can ever be infinite.
3. Therefore, the series of past events must be finite.

The meat of this argument is in premise two, which says that you can't get to infinity by counting 1, 2, 3, ... This is easy to see. No matter how high you count, you could always count one higher. No matter how high you count, there will always be an infinity of numbers left for you to count. You will never reach an *actual* infinite.

You can think of the passage of time and events like dominoes falling. Each event in the past series of events is like a single domino falling. Well, if an infinite number of dominoes had to fall in order to get to today, then today would never have arrived. But, you're obviously reading this, so today is here! Which means, the past cannot have been infinite. It must be finite, and it must have had a beginning.

Kalām Application

We have proven that the universe had a beginning, and we've seen that this is supported by both modern science and philosophy. All that's left is to show how this relates to God.

All matter and time came into existence at the start of the universe, and prior to this point there was no matter, and there was no time. Since the universe had a cause, that cause must have been *timeless* and *immaterial*, since neither time nor material existed before the universe came into being.

The cause of the universe must also be very *powerful, personal,* and *intelligent*. If you ask someone what they call a timeless, immaterial, powerful, personal, intelligent being, they will most likely say, "god."

That is what the Kalām Cosmological argument proves — that there must be a god. It does this using rational thought, logic, science, and philosophy. There hasn't been a Bible verse in this chapter (so far), and there didn't need to be. Combine some observation, and critical thought, and you arrive at the conclusion that there must be a god. However, it's interesting to note that Paul makes the same point when writing to the Romans: "Since the creation of the world his invisible attributes – his eternal power and divine nature – have been clearly seen, because they are understood through what has been made." (Romans 1:20)

Since we've covered the most powerful argument for God's existence, we can make our case even stronger by introducing additional and independent lines of evidence and argument. Arguing that universes don't just pop into being without a cause is a great strategy, and it's usually my first move.

There are times, however, when you're talking with someone who doesn't care about science and doesn't appreciate a good logical argument. When you encounter this type of person, you need a different type of argument. The moral argument is often just the sort of thing that will be compelling to such a person, and it's included in the chapter on morality.

It's important to understand the function of the Kalām Cosmological Argument. Since it doesn't have a Bible verse in it, it cannot point someone directly to Jesus, and thus salvation. But, for someone who starts out as an atheist, it's a big step to come to the belief that there is *a* god out there. From there, you would need to talk with this person further in order to convince them the Bible is true and that Jesus is the only means of true hope and salvation.

WHAT WE LEARNED

- ❖ The existence of the universe is the most powerful proof for the existence of God.
- ❖ The past is not infinite and objects do not come into existence without a cause.
- ❖ That cause must be timeless, immaterial, powerful, personal, and intelligent.
- ❖ It is more reasonable to believe in a grand being than to believe universes can pop into existence from nothing and without a cause.

5

IS EVIL A PROBLEM?

One of the most common and powerful arguments against God is as follows:

> The Bible says God is all-good and all-powerful. So, God would want to and be able to prevent evil. But we see evil all around us. Therefore, God does not exist.

This world is full of hurt and heartache; it's full of evil, and it's easy for the non-Christian and Christian alike to wonder how all of this evil could possibly exist if God actually existed. You or someone you know has probably been the victim of an evil act or experienced deep suffering in life.

Where is God in all of this? Does he care? Is he powerless? Does he exist?

The first thing to point out is that this is a problem that confronts every single religion and person — *including atheists*. Every worldview needs to explain why evil exists and how we know to recognize it as such. We'll look at this in detail later.

THE ARGUMENT IS INSUFFICIENT

This argument against God fails on many levels. First, God could very well exist and simply not be powerful enough to stop all evil. Or God could exist and not be *totally* good. These are possibilities that must be considered. So, from the start we see this argument doesn't necessarily disprove the existence of a god. It only could, at most, say something about his characteristics. However, the problems don't stop here.

The problem of evil can be succinctly summarized as follows:

Statement 1
1. God is all-good.
2. God is all-powerful.
3. God created the world.
4. The world contains evil.

However, when people use the problem of evil to try and disprove God's existence, they usually have something such as the following in mind, even if they don't vocalize it this way.

Statement 1a
1. God is good.
2. God is all-powerful.
3. God created the world.
4. *The world shouldn't contain evil.*
5. The world contains evil.

People implicitly include point number four in their argument, but they rarely state it. However, this point is an assumption; it must be proven before the argument is actually valid and sound. Without point four and its proof, there is no logical problem in the "problem of evil," as described in Statement 1. People assume that God must eliminate or prevent all evil. If we can demonstrate that there is no logical contradiction in God being all-good and all-powerful and the world containing evil, we will have removed the problem of evil and taken a big step closer to the gospel of Jesus Christ.

We must keep in mind that addressing the logic of the situation is most likely not going to be emotionally satisfying to someone troubled by the evil in the world. But, it is still necessary to point out that the existence of evil and the existence of God are not incompatible.

When people comment that there is *too much* evil in the world, we could ask, "How much evil would be just enough?" This points out a problem in the perspective of the questioner. For example, if there were 100 units of evil in the world and God reduced it to 75 units, then, moving forward, 75 would seem like 100 to us, since we would have known no differently. If you keep playing this out, you arrive at God needing to remove all evil in order for us to not have anything to complain about. I totally understand people who say that any evil is too much evil. However, God is not to blame, and Christianity doesn't teach that evil shouldn't exist.

In fact, the Christian account of history, the Bible, tells us how evil came into the world. Due to the consequences of Adam and Eve's first wrongdoing and the resulting sin nature of man, Christians understand that people are pointed toward evil.

Evil came to be and continues to occur, *due to the actions that you and I commit.* So, to answer the question, "Why is there so much evil in the world?" we have to say, "Because we commit so much evil as a people." We do. All of us. It's really easy to blame evil on God, or other people, but the truth is that all of us do wrong against others (and ultimately God) every day.

This issue of evil really does come down to the choices people make. Some of these choices result in good and some result in evil. But they all stem from choice, nonetheless. The only way for God to have prevented evil would be for him to have made us without the ability to make choices. There is no other way around this. God made a moral creature who had the power of choice, and that creature, in exercising his will, brought evil into the world.

Consider: what would it be like if we didn't have the power of choice? We would be robots! There is actually a group who believe that everything is determined — that we don't have the ability to choose.

The *typical* atheist doesn't believe in the existence of the soul/mind, so our "choices" are just the results of molecules in motion. Our decisions are just the result of chemical reactions. Choice is an illusion. There is no immaterial self who is guiding our physical body and making actual choices. If this is true, then we must ask what is the atheist actually complaining about when he speaks of "evil"? Without choice, there is no responsibility for good or bad actions. And, on that view, we also don't have a choice in coming to call the actions bad or good. Those end up becoming completely arbitrary labels.

The existence of evil is a much larger problem for the atheist than it is for the Christian. The concept of evil doesn't fit in the atheistic worldview, it's borrowed from the Christian worldview. There can be no evil if good does not exist, and there can be no good without God. To be clear, people can do good *actions* without believing that God exists, but the existence of good is contingent on God's existence.

There must be a standard and authority that is external to us or a person is just emoting when they claim that such and such is evil. If there's no God, a person is really saying nothing more than, "I don't like such and such." It's like making up your own rules during a game and then claiming people are wrong for breaking your personal set of made up rules. My grandmother used to get upset with me for doing this very thing. Without an external standard, all claims about the rightness or wrongness of an action are meaningless.

So, if evil can't actually fit in an atheistic worldview, then why do atheists seem to complain about the problem of evil more than any other point? Their moral outrage points to their innate moral knowledge. Most atheists genuinely know right from wrong; they just haven't realized that morality has no place in their worldview. This is extremely important. Recognizing this, we can actually use the problem of evil to argue for God's existence — we can turn around one of the atheist's most powerful and compelling arguments and use it as an argument for God.

THE MORAL ARGUMENT

What follows is the Moral Argument for God's Existence.
1. If God does not exist, objective moral values do not exist.
2. Objective moral values do exist.
3. Therefore, God does exist.

This is a logical argument; if the premises (points one and two) are true, the conclusion *must* follow. So, let's look at supporting those points with other arguments and evidence.

1. If God Does Not Exist, Objective Moral Values Do Not Exist

Said more simply, *morality requires a grounding.* A moral standard must be external to us for it to be universally binding and have actual meaning. The being that created us is the most reasonable candidate to dictate morality for his creation. This is the same concept as a father setting rules for his children, or a pet owner setting the rules for her pets.

Relativism

Some people will disagree that a god is the only thing that can account for morality. Many people want to say that there is no such thing as objective morality, which is morality that applies to everyone the same way. Instead, these people want to say that morality is relative — that is, it depends on a person. So, relativism holds that the rightness or wrongness of an action is dependent on how the person doing that action feels about it. On this view, rape wouldn't be wrong if the rapist didn't think it was wrong. Now, it would certainly be wrong to me, because I think it's wrong, but it wouldn't be wrong for the rapist. Relativism says that morality is relative to the person, and we all just decide for ourselves.

However, most of the time, people who hold to relativism speak and act like morality is objective. For instance, these people are often very sensitive to social justice issues like sex trafficking, genocide, poverty, and more. When they talk about these *evils*, they can be very convincing that something actually wrong is happening. I think they're actually convinced too — they just won't admit it. You see, based on their view of relativism, nothing actually wrong is happening, and when they say something is wrong, they're just expressing an emotion — "I don't like it." Their passion and actions betray their intellectual commitments, though, for many times they speak of evil the same way they speak of gravity — as something that they're convinced actually exists in the world.

We need to be able to demonstrate that relativism doesn't work and can't explain truth or morality. We can do that in conversation by getting people to show just how strongly they're attached to their moral commitments. We can also do this by pointing out, "If everyone gets to decide what truth is for themselves, what if I decide that that isn't actually how we find truth?" A system that allows for such contradictory statements cannot be a good system. Relativism is incapable of being practically enacted and applied. It's a bad grounding for morality

Social Contract Theory

Another proposed grounding for morality is Social Contract Theory. In this view, a society decides for itself what is right and wrong, or at least the majority in that society does. Hopefully you see that this is just a bigger, more organized, form of relativism, though it does have its own unique problems.

In this view, Americans decide what is right for Americans. But they have no ability to speak to the rightness or wrongness of another country's actions, since that society would also be deciding for itself what is right and wrong. Things get more convoluted still, for there are societies within societies that could also decide on a moral code for themselves, and so on. There are countries within continents, states within countries, counties within states, cities within counties, neighborhoods within cities, and so on. Who decides how large a group must be before they can decide morality for themselves?

There are other, larger, problems though. Social contract theory makes Dr. Martin Luther King Jr.'s actions immoral. Consider: he rejected the established moral views of the day, as set forth by the majority. The society at large said that blacks weren't equal with whites, and King opposed that and took actions to change it.

But why stop there? In social contract theory, there is nothing wrong with the treatment of women in the Middle East. They have few (if any) rights, are subjected to physical abuse, oppressive standards of dress, and more. But according to social contract theory, all of these things are morally right because that's just how their society is setup.

Since it has the same base problems as relativism, and suffers these additional problems, Social Contract theory is also a bad grounding for morality.

Evolution

The last proposed grounding for morality that we'll look at is evolution — the Darwinian Theory that life has developed through the combination of random mutation and natural selection. In an attempt to explain the innate moral knowledge that humans have, some[1] will try to say that this is the result of millions of years of evolution. In addition to making us more advanced in a physical sense, evolution has also created and increased our moral knowledge along the way.

Right from the start we have an issue. Morality is immaterial; it isn't made of physical "stuff." So, how does a physical process that only works on material create immaterial things like moral values? It can't. Additionally, immaterial realities have no place in an atheistic worldview.

There are other problems too. By using observation (one of the bedrock tools of science) we come to see that evolution puts "me" first. This stands in stark contrast to morality, which puts others first. Evolution is about *my* survival, so that *I* can pass on my genes to the

40

next generation, but morality is generally about putting myself second, about sacrificing myself for the well-being of others.

The atheist's argument is that evolution somehow has favored individuals who are more moral, so these moral characteristics are more likely to be passed on to the next generation. But how? If morality makes me more loving and self-sacrificing, how does this make it more likely that I'll pass on my genes? It doesn't; it makes it much less likely.

The individual who, in a split-second, makes the choice to jump on a grenade to save his fellow soldiers is by definition giving up his chance to pass on his genes. So, when philosopher and promoter of evolutionary theory, Michael Ruse says, "Morality is just an aid to survival and reproduction, and has no being beyond this"[2], we should be able to see right through that, because *it doesn't explain reality.* It doesn't explain the acts we *know* to be moral that don't aid in survival or reproduction.

This view of morality also fails to explain why some actions such as rape are wrong. Almost without exception, people condemn rape as a horribly immoral action. However, from an evolutionary perspective, rape would be a good thing; it aids in the reproduction of the rapist. You see, if morality is explained by survival of the fittest, there are many actions that are actually *moral,* such as rape, murder, theft, and genocide.

We see that there are many problems with using evolution as a grounding for morality. Immaterial things can't be created by evolution, and they don't even fit into an atheistic worldview. Additionally, evolution can't explain how we know that certain actions are wrong, if they aid in survival, or how self-sacrifice is right, when it doesn't aid in survival.

God

All of these failed groundings bring us back to the idea of a god. The first premise of the Moral Argument states, "If God does not exist, moral values do not exist." Morality requires an external, authoritative foundation, and as we have seen, apart from a god, morality has no plausible grounding.

This leads us to the second premise that we need to support.

2. Objective Moral Values Do Exist

There are actions in this world that are actually morally right and morally wrong. Now, for some people there will be no disagreement with this point. Such a person might try to ground morality on one of the aforementioned methods. But on the other hand, others will say that morality doesn't exist at all. If you're speaking with the former, you won't have to do much work proving this premise. So, we'll concern ourselves with those who deny the existence of objective morality. I'll frame the argument through a hypothetical conversation.

The first thing to do when you're talking with someone who says that morality doesn't exist is to pay attention to how they talk. Ask the person what their thoughts are on religion, maybe even on the Crusades. Usually, atheists are quick to say that religion is harmful and dangerous (famous atheist Richard Dawkins definitely thinks so). Getting them to admit this is actually a good thing!

If the person doesn't bite on that issue, ask about the Holocaust, genocide in Africa, persecution of atheists, murder, or human trafficking. Our goal is to get them to say that *something is actually wrong*. The best way to do this isn't right after they've denied that morality exists — they will probably see that coming. Instead, after the denial, change the topic, but weave in questions so that you can come to understand how they view some important issues.

You don't have to just ask about negative things — you can also find things that they believe to be actually good. Affirmations of either good or evil will help us with our next step. If you can't get them to admit to any action being good or bad, you might have to make the situation more personal. You can ask questions such as, "If *your* child were severely beaten, would you say something actually wrong took place?" or "Would it actually be wrong for someone to murder your wife?" I know these are difficult and invasive questions, and, if you choose to use questions like these, you need to do so in a confident and yet very *sensitive* way. These types of questions can be all the more persuasive if they're used in front of other people. The intention isn't to offend the person, or make them feel trapped. Instead, the intention is to lead them to the realization that they hold two contradictory views – their worldview has a problem that Christianity has a solution for.

Some people will not affirm that morality actually exists, no matter what examples you use and how bad they look for their answers. If you're talking to such a person, there isn't anything else you can do but pray for them. And I don't say that flippantly — that person needs the supernatural work of the Spirit in their life.

Now let's address those people who do acknowledge that some things are morally right or wrong, even if they've said that morality doesn't exist. You can now ask the person something such as, "What did you mean when you said _____ was wrong? Did you mean that _____ was immoral?" If the person says that they do think an action is immoral, then they have admitted that morality exists, which is what we're trying to prove. If they don't, we have a few more questions we can use.

"If _____ isn't morally wrong, are you only saying 'I don't like it'?" If they say "yes," then they've admitted that they don't think morality exists, and they're doing nothing more than emoting when they say things are right and wrong. At this point, if appropriate, you can now use the more personal questions we looked at above.

To be clear, the goal is to get the person to the point where they realize that they firmly believe certain things to be right and other things to be wrong. Keep in mind that it will sometimes be obvious to you (and probably to them) that they believe this way, even if they won't admit it. That's okay. You'll be leaving this person with something to mull over once your conversation is done.

Once you've gotten a person to realize and admit that they believe an action is moral in nature, you need to ask them how they account for moral values. Where do they come from? How are they grounded? What's the external standard? You can use the information we covered when looking at premise 1 — "If God does not exist, objective moral values do not exist" — to address whatever grounding they bring up.

The overarching question the person needs to answer is: **"Since you believe morality exists, what best explains the existence of moral values *and* your innate ability to know them?"** They might not have an immediate answer, and that's okay. Weighty issues such as these should be pondered at length, and leaving someone with something to think about is a great tactic.

Here is a summary of the conversation flow we went through for premise 2:

Do you believe morality exists?
- ❖ Yes
  - ▪ "Since you believe morality exists, what best explains the existence of moral values and your innate ability to know them?" A god is the best explanation for the existence of both moral values and our ability to know them.
- ❖ No
  - ▪ Use examples of actions such as genocide, rape, murder, persecution, the Crusades, etc. to see if they'll bite and say that any of those are wrong. If not, go to the next step.
  - ▪ Make your questions more personal.
  - ▪ If they still don't affirm morality, walk away from this issue, and possibly the conversation. You can't win them all!

3. THEREFORE, GOD EXISTS

God exists. This is the conclusion of the moral argument. It follows from the two premises and is the natural conclusion to this valid and sound argument. We have seen how each of the premises can be supported and defended. Moreover, the existence of morality is in line with what we *observe* about the world and our innate reactions and intuitions.

Now, it is important to note that that this argument does not prove the exclusive existence of the God of the Bible. For that, you will need to demonstrate that the Bible is trustworthy and the resurrection occurred. However, taking someone from atheism to theism is a large step!

WHAT WE LEARNED

- ❖ Evil does not defeat Christianity; the existence of evil in no way means that God doesn't exist, God isn't all-good, or God isn't all-powerful.
- ❖ There is no logical contradiction in the statement of the problem of evil.
- ❖ Every worldview must explain how evil exists, not just Christianity.
- ❖ Christianity provides the best explanation for how evil exists and what will be done about it.

❖ **The Moral Argument**
  - "If God does not exist, objective moral values do not exist."
  - "Objective moral values do exist."
  - "Therefore, God exists."

6

CAN WE TRUST THE BIBLE?

Christians base their life on a single collection of documents. However, is the life-changing faith that they place in these ancient writings actually justified, or is it blind? If you're going to base your life on something, you should want to know that it's true and not a fairytale.

POPULAR REASONS FOR TRUSTING THE BIBLE

It's common to hear people say that they trust their religious book because it has positively affected their life. "I find comfort in it." "I've gained wisdom that has helped my business flourish." "It's made me a more peaceful person." Comfort, wisdom, and peace are great things, and these types of claims certainly combat the stereotype that religion only causes harm. However, we often gain comfort from lies, and false beliefs can bring peace to those who believe them. So, those aren't good reasons to base one's life on a book.

I also frequently hear people say that they trust the Bible "because it is the word of God." When I ask how they know this, they usually reply, "Because the Bible says so." Generally, they have 2 Timothy 3:16-17 in mind, which says, "Every scripture is inspired by God and useful for teaching, for reproof, for correction, and for training in righteousness, that the person dedicated to God may be capable and equipped for every good work."

However, this is a circular argument — "I believe the Bible because God wrote it, and I know God wrote it because the Bible says so." This is not a good way to support the truthfulness of Scripture. Leading off with a logical fallacy will get you nowhere with people who value reason.

So, if we shouldn't defend the truthfulness of Scripture on the basis of lives that are changed or because it says God wrote it, how should we contend for its reliability? In this chapter we will make a case using multiple types of evidence and arguments which, when taken as a whole, leave little doubt that the Bible should be trusted. While any single piece of evidence will probably not move an individual to believe the Bible, the overwhelming persuasive weight of the complete case is hard to deny.

A PERSUASIVE CASE

Life-Changing Nature and Self-Attestation

The first step in our case is to acknowledge that the Bible claims to be written by God and to have life-transforming power. Huh? You're probably wondering why it seems as though I've flip-flopped. Well, neither of these points is compelling on their own, but if the Bible didn't claim to be God's word, we wouldn't be justified in regarding it as such. If it's just a self-proclaimed tall tale concocted around a campfire, no one should base their life on it. So, the fact that the Bible claims divine origin is very important. This is called self-attestation — the Bible attests, or speaks for, itself. Remember, this doesn't mean that it *is* true, but it's an initial piece of the puzzle. Additionally, if it didn't change lives, while claiming to do so, it would show itself to be untrustworthy.

Once again, just because something changes lives, that doesn't mean it's true. However, it does give us a reason to consider it more strongly.

The Bible Is Unique

The Bible wasn't written cover to cover by one author or in chronological order. In fact, the Bible is 66 different documents that were written by more than 40 authors on different continents during a 1,500-year period (roughly 1400 BC to 95 AD) in more than eight genres.

What's remarkable is that, despite these facts, *the Bible tells a unified and internally consistent account.* Though some would point to apparent contradictions such as the number of people present at the empty tomb, the majority of "contradiction" claims can be dealt with simply by demonstrating that the details in question are complementary, not contradictory. No Gospel writer makes the claim that he is including an exhaustive list of who was at the tomb; each of them choose to highlight certain individuals. Matthew includes two people (Matthew 28:1) whereas Mark lists three people (Mark 16:1)

The description above makes it obvious that the Bible is quite unique; there is no other collection of documents like it. It should be said that simply telling a unified, internally consistent story doesn't make that story true; fiction writers and playwrights do this all the time. But the Bible claims to be fact, not fiction, and it makes historically verifiable claims, which we will examine shortly. And when we consider how many different people wrote these documents over such a protracted and geographically separated time period, we can start to appreciate how remarkable it is that all of these documents fit together so cohesively.

The Bible's unique and internally consistent nature is another piece of our case for its trustworthiness.

The Evidence Is Early

We all know that the further from an event we get, the worse our recall of that event's details become. It follows that when analyzing someone's account of an event, it's helpful to know how soon after the event the account was written down. Also, were there other eyewitnesses still around when the account was written — people who could confirm or contradict the details of the account?

There is early evidence for the Bible. Though not all scholars agree, some of the manuscripts we have for parts of Mark, Acts, Romans, 1 Timothy, 2 Peter, and James date to between AD 50 and AD 70. These were found as part of the Dead Sea Scrolls. We have documents that attest to the Jesus' death and resurrection that were written within 20 to 40 years after the events they describe. For an event that happened 2,000 years ago, that's incredible! The earliest parts of John also date to AD 117–138.

It's helpful to know the copy time gap for a document when its trustworthiness is in question. The copy time gap is the amount of time that elapsed between the initial writing of the document and the age of the oldest copy we have. For example, if a document was originally written in 1980, but the oldest copy we have is from 1997, then there is a copy time gap of 17 years.

For some of the biblical documents, we have a copy time gap of 25 years. When we compare this to other ancient works, the Bible is seen to stand in a class all its own. For instance, the *Iliad* by Homer has a copy gap of 500 years. Below is a graph[1] showing renowned ancient authors and the copy time gaps of their works.

As you can see, it is remarkable just how close to the source the biblical manuscripts are.

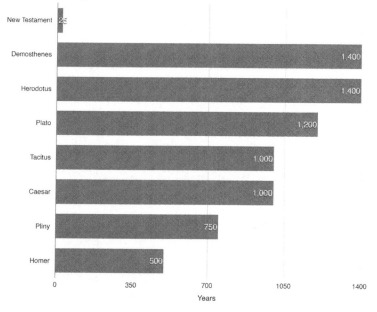

The Evidence Is Written by Eyewitnesses

Hearing something directly from the source gives us more confidence in it than if we heard it from someone who wasn't an eyewitness. In the same way, we should value the Gospel accounts since they were written by eyewitnesses during the lifetime of other eyewitnesses.

Peter makes this very clear in 2 Peter 1:16 when he says, "We did not follow cleverly invented stories when we told you about the power and coming of our Lord Jesus Christ, but we were eyewitnesses of his majesty." Reading on a little further, we see that he makes this clear because false teachers will come and spread "destructive heresies." It was imperative to early Christians to know both the truth and that the truth wasn't a "cleverly invented story," and it should be imperative to us too.

In Acts 2:32 Peter also claims to be an eyewitness: "This Jesus God raised up, and we are all witnesses of it." Luke, who is writing Acts, understands the importance of eyewitness testimony, as we see in the opening chapter of his first work that bears his name.

> Now many have undertaken to compile an account of the things that have been fulfilled among us, like the accounts passed on to us by those who were eyewitnesses and servants of the word from the beginning. So it seemed good to me as well, because I have followed all things carefully from the beginning, to write an orderly account for you, most excellent Theophilus, so that you may know for certain the things you were taught. (Luke 1:1–2)

Now, *saying* that you're an eyewitness and *being* an eyewitness are two very different things. So, why should we believe that they were indeed eyewitnesses? One reason is that they correctly cite locations, dialects, authorities and officials, and current events.

Colin Hemer is a historian who has gone through Acts verse by verse and confirmed 84 facts just in the last 16 chapters of the book[2]. These are details Luke includes that we can verify by third-party historical and archaeological evidence. Luke correctly cites the language spoken in remote regions, the correct locations of rivers and cities, the best routes to sail depending on weather conditions, the legal procedures in small providences, the governing officials in many places, cultural perspectives, and so much more.

If someone were to manufacture a story and include so many specific details, they would certainly get many things wrong. Bible scholar F.F. Bruce says this well.

> A writer who thus relates his story to the wider context of world history is courting trouble if he is not careful; he affords his critical readers so many opportunities for testing his accuracy. Luke takes this risk, and stands the test admirably."[3]

There's a reason that most lies are filled with vague generalities; it's much harder to get caught if you don't include many specifics. However, the gospels are full of detailed descriptions that have been confirmed from extra-biblical evidence and sources.

The Evidence Is Embarrassing

Historians have a principle that helps them determine whether or not something is true. It's called the principle of embarrassment: *any details embarrassing to the author are probably true.*

When you make up a story, you're not only going to avoid specific details, but you're also not going to include embarrassing details about yourself or the people you care about. However, the Gospel writers include many embarrassing events, and not funny ones such as passing out on your wedding day or that you walked around all day with a "Kick Me" sign on your back. Let's look at some of these embarrassing details. When you read these, ask yourself, "If I were in their position, would I have included these statements *about me?*"

Details about the authors

- ❖ The authors are portrayed as being dim-witted — numerous times they fail to understand what Jesus is saying (Mark 9:32; Luke 18:34; John 12:16).
- ❖ They seem to be uncaring — they fall asleep on Jesus twice when he asks them to pray (Mark 14:32-41).
- ❖ They are sometimes cowards and doubters (Matthew 26:33-35; John 2:18-22; 3:14-18).

These are but a few of the details, but they are a big deal! Let's confront these realities. The Gospel writers believed Jesus to literally be God, yet they write about their doubt, their uncaring behavior, and cowardice regarding him. Additionally, Peter is called "Satan" by Jesus. If you're trying to start a false religion and you're making up all of this, why on earth would you say that God called you Satan? That's not going to help your cause as you try to convince people that you're an authority on God.

But what we see repeatedly is that the Gospel writers include the good *and the bad* about themselves and about Jesus.

Details about Jesus

- ❖ Jesus is considered "out of his mind" by his mother and brothers (Mark 3:21, 31).
- ❖ He is not believed by his own brothers (John 7:5).
- ❖ He is called a "drunkard" (Matthew 11:19).

- He has his feet wiped with the hair of a prostitute (an event that could have been perceived as a sexual advance — Luke 7:36-39).
- He is crucified by the Jews and Romans despite the fact that "anyone who is hung on a tree is under God's curse." (Deuteronomy 21:23; cf. Galatians 3:13)
- He is buried by a member of the group that sentenced him to death (John 19:38).
- He first appears to women (who had no legal standing or societal credibility — John 20:10-18).

To put this in context, the Gospel writers are trying to convey that Jesus is God, and they include very embarrassing details about him. His own family didn't believe him before his death (though, after his resurrection he appeared to his brother, James, who went on to lead the Jerusalem church and would ultimately be stoned for his faith). Including all of this makes no sense if you're making up a story, because these events serve to raise questions about Jesus' divinity, not reinforce it.

There Is Extra-Biblical Evidence

We've examined some of the statements that are included in the Bible, and we've seen that the most reasonable explanation for their inclusion is that they were true. In addition to the biblical evidence, we also have evidence from non-biblical sources.

Flavius Josephus, who lived from 37 AD to 100 AD (approximately), was the greatest Jewish historian of his day. One of his three main works, *Antiquities of the Jews*, which he finished around 93 AD, has quite a bit to say about Jesus and the Christian movement.

At this time [the time of Pilate] there was a wise man who was called Jesus. His conduct was good and (he) was known to be virtuous. And many people from among the Jews and the other nations became his disciples. Pilate condemned him to be crucified and to die. But those who had become his disciples did not abandon his discipleship. They reported that he had appeared to them three days after his crucifixion, and that he was alive; accordingly he was perhaps the Messiah, concerning whom the prophets have recounted wonders.[4]

Josephus is just one of ten known non-Christian writers who mention Jesus within 150 years of his life. If you include Christian sources, the total rises to 43. Compare this to only nine sources that mention Tiberius Caesar.

From all of these extra-biblical sources, we know that Jesus:

- ❖ lived during the time of Tiberius Caesar.
- ❖ lived a virtuous life.
- ❖ was a wonder worker.
- ❖ had a brother named James.
- ❖ was acclaimed to be the Messiah.
- ❖ was crucified under Pontius Pilate on the eve of the Jewish Passover.
- ❖ was believed by his disciples to have risen from the dead.
- ❖ was worshiped as God by his disciples who denied the Roman gods.
- ❖ had disciples who were willing to die for their belief.

All of these details confirm what the biblical writers said, and none contradict it. This is very important, for while the internal biblical evidence that we've looked at is a good foundation, third-party evidence serves to make our case even stronger.

The Evidence Is Deadly Serious

Many of the New Testament believers were Jews who then came to Christianity. However, this wasn't an easy transition — the two religions are *very* different. Jews of that day were much more devout than your average church-goer today, and their culture and religion where much more closely joined. For people like this, changing religions would have been extremely difficult. There would have been a large social cost. Additionally, these were people leaving Judaism to follow a man who had just been killed by the Romans in a manner that according to the Old Testament would have left him "cursed." This was not the easy or popular way to go.

To change from being Jewish to Christian required a massive shift in thought and lifestyle. Jews believed in the necessity of animal sacrifice for the forgiveness of sins. The Christians — Jews turned followers of Jesus — now believed that Jesus' sacrifice was the basis for their forgiveness, not animal sacrifice. To a devout Jew, this would be heresy; they were forgoing their only method of restoring right-standing with God. You would only do this if you were certain that you were right.

Additionally, for thousands of years the Jews had been looking forward to the Messiah — their savior. They expected this person to defeat their enemies and restore Israel to its former sovereign glory by delivering them from the Romans. They expected a conquering messiah. Instead, they got a sacrificial lamb.

While Jesus didn't defeat the Romans, he actually did defeat the Jews' greatest enemy — sin — once and for all. They just didn't understand because this suffering savior didn't resemble the person they had been anticipating for so long. What's important to note here is that a Jewish convert to Christianity would have had to be very convinced that Jesus was indeed who he claimed to be, since he didn't resemble the military leader his people had expected.

All of this points to the Gospel writers and new Christians having such a conviction in the historical resurrection that it couldn't help but change their lives. But, their religious changes, which are also attested to by extra-biblical evidence, aren't the only reason we should believe what the authors have to say.

All of the apostles were either tortured or murdered for their convictions. James was killed "with the sword" — most likely beheaded. Peter and Andrew were crucified. "Doubting" Thomas was burned alive, and all the others, except for John who was tortured, were also killed for their faith. There is no more incredible display of testimony than to be martyred for one's beliefs.

Now, when you use this argument in conversation, someone will inevitably point out that today's religious extremists are also willing to die for their beliefs. And such a person would say, by extension, that since many different religious all have their own extremists, nothing is unique or noteworthy about these early Christian martyrs.

However, the person voicing this objection is missing a crucial point. Many people will die for something they *believe* to be the truth, but no one dies for something they *know* to be a lie. The Gospel writers were in the position to know if their beliefs were accurate or not — if Jesus really did rise from the dead — and they chose to die defending and testifying to the truthfulness of an actual bodily resurrection.

No one would die defending a lie like that. It didn't bring them wealth or power. It didn't bring them peace or a better life on earth.

They gained nothing, but gave everything because *they were convinced that Jesus was who he claimed to be.* They had something that no jihadist has today: first-hand knowledge of the events they claimed to know. Being eyewitnesses gave them the privileged position that no other religious followers can claim to have.

The case for the reliability of the Gospels is very strong. We can have assurance beyond a reasonable doubt that what the Gospel writers describe is accurate and trustworthy. The foundation for the Christian's faith is very firm!

WHAT WE LEARNED

- ❖ Don't use circular arguments for the reliability of the Bible.
- ❖ The Bible is a unique and cohesive collection of historical documents that tells a unified and consistent account.
- ❖ We have *early* evidence for the events the Bible describes. It wasn't written hundreds or thousands of years later.
- ❖ This evidence is from *eyewitnesses.* They include details that correctly describe the cultural surroundings of the day.
- ❖ The authors write embarrassing things about themselves and Jesus, giving their accounts credibility.
- ❖ Most importantly, they endured torture, and were willing to die defending the events *they were eyewitnesses of.*

7

SHOULD THE BIBLE BE
TAKEN LITERALLY?

Do You Take the Bible Literally? You might have been inclined to answer yes, but then you paused and thought about it and suddenly, this feels more and more like a trap! It's like being asked if you've stopped beating your wife. You don't want to say, "no" and you also don't want to say "yes" because each answer would affirm something that isn't true.

In the same way, most people don't want to say that they take the Bible literally, because most of us still have two hands — we haven't chopped one off yet. But, didn't Jesus say something about cutting off your hand if it causes you to sin? So we don't want to say that all of the Bible is literal but we also don't want to say that it isn't literal because we really believe that Jesus lived a perfect life, died, and was raised - that *literally* happened, otherwise our faith is in vain, and we are to be pitied (1 Corinthians 15:12-19).

So what do we say when someone asks this question? How about: *"I seek to read it contextually."* It's kind of long, but it's shorter than "I take it literally where it's intended to be literal and figuratively where the original intent is figurative." Expecting the entire Bible to be able to be understood in a single way is rather absurd, after all. It's a library of separate books, poetry, historical narratives, and letters written by at least 40 authors over a period of 1,500 years. You wouldn't go to your local library, check out multiple books in different genres, eras, and languages, and still expect them to all be written the same way. That's not a reasonable or realistic approach to take with the Bible either.

It's interesting that people want to make an issue out of taking Scripture literally or not, because every one of us is very comfortable understanding what we read with varying degrees of literality. I've never known anyone who, upon reading a sports headline in the newspaper, called 911 and said, "I'm appalled at the mass murder that occurred in the football stadium this past weekend when the Knights *killed* the Trojans! What's being done about it?!" We understand that figures of speech such as simile, metaphor, and hyperbole are frequently used by writers to make a point. This is the most important idea you could ever understand! (See, that's hyperbole.)

A literal reading of Scripture would lead us to believe that the sun revolves around the earth since "The sun rises and the sun sets" (Ecclesiastes 1:5). A literal reading would also mean we should cut our hands off if they're involved in sin (Matthew 18:8), or that Jesus is an actual vine (John 15:5) and I'm somehow a wooden branch, even though the mirror shows me otherwise. As you can see, taking all of the Bible literally, is *literally* a big problem, if we want to understand the life-changing meaning that these inspired words convey.

Many atheists like to attack Christians' commitment to the historical Jesus by using some of the passages quoted above. After pointing out that these passages make less sense when interpreted literally, they usually move on to argue that many other parts of Scripture shouldn't be interpreted literally either. How about the virgin birth? Or the resurrection? Or creation? Or God himself? If we can't understand and defend a correct contextual reading of Scripture, we won't have solid ground to stand on when confronted. We also won't have a hope of getting such a person to even listen to the gospel.

WHAT IS LITERAL AND WHAT IS NOT?

I've made the case for not taking all of Scripture literally, but how do we know which sections are literal and which aren't? We can generally use the same clues that we use when reading English. For instance, when we read poetry today, we expect the writer to use exaggeration and figurative language. We're comfortable with that. We need to be comfortable with that in the Bible too.

Now, you might ask, "How do we know when a Scripture passage is poetry?" That's a good question! Many modern translations such as the NET and the ESV format poetry very differently from normal text, much as modern poetry is formatted. This is an obvious clue.

Another simple tip to remember is that, when we read history, we should tend toward a literal interpretation of Scripture, where a tree is a tree and a branch is a branch. But when we read Jesus and the other prophets, metaphor, exaggeration, and irony abound. Half of the time, Jesus refuses to give straight answers to the questions put to him, and a lot of the questions Jesus asked were loaded. Additionally, sometimes he explains a parable after he gives it (Matthew 13:1–23), and other times he leaves us wondering (Matthew 13:33).

While Paul and Moses have a straightforward style, Jesus and most prophets invite us to *think* by making liberal use of poems, parables, and analogies. In these contexts, a tree might be a person (Luke 6:43), and a branch might be a Christian (John 15:5).

Some translations include footnotes that can be invaluable in understanding some of the background and nuances of the text. Every Christian's library should contain commentaries along with their Bible. Our goal should always be to understand the original intent that God and the authors had in mind when the words were penned.

Also, you can use two or more translations to help gain a more comprehensive understanding what a passage is saying. For example, try pairing one of the ESV, NASB, or NKJV translations with one of the NET, NIV, or NLT translations so that you can see both a more word-for-word translation alongside a phrase-for-phrase translation. This will greatly aid in your study efforts.

ORIGINAL INTENT

Original intent is extremely important! A passage of Scripture cannot *mean* something that it never *meant*. In other words, as a rule, if our interpretation of a passage doesn't match the meaning the author had in mind, we have made a mistake. Scripture isn't just composed of the individual words of God; those original words accurately express the thoughts of God — the heart of God. If you arrive at an interpretation of a verse that doesn't match the original, you haven't learned what God thinks; you've learned what you think.

Christians should not hold the view that there are "special messages" in Scripture just for them. There is no room for a "personal meaning" different from the original meaning. God had *one* message and *one* meaning in mind when he inspired the authors to write what they did. This inspiration was a work of the Holy Spirit in their lives.

And still today, the Holy Spirit works in the lives of Christians to help bring them to a clearer and more accurate understanding of Scripture — to *illuminate* it. We can be totally confident that the Spirit gives us understanding of the Word sufficient for bringing us to salvation. However, beyond this, we have no guarantee that we will arrive at the correct interpretation of a passage, no matter how much we pray or study. This is due to us being non-omniscient, fallen, imperfect beings.

Our lack of ability to always arrive at the correct interpretation of a passage seems obvious because some of the most notable figures and fathers of the church and our faith arrived at different conclusions about certain passages and theological concepts. These great men of God prayed and studied, but they arrived at different conclusions nonetheless. For example, still today we disagree about aspects of salvation. Is it God's sovereign act, or man's freewill choice? Is it both or neither? Can it be lost? Are some predestined for hell and some for heaven? Such questions represent only one of many areas of disagreement founded on differing interpretations of the same texts.

Many such disagreements may be laid at the doorstep of the modern-day reader's distance from the original culture and languages. Furthermore, many of Paul's letters were written in response to situations and contexts that he assumes his readers will know which modern readers will not. Think of listening to one side of a telephone conversation: you can get a good idea of what's being discussed, but some of the specific details may be hard to pin down.

This kind of one-sided conversation transpires in epistles such as 1 Corinthians and Galatians. Paul is addressing specific situations, and we need to be careful not to extrapolate his counsel to other contexts where such application could be unwarranted.

For example, Paul says we are justified by faith: "For we hold that one is justified by faith apart from works of the law" (Romans 3:28 ESV), but James says we are justified by works: "You see that a person is justified by works and not by faith alone" (James 2:24 NET). At first blush, this seems to be a. However, let's look at the *context* of each of these.

FAITH VS. WORKS

The first step toward understanding this apparent contradiction is to look at other passages — use the Bible to interpret the Bible. Ephesians 2:8-9 says, "For by grace you are saved through faith, and this is not from yourselves, it is the gift of God; it is not from works, so that no one can boast." So, if you're keeping score, that's two tallies for "faith" and one tally for "works." And indeed, if we were to survey more of the NT, we'd find a preponderance of verses saying that salvation is through faith, not works. Does this mean James is wrong? Let's move on to the second step to find out.

When looking at a passage of Scripture, you must also consider the context; in this case, the audience. James was writing to people who thought their faith was just something to sit around and think about — no action was required. These practitioners of antinomianism[1] believed they didn't need to follow any moral code or do good works; they just needed faith. However, this flies in the face of Jesus saying, "If you love me, you will obey my commandments" (John 14:15). It also goes against Jesus' teaching on the beatitudes — help the brothers who are poor, hungry, thirsty, etc.

Most would agree that the faith Jesus and Paul taught about was one of action, of "bearing fruit." Now that we understand more of the context, it's starting to look like James was right to correct these people and their misunderstanding of faith and works. However, did he err too far on the side of works? In step three, we will look more closely at the specific works that James chose to convey this idea.

The Oxford English Dictionary contains 171,476 words, and the English language has many more words than other modern languages. However, even with all of our unique words, we still use the same word to refer to *different* ideas. This is what is happening with James and Paul.

We need to consider how these different authors are using the word "justified" because, contrary to what many of use were taught throughout our lives, words don't have meanings — they have *usages*. If I say the word "milk," you would have no idea what I meant. Was I referring to the white tasty drink (noun)? Or did I mean, "To exploit or defraud someone" (verb)? Without me using the word in a sentence (its context), you can't know.

When Paul speaks of justification, he means, "To declare free of blame, or absolve of guilt." James, on the other hand, isn't writing about removing our guilt in the eyes of God — he is speaking of how we, "show, or exhibit, our right standing" with God. These are very different usages. When we understand these verses in their contexts, we see that they are complementary, rather than contradictory.

Christians were justified (in the guilt sense) once and for all when they received salvation, and they continue to justify themselves (in the exhibiting sense) by following Christ's commands.

So, when you want to understand a passage:

❖ Consider what other related passages with more clarity say.
❖ Consider the context — author, audience, genre, and time period.
❖ Consider that a word's meaning in a passage depends on its usage, not its dictionary definition.

These three steps aren't exhaustive, but they are a great start.

CONFIDENCE AND HUMILITY

Two things need to be understood in all of this. First, *there is one correct interpretation of a passage of Scripture.* Even though we cannot know with total certainty that we have arrived at that correct conclusion, we need to remember that there is indeed a right view and there are many wrong views. A view is not correct just because "that's what it means to me."

Second, *we need to strive to be confident and humble in the positions we take on a passage.* A non-confident Christian is an ineffective Christian. We need to study, pray, and try to arrive at correct conclusions about a passage. We need to apply sound principles of interpretation such as considering how it would have been understood by the original audience in its context. If we haven't considered these items, we shouldn't be confident about our view on a passage.

However, we *need* to be confident so that we will stand firm in our beliefs and convictions. This is why it's so important for us to arrive at the meaning of the text by using sound methods of interpretation. The Bible was written, in part, so that we *know* the truth, and in knowing, have faith. Christians who *know* the "what" and "why" of their beliefs are much more likely to be effective and confident.

This confidence must also be tempered with equal parts of humility. We need to be conscious of our fallen condition. We need to acknowledge and internalize that we *could be* wrong in our convictions and interpretations. Christianity does have a corner on truth, but, as individual Christians, we have no guarantee of coming to correct interpretations on nonessential matters like whether or not the rapture is before the tribulation, or if infants should be baptized or not.

There is nothing wrong with being honest about the uncertainty in our position. In fact, that is the most truthful thing we can do. Humility requires us to not esteem our own opinions and conclusions more highly than we ought. It is possible that we are mistaken in our beliefs about the Bible's inerrancy and Jesus' resurrection. Is it plausible? No. And, it certainly isn't probable.

WHAT WE LEARNED

❖ The Bible contains both literal and non-literal passages.

❖ We can use the context and formatting of a passage, along with other clues and logic, to get a good idea of which passages should be understood in a literal way, and which shouldn't.

❖ When someone tries to say that, because some passages are non-literal, the whole Bible is non-literal, we can point out that our Bible is a literary collection of 66 different documents, in different genres and languages, written by many different authors over a long time period. We wouldn't expect any other collection with similar characteristics to be understood in a single way, and we shouldn't expect this of the Bible either.

❖ There is one correct interpretation for each passage. We need to try to arrive at the correct understanding of God's original intent and have confidence and humility in our position.

8

DID JESUS PHYSICALLY RISE FROM THE DEAD? PART 1

Christianity depends on the God-man – Jesus Christ – living, dying on a Roman cross, and then rising from the dead. Virtually all historians (even secular ones) affirm those first two events: the life and death of a real person named Jesus. However, the claim that Jesus rose from the dead is hotly contested.

WHY DOES DISAGREEMENT PERSIST?

The first possible reason for dismissing the resurrection is naturalism. If you believe that there is no such thing as the supernatural, then a resurrection (which is by definition a supernatural event) could not have taken place. To a naturalist, a resurrection is as absurd as saying that a square circle exists. As I have pointed out previously, the naturalist's position is almost always a *starting* point, and not a conclusion.

The second reason might be that a person thinks that we are too far removed from the original events to know what actually happened. Usually at the heart of this objection is the belief that the Bible is not trustworthy. However, as we saw in the "Can We Trust the Bible?" chapter, we have good reasons for believing what the NT writers said.

What's interesting to note is that many scholars (even secular ones) believe the Gospel writers gave honest accounts, in which they wrote down what they believed to have happened. Now, some of these scholars don't think the resurrection actually happened, only that the

NT authors *thought* it happened. In this view, the Gospels are not Holy Spirit-inspired truth but instead are just accurately preserved documents written by normal men that convey their experiences from their point of view.

There are two things that must be true for us to be justified in believing the resurrection.
1. The tomb Jesus was buried in must have been empty.
2. People believed they saw Jesus after his very public death.

THE EMPTY TOMB

The first event we need to analyze is the claim that the tomb was empty. A very commonsense starting point is that the tomb must have been empty when the disciples started preaching. Since people claimed to have seen Jesus physically resurrected in the same city in which he was killed, if his body were still in his tomb, it would have been easy to demonstrate. There's no better way to quash the claim that a dead guy is now alive than to show people the body!

Independent Sources in Agreement

There are also multiple *independent* sources that attest to the tomb being empty.

❖ Mark (Pre-70 AD)
❖ Paul (36 A.D., on his visit to Jerusalem)
❖ John
❖ Matthew & Luke

Most scholars believe that Matthew and Luke relied heavily on Mark's Gospel when writing their own. However, both Matthew and Luke contain unique details that indicate that they are not entirely based on Mark. Then, there's the Gospel of John which gives all indication of having been written independently from Mark. Lastly, while Paul's much shorter account in 1 Corinthians 15:3-5 was most likely received from the disciples on his visit to Jerusalem in AD 36, it gives all the essential details that the others contain, and more.

These five independent accounts all state that Jesus was buried. Now, some people will say that we can't trust the Bible because its Christian authors are biased. However, this objection is simply ridiculous. The same logic would have us not believing anything written about the Holocaust by Jews because they must be biased too! What such an argument really says is that we can't trust things written by people who believe what they write. Hopefully you see how absurd this is.

We should evaluate the biblical documents just as we should any other documents — on their merits. Such an approach, the same as is taken by historians, leads us to the conclusion that the authors wrote down what they really believed took place. It's up to us to see if that actually makes sense.

John A. T. Robinson of Cambridge University says that Jesus' burial by Joseph of Arimathea is "one of the earliest and best-attested facts about Jesus."[1] There are also other reasons to believe what the NT authors wrote. Mark's Gospel is simple and understated. He doesn't embellish but rather is very matter-of-fact. This stands in stark contrast to the second-century, faked, Gospel of Peter which describes "Jesus' triumphant exit from the tomb as a gigantic figure whose head reaches above the clouds, supported by giant angels, followed by a talking cross, heralded by a voice from heaven, and all witnessed by a Roman guard, the Jewish leaders, and a multitude of spectators!"[2] This is the type of description we find in accounts that are obviously false. However, Mark's description of events is very plain and straightforward, which is characteristic of accurate historical accounts.

Women

Another piece of evidence that lends credibility to the Gospel accounts is the gender of those who first discovered that the tomb was empty. They were women. In our modern culture, most people seem to think nothing of this. However, in Jesus' day, women held extremely low social standing, and their testimony wasn't considered credible in court. In fact, their social position was so low that one of the daily prayers of a Jewish man was "Blessed are you, Lord our God, ruler of the universe, who has not created me a Gentile, a slave, or a woman."

Before we continue on with the significance of this, it needs to be pointed out that, while God's people held this incorrect view of women, God did not and does not hold that same view. Even though the Israelites were God's chosen people, they weren't immune from perverting moral ideals such as the equality and equal worth of men *and* women.

If the Gospel writers were fabricating the whole story, they would not have had women discover the empty tomb. When you're trying to get people to take you seriously, you're not going to base a large part of your story on people who society and the legal system consider to be unreliable witnesses, *unless it actually happened that way*. We've discussed the principle of embarrassment before, and this is certainly another application of it. The embarrassing detail of women discovering the empty tomb is most likely true.

No Denial

We have evidence that the Jewish authorities of the day couldn't deny that the tomb was empty. In fact, they tried to cover it up. Matthew describes this in chapter 28 of his Gospel.

> While they were going, some of the guard went into the city and told the chief priests everything that had happened. After they had assembled with the elders and formed a plan, they gave a large sum of money to the soldiers, telling them, "You are to say, 'His disciples came at night and stole his body while we were asleep.' If this matter is heard before the governor, we will satisfy him and keep you out of trouble." So they took the money and did as they were instructed. And this story is told among the Jews to this day. (Matthew 28:11–15)

Here we see that Matthew was concerned about refuting a widespread Jewish explanation of the resurrection. Since the Jews were trying to circulate this story about the disciples stealing the body, we can easily infer that the Jews knew the tomb was empty. There would be no need for a cover-up if Jesus were still in the tomb!

Empty Tomb Summary

In a survey of over 2,000 documents, scholar Gary Habermas has found that 75 percent of scholars, including non-Christian scholars, who have written on the subject of the resurrection accept the historical reliability of the women's discovery of the empty tomb. Additionally, Jacob Kremer, a New Testament critic who has specialized in the study of the resurrection, says, "By far most exegetes hold firmly to the reliability of the biblical statements about the empty tomb."[3] An "exegete" is someone who studies the biblical texts.

It's no wonder that such large numbers of educated people believe the tomb was empty, for the evidence is excellent. We have multiple, distinct, and yet cohesive accounts of the same event. These accounts include embarrassing details, and they show us that the authorities could not deny the most important fact: the empty tomb.

As we're about to see, once you establish that the tomb was empty, the case for the resurrection is pretty much a slam dunk. This is why people who want to deny the resurrection usually start by denying the empty tomb. But as we've seen with even our brief survey of the evidence, it is much more likely that the tomb was empty than that it wasn't.

JESUS' APPEARANCES AFTER HIS DEATH

The disciples moved from a belief that Jesus was dead, for they saw him die, to a belief that he was alive because they saw him, talked with him, and ate with him. If you were to share a meal with someone or see them walking around, you aren't going to believe that person is dead any longer. Let's look at the multiple accounts of people who saw Jesus after his death.

> For I passed on to you as of first importance what I also received — that Christ died for our sins according to the scriptures, and that he was buried, and that he was raised on the third day according to the scriptures, and that he appeared to Cephas, then to the twelve. Then he appeared to more than five hundred of the brothers and sisters at one time, most of whom are still alive, though some have fallen asleep. Then he appeared to James, then to all the apostles. Last of all, as though to one born at the wrong time, he appeared to me also. (1 Corinthians 15:3—8)

Peter

Here, Paul is passing on what he knew from talking with people who were eyewitnesses. The Gospels don't detail the appearance to Peter (also known as Cephas), but Paul includes it here since he most certainly learned of it directly from Peter when they spent two weeks together in Jerusalem, three years after Paul's conversion on the Damascus road. Additionally, Luke independently includes this in his Gospel: "The Lord has risen indeed, and has appeared to Simon!"

(Luke 24:34). This is the same person — *Simon* Peter — who was also called Cephas.

So, we have multiple early and independent sources attesting to Jesus' appearance to Peter, and virtually all New Testament scholars agree (for varying reasons) that Peter did see a post-mortem appearance of Jesus.

The Disciples

The second group Paul mentions is "the twelve." This refers to the original group of twelve disciples that were chosen by Jesus. Even though Judas is missing, which technically makes eleven disciples, this doesn't affect the formal title of the group.

This resurrection appearance is the best attested to. Paul had personally talked with members of the twelve, and this appearance is independently reported in Luke 24:36–42 and John 20:19–20.

The Five Hundred

The Gospel writers don't include the details about the 500 witnesses. However, these were personally known to Paul, since he knew that some of this group had since died, though most were still alive. While it's true that 1 Corinthians 15 is the only place in the New Testament where this detail is found, it is inconceivable that Paul would make this up. By including this detail Paul is effectively saying, "There are hundreds witnesses out there, *go talk to them.*" 1 Corinthians is Paul's public letter to the church at Corinth, and it would be foolish to write a letter filled with lies to a large group of people that invites those people to go talk to the supposed witnesses! The only reasonable conclusion is that the event actually happened.

This appearance to the 500 most likely happened in Galilee because the progression of appearances goes from Jerusalem to Galilee and back to Jerusalem. A large gathering on a hillside in Galilee is the most likely place for this appearance because it was probably the same hillside where thousands of people came to hear Jesus teach earlier in his ministry.

When Mary Magdalene and Mary, the mother of James and Joseph, encounter Jesus after they leave the tomb, he says to them, "Do not be afraid. Go and tell my brothers to go to Galilee. They will see me there" (Matthew 28:10). The appearance to the 500 could have been the very appearance that the angel at Jesus' tomb predicted.

James

In Mark 3:21, toward the beginning of Jesus' ministry, we see that his own brothers don't believe him to be a prophet or the Messiah. Instead, they believe that "he is out of his mind." According to the principle of embarrassment, we can hold this claim as historical fact. Manuscripts do exist in which scribes removed this section about his family believing him to be crazy because the scribes understood just how embarrassing that would be.

However, the Bible contains more detail about Jesus' brothers. James, Jesus' younger brother, is part of the gathering of the disciples in the upper room after Jesus' death (Acts 1:14), and through Paul's later writing we come to understand that Paul views James as an apostle. In fact, on Paul's second visit to Jerusalem (fourteen years after his first visit), he refers to James as one of the three "pillars" of the Jerusalem church (Galatians 2:9).

All of that makes it clear that James changed his beliefs about who his older brother was. We can be certain that he believed Jesus to be the Christ because as Jewish historian Josephus chronicles, James was illegally stoned *for his faith in Christ* by the Sanhedrin (Jewish religious leaders) sometime after A.D. 60. He was stoned for claiming that his older brother was God — the same older brother he used to believe was insane.

What could account for such a change? There can be little doubt that the reason was, as Paul wrote, "[Jesus] appeared to James" (1 Corinthians 15:7) after his resurrection. Little else would result in such a drastic change of belief. James moved from believing that Jesus was a *lunatic* to calling him *Lord*. According to the skeptical New Testament critic Hans Grass, James' conversion is one of the surest proofs of Jesus' resurrection.[4]

Conclusions about Jesus' Appearances

The Gospels aren't the only historical documents to chronicle the post-death sightings of Jesus. Flavius Josephus, writing in his work *Antiquities of the Jews*, includes the following:

> Pilate condemned him [Jesus] to be crucified and to die. But those who had become his disciples did not abandon his discipleship. **They reported that he had appeared to them three**

days after his crucifixion, and that he was alive." (Emphasis added)

We have seen that multiple accounts written independently of each other all make the claim that Jesus rose from the dead. There can be no denying that, at the very least, hundreds of people *believed* that he wasn't in the grave. Critics can try to explain away how these appearances may have happened — maybe they were hallucinations — but what they cannot reasonably do is claim that people didn't sincerely believe that Christ rose from the dead. As the skeptical German critic Gerd Ludemann emphatically states, "It may be taken as historically certain that Peter and the disciples had experiences after Jesus' death in which Jesus appeared to them as the risen Christ."

THE RESURRECTION AS A FOUNDATION

While it is common knowledge that Christianity leapt into existence in the middle of first century AD, we must answer the question of *why* it came into existence. While on earth, Jesus claimed to be the Messiah who had been prophesied long before. But then he was killed. His death at the hands of the Romans in no way fit with the understanding the Jews had about their future king and savior. They expected a military leader, not a suffering servant. They expected the Messiah to deliver them from Roman oppression, not for him to be killed by those very Romans. In other words, Jesus in no way embodied what the Jews expected in a Messiah.

So why did hundreds upon hundreds of Jews start converting to Christianity, and begin claiming that Jesus was the Messiah after his death? The only answer that makes sense is the resurrection. You're going to have a hard time creating a new religion around a man who was supposed to be God if that man got killed and stayed dead. However, the resurrection set right everything that was wrong as a result of Jesus' death. Now, due to seeing Jesus alive in the flesh, the disciples fully believed he was God — the Messiah — who he had always claimed to be.

Without the resurrection, no one, least of all the Jews, would have believed Jesus was God. We don't trust people who are dead to save us; only someone who is alive can do that, and the Jews understood this.

Without the resurrection and the post-death appearances, there would be no Christianity today.

WHAT WE LEARNED

❖ The tomb must have been empty when the disciples started preaching.

❖ The authorities could not demonstrate that Jesus was still in the tomb.

❖ Multiple independent sources attest to the empty tomb and post-mortem appearances. What they say is in harmony with the extra-biblical data.

❖ It is certain that the disciples talked and walked with the risen Christ.

❖ Only a bodily resurrection explains the start of Christianity in a Jewish culture.

9

DID JESUS PHYSICALLY RISE FROM THE DEAD? PART 2

Christians do not make up the whole world because some people have never had the opportunity to hear about Jesus and others think that God doesn't exist. But, I would say that the main reason people don't believe Jesus is God is that they don't think he actually rose from the dead. There are even many who have seen the excellent evidence for the resurrection but still don't believe. This is because there are quite a few other hypotheses for the post-death sightings of Jesus. In the following section we're going to examine some of the popular ones.

Historians take into account multiple factors when evaluating proposed explanations for an event. A good explanation:

❖ Explains more of the evidence than competing explanations.
❖ Makes the evidence more probable.
❖ Fits better with true and accepted current beliefs.
❖ Requires adopting fewer new beliefs for which there is no independent evidence.[1]

Here's an example of how we could use one of these principles. In the television show *The Big Bang Theory*, Sheldon, a theoretical physicist, is explaining to Leonard, his roommate and an experimental physicist, about his recent work in string theory. Here is a sample of their dialogue:

Leonard: At least I didn't have to invent 26 dimensions just to make the math come out.

Sheldon: I didn't invent them. They're there.

Leonard: In what universe?

Sheldon: In all of them, that is the point!

Sheldon *could* be correct in his hypothesis, but, as Leonard pointed out, his explanation requires adopting many new beliefs (like the 26 new dimensions) which don't have independent evidence. In Leonard's mind, this makes it a less likely explanation. Historians would agree.

The Conspiracy Hypothesis

The disciples stole Jesus' body from the tomb and then lied to people about his appearances, so that the whole resurrection was a hoax.

This is, perhaps, the oldest of the proposed explanations, since, as we saw, Matthew mentions that the Jews started circulating the story that the disciples stole the body to cover up the fact that they didn't have it. This hypothesis may have been persuasive back then, but modern scholarship has totally abandoned it today. As we examine how this theory stands up to the criteria above, you'll see why.

The one thing this explanation has going for it is that *it explains all of the evidence*. The tomb was empty because Jesus' body was stolen, and when the disciples claimed to see him after the "resurrection," they were simply lying.

But, we must ask ourselves, is this explanation probable? *There are many details this theory does not explain*. If the Gospel writers were making up everything in their Gospels, why would they write that women discovered the empty tomb, when most Jews wouldn't have believed what the women said? Any Jew would know better than to fabricate this detail. Additionally, serious questions can be raised about how the 500 people who claimed to be witnesses could have been in on the conspiracy.

The biggest problem with this hypothesis is that it fails to explain why the disciples believed that Jesus rose from the dead. If you want to know what someone believes, don't just read what they wrote. You should also examine how they acted. Even a superficial look at the lives of the disciples shows that they were convinced that Jesus was alive because they were willing to *die* while holding to that very claim. No one is going to die for a lie that gains them nothing. This is why scholars who study Jesus' resurrection have universally recognized that there is no way to plausibly deny that the early disciples at least sincerely *believed* that Jesus had been raised from the dead.

The conspiracy theory assigns motives and actions to the earliest disciples for which we do not have a shred of evidence. It's completely anachronistic to imagine that first-century Jews would make up and rally behind the resurrection of a man that died claiming to be the messiah. Jewish theology had no concept of the isolated resurrection of a single individual. So, it would make no sense for the Jewish writers to say this unless it happened, since they were writing to a largely Jewish audience.

The Conspiracy Hypothesis is a poor explanation for the evidence, which is why it has been discarded by scholars. This theory, like most conspiracies, unravels under the strain of time and examination.

The Apparent Death Hypothesis

> Jesus swooned on the cross; he wasn't really dead. After he was buried, he escaped and convinced the disciples that he had risen from the dead.

This view was introduced by critics around the early 19th century, and a cursory evaluation reveals that *it does explain most of the evidence.* The evidence that shows he was buried is correct because he actually was buried. The tomb was found to be empty because he had left. People claimed to see him alive because he really was alive.

What we must consider, though, is how *probable* is this explanation? Are we really supposed to believe that Jesus survived a Roman execution by chance? How did a man who barely survived his execution roll away the stone covering the tomb *while he was on the inside*? And most damningly, how would a half-dead Jesus have convinced anyone that he was God and had just conquered death, when he would have been barely clinging to life, desperately in need of medical attention? Nothing about the apparent death hypothesis inspires the life-changing belief that he had gloriously risen from the dead!

It was the sole job of Roman executioners to ensure that their victims were dead. Since it could be hard to determine the moment of death, they would sometimes thrust a spear into the condemned man's side to ensure that he was dead. We see a description of this very act in John 19:34. "But one of the soldiers pierced his side with a spear, and blood and water flowed out immediately." The preceding verse tells us that they knew Jesus was already dead, but they stabbed him anyway.

There's something very interesting about this description in John 19:34 that "blood and water flowed out." Early Christians, and indeed many today, weren't quite sure what to make of this, and when the church fathers were writing commentaries on this section around the second century they weren't sure how to interpret it either. People back then weren't familiar with blood and water flowing out of a person when they were stabbed.

The church fathers thought that maybe this was symbolic, where the "blood" is a reference to the "flesh" and the "water" is a reference to the "Spirit," or where "water" is a reference to "baptism" and blood to "the mysteries of the faith."[2] In fact, there are some commentators today who also take this symbolically.

However, there's another explanation for why John writes that "blood and water flowed out." It's probable that blood and water *did* actually flow out of Jesus when he was stabbed. Our 21st century medical knowledge is extremely advanced compared to that of the first century, and John's description fits with what medical science would predict for a person who had been lashed 39 times, forced to carry his cross, and then hung on that very cross.

Jesus most likely had a pericardial and pleural effusion.[3] "Pericardial" refers to the heart, and "pleural" to the lungs. A pericardial effusion is when fluid leaks into and pools around the heart, and a pleural effusion is when that happens around the lungs.

People who were flogged would often go into hypovolemic shock. In other words, they would lose so much blood that their heart would race to pump much needed blood, even though there wasn't much blood to be pumped. The kidneys would shut down to help preserve fluids, and because of this, the person would experience an intense desire to drink and replenish lost fluids.

We would expect Jesus to have suffered from this because of how he was flogged, and we also see evidence of it in the Gospels. He collapsed while carrying his cross — an indication of low blood pressure — and he asked for a drink while on the cross: "I thirst" (John 19:28).

The sustained rapid heartbeat caused by being in shock also causes fluid to gather around the heart and lungs. So, when the Roman solider pierced Jesus with a spear in his [probably left] side, blood and water flow out because those fluids had gathered and pooled around Jesus' heart and lungs, which would both have been punctured by a spear thrust to his left side.

This is a great example of how modern science can help confirm the most important claim of Christianity — the resurrection. We now understand this event better in some ways than even those who witnessed it.

What this evidence shows is just how inadequate the Apparent Death Hypothesis is. As we've seen, Jesus' physical state of health was horrible, and there's little chance he would have survived a crucifixion, much less escaped to convince those who knew him best that he transcended death and was the prophesied messiah, come to reign for all eternity.

This inadequacy is the reason that this hypothesis has virtually no New Testament scholars defending it today!

The Hallucination Hypothesis

All of the resurrection appearances were actually hallucinations.

In my experience and lifetime, this seems to be the theory that most people have heard of, and it dates back to 1835, when the book *The Life of Jesus, Critically Examined* was written by German Bible critic David Friedrich Strauss.

This hypothesis *does not explain much of the evidence.* It fails to explain why the tomb was empty, and that's quite a large failing. Was this also a hallucination by the disciples, *the Romans, and the Jews?* Remember that no group denied the tomb was empty.

Additionally, this theory doesn't explain why the disciples believed that Jesus was resurrected. Scholar N. T. Wright points out that, for someone in the ancient world, visions of the deceased were not taken as evidence that the person was alive, but as evidence that he was dead![4]

Today, a surprisingly high percentage of people who have just suffered the loss of a loved one see a vision of that person.[5] However, these visions do not convince the seer that the departed person has come back to life; quite to the contrary, they are a reminder of the person's deceased state.

Because of the Jewish beliefs of the day, the empty tomb greatly predisposed the disciples to believe that God had taken Jesus to heaven, not that Jesus had been resurrected to life and was still on earth.

The hallucination hypothesis *doesn't seem very probable in explaining their belief.* Let's say, for the sake of argument, that Peter, moved by his guilt at having denied Christ, has a vision of Jesus. Or, more probably, he had a vision just as others do who have lost loved ones. Even if Peter had such a vision, would it be powerful enough to explain his belief in Christ's resurrection? I think not.

Jesus appeared multiple times, to multiple people, in multiple places, in multiple circumstances. He appeared to individuals and to groups, to his followers and others. Even if you say that, by some unexplainable cause, the hallucinations moved like a virus from disciple to disciple, this fails to explain why James claimed to see Jesus (1 Corinthians 15:7), since he was not a disciple, and he didn't think Jesus was God.

The hallucination hypothesis *is also quite implausible.* The psychoanalytic basis for it is rooted in some of the theories of Jung and Freud — theories that have since been widely rejected. As William Lane Craig points out, "Psychoanalysis is difficult enough to carry out even with patients on the psychoanalyst's couch, so to speak, but it's next to impossible with historical figures. That's why historians reject the genre of psychobiography[6] today."[7]

The hallucination hypothesis is still in circulation today, unlike the other hypotheses that have come and gone. However, I hope you see that it has numerous problems which make it a poor theory. But the main question is: How do all of these hypotheses stack up against the Resurrection Hypothesis?

The Resurrection Hypothesis

Jesus died on a Roman cross, was stabbed in the side, buried in a borrowed tomb, raised to life three days later, and appeared to hundreds of people.

The resurrection hypothesis *explains all of the evidence,* which is more than can be said of some (but not all) of the other proposed explanations. It also makes the evidence seem very probable, and it is the most plausible hypothesis of them all.

This hypothesis does require adopting the belief that God exists. But this is only one new belief, whereas most of the other theories require adopting many new beliefs. Also, before trying to convince someone of the truthfulness of the resurrection, the arguments that we have covered in previous chapters for the existence of God can be used to convince a person that belief in God is a logical and rational conclusion.

As William Lane Craig points out, "It should be noted, too, that scientific hypotheses regularly include the supposition of the existence of new entities, such as quarks, strings, gravitons, black holes, and the like, without those theories being characterized as contrived."[8]

Is it unreasonable to suggest a supernatural explanation here? Are we saying, "We don't know what happened, so... God did it."? No, we aren't.

Based on Jesus' exceptional personal life and ministry, and his claims about who he was and who his Father was, we must be open to considering a supernatural explanation for the evidence. Anyone who fails to consider this as an option does not do so because they have come to the conclusion that it is a poor explanation. To the contrary, *for someone familiar with the evidence*, a rejection of the resurrection hypothesis is almost always the result of a commitment to naturalism/materialism.

On the other hand, those who have a sketchy acquaintance with the evidence dismiss the idea of Jesus' resurrection. However, you are now equipped to talk about this and explain the evidence to such a person, just as you are more equipped to discuss the outright rejection of the idea of God. Once you convince someone that there is a God, you can then look at the evidence for the resurrection.

WHAT WE LEARNED

- ❖ The Conspiracy Hypothesis fails to explain why the disciples would die for a lie; it assigns motives to them for which we have no evidence.
- ❖ The Apparent Death Hypothesis is contradicted by modern medical science and fails to account for the confidence the disciples had in the power of Jesus over death.

- ❖ The Hallucination Hypothesis has no credible modern psychological evidence to support it, and there has never been a documented case like it.
- ❖ There are no good hypotheses for the empty tomb and post-mortem appearances *except* for God the Father raising Jesus to life!

10

THE TRINITY: THREE GODS IN ONE?

The Trinity is perhaps the most difficult Christian doctrine to understand and explain without introducing some sort of heresy. Since none of us wants to be a heretic, we're going to look at what the Trinity actually is, critique common analogies, and develop a way of describing the Trinity to others.

THE DOCTRINE OF THE TRINITY

While the Bible never uses the word "Trinity,"[1] the Christian doctrine of the Trinity is firmly rooted in what Scripture teaches.

Here is what the Bible teaches about God, and by extension, the Trinity.

God is one being comprised of thee equal and distinct persons, the Father, the Son, and the Holy Spirit. All persons are of the same substance; all persons are fully God; all persons have always existed, none are created; all persons are equal in power and in glory.

Now, we're going to examine each statement and the scriptural support for it.

God Is One Being Comprised of Thee Equal Persons

It is common to hear atheists (and even some Christians) say, "The Trinity is three beings in one being." Generally, the person will go on to say that this is a contradiction, similar to saying that there can be a "square circle." Some Christians, not realizing that they just got painted into a corner, will reply, "Well, it's just something you have to take on faith." But is that the correct response? Not quite.

The Christian who accepts the atheist's definition ("three beings in one being") without realizing that the definition is incorrect has few responses available to him. However, the Christian definition of the Trinity is that God is three *persons* in one *being*. That is a huge difference. If the atheist is correct, and the Trinity is three beings in one being, then that would be a contradiction — he's absolutely right about that.[2]

In order for there to be an actual contradiction, the Law of Non-Contradiction — the second law of logic — must be violated. If you'll remember back to the Truth chapter, the Law of Non-Contradiction states that:

A thing cannot be what it is, and what it is not, at the same time, and in the same way.

So, God cannot be three beings and also be one being. He can't be three persons and also be one person. However, neither of these should cause trouble for the Christian. Our God — the only true and living God — is not three in the same way that he is one. Our God is **three** in *person* and **one** in *being*.

This statement is perhaps the most difficult to understand. We're only used to one being existing as one person.[3] For example, your mother is one being, one person. Besides God, there are no other real-world examples of beings who are multiple persons. That's what makes describing God so difficult.

Let's look at a passage that speaks to the three distinct persons in the Trinity.

After **Jesus** was baptized, just as he was coming up out of the water, the heavens opened and he saw the **Spirit of God** descending like a dove and coming on him. And a voice from heaven said, "This is my one dear Son; in him **I** take great delight." (Matthew 3:16–17, emphasis added)

Here we see all three persons at once: Jesus is baptized, the Holy Spirit descends, and the Father speaks from heaven. Note that nothing in the text even suggests that Jesus is actually the Father, or that the

Father is actually the Spirit. Quite the contrary, all members of the Trinity are presented as separate and distinct from each other.

The heresy known as modalism says that God is one person who presented himself in three different modes throughout history. In the Old Testament, God presented himself as father. Then, he came as Jesus, and then as the Holy Spirit. However, this was condemned by the early church, and for good reason. It contradicts the clear teaching of Scripture where we see all three persons of God presented distinctly, as in the Matthew 3 passage above or when Jesus prays to the Father. The church father Tertullian said, "If you want me to believe him to be both the Father and the Son, show me some other passage where it is declared, 'The Lord said unto himself, I am my own Son, today I have begotten myself.'"[4] United Pentecostals represent a modern group of modalists because they deny the Trinity.

Let's look at two passages that show God to be one being.

"Listen, Israel: The Lord is our God, the Lord is one!" (Deuteronomy 6:4)

"The Father and I are one." (John 10:30)

In the John 10 passage, we see Jesus saying that he and the Father are one. Now, that shouldn't be understood to mean that Jesus and the father are identical, but rather that they are one "thing" or substance. The Greek grammar of this and other passages doesn't allow for an interpretation that says the Father is identical to Jesus.

So, we see that God is one being who is three distinct and non-identical persons.

All Persons Are of the Same Substance

When we speak of the substance of God, we do not mean that God is physical, for he isn't. God exists as a mental or spiritual substance – a divine substance. All of the members of the Trinity are of this same substance, meaning that all are fully God. None is more God than another.

All Persons Have Always Existed

God, and by extension all of the members of the Trinity, is the uncreated creator — he has no beginning and has always existed.

Even before the mountains came into existence, or you brought the world into being, you were the eternal God. (James 1:17)

Some cults, such as Jehovah's Witnesses, would say that Jesus is a created being. They base from a reading of Colossians 1:15.

He is the image of the invisible God, the first-born of all creation. (Colossians 1:15)

However, the Greek for "first-born" [πρωτότοκος] means pre-eminent, or sovereign. In other words, Jesus is sovereign over all of creation. And, if we continue reading, we see clearly that Jesus isn't created.

For all things in heaven and on earth were created by him — all things, whether visible or invisible, whether thrones or dominions, whether principalities or powers— all things were created through him and for him. (Colossians 1:16)

Paul goes to great pains to say that *all things* were created by Jesus. If Jesus created everything that exists, then he can't be part of that group of created things, or he would have created himself. And that is just as logically preposterous as saying the universe created itself.

Additionally, we have parts of John's Gospel that make this clear.

1 In the beginning was the Word, and the Word was with God, and the Word was fully God. 2 The Word was with God in the beginning. 3 All things were created by him, and apart from him not one thing was created that has been created. 14 Now the Word became flesh and took up residence among us. We saw his glory — the glory of the one and only, full of grace and truth, who came from the Father. (John 1:1–4; 14)

John says that the Word was fully God (v.1) and that the Word came from the Father and took on flesh (v.14). In other words, Jesus (called "the Word" here) existed as spirit before he came to Earth and took on flesh. And, just as Paul does, John makes it clear that *all things* were created by Jesus and that nothing was created apart from him. If Jesus created all things, then Jesus cannot be a created "thing."

All Persons Are Equal in Power

Since all persons of the Trinity are fully God, there is no difference in their power or greatness. It is a mistake to think that Jesus is greater than the Spirit, or the Father greater than Jesus. Perhaps you're thinking *but didn't Jesus say he wasn't equal with the Father?* Indeed, he did. However, there are two ways to look at a person.

The first is how they actually exist, in and of themselves. As a person who is created in the image of God, you are just as innately valuable as the President. He is no more or less valuable than you in this way. It doesn't matter if you're sick or healthy, rich or poor, you are equally valuable *in how you actually exist.* In this way, the Father, the Son, and the Holy Spirit are all equally powerful, important, and worthy of glory — there is no hierarchy.

The second way to look at a person is economically — by considering how they function and the role they play. In this view, an employee is worth less than her boss. The boss has more authority and power, and therefore makes more money. In the same way, economically, there is a hierarchy in the Trinity. The Father sends the Son, and the Son sends the Spirit. The Son and the Spirit both willingly do the will of the Father.

Now, let's address John 14:28 where Jesus says, "The Father is greater than I am." Jesus willingly humbled himself when he came to earth, and gave up the free and independent exercise of his power, doing all things in reliance on the Father. This is why, when asked, Jesus didn't know the time of his second coming.

Having humbled himself, he had no access to that information since the Father had not revealed it to him. We also see this in Philippians 2:6, where Jesus "did not regard equality with God as something to be grasped." He didn't regard it as something to be *held onto* when he came to Earth. After the resurrection, once Jesus was glorified, he regained his former power and glory as he had before the incarnation.

When we look at Jesus in Scripture, it's very important to note where in time a statement about him is being said. Is it referring to him pre-incarnation (before he took human form), during his time on earth, or after his glorification by the father and ascension to heaven? Jesus' situation and some characteristics differ in all of those. Jesus makes this clearer in John 14:10, where he says that he doesn't perform miracles or speak on his own power but on that of the Father's.

TRINITY ANALOGIES

Many Christians feel as if they need to give analogies for the Trinity when talking with or teaching others, and this feeling is quite understandable. It can be difficult to wrap your mind around three persons in one being. In order to make the Trinity easier to understand, we try to leverage a concept people are already familiar with. Usually, however, these analogies can give rise to views that have been condemned by the church as heresy!

Let's examine a few common analogies.

The Trinity is like water; there are three states: liquid, solid, and vapor. Yet, all three are water.

This actually teaches the heresy of modalism, which as noted above, says that God is one person who presented himself in three different modes throughout history.

A molecule of water cannot be liquid, solid, and vapor all at the same time. It only can exist in one state at a time and only reaches different states by changing form. To contrast, all three persons of the Trinity have existed concurrently for all eternity. The water analogy fails to capture this aspect of the living God, and should be avoided.

The Trinity is like an egg. You have the whites, the yoke, and the shell which comprise one full egg.

The problem with this analogy is that it teaches partialism, that each member of the Trinity is only part of God. This clearly contradicts the biblical teaching that all members are fully God. The yolk is not fully an egg, but only part of an egg. And the whites are not the same substance as the shell or yolk. God is not the sum of the persons of the Trinity.

The Trinity is like a man who is a father, husband, and son.

Here there is one person, but three roles. But this is just modalism repeated, and it breaks down for the same reasons as the water analogy. God exists as three persons in one being, not one person with three roles. A man can't simultaneously be a father, husband, and son to the same person.

The Trinity is like a three-leaf clover.

Take a minute and see if you can determine what's wrong with this one. It's partialism again. Just like the yolk and the egg, a leaf is not a clover. Each leaf is one-third of a clover, but Jesus is not one-third of God. He is fully God.

> The Trinity is like the sun. There is the star, the heat, and the light.

This analogy contains several different problems. The first is that this describes "logos christology," which was condemned by the church in the second century. Logos christology teaches that the Son and the Spirit have not always existed, but, instead, that they proceed from the mind of the Father. Obviously this has problems, since Scripture teaches that Jesus is coeternal with the Father.

Heat and light proceed from the sun and do not exist independently of it; hence the problem with this analogy. Additionally, neither heat nor light is a sun, so we would seem to have partialism here too.

The sun analogy could also reflect Arianism, which teaches that Jesus was the Father's first creation. This is very close to what Jehovah's witnesses believe. And as we saw when critiquing the view that Jesus is created, it falters under the weight of the scriptural evidence too.

SUMMARY

I hope you see that Trinity analogies are more trouble than they're worth and can actually do a lot of damage. I've talked with people who, when I gave them the doctrinal statement of the Trinity written above (see: The Doctrine of the Trinity), were very confused. It contradicted what they understood the Trinity to be, *based on an analogy they had found to be compelling and easy to understand.* For us to fully comprehend how an infinite being exists and functions is most likely not even possible, but we must attempt it and not settle for easy-to-understand half-truths. Should we really be surprised that using examples of created things inadequately describes their creator?

Our goal isn't to arrive at comfortable ideas but to arrive at truth. And sometimes, especially when dealing with God, this truth can require some straining in order to fully grasp it.

I don't recommend using analogies to explain the Trinity; instead, use the doctrinal statement.

> God is one being comprised of three equal and distinct persons, the Father, the Son, and the Holy Spirit. All persons are

of the same substance; all persons are fully God; all persons have always existed, none are created; all persons are equal in power and in glory.

This is the culmination of Scripture's teaching on the Trinitarian nature of God. We want to be careful not to speak too much where Scripture speaks less.

I find this situation to be similar to our understanding of gravity. We know *that* gravity exists — I'm firmly planted on the couch as I write this, due to no effort of my own. But, with all of our scientific advancement, we currently don't know *why* gravity exists.

The first time I realized this, I found it quite ironic. Many people want to say, "You aren't justified in believing in God if you can't explain everything about him and how he exists." However, even while they're uttering those words, they're firmly planted on the ground due to a force neither they nor anyone else can explain, but which they surely believe in! Modern science has some guesses about how gravity might work, but nothing that has been proven. All of this goes to show that you can be justified in believing "that" without knowing "how."

How the Trinity works is something we must take on faith (active trust in what we have good reason to believe is true). We have good evidence for the New Testament, and by extension, for the Trinity. However, knowing *that* the Trinity exists is not the same as knowing *how* the Trinity exists. Like I said, we should try to strain toward a better understanding, knowing that we must be comfortable with only what Scripture teaches. There can be no better way to love God with our minds, than to continually pursue a deeper understanding of him.

WHAT WE LEARNED

- ❖ God is *one being* comprised of three equal and distinct *persons*, the Father, the Son, and the Holy Spirit. All persons are of the same substance; all persons are fully God; all persons have always existed, none are created; all persons are equal in power and in glory.
- ❖ There is no logical contradiction in the Trinity.
- ❖ Common analogies to explain the Trinity do more harm than good. Avoid them.

11

IS BIBLICAL FAITH BLIND?

Faith is the distinguishing trait of spiritual people. It's also the "soft" target atheists shoot at. They say our faith is blind, a leap, a belief in spite of evidence, a fantasy. They attack the source of our faith — biblical accounts and personal experience — by saying that the Bible is an ancient book that has been changed more times than there are years since its penning and that many people besides Christians have personal experiences that move and shape their lives.

What did the Gospel writers have in mind when they spoke of faith? Did Jesus mean we should believe *in spite* of the evidence? Are faith and knowledge opposite ends of the spectrum so that if you know more, you must have less faith?

Sadly, this is one of the areas where many Christians are woefully misinformed as to what Scripture has to say. And, like all bad theology, misinformation leads to bad choices and thinking. So let's examine what biblical faith really is.

DEFINITIONS

Broadly speaking, there are two different *major* definitions and usages of the word *faith*.

❖ **"A system of religious beliefs."** This is the definition being used when someone speaks of "the Christian faith." It is also not the controversial usage.

❖ **"A strong belief or trust in someone or something"** Here is where the controversy lies! This is the usage we will concern ourselves within this chapter.

THE BIBLICAL EVIDENCE

Since we want to determine what the biblical concept of faith is, we need to look at the relevant biblical data. I've listed some of the relevant passages below. Emphasis has been added.

❖ "Which is easier, to say to the paralytic, 'Your sins are forgiven,' or to say, 'Stand up, take your stretcher, and walk'? But so that you may *know* that the Son of Man has authority on earth to forgive sins," – he said to the paralytic – "I tell you, stand up, take your stretcher, and go home." (Mark 2:9–11)

❖ Peter makes a case for the gospel, and then he says, "…Therefore let all the house of Israel *know* beyond a doubt that God has made this Jesus whom you crucified both Lord and Christ.' Now when they heard this, they were acutely distressed and said to Peter and the rest of the apostles, 'What should we do, brothers?' Peter said to them, '*Repent*, and each one of you be baptized in the name of Jesus Christ for the forgiveness of your sins, and you will receive the gift of the Holy Spirit.'" (Acts 2:36–38)

❖ "You will *know* the truth, and the truth will set you free." (John 8:32)

❖ "In a little while the world will not see me any longer, but you will see me; because I live, you will live too. You will *know* at that time that I am in my Father and you are in me and I am in you." (John 14:19)

You might be wondering if you missed the word "faith" in those verses; you didn't. Faith is used sometimes when salvation is in view, but many times, the words "know" and "repent" are used together. Both of these involve the mind. In the case of "knowing," a person comes to believe in the truthfulness of an idea. The original Greek word used for "repent" in the Bible is μετανοέω [metanoēō], which means "to change one's mind." It doesn't mean to say, "I'm sorry" or to "change direction" as is so often taught today. However, both of these things *should* follow from a mind that has truly been changed.

KNOWLEDGE VS. FAITH

Belief and action are what connect knowledge and faith. A good definition of knowing is "justified true *belief.*" And, when the New Testament writers use the word "faith" they usually mean "conviction of the truthfulness of something" or once again, "trust." In other words, when you come to the word "faith" in Scripture, you can usually replace it with "conviction" or "trust." This will *start* to capture the meaning much more accurately.

However, knowledge and belief on their own don't rise to the level of biblical faith, because faith requires *action.* You may have heard sermons on "active faith" before. But as far as Scripture is concerned, this is just as redundant as saying, *wet water.* Faith, by its very nature, requires action! This is what James is arguing when he says, "Faith, if it does not have works, is dead being by itself" (James 2:17). In Mark 11:22, Jesus said to the disciples, "Have faith in God." Here, he is telling them to stand firm in their convictions and *act* on them in trust.

If your faith is *just* something you sit and think or talk about, it's dead. If your actions don't match your faith, it's dead. If your political views don't match your faith, it's dead, or at least not as alive as God expects it to be. It was this concept of faith — something we sit and simply ponder — that James is writing against in chapter 2, verse 17. Those who practiced antinomianism believed they didn't need to follow any moral code or do good works; they just needed "faith." And make no mistake, an action-less "faith" is what society wants from you today.

Have you noticed the reframing of our first amendment, freedom of religion?[1] The secular public and media now refer to it as "freedom of worship." Freedom of religion protects the *actions* that naturally flow from your religious beliefs. This is a right to be left alone — you don't have to violate your religious or moral convictions. On the other hand, freedom of worship refers to your right to attend worship services with people of like belief. This "right" protects only your ability to gather together. It doesn't protect the actions that naturally follow from religious and moral views.

For instance, the original concept of freedom of religion protected business owners from being compelled to participate in actions that violate their moral beliefs and conscience, such as providing services for same-sex weddings. However, now due to this cultural redefinition of our first amendment rights, Christians can no longer refuse to provide services for same-sex wedding ceremonies. They have consistently lost court cases when sued because of denying these services.

For example, in 2006 Elaine Huguenin, of Elane Photography in Albuquerque, New Mexico declined to photograph a same-sex ceremony stating, "the message a same-sex commitment ceremony communicates is not one I believe." After an eight-year court battle, she finally lost and was fined thousands of dollars. A second example would be Sweet Cakes by Melissa, a cake baking business who, in 2013 declined to bake a cake for a same-sex ceremony. After 2 years in court, they were fined $135,000 *from their personal*, not business, assets. These are just two of many such cases.

The key point to understand is that these Christian business owners were living out their faith, something the Bible demands of all Christians. They weren't objecting to providing services to gays — many had before and planned to continue doing so — instead, they rejected the idea of participating in *celebrating* what God calls sin. This type of objection used to be protected by our constitutional rights, but no longer.

The stakes are getting increasingly higher for those who choose to not let their faith be a mere thought exercise but instead choose to *act* out their beliefs as their love for God compels them. Do not be mistaken: God expected action from Abraham because of his faith (Hebrews 11:8), and he still expects the same of us today.

EXHIBITING FAITH

How does one exhibit faith? How is it put into practice, and what does it look like? It looks like *trust*. Greg Koukl defines faith as "active trust in what you have good reason to believe is true." You can know something, but not act on it. It isn't until you act on your beliefs — your knowledge — that you exhibit faith (trust).

It's very much like the transition from engagement to marriage. When I was engaged, I had good evidence to suggest that my fiancée would make a good wife; I believed that and was fully convinced of it (or I would not have proposed to her!). However, I didn't exhibit faith in her until I said, "I do."

At that point, I was taking a step, not a leap, of faith, and it was a logical step. She was a kind, God-loving, hard-working woman, and after all our time together, marriage, while uncharted territory, was but a small *step* of faith. In the same way, our faith in Christ should be a small step from our current location.

After considering how the universe came to exist, I can't help but conclude that a god exists. What other reasonable explanation could there possibly be for how everything came to be out of nothing, besides a timeless, immaterial being (See the chapter "Is There a God")? After examining the evidence for the reliability of the Gospels and the historical evidence for the resurrection (See the chapter "Did Jesus Physically Rise from The Dead?"), I find the next logical step is to conclude that Jesus, and the other two members of the Trinity, are that God.

If all I did was come to that conclusion, if I only came to know and believe, that still wouldn't be enough, because salvation comes "through faith" (Ephesians 2:8). I need to exercise and exhibit *active trust* in these things that I have good reason to believe are true. That trust looks like committing to follow God and his word and commands, and surrendering to his lordship. Martin Luther has a simple way of wrapping this up: "It is therefore faith alone which justifies, and yet the faith which justifies is not alone."[2]

Since faith is based on what we know, we need to make sure that we *know* the truths of Christianity. How can you have a "conviction of the truthfulness of something" if you don't know anything about that thing? You can't. Faith without knowing is blind, and some Christians' faith is a leap. But that isn't the biblical model of faith. Our faith isn't supposed to be blind because God has given us eyes to see. It isn't supposed to be a leap, only a step from a firm foundation.

In John 4:24 Jesus says, "God is spirit, and the people who worship him must worship in spirit and truth." If our worship is supposed to be based on truth, that means our beliefs and convictions should be too. You can't worship God in truth if you don't know the truth!

If someone defines faith as believing in spite of evidence, then the best thing for that person's faith would be for us to discover the bones of Jesus! Then, they could have even more faith, in spite of the evidence. But, obviously this is absurd! Faith and knowing aren't opposites on a continuum. Like we've seen previously, faith, *as action*, should flow from what we know.

Contrary to what the non-Christian culture believes, the biblical model of faith isn't believing *in spite* of evidence, or believing *in the absence* of evidence. Biblical faith is *acting **because of** evidence*. This is why in Mark 2:10-11 Jesus says, "'So that you may know that the Son of Man has authority on earth to forgive sins,' — he said to the paralytic — 'I tell you, stand up, take your stretcher, and go home.'" Only God can forgive sins, and to prove that he was God, Jesus showed his authority over the natural world by healing the man. This is just one of many examples where evidence and reason precede a call to action.

IN THE UNKNOWN

It does need to be said that most times when we exhibit trust, we are doing so in a situation where we don't have total knowledge. Think of a parent leaving an older sibling alone at home to watch the younger one for the first time. When we act in such a situation, we are exhibiting faith in the areas where we don't have knowledge *because of* the areas in which we do have knowledge. Christians aren't the only ones who make trust decisions like this; *everyone does*. For example, the atheist believes his car will start in the morning, though he can't know that it will; and the scientist believes in Darwinian evolution because of how he looks at the evidence, in spite of never having observed macroevolution. Both of these people are exhibiting trust in something without total knowledge of the foundation for that trust.

SUMMARY

The concept of biblical faith that we've developed here is very different from the way culture understands and uses the word. Because of this, I would encourage you to remove the word faith from your conversational vocabulary — it simply doesn't communicate well in today's culture. You *say* "faith" and people *hear* "blind faith" or "leap of faith." I recommend saying, "my convictions" or "trust" instead of "faith." Non-Christians have convictions about things such as animal rights, women's rights, rape, murder, and genocide. Society better understands conviction as something that you act upon, and this phrase tends to communicate much more clearly the idea of faith you're trying to convey.

Jesus' miracles and Paul's arguments gave witness to the truthfulness of the gospel, and the precedent that they set of giving evidence for the trustworthiness of the gospel hasn't changed. The church of today must embrace apologetics — the practice of giving a defense for Christianity. She must realize that a lack of knowledge and an uninformed "faith" are weak foundations that will be torn down by today's ever increasingly hostile culture. We do our children and new Christians a disservice when we fail to equip them with the truth to fuel a deep and powerful faith in Christ.

Go. Trust. Act.

WHAT WE LEARNED

❖ Biblical faith is a combination of knowing, believing, and acting — "active trust in what you have good reason to believe is true."

❖ Knowledge and faith are not opposites, but are complementary.

❖ Faith is **acting** *because of* evidence, not **believing** *in spite of* evidence.

❖ In order to better communicate the biblical concept, say "my convictions" instead of "faith" when speaking with non-Christians.

❖ Make sure your "faith" is marked by *acting* in trust!

12

IS ABORTION
A COMPLICATED ISSUE?

Abortion remains one of the most divisive issues in America, and while the divide is generally along party lines, it is much more than a political issue for the majority of people.

Before we get too far into this, we need to briefly cover the role of emotions. They can be remarkably powerful and persuasive, and I want you to understand that I'm sensitive to the fact that this is a delicate issue. Based on statistics, a large portion of the nation has been affected by abortion, either as those who have had them, or as friends, family, spouses, and more.

While this is often a topic where rhetoric is used to move people, and often times *obscure* the truth, in this chapter we will be concerning ourselves with the facts. This approach can sometimes be taken as insensitive, which is why it's important for me to clarify that I am not cold or indifferent toward those who have been affected by abortion.

Any time we're trying to uncover the truth in a situation, we need to be conscious of how our emotions affect our rationality. The fact that we dislike an idea doesn't, in and of itself, tell us anything about the correctness of the idea. A patient may be told by her doctor that she has cancer. She will certainly not like this, but her emotional response doesn't in any way call into question her doctor's diagnosis. While facts are often thought of as "cold", they don't have to be presented in a cold way. The information we present may be disliked, but our manner and character shouldn't be.

We are told that all the considerations surrounding abortion make it a very complicated issue: women's rights, the interest of the state, effects on society and crime, women's health, father's rights, "religious" perspectives, and the rights of the child (depending on who you ask).

If you were to look at that list with no other context, that might indeed seem like a complicated mess. However, not all considerations should receive equal weight. For instance, if I'm looking for a place to eat, I might have some requirements such as proximity, menu, casual dress acceptable, etc.

However, all of those considerations do not receive equal weight. I'm willing to drive much farther to get the type of food I want, even though I prefer closer restaurants. So, the location isn't as important as the menu

In the same way that my restaurant considerations do not get equal weight, neither do all of the considerations surrounding abortion. To put this issue in its proper perspective, we need to ask and answer one question.

What is the unborn?

Abortion requires killing something that's alive, so before we can applaud it or condemn it, we have to know what that "something" is. Some people say that it's nonviable tissue mass, a potential human being, a human that's not a person, or just a fetus.

If the unborn is any of those things, then no one needs to give a reason why it can be disposed of. We don't need proper justification to get rid of warts or have our hair cut. However, if the unborn is in fact a genuine human being, then there is no reason good enough to allow their institutionalized mass murder to continue. As you can see, this issue really does come down to just one question - "What is the unborn?"

We can demonstrate that all of those descriptions of the unborn are woefully inadequate and incorrect.

THE UNBORN IS A HUMAN BEING

Is the Unborn Alive?

Some people will say that the unborn isn't alive. This position is not rooted in even the most basic medical science or biology. The unborn is the product of a *living* sperm joining with a *living* egg. The resulting zygote (fertilized egg) then grows and continually gets bigger by the continuing division of cells.

What about this process makes it seem like the zygote isn't alive? How do two *living* cells come together and not make something that is itself *alive*? And what are we to make of something that takes in nutrients and expels waste, all the while it is growing?

Also, if a baby is considered to be alive after birth, at what point is it considered to have gained its "alive" status? When it travels seven inches down the birth canal? If so, that is an extremely artificial and arbitrary qualification. It is simply indefensible to hold to the position that the unborn is not alive.

Is the Unborn Human?

We've established the point that whatever the unborn is, it is alive. The biggest question, though, is whether "it" is a human being. There are a few ways to address this question.

I have a good friend who, in his college days, was having a conversation about abortion with a classmate. They were discussing this very question — the nature of the unborn. This classmate, though not exactly sure what the unborn was, nonetheless held the position that it certainly wasn't a human being.

My friend's response interjected some common sense into the conversation. He said, "You don't think it's a human being? Well, what is it? Is it a turtle that's growing in there?" Let's think about it: two birds mate and they make a bird; two turtles mate and make a turtle. But, when asked what two mating humans produce, people suddenly aren't sure. Doesn't that just seem silly? 100 out of every 100 human births result in a *human* child. Two members of any species always produce something of the same species when they reproduce.

Is Killing Wrong?

We've seen that the unborn is alive and that it is human. Next we need to establish whether or not killing, in general, is wrong. Then, we'll consider if killing the unborn is acceptable.

Any discussion about the value of life needs to be in the context of an *objective* standard such as the Bible. Throughout history, our species has not had a great track record when it comes to human rights, but the Bible has been consistent on them from the very beginning, in the book of Genesis.

God created humankind in his own image, in the image of God he created them, male and female he created them. (Genesis 1:27)

When society today considers how we should treat other people, something like the "Golden Rule" is generally presented: "Do unto others as you would have them do unto you." However, this puts *me* in the position of authority to determine what is right and wrong, and that's a *subjective* position.

On the other hand, the objective biblical standard is based on a recognition that all people are created in the image of God with intrinsic dignity and worth, and we should treat them as such. Since people are image bearers of God, indiscriminately killing them flies in the face of claiming that they have intrinsic dignity and worth. So it shouldn't be allowed.

However, there are times when killing is acceptable, or even is the greater good such as in situations of self-defense. This is why we separate killing and murder. *Killing becomes murder when innocent life is taken without proper justification.*

The unborn child is alive and is certainly innocent, by any standard imaginable, so killing it without proper justification is wrong. Since it is an innocent human life, the types of proper justification required for its death should be the same as those for any other human.

SLED

In his book *The Moral Question of Abortion*[1], Stephen Schwarz describes the only four areas in which the unborn differ from toddlers. We will examine these and see if they're large enough differences to warrant being allowed to kill the unborn.

An easy way to remember them is with the acronym "SLED"

❖ Size
❖ Level of development
❖ Environment
❖ Degree of dependency

Size

> The unborn is too small to be a person; it is just a clump of cells!

That statement definitely has some rhetorical force, and many times when people are confronted with a powerfully persuasive statement, they retreat to using "feeling" or "belief" language. For instance, "Well, I can't prove it's a person; I just feel/believe that it is wrong to kill it." However, we should not just accept all the claims levied against us!

Instead, you could respond with: *Based on what evidence should we believe that microscopic human beings aren't actual human beings?* Is it really our size that gives us our worth? Are big people more valuable than small people, and if you're small enough, you just don't count at all? If our worth is related to our size, the average male is 26 times more valuable than the average newborn. Don't most parents (even pro-choice ones) tell their children not to pick on people who are smaller than they are? If we can't pick on people smaller than we are, why should we be allowed to kill them if they're "sufficiently" small?

Level of Development

> The unborn can't think, feel pain, or know that it exists.

What such a perspective is really saying is that our worth is based on our abilities. But this seems like a horrible and unenforceable standard. Are people who are blind less human than the rest of us? How many of your senses do you have to lose before you're not a person anymore? For example, consider Jane, a 35-year-old mother of two.

It's possible that Jane has a condition known as congenital insensitivity to pain (CIP). People with CIP cannot and have never felt physical pain. How cool is that!? Running through walls, never hurting your thumb when you hit it with a hammer, etc. Actually, this condition is very dangerous. Without a feedback loop between their body and their brain, and no pain response, people with CIP can and do certainly get hurt.

When they wake up in the morning, they have to check their eyes to make sure they didn't get scratched in the night, since they couldn't feel it if they did. They can't really play sports, or have to be really cautious if they do, since they could break a bone and never know.

What are we to make of such people, if it's true that they're not as valuable as the rest of us since they can't feel pain? What about people in comas? They can't think, feel pain, or know they exist - do they cease to be a person when they go into a coma?

How would that work? You're not in a coma, so you're a person. Then you go into a coma, and cease to be a person. Finally, 10 years later you come out of the coma, and you're a person again? That seems ridiculous.

Additionally, the unborn *can* feel pain. An unborn baby at 20 weeks of gestation "is fully capable of experiencing pain... Without question, [abortion] is a dreadfully painful experience for any infant subjected to such a surgical procedure," said Robert J. White, M.D., PhD., professor of neurosurgery, Case Western University.

All of this goes to show that a person's level of development has nothing to do with their worth.

Environment

The unborn is not in the world yet — it's in a different environment. It doesn't even breathe air.

There's a certain age at which a child can be easily fooled. You can show them a coin, then cover it with you hand, and they think it has disappeared; they don't understand that it is under your hand. As children grow up and experience the world, they are not so easily fooled.

Well, it seems as though some adults are still falling for the coin trick. "We can't see the fetus, so it isn't in the world yet." But if the "fetus" isn't in the world, where is it?

This just amounts to a word game. The unborn is very much in the world, in *our* world. And it is interacting in an age-appropriate way. A healthy pregnancy, in part, is one in which the unborn child "acts its age (or developmental level)." For instance: sucking their thumb, kicking, blinking, moving, and turning. Why are people marginalizing the unborn for acting just as it should in its current developmental stage? If it talked to us, everyone would be freaked out!

Lastly, is it really the use of our lungs that gives us our worth? If you only have one lung, are you half as valuable? It's also worth pointing out that the unborn does breathe, in that its cells undergo respiration, the process by which oxygen and other nutrients are transformed into energy. If your body can't do this type of respiration, you'll die. However, if you can't use your lungs, you can still live as long as your body's cells can receive oxygen through the use of a ventilator or the injection of oxygen into the bloodstream.

Degree of Dependency

The unborn is totally dependent on only one person.

Remember, these four categories of "differences" are ways of making the unborn seem "less-than" *as justification for ending its life.* To me, this one makes even less sense than the others. It also broadens the issues to include much more than just the unborn.

If we really should be able to kill a person because they are totally dependent on others, then newborns would be fair game. So are veterans who have been severely wounded in combat along with people in comas as well as people with severe forms of cystic fibrosis or cerebral palsy.

Additionally, how would this work out in real life? Picture a pro-choice person, Dave, who believes this line of thinking, sitting by the pool on a warm summer's day. A nearby mother has her two children with her. James, 8 months, and Peter, 5 years. Peter starts to pitch a hysterical fit, and while trying to deal with him, the mother doesn't see little James crawling toward the pool and doesn't see him fall in.

What should Dave's response to this be? *If he's consistent,* he would just keep reading his book. He wouldn't get up or say anything. After all, James is totally dependent on only one other person, and as such, isn't a valuable human being. This is what logically flows from a position that is based on degree of dependency.

If someone tries to say that we can kill the unborn based on size, level of development, or degree of dependency, then such a person is most likely making an argument, albeit unknowingly, for killing toddlers too, for they are much smaller than adults, they are certainly less developed, and they have a high degree of dependency!

WHAT WE LEARNED

- ❖ The unborn is a *human being* that is *alive*.
- ❖ Murder is the unjustified taking of innocent life. Abortion is murder.
- ❖ **Size**, **Level** of **Development**, **Environment**, and **Degree** of **Dependency** are bad reasons for saying that we can kill the unborn. Those reasons, except for environment, would support killing toddlers, too.

13

WHEN IS ABORTION JUSTIFIABLE?

While we've established that abortion is wrong, in general, pro-choice advocates will often pose some specific scenarios to try to prove their case that abortion should be legal. Most of these situations are what we might call "hard cases" where there seem to be no good options. They are also emotionally moving. The abortion advocate will say that while there are no good options, abortion is the lesser of two evils.

As a point of principle, policy decisions should not be based on hard and difficult cases. We should strive to make laws that work for the majority of people the majority of the time.

RAPE

The most difficult case is that of rape. Rape is a heinous crime that takes physical assault to a more extreme degree due to its sexual nature. Please understand that nothing I say here is intended to diminish the savage behavior of those who commit rape.

The real question when it comes to considering abortion in the context of rape is:

> How should we treat an innocent human being who reminds us of a horribly traumatic experience?

The argument being advanced here is that it's acceptable for a mother to kill her child if she didn't have a choice in that child's conception, or if the child reminds her of the rapist. A similar argument is used for allowing abortion in the context of incest.

But neither argument should be persuasive because if taken to its logical conclusion, it would be just as justifiable for the mother to kill her toddler, too. We're confronted with the question: How old is too old for her to kill her child?

Additionally, how does murder in any way redeem the rape? It is not morally acceptable to intentionally kill an innocent person just because you are attacked. Moreover, a child should never be murdered to pay for the crimes of its father.

Many women have found that bringing their child to term and then putting it up for adoption was their way of bringing some good into the world after the atrocity that was done to them. There are scores of heart-warming accounts from mothers *and* children who were affected by rape, but didn't decide to make the situation worse by killing the child. Instead, they chose life!

Of women who were sexually assaulted, 70 percent chose to keep their baby and didn't regret that decision. As for those who aborted, 78 percent of women had regrets and said they made the wrong decision.[1]

THE CHILD IS UNWANTED

It is never morally acceptable to take someone's life simply because they are unwanted. If parents shouldn't be allowed to kill their toddler when they don't want it anymore, they shouldn't be allowed to kill their unborn child either.

We shouldn't even accept the premise of this argument. Children *are* wanted, certainly by infertile couples who spend a decade or more and thousands of dollars on fertility treatments and in vitro fertilization. Many couples are waiting until later in life to start their families, and often times they are adopting children. Someone wants that child. Even if a child isn't adopted, and is instead placed in foster care, that is still much better than being murdered because EVERY LIFE IS VALUABLE.

More importantly, if people don't want children, they should abstain from sex. Anyone old enough to have sex must take responsibility for any and all consequences. Our culture saturates us with the idea that sex is primarily about pleasure and children are a burden, preventable by several methods of birth control. This is backwards! God's design for sex puts others above self. It's an expression of love and loyalty within marriage, and its end purpose ultimately creates new life

UNWANTED CHILDREN CREATE A DRAIN ON THE ECONOMY

It is not morally acceptable to kill people when they get expensive. If it were, who would get to set the quota of how much a person can cost before they got murdered? What would be a reasonable amount? In such a society, statements such as, "You're close to crossing your cost threshold, be careful!" would be commonplace, but such a society could not be more cold and heartless.

It has in fact been demonstrated[2] that, when abortion was legalized, it had a very positive effect on the crime rate many years later. The children who are most likely to be aborted are also more likely than the average child to grow up to commit crime.

However, we can't kill people because they are costly, and we also can't kill people because of the actions they may commit one day.

MAKING ABORTION ILLEGAL FORCES WOMEN INTO BACK ALLEYS WITH COAT HANGERS

Please forgive the graphic image, but this is the extreme situation often used to lobby for keeping abortion legal. Women will be in danger if we outlaw abortion. Well, they would only be in danger if they were breaking the law, and more importantly, *while they were killing another person.*

Why should the law be faulted for making it harder to kill an innocent person? As a rule, we oppose making it easier for people to commit crime and evil. For instance, what would we think about someone who said that we should make bank robbery legal, because if it isn't, bank robbers could get hurt while robbing banks. Obviously, that is foolishness, but this is the same line of reasoning used to support abortion.

A WOMAN HAS THE RIGHT TO CHOOSE

All people have a right to make their own choices. However, there must be limits on these free choices such that the actions of an individual will not infringe on the rights of another. A mother's "right" to choose to end her child's life is a radical violation of that child's most basic rights:

> We hold these truths to be self-evident, that all men are created equal, that they are endowed by their Creator with certain unalienable Rights, that among these are Life, Liberty and the pursuit of Happiness." (The Declaration of Independence, emphasis added)

Our very Declaration of Independence affirms that all of us are created equal. Not *birthed* equal. *Created.* This obviously includes the unborn too. There can't be a more basic set of rights than these. The right to life, not the right to murder. The right to be born is the most basic of all human rights.

It's common to hear that it's "the woman's body" so she should be able to do with it as she pleases. From a certain perspective this could be considered a sticky wicket. All of the cells that comprise that child, save for half of one, have come from the mother. However, just because the components of thing A have all come from thing B, this does not mean that thing A is the same as thing B. In reality, the child is a distinct person, and while it has come from the mother, it is not the mother.

THE UNBORN IS JUST PART OF THE MOTHER'S BODY

Should the unborn be able to be killed because its "just part of its mother's body?" This is a medical and scientific claim, and it is incorrect. While pregnant, a woman does not have two hearts, four hands, two brains, etc. She has her set of organs and appendages, and the child has its. When she gives birth, she doesn't go from having four feet to having two.

We can go on to make an even stronger case than that. All of the cells in a non-pregnant person's body have the same DNA. This DNA is one of the things that makes you, uniquely you. The unborn child has its own unique and distinct DNA too, which is separate from the mother's.

Perhaps most strikingly of all, the fetus' blood and the mother's blood cannot mix without serious consequences. In the placenta, the child's blood and the mother's blood come close together, and if they mix, the mother's body mounts an immune response in reaction to the child's blood. It sees the child's blood as a threat, as something foreign, *as something separate from the mother's body.* The mother's body never attacks its own kidneys, feet, or blood, because those are all parts of its body. But the body knows that the fetus is separate from itself.

We can also come at this from at least one other perspective. A child can be created through in vitro fertilization, where a sperm and egg are combined outside of a body in a laboratory dish. This embryo is then transferred to the uterus of a woman. An in-vitro embryo wasn't created in the woman, so how can it be *only* a part of the woman?

You can actually take a sperm from an African America man, an egg from an African America woman, combine them, and then implant that embryo into a Chinese woman. This results in a 100 percent African American child growing in a Chinese mother. The child is a totally different race and ethnicity than its mother, once again proving that the child isn't just part of the woman's body. It is a distinct living and growing person all its own.

THE MOTHER'S LIFE IS IN DANGER

This is the only circumstance in which it *may* be permissible for a woman to get an abortion. If it is reasonably certain that, in the process of carrying the child, the mother's life will be lost, then it is morally acceptable to end the life of the child. Please understand that this isn't morally required but rather simply permissible; and the goal isn't to kill the child, *it is to save the mother.* It is better for one person to live than for two people to die.

What this line of reasoning doesn't support is killing the child because it *might* have a disability like Down syndrome or a physical deformity. If it isn't okay to kill mentally or physically disabled 10-year-olds, it isn't okay to kill the unborn for those reasons either.

ABORTION IS OKAY BECAUSE _____

While we have addressed most of the common reasons given in support of abortion, one day you might hear one that wasn't covered. Always ask yourself, "How relevant is this objection, if we're talking about an actual human being?" Always return to the central issue and question: *What is the unborn?*

This approach will bring clarity to the situation. It doesn't make difficult situations easier, but it does help us reason through them.

GRACE AND THE GOSPEL

No discussion of abortion is complete without the inclusion of the gospel. When we convince someone that abortion is wrong, we have just convinced them that children are being murdered; that a person, or people they know, may have been complicit in the murder of a child. If the conversation simply ends in agreement about the wrongness of abortion, we haven't said nearly enough.

In Christ, and in Christ alone, there is grace and forgiveness for the sin of abortion. The whole function of apologetics is not to win arguments and tear people down, but to tear down obstacles and arguments that *stand in the way of the gospel.*

We must always be conscious of the fact that abortion causes pain and suffering for anyone close to it: the mother, the father, the parents of the mother, and more. There can be deep wounds that will only heal with time and the Holy Spirt's restorative work.

When you have the opportunity to discuss abortion and contend for the unborn lives that don't have voices, always conclude with the gospel – the undeserved offer of forgiveness and grace provided for by an innocent who, like aborted children, was also wrongly killed: Jesus Christ.

WHAT WE LEARNED

- ❖ Killing an innocent is never okay, even if a woman becomes pregnant as a result of the heinous crime of rape.
- ❖ We don't kill people when they get expensive.
- ❖ The law shouldn't make it easier for people to commit crimes like murder.
- ❖ Mothers don't have the "right to choose" to kill their children. Even the unborn have the "right to life."
- ❖ The unborn is distinct, unique, and separate from the mother — not *just a part of her body.*
- ❖ Abortion can be permissible when the mother faces certain death as a result of the pregnancy.

❖ For all objections, restore clarity to the situation by examining the objection in light of the unborn being a human being that is alive.

❖ Don't let conversations about abortion end with just the moral question, always include the gospel.

14

ARE CHRISTIANS SUPPOSED TO BE TOLERANT?

Tolerant. It's vogue to be tolerant. You're either tolerant of others' beliefs and values, or society brands you as being bigoted, hateful, or worse. People have lost their jobs, and have been sued and threatened, all because they were "intolerant."

HOW SOCIETY VIEWS TOLERANCE

Poll a random person on the street, and chances are, they will tell you that tolerance involves accepting others' beliefs as just as valid and correct as your own. This is the "new tolerance" of today. New tolerance demands that we not say someone's beliefs are incorrect or morally wrong. What makes this so new is that this wasn't always the use of the term.

The word "tolerate" used to be defined as:

To allow or permit, to recognize and respect others' beliefs and practices without sharing them, to bear or put up with someone or something not necessarily liked.

Doesn't this sound a lot like the values on which America was founded? Mutual respect, *not* mutual acceptance. The freedom to speak, not the compulsion to agree. However, all this has changed.

I'm sure you've noticed that it's not acceptable in non-Christian culture to say statements such as: "Jesus is the only way to heaven," "Jews are wrong for rejecting Jesus," or "Homosexuality is wrong." Isn't this confusing, though? For a secular society that prides itself on "accepting others' viewpoints as equally valid" it sure doesn't accept *those* viewpoints. Doesn't that seem hypocritical and maybe even... *intolerant*? That is the problem with the new tolerance — it doesn't follow its own standards.

The new tolerance is also incapable of being faithfully enacted. If every behavior has to be viewed as equal, we can't say that murder, rape, or racial discrimination are wrong. At best, we can say, "We don't like those actions." But even that response falls short of accepting those behaviors and beliefs as equal.

Perhaps most damning to proponents of the new tolerance is their condemnation of those who they consider to be intolerant. Since the new tolerance says that all views are equal, a person is actually being intolerant when they accuse you of being wrong for saying someone else is wrong.

In a talk he gave a U.C. Berkley in 2004, Greg Kuokl made this easy to understand with a simple example. He offers the following two statements:

1. "All views are equally valid; no view is better than another."
2. "Jesus is the only way to heaven, and Jews are wrong for rejecting him."

He then asks, "Which of these statements do you agree with?" Most non-Christians will agree with statement one and not statement two. Next, he asks, "Do you think that statement two is wrong and that people shouldn't say it?" Most will answer "Yes" to this. Here is where it all gets tied together. Since it is a view that "Jesus is the only way to heaven" and since you agreed with the view that "All views are equally valid; no view is better than another" why do you say that statement two is wrong? Isn't it a view just as equal and valid as any other? Now the person is caught between those affirmations, and you have shown how contradictory the new tolerance is.

When someone says that you are intolerant for making a moral judgment, try *gently* walking them through the above train of thought; just substitute the statement they disagreed with for statement two.

Here's another view: "It's intolerant to say that a person shouldn't eat large amounts of sugar regularly. That person will most likely become overweight and/or get diabetes." This probably sounds very silly to you, since many people would classify this statement as a scientific claim, and most would agree that scientific claims can't be tolerant or intolerant. In the same way, it isn't intolerant for your doctor to tell you that you have cancer, if indeed you do. Or for a parent to tell a child that, if she steps off the ladder, gravity will swiftly bring her to the floor.

So, if those claims aren't intolerant, why is saying that, "Jesus is the only way to heaven" considered to be intolerant? Relativism. It's the mistaken thinking that something can be true for you but not for me. This is the category in which today's society places religious truth claims. Somehow, it escapes their grasp that contradictory claims cannot all be true.

From a relativistic perspective, the phrase "Jesus is the only way to heaven" really means "Jesus is the only way to heaven **for me**." Allah might be your way to heaven. Or Buddha. Or unicorns. It's just like saying, "Chocolate Moose Tracks® ice cream is the best flavor of ice cream [**to me**]."

Unsurprisingly enough, you were either born, or you weren't. Your birth was a real event that happened and is "true" for everyone, or it didn't happen at all. I can't say it didn't happen just because I don't like you; that would be nonsense. It isn't intolerant to state historical or scientific fact. The "intolerant" label doesn't apply.

Here's where this all comes together: Christianity is based in its entirety on historical fact. Just like your birth, that either happened or it didn't, Jesus was resurrected, or he wasn't. He performed miracles, or he didn't. These are historical claims. They're the type of claims that are either true or false, but they are *not* the type of claims that can be true for you and not for me. There is no middle ground with them. Since those events happened, we have excellent reasons to believe that, when Jesus claimed to be God, he was telling us something true and accurate.

When Christians say that "Jesus is God," they are also intending to communicate something true about the nature of reality in the same way that someone who says, "The sun is the center of the solar system" is communicating a universal truth.

So, the next time that someone tries to silence you by claiming that you aren't tolerant, point out that historical events are not the types of things to which tolerance applies (use the birth analogy), and Christianity is grounded in such historical truth.

It should be said that people may not accept your assertion that the Bible is historically accurate. This is to be expected, and it allows for a natural transition to focusing on the evidence for the reliability of the Bible. However, a difference of opinion or a disagreement about how compelling certain evidence is doesn't make someone intolerant. There are multiple scientific studies that contradict each other (just look at the area of nutrition), but the idea that the study authors are *intolerant* for claiming their study is correct (and by extension, that others are incorrect) isn't even a topic of conversation in the scientific community.

SHOULD CHRISTIANS BE TOLERANT?

So, should the Christian be tolerant? That depends on which definition of tolerance we're considering. As was previously shown, the new tolerance cannot actually be put into practice. But Christians do need to be tolerant in the classic/original way. This seems to be what God had in mind in 1 Corinthians 13:7, where Paul writes that love "endures all things." This does not mean that love agrees with all things or considers all things equally valid. The word *endures* matches the dictionary definition in the first paragraph of this chapter: "to allow or permit, to recognize and respect others' beliefs and practices without sharing them, to bear or put up with someone or something not necessarily liked."

However, this shouldn't be understood to mean that we aren't to make moral judgments. As was discussed in the chapter on truth, judgment does have its proper place in the Christian's life. We need to be able to distinguish truth from error and right from wrong. This requires making a judgment. In fact, the phrases, "people shouldn't judge" and "it's wrong not to be tolerant" are themselves judgments.

It's also worth noting that our federal and state laws are judgments that certain behaviors are wrong (for instance, theft), and most people are comfortable with that.

CHRISTIANS VS. NON-CHRISTIANS

Tolerance and the Christian

How we treat a person's actions should also be dependent on whether or not that person is a Christian. In 1 Corinthians 5, the apostle Paul instructs Christians not to associate with other Christians engaged in prideful, habitual, unrepentant sin. Don't eat with them. Remove them from your midst. This, of course, is the final action, after attempting reconciliation to righteousness. This process is described by Jesus in Matthew 18:

> If your brother sins, go and show him his fault when the two of you are alone. If he listens to you, you have regained your brother. But if he does not listen, take one or two others with you, so that at the testimony of two or three witnesses every matter may be established. If he refuses to listen to them, tell it to the church. If he refuses to listen to the church, treat him like a Gentile or a tax collector. (Matthew 18:15–17)

Paul makes it clear that Jesus doesn't tolerate prideful sin in his church. This is where church discipline comes in, as is described in Matthew 18 above. This concept rubs some people the wrong way. After all, as some will say, "Isn't church supposed to be all about love?" Actually, these people are right; it is about love! However, our first priority, and indeed the first commandment,[1] is to love God, not please people. Loving people comes second, but not at the expense of loving God. Many of the missteps of the mainline church today are the result of putting the second command before the first and greatest commandment.

The way we show our love for God is by following his commands.[2] One such command is to attempt restoration for those stuck in sin and if that fails to remove the person from the church. This is a foreign concept to many of us today. So, let's put it in terms most people will be familiar with.

Let's say you create a non-profit organization that provides temporary shelter to at-risk teens. Your goal is to help these kids by giving them a safe environment and support as they finish high school. You would most likely set up some ground rules: no drugs, no fighting, no disrespect to the staff, etc. If a teen, Mark, didn't follow the rules, you would likely try to work with him and get him to fall in line. After all,

Mark is a troubled kid — he has some issues to work through, and you're there to help him with those issues.

However, if Mark repeatedly breaks the rules and is disrespectful and prideful about his behavior, the right thing to do is to have him leave. As painful as that might be, you can't risk having him corrupt the other teens that you also care about also. To preserve the integrity and effective purpose of your organization, you would sometimes need to have people leave. Unfortunately, as 1 Corinthians 15:33 says, "Do not be deceived: 'Bad company corrupts good morals.'"

Our example with Mark and the teen shelter is just like the unrepentant Christian and the church. The shelter has ground rules to protect the teens, and Jesus' rules for the church are to protect it from "bad apples."

So, should we tolerate prideful sin in the church? Absolutely not. Our love for God and our Christian family should compel us to attempt reconciliation. However, that same love for God requires that we follow all of Matthew 18, even to the point of removing people from church, if necessary.

Tolerance and the Non-Christian

What about the non-Christian? Do we shun them too? No. Paul is also clear about this in 1 Corinthians 5. If we shunned non-Christians, we would never be able to share the gospel with them. We shouldn't expect those who are dead in sin (Ephesians 2:5) to act as though God has breathed new life into them. Non-Christians haven't been set free from the bondage of sin yet (Galatians 5).

The misstep of those who espouse the new tolerance is their belief that a person's worth and identity are only the sum of their actions, and, by extension, that a rejection of an action is a rejection of the person doing the action. But a person's value isn't related to the sex of the person they marry, their religious beliefs, political views, or food preferences. However, this is exactly how the new tolerance believers act — we are simply the culmination of our preferences.

We need to view non-believers as God's image bearers because they, like you and me, were created in God's image with intrinsic worth and dignity. All people are the same in the eyes of God, but all actions are not the same. We need to love and respect all individuals without accepting their wrong behaviors.

Loving them means trying to see them and treat them as a valuable creation of God — to take actions toward their good and betterment. Be kind. Don't repay insult for insult, but instead return grace. Be winsome. This shouldn't be understood to mean that we ought not point out wrongdoing. In order to get someone to see the need for the gospel, that person will first have to understand that they are utterly incapable of righteousness on their own.

In 2 Peter 3:15, Peter tells Christians to be prepared to defend the gospel. Then, in verse 16, he says to "do it with courtesy and respect, keeping a good conscience, so that those who slander your good conduct in Christ may be put to shame when they accuse you." You may have heard the phrase, "You can't out-nice a Mormon." Why isn't it "you can't out-nice a Christian?" Maybe because, though we do sometimes stand up for truth, we do it in an ineffective way — we leave out the courtesy; we leave out respect.

In Colossians 4:6 Paul says, "Let your speech always be gracious, seasoned with salt, so that you may know how you should answer everyone." Salt makes food attractive, and in the same way, our speech should help make the gospel attractive. Or, at least it shouldn't tarnish it. Paul is saying that a Christian's words should be marked by a grace that demonstrates patience, respect, and undeserved favor.

HOW CAN CHRISTIANS USE SOCIETY'S CONCEPT OF TOLERANCE?

While our culture has certainly perverted the true and noble concept of tolerance, there are times when we can use this distorted concept to our tactical benefit.

For example, imagine coworkers sitting around the break room during lunch. Jim is reading the news on his phone when he comes across a story about Christians opposing same-sex marriage. Jim knows that Kyle is a Christian. So, he says, "Hey Kyle, are you one of those Christians who thinks gays shouldn't be able to marry the people they love, just because they're of the same sex?"

Kyle is in the hot seat now. This is lunch time, so there's an audience in the break room. Kyle doesn't want to be thought of as hateful or as a bigot, but he wants to faithfully represent Christ and the biblical view of homosexuality. So, what can he do?

In many conversations, the difference in a positive outcome and a negative one is not what information is shared, but *how that information is shared*. Here's how Kyle should set the stage for his answer. "Jim, that's a good question, and I'll answer it in a second. But first, I have a question for you. Do you consider yourself to be a tolerant person? Would you be accepting of people who share different viewpoints than you?" Now, Jim is sharing the hot seat with Kyle. He doesn't want to look intolerant in front of his coworkers. So, he will probably tell Kyle that he is a tolerant person.

At that point, Kyle can go ahead and talk about his views on marriage. (Hopefully he has read the chapter on homosexuality, and one of his points will be that marriage is not primarily about love, at least not from the government's perspective.) If Jim starts to push back about how that's intolerant or hateful, Kyle can remind him that just seconds earlier, Jim said in front of everyone that he is a tolerant person who accepts people who have views different than his own.

We can use others' fear of looking intolerant to our benefit. When you feel like you're being set up to look bad to others based on how you answer a question, put the other person in the hot seat too by asking them if they're a tolerant person *before you answer their question*.

WHAT WE LEARNED

- ❖ The "new tolerance" is self-refuting and can't actually be put into practice without being hypocritical.
- ❖ True tolerance involves respecting others, even when you disagree with them — a "live and let live" approach.
- ❖ Christians should not tolerate unrepentant sin in the church.
- ❖ Christians should not expect non-Christians to live like Christians.

15

HOW OLD IS THE EARTH (AND DOES IT MATTER)?

Thousands, millions, or billions of years seem to be the most popular numbers when it comes to the age of the universe and earth. People who hold to a "young earth" view believe that the earth is 6,000 to 15,000 years old whereas people who hold an "old earth" view would say that the earth is billions of years old. These are incredibly different positions, and the disagreement over this issue can get quite heated.

However, the age of the universe is not that important; most of the disagreement centers on *how* you reach your conclusion. Most of the young-earth people are going to be Bible-believing Christians who read Genesis 1 in a literal manner.

So for them, if you think the universe is billions of years old, you aren't treating the Bible as your primary authority. On the other side, the old-earth people don't understand how someone could believe some book that is thousands of years old instead of the clear findings of modern science.

My goals in this chapter are three-fold:
1. Show that the Bible, and more specifically Genesis 1, doesn't speak to the age of the earth.
2. Convince you that this shouldn't be a big or contentious issue.
3. Demonstrate the important points we should take away from Genesis 1 and 2.

A "LITERAL" GENESIS?

When I speak on creation, one question I like to ask the audience is "Which biblical creation story do you believe?" Most people are confused right from the start because they don't realize that, on the face of it, Genesis 1 (Genesis 1 – Genesis 2:3) and Genesis 2 (Genesis 2:3–25) tell very different accounts of how creation happened.

The differences are fairly major. For example, in Genesis 1 man is created last, as the pinnacle of the creation "week", but chapter 2 has man's creation happening first: We have two questions to answer. 1) Does Genesis describe literal events and steps? and 2) Does Genesis claim that God literally created the universe, earth, and life?

A Non-Literal Account

Since the *ordering* of events in Genesis 1 and Genesis 2 contradict each other, they can't both be literally true, and I will demonstrate why a non-literal reading is the most intuitive. However, this doesn't mean that they can't *communicate* something that is literally true. (More on this in the next section).

There are other issues that point to a non-literal intent:
1. There was light/darkness before the sun was created.
2. There was evening/morning (which would be marked by sunrise/set) but there was no sun.
3. There were plants before the sun.
4. The "days" end with a common formula, "a ____ day"
5. The parallelism of days 1–3 and 4–6.

The Issues Surrounding the Sun

It makes no sense to say there was a "day" if there was no sun. What would the earth be revolving *around*? What would be marking the evening and morning the text speaks of? There would be nothing! Also, how do you have light without the sun?

To be fair, many have proposed solutions to these issues. For instance, some say, "God was the light before the sun." But ideas like these have little to no biblical support and seem less likely than a non-literal reading.

"A ____ day"

Each of the creation "days" ends with a final formula that goes something like "there was evening, there was morning, a ____ day." Now, your translation might say "the ____ day" However, the first five days lack the definite article "the." So, they should be translated and read as "one day" or "a second day".

A better understanding points to the days not being literal, 24-hour, solar days (and what's a solar day without a sun anyway?). It also implies that the days aren't necessarily in direct succession, where one comes right after the other.

Days six and seven *do* have the definite article "the" with them, thus setting them apart. On the sixth day, God creates man, who is his prized creation, formed in his image, to bear his image, and on the seventh day, God rests.

Additionally, day seven doesn't include, "there was evening, there was morning," thus pointing to the seventh day — God's rest — still being in progress.

The Parallelism of Days 1–3 and 4–6.

Another clue pointing to a non-literal interpretation of Genesis 1 is the use of parallelism between days 1–3 and 4–6.

On days 1–3, God creates by separating, and on days 4–6, God fills the voids from days 1–3 with life.

- ❖ On day 1, God separates light from dark, and on day 4 he fills the sky with lights.
- ❖ On day 2, God separates sky from waters, and on day 5 he populates the sky with birds and the waters with fish.
- ❖ On day 3, God separates land from water, and on day 6 he populates the land with animals and man.

This type of parallelism was common in ancient Hebrew literature and can hardly be considered an accident.

Genesis 1 Is neither Literal nor Scientific

I have presented several reasons here for why I believe that Genesis 1 was not intended to be taken literally. While there are more, I think these are sufficient to make someone at least consider the possibility that it wasn't intended to be a literal document. Even still, much more could be said about each of the areas I briefly covered.

Before we continue, I would like to address a common claim used by young earth believers: "Your interpretation contradicts the Bible, and so it must be wrong."

This might sound compelling to some, but it has a large problem. When these believers read the bible, they are *interpreting* it. So, when you disagree with them, you are disagreeing with their *interpretation*. What's actually being compared is your interpretation with their interpretation.

Some interpretations are better than others, and some have better support and evidence than others. But no one just reads the Bible and arrives at absolute truth without going through the step of interpretation. For some, this step isn't always a conscious one, but it always present, nonetheless.

So, Genesis 1 isn't literal, but it isn't scientific either. And really, why should we expect it to be? Would ancient Israel have understood anything about string theory, dark matter, quarks, or gravity waves? No. Most people today haven't heard of them either, and much fewer actually understand them.

In Genesis 1, God was more concerned with correcting bad *theology* (ideas about himself) than he was with correcting faulty *scientific* ideas. To understand this, we need to know the context of Genesis 1. Knowing the context of a passage should always be our first step when we want to understand it correctly.

The Israelites Were Captives

Around 1,400 BC, when Genesis 1 was written, Israel had just come out from under 400 years of Egyptian captivity. They had worshiped Egyptian gods, and they took those gods with them when they left Egypt for Canaan.

In fact, while they were still in Egypt, Moses says to God, "If I go to the Israelites and tell them, 'The God of your fathers has sent me to you,' and they ask me, 'What is his name?' – what should I say to them?" (Exodus 3:13) They didn't even know God's name! You can't be much less familiar with a person then when you don't even know their name.

This was the state in which Genesis 1 was written: His people have forgotten who their God is, and they are worshiping false gods. When we approach Genesis 1, we need to keep this in mind.

What Did Egyptians Believe?

Since I said context is important for biblical understanding, you might be wondering what Egyptians believed about God and creation. If you were, you're on the right track!

Since Moses is correcting bad theology (ideas about God), we need to understand what those ideas were. Just what did the ancient Egyptians believe about God? The chart below compares some of the specific Egyptian beliefs with specifics from Genesis 1.[1]

	Genesis	Egypt
Initial Conditions		
	Formless, void, darkness, deep	Watery, unlimited, darkness, imperceptibility
	The Spirit of God was hovering over the face of the waters	The god of wind/breath on the waters
Means of Creation		
	God creates by divine command	Atum (or Ptah) speaks creation into existence
Separation		
	Light is created before the sun is in place	Light is created before the sun rises in its place
	God creates by separating the waters to create an atmosphere	The gods create by separating the waters to create an atmosphere
	God creates by separating the land from the waters	The first little hillock of land (primordial mound) rises out of the water

Creation of the Sun		
	God creates the sun (day 4) after the light (day 1)	The sun rises on the first day
Creation of Mankind		
	God creates mankind in his image	The gods create man in their image, formed out of clay
God Rests		
	After completing the work, God rested	Ptah rested after completing his work of creation
Purpose of Creation Account		
	God as creator claims sovereignty over all creation and so all nations	The creator god claims sovereign rule of state

Remember, the Egyptian beliefs predate Genesis 1. I imagine that you might be confused now. After all, if you were a teacher who assigned a writing project to her students, and you had two papers that were as similar as these two accounts are, you're going to accuse those students of plagiarism.

What are we to make of the unmistakable similarity? On the surface, it looks as if Moses just copied the Egyptians and then attributed everything to God. However, when we look at the differences, we start to see why Moses used the Egyptian beliefs for a foundation, and we also see what makes Genesis unique and distinctive.

What Is Distinctive in Genesis 1

The first thing to note is that the Egyptians believed god was not eternal — he had not always existed. Additionally, he created himself, which is logically impossible. This stands in contrast to Yahweh, who has always existed.

We also see Genesis affirm that God, and God alone, is deity. There aren't multiple gods, there is one God, and Yahweh is he.

In Genesis, the sun is presented very differently. The sun was a god to the Egyptians, and so they and the Israelites would not have missed how heavily deemphasized the sun is in Genesis. It isn't created first. It isn't a force over other gods. It's just another creation, and it doesn't even get a formal name! You can't deemphasize something much more than that.

Most importantly, mankind replaces the sun as the central focus of creation, and in fact, mankind is created to bear the image of their creator God and to enjoy fellowship with him.

Remember when we looked at the final formula of each day — "There was evening; there was morning"? This makes much more sense when we consider the Egyptian beliefs about the world. They believed that there was a cosmic struggle every night as the sun god, Re, descended into the primeval ocean to fight Apophis. Gods fighting every night? That can't have given their followers peace as they lay their heads down to sleep, not knowing if tomorrow would come.

Contrast that to the picture we see in Genesis. Instead of chaos, God is bringing order. There is no fighting, for nothing and no one can hope to contend with God. Moses tells us that God, and God alone, was in sovereign control as he created and brought order to the cosmos.

So how should we interpret Genesis 1? *Theologically*, not literally or scientifically. And doesn't this make sense? God's people didn't know anything about him, not even his name, and we're expected to believe that his first goal was to give them a science lesson? No. It's far more likely that God's first order of business was to correct their bad theology and ideas about him.

Genesis 1 and Genesis 2

The easiest way to look at the functions of the first two chapters of Genesis is to consider that they affirm the same ideals, but from different perspectives. Chapter 1 tells us about creation from the perspective of the universe, and chapter 2 speaks about creation from the perspective of man.

There is only a contradiction here if we insist on interpreting these passages literally, and as we covered in the chapter on literal biblical interpretation, this is not always the correct means of understanding.

SCIENCE

In some circles, *science* is the seven-letter word that might as well be a four-letter word. "You believe science? Well, I believe my Bible." Remember, though, that what's really being compared are interpretations of the Bible. But more than that, I hope I've shown that there are compelling reasons to treat the biblical creation stories as theological, and not scientific. Let's not abuse the Bible by treating it in a way it wasn't meant to be understood.

So, how should we view the scientific evidence about the age of the universe? With an open mind. If I want to know which musical scale to play over a dominant fifth chord in a blues tune, I ask a musician, not my Bible; if I need to know the best way to invest for retirement, I ask a financial advisor; when I wish to know something about the *physical* world, I ask a scientist.

This doesn't mean that scientists are all unbiased or correct, but I have a better chance of getting the correct answer to scientific questions from a scientist than I do my Bible, unless there are compelling reasons to believe otherwise.

Modern science points to the universe being 13,400,000,000 years old (13.4 billion) and the earth being 4.54 billion years old. The Bible doesn't affirm or contradict either of those ages. And just to muddy the water, there is a third age to consider: the age of life.

From a logical perspective, everything could be young or the universe could be old and the earth and life could be young, or the universe and earth could be old and life could be young, or everything could be old.

It doesn't really matter to me! I don't care about the age of everything, but do I care that God did the work. It doesn't matter to me if life is old; it only matters that God planned for all of this before there was time.

While the age of everything isn't that important, we must be clear on a few things:

- ❖ **God did the work.** He is very clear about this, and we'll revisit this point in the chapter on evolution.
- ❖ There is only one God: Yahweh – the God of the Bible.
- ❖ The age of the universe is something we can disagree about. There is no need for breaking fellowship or arguing. There

should always be room for healthy, challenging, debate, though.

WHAT WE LEARNED

❖ Context is key in understanding Genesis 1.

❖ Genesis 1 was written after, and because of, Israel being under Egyptian rule for 400 years while adopting Egyptian religious beliefs.

❖ There are many reasons to believe that Genesis 1 and 2 are non-literal and convey theological, not scientific, truth about God and creation.

❖ This is not something we should fight over as Christians.

16

CAN EVOLUTION EXPLAIN THE ARRIVAL AND FLOURISHING OF LIFE?

The Theory of Evolution is one of the issues at the center of the divide between those who look to science for answers and those who look to the Bible for answers, though there are many people in between. For example, some see science as an authority or at least a valuable tool, but do not think evolution is an adequate explanation for the arrival and flourishing of life.

There are also Christians who disbelieve evolution simply because they believe it runs contrary to the Bible. However, there are additional reasons why evolutionary theory is not true, and we're going to look at those reasons in this chapter.

But first, let's address one thing. You can't try and fight evolution by saying, "It's only a theory." This is a mistake because you're using the word "theory" in a different way than scientists use the word. Most people use the word *theory* as a synonym for an educated guess. For instance, when you say, "I have a theory about why Jane was late this morning," you have a guess.

On the other hand, when scientists use the word theory, it's often used to describe generally accepted scientific principles that have explanatory power. Think of this as a capital T Theory, as opposed to the lowercase t theory we usually use.

The Theory of Gravity is an example of one of these sets of widely accepted scientific principles, and it has great explanatory power: I drop my pen, and it goes to the floor. Every time. To most scientists, the Theory of Evolution is such a theory. So, when you discuss the Theory of Evolution, don't lead off by saying something like, "Well, it's just a *theory*, so why should we believe it?"

Just because something is a Theory doesn't mean it's true, but it does mean many people have put a lot of time and effort into testing it. You just shouldn't dismiss that offhand.

TERMS

The topic of evolution, like many, *requires* those who discuss it to first define their terms. It's common for a Christian to say, "I don't believe in evolution," and for someone else to say, "Don't you believe things change over time? Well, that's what evolution is." All those two people have succeeded in doing is talking right past each other.

One use of the word *evolution* is simply "change over time," and everyone agrees that things can change in some way over time. Another way the term is used is to describe "small adaptive changes over time," something that might better be called "microevolution." Lastly, there's the usage that is most common today, the one that refers to "large change over time" — macroevolution.

Macroevolution has been expanded over time (it has "evolved") to a more robust theory, called the "Neo-Darwinian Synthesis." To put it in a more simple and amusing way, it's the view that life came about "from goo, through the zoo, to you!"[1]

In other words, at one point in time there were no living things. Then, single-celled life was formed purely by accident. And over time, life became more and more complicated as it reproduced. This happens because of mutation and natural selection.

When life forms reproduce, they are creating a copy of all or a part of themselves. Problems can arise in this copying process, so that the copy isn't a perfect match to the original. In such a case, a "mutation" would have occurred. There is no purpose or design to these mutations, so they could be harmful or helpful to the survival of the resulting life form.

This is where "natural selection" comes into play, or so scientists say. Organisms that contain mutations that make them more likely to survive are more likely to pass that mutation on to their offspring, which makes their offspring more likely than the others to survive and pass on their genes, and so on.

On the other hand, mutations that are harmful are less likely to be passed on. Either the organism is never viable, or it is less equipped for survival than its kin, so it is also less likely to pass on its negative mutation.

When I speak of evolution, it is this process of mutation and natural selection that I'm referring to.

PROBLEMS

Before Charles Darwin, atheists had a problem. They had no good explanation for how life came about without God. That all changed when Darwin theorized that organisms change over time because some of them were more fit for their environment as a result of mutations. As Richard Dawkins said, "Darwin made it possible to be an intellectually fulfilled atheist."[2]

Evolution Is Not Observable

It is often pointed out that different bird populations develop different physical characteristics that make them more fit to survive in their specific environment. For instance, birds with thin, sharp beaks are more likely to survive in an environment that is rife with insects, whereas birds with large, sturdy breaks are more likely to prosper in environments where nuts are prevalent.

The birds with large, sturdy beaks are less likely than their sharp-beaked relatives to survive in environments with many insects and few nuts. This is how mutation and natural selection is documented to work. This process has been observed.

Science itself is based on empiricism – what you can observe and measure. We have examples of microevolution — birds' beaks changing, bacteria becoming resistant to antibiotics, etc. But there are no examples of any organism changing from one kind to another. Macroevolution has never been observed. We have zero examples of a bird changing into something besides a bird. No examples of bacteria evolving into something that is not bacteria. It is an inappropriately large "leap of faith" to jump from microevolution to macroevolution.

We can observe gravity at work. We can observe and test most of the other theories of science as well, such as those in the areas of electricity and magnetism, but this is not the case with evolution. And, in a culture where seeing is believing, why do most people believe in a theory based on something that has never been observed? I firmly believe it is their precommitment to naturalism.

As Dawkins said, the theory of evolution negates the need for a creator — with the Neo-Darwinian Synthesis, you can be intellectually fulfilled as an atheist. Or can you?

Darwinists Must Prove Two Things

In order for evolution to be true and viable, proponents of it must be able to prove two things. First, that life can come from non-life, and second, that life forms can change over time in substantive ways.

1. Life Can Come from Non-Life

Picture with me if you will, a primeval earth filled with a soup of chemicals. Over time, and with the interjection of electricity, these chemicals slowly form amino acids, which then form proteins, and so on, until you end up with the first life form. Something like that is how some scientists imagine life to have come about.

There are several problems with this idea. First, no evidence exists to show that it is possible for life to come from non-life; it has never been observed or proven. Scientists are working on proving this, and it just might be that you will see a new headline claiming, "Scientists have proven in the lab that life can come from non-life."

Think about that type of claim for a moment. What has actually been proven? Intelligent design! I guarantee that those scientists will want to take the credit for designing the experiments, running the test, carefully tweaking the conditions, until, viola, life was *created*. The only way around this would be for the scientists to claim that they aren't intelligent, so that no intelligence actually created life. I don't see that happening.

There is no other way around this: if you create situations and carefully manipulate variables with the end goal of creating something, and then you end up creating that thing, then you are the intelligent designer.

However, there is an even greater issue with evolution: Where did the raw materials come from? This was covered in the "Is There a

God?" chapter, but what generally goes along with a belief in evolution is a belief in the Big Bang Theory. But, it makes no sense to believe everything came into existence, uncaused, and from nothing. Creation from nothing and evolution usually come hand in hand.

Mutation and natural selection have to have material — DNA — on which to work. Even more important, where did the elements that comprise DNA come from? We don't know. Often, when Christians believe God has done something, when there isn't evidence for it, they're accused of using a "God of the Gaps" argument. Basically, it's said, that when Christians have a gap in their knowledge or they lack an explanation, they just stick God in that "gap" as the explanation.

It seems to me that non-Christians do the same thing. They exercise "faith" in that, though they don't know something now — such as how life can come from non-life — they believe science will show them in the future. This is a "Science of the Gaps" argument.

However, Christians shouldn't use a "God of the Gaps" argument. We should form our beliefs from the foundation of Scripture, understood through the God-given ability to reason. If we use a "God of the Gaps" argument, we may end up sticking God in a place where he doesn't belong.

In the same way, we shouldn't accept a "Science of the Gaps" argument from non-Christians either. Statements like, "We don't know how it works or where it came from, but Science will show us one day" are examples of poor argumentation.

2. Life Can Change over Time

We have seen that there is no reason to believe that life can come from non-life, but let's pretend for a moment that it could (for the sake of argument). The initial life form would need to be able to change and become more and more complicated over time, until taking human form.

In order for life to become more complicated, there has to be an infusion of new information from somewhere. All of the structures and systems in a living being are coded for by that being's DNA. It is DNA that contains all of the *information*.

In order for organisms to evolve to be more adaptable, their DNA would need to become more complicated. You don't go from a single-celled organism to a sheep without more DNA getting more complicated. Where does this new information come from?

Evolutionary theory would say that mutation produces the changes and then natural selection makes the advantageous changes more likely to be passed on to positively affect future offspring. That sounds all well and good on the face of it, but I have never experienced or seen nature taking the simple and making it complex. Left alone, nature will turn a house into a pile of bricks, but it will never turn a pile of bricks into a house.

I am a software developer — I write computer code as a large part of my day. This code is similar to DNA in that it is information that controls a process toward an end. Bill Gates has said, "DNA is like a computer program but far, far more advanced than any software ever created."[3]

When I consider the hundreds of thousands or millions of lines of code I've written in my life, I realize that it pales in comparison to the size and complexity of our human genetic code. I can tell you that, if I just open a program file, and type just one character at random somewhere, the chances of me even getting a program that runs are very small. It is basically impossible to do this over and over again and get a program that is more complicated in a beneficial way. But this is how we're told that life has gotten more complicated, by successive *random* changes.

Almost the entirety of these random changes are not going to be helpful to the survival of the organism, and most would be detrimental to it. There are so many more ways to break something that is working, than there are ways to improve it or simply keep it running.

Many scientists, including some secular scientists, think that there has not been enough time to account for the complexity of life on an evolutionary model, based on the estimated age of the earth. It would simply take far too long, if it were possible at all, for life to advance as far as it has, without the infusion of information from some other source.

If evolution works as it is purported to, these changes would create what are called *transitional* forms — forms that are between other forms. Darwin said, "The number of intermediate and transitional links, between all living and extinct species, must have been inconceivably great."

However, the fossil record *does not* testify to this at all. And, in fact, we don't see anything close to what we would expect from the evolutionary process, which should create many more duds than success stories.

Since the changes that are occurring — mutations — are random, there will be both helpful and non-helpful ones. Well, where are the fossils of the organisms that were the result of the non-helpful changes?

We have *no* fossils from non-viable transitional forms — those animals that were the result of detrimental mutations and that couldn't survive. For example, where are the fossils with feet coming off of their back or something like that? Since evolution will result in a disproportionately large amount of non-helpful mutations, we would expect a large amount of non-viable animal remains. We don't have them.

The fossil record is full of viable forms. But more than that, it lacks the forms that come *between* other forms. If you took all of the fossils we have and arranged them in the order in which evolutionists say they evolved, you would be left with huge "holes" — large gaps between each of the forms.

The currently accepted evolutionary model is thought of as a *tree*, where there are branches, and branches off of those branches and so on. However, it has been said that the fossil record looks more like an *orchard*, with many distinct trees growing separately from one another, than it does a single tree with many branches.

The fossil record presents another great challenge to traditional evolutionary theory. There are times when nothing happens for long stretches, followed by times of quick leaps forward, where much change happens and life becomes more complicated relatively quickly.

One such time period is known as the Cambrian Explosion. In this period of time, which took place during the Cambrian era about 542 million years ago, we see evidence of the rapid appearance of most major animal phyla (types of animals) in the fossil record. There was a proverbial *explosion* of diversity in life. Before about 580 million years ago, most organisms were simple, composed of individual cells, but this changed with the Cambrian Explosion. In fact, all currently present phyla appeared within the first 20 million years of the period.

The significance of this cannot be overstated. Evolution is not capable of explaining large leaps forward in small periods of time. Twenty million years may seem like a long time to us, but from an evolutionary perspective, it's a very short period of time, and yet, *all current types of life appear during this time.* That sounds miraculous, doesn't it?

Now, I'm not simply claiming that "God did it!" just because science can't explain it. A well-reasoned examination of the evidence leads me to believe that God's intentional and continuing act of creation was the cause of this infusion of new life and genetic information. So, when in the Bible God says, "I created everything" I'm inclined to believe him. And this is only further confirmed by what scientific evidence and a well-reasoned evaluation bring me to.

Theistic Evolution (or Evolutionary Creation)

Is there any way to marry the science of evolution with the teaching of Scripture that God did the work of creation? Some have tried to do this, and the result is "Theistic Evolution." Some Christians don't like how the name "Theistic Evolution" puts the emphasis on the "Evolution" part, so they prefer to call it "Evolutionary Creation", believing that this puts more of an emphasis on the "creation" part.

There is a major issue with this view, no matter what you call it. Both of these names are comprised of contradictory terms. Just ask any evolutionary biologist and they will tell you: Evolution *by definition* is a totally natural, *unguided* process. There is no room for God in this process, at all. Evolution is a system that works on chance.

What does it even mean to say, "God created everything by chance"? I think this means nothing at all. "Creation by chance" is a contradiction in terms. To create is to plan and execute, to craft something. Chance involves none of that. If someone claims to have created something by chance, you'd be justified in saying *you didn't build that*.

In short, there is no room for God in evolution, and since God claims to have done the work, there is no room in Scripture for evolution either. If evolutionary theory is not sound, baptizing it with "God" does nothing to change that, and if it is sound on its own, adding God changes nothing.

Adam and Eve

If evolution is correct, then who were Adam and Eve? There are various views on this, but most people who believe in evolution do not think that they were the first humans, or that they even existed at all. Some will say that they were the first humans who had a soul, but this seems somewhat arbitrary to me.

From a biblical perspective, one of the issues with evolution is that it leaves little to no room for Adam and Eve to be real, literal people, but the Bible presents them as such.

The Fall

The fall is the event in Christian/biblical history where sin entered the world when the first human willfully disobeyed God's command. This is described in Genesis 3, where Adam eats the fruit from the tree of the Knowledge of Good and Evil, and so alters the course of all those who will be his descendants. Sin entered the world though Adam, and death entered the world as a result of his sin. All of his children (including us) inherited a sin nature as a result of this — we gained a nature that is pointed toward sin.

There are no good ways to explain the overarching narrative of Scripture without the fall occurring. Indeed, the majority of the Bible describes God's outworking of his plan of redemption for fallen man, which ultimately comes to fulfillment at the cross. Without the fall, much of Scripture doesn't make sense.

It specifically doesn't make sense when Paul, writing under the inspiration of the Holy Spirit, speaks of Adam *repeatedly* as a real person who made a real choice, which had real consequences, which led to Jesus' real crucifixion. Paul grounds the need for Jesus' death *in the fall* originating with Adam and Eve.

> So also it is written, 'The first man, Adam, became a living person'; the last Adam became a life-giving spirit" (1 Corinthians 15:45)

> Yes, Adam's one sin brings condemnation for everyone, but Christ's one act of righteousness brings a right relationship with God and new life for everyone. Because one person disobeyed God, many became sinners. But because one other person obeyed God, many will be made righteous. (Romans 5:18-19 NLT)

Paul speaks of Adam as a historical person. Much of Romans 5 is a comparison of the *person* of Adam with the *person* of Christ. And in Matthew 19, Jesus grounds marriage in the way God *created* Adam and Even, by quoting from Genesis 2.

If evolution is true, Adam is likely a fictitious person at best. This creates large issues for claiming that Scripture is true.

COMMON DESCENT VS. COMMON DESIGN

Often, evolutionary proponents will point to the similar features in many different living organisms as evidence that these organisms are related on the evolutionary tree. These are called homologous structures. Animals that share *common* traits *descended* from a *common* ancestor. For example, many animals have eyes, so it would seem as though the eye evolved and was kept by animals as they experienced further evolution into more complex organisms. Evolutionists claim that physical structures like the eye are evidence of all life having a common ancestry. They also cite feet, fins, ears, etc. as similar examples.

There is another explanation that makes sense of the evidence. If everything were created by the same person, or group of persons (The Trinity), then we would expect there to be common traits and structures that were put to use in similar ways, but in different organisms.

In fact, I think this is a more natural view of the world than the alternative. Studies[4] have shown that children, even those not raised in religious households, see almost everything as being designed for a purpose. This is one of the results of being created in the image of God. Our understanding of beauty, justice, good, evil, and design point to our having been created intentionally with those instincts and knowledge of those concepts. They don't make sense in a naturalistic worldview.

Since most humans seem to see the world as designed, evolutionists can't say that their model of common descent is the most natural model to believe. In fact, you would only come to believe that model after believing evolution for other reasons, because if you looked at the world around you, you're more likely to believe that a designer created everything.

If you designed the structure of an eye, and it was good enough to use once, then it makes sense to use it again, though after adapting it for your specific application. Some evolutionists actually used to use the example of automobiles "evolving" over time to help prove their point about life evolving. Cars in the 1940s were simpler than today; they didn't have A/C or the sleek curves like the cars we have now.

As the evolutionists told it, the cars changed over time, and became more refined, and more complicated. They ran better. Some disturbing mutations occurred (like cars with a fifth wheel to supposedly aid in parking), but these were not "selected for", so they didn't survive.

For a second, that might make sense to you, until you realize that *cars are designed!* Automobile designers make use of common parts, like wheels and doors, for the same purposes, Their use is evidence of design, not common descent. Evolutionists don't use this example anymore, because they realized their error. Still, it's a fun reminder of how they made a great point — the most straightforward explanation for the common attributes in organisms is that life has been designed.

ARRIVAL VS. SURVIVAL

Evolution is said to explain the arrival of the fittest, but as we have seen, it doesn't seem to do a very good job of that. Evolution presents no good explanation for how life could come from non-life, and there is little evidence supporting the idea that the initial life forms changed over time from the simple to the complex.

It seems more accurate to say that evolution — mutation and natural selection — can explain the *survival* of the fittest organisms, but not their *arrival*. It makes sense that organisms that gain beneficial traits are more likely to pass those on.

The large leap of faith comes into play when someone says that this totally natural, unguided, process can account for the *arrival* of life and its constantly *increasing* complexity through natural selection and random mutation.

So Darwin may have "made it possible to be an intellectually fulfilled atheist" as Richard Dawkins says, but only if you don't examine the whole system too closely or delve too deeply into the details.

WHAT WE LEARNED

- ❖ "Evolution" means change over time, but to scientists, it refers to the combination of natural selection coupled with random mutation.
- ❖ Evolution is not observable or testable.
- ❖ Evolution requires that life can come from non-life, something that has never been demonstrated.

❖ Evolution requires that life can become more complicated
(not just that it can change) on its own, something that has
never been demonstrated.

17

WHAT DOES THE BIBLE SAY ABOUT HOMOSEXUALITY?

In recent years, the issue of homosexuality and what Christians have to say about it has received almost constant front page attention from religious and secular press alike. Some preachers won't talk about it, believing it to be too divisive, and some speak on it almost exclusively. What about you? Where do you stand on this issue? You might not care — "If it doesn't harm me, why get involved?" But, as some have said, *at some point, you will be **made** to care*, if you don't now.

ACTIONS VS. ATTRACTIONS

As always, let's be straight on the terms we're using and what they mean. When I use the term "homosexual," I'm referring to someone who is *attracted* to a member of the same sex. And when I use the term "homosexuality," I'm referring to sexual *activity* between two members of the same sex.

We need to understand the distinction between an innate attraction to members of the same sex and sexual actions between members of the same sex. While both the attraction and action are sinful, they are not sinful to the same extent, and the passages we are about to examine will deal largely with the *action* of homosexuality. Even though my purpose in this chapter is not make the case for the sinfulness of same-sex attraction, I do think it warrants a brief discussion.

Generally, the argument that same-sex attraction isn't sinful points to the non-lustful attraction between heterosexual people. This attraction is not innately sinful. So, if heterosexual attraction isn't sinful, why is homosexual attraction sinful? First, we must consider what same-sex attraction fundamentally is: a disordered desire that has no possible righteous, God-honoring fulfillment, which denies the natural and created order, as God designed it. Any attraction that has these characteristics cannot be holy or good; it must be sinful.

While not a popular notion, the Bible's view of man and sin fundamentally rejects the idea that only freely chosen acts and desires are morally blameworthy. Man is a slave to sin before salvation (John 8:34). He has an inherited guilt and sin nature from Adam (Romans 5:18). He did not choose any of these, though God rightfully holds man accountable for his actions and desires. This isn't unique only to same-sex attraction.

IS HOMOSEXUALITY WRONG?

Now that we have appropriately described the distinction between action and attraction, we need to determine if the *action* of homosexuality is wrong.

The Levitical Law

There were 613 laws in the Torah (the first five books of the Old Testament) that the Jews were supposed to obey. We will look at some of them here.

> You must not have sexual intercourse with a male as one has sexual intercourse with a woman; it is a detestable act. (Leviticus 18:22)

> If a man has sexual intercourse with a male as one has sexual intercourse with a woman, the two of them have committed an abomination. They must be put to death; their blood guilt is on themselves. (Leviticus 20:13)

> You must not allow two different kinds of your animals to breed, you must not sow your field with two different kinds of seed, and you must not wear a garment made of two different kinds of fabric. (Leviticus 19:19)

What Does the Bible Say about Homosexuality?

Matthew Vines, author of *God and the Gay Christian*, and others would say that Jesus came and "fulfilled the law"[1] and that therefore the law doesn't apply to us anymore. Additionally, how are we supposed to take the law seriously when it tells us to not wear clothes with mixed fabrics at the same time it says homosexuality is wrong?

Before we can make a determination on how to answer these questions, we need to learn more about the law. There were, in fact, three types of laws that ancient Israel had to obey: ceremonial law, civil law, and moral law.

The ceremonial laws, which included instructions on animal sacrifice, circumcision, feasts, dietary restrictions, etc. had a purpose for Israel *at that point in their history*. They were intended to keep them separate from the other nations who practiced idolatry, and to *remind* them that they were to be a separate — called out — people. These types of laws pointed toward the future when a messiah would come and once and for all atone for their sins.

Civil laws, as you might have guessed, detailed how civil affairs should be handled. Examples include what happens when an innocent third party is injured in a fight, how inheritances work, property rights, punishment for crimes, etc.

On the other hand, there is the moral law which wasn't just binding on the people of Israel at that time, but was an outward reflection of the character of God and expressed timelessly true moral requirements such as don't murder, steal or commit adultery. Of course, there are the rest of the ten commandments[2], along with many other moral laws expressed in the rest of Leviticus.

When Peter had his vision in Acts 10, where God told him to eat animals that the ceremonial law forbade, Peter understood that keeping the ceremonial law was no longer required. Paul also said in Galatians 3:24–25: "Therefore the Law has become our tutor to lead us to Christ, so that we may be justified by faith. But now that faith has come, we are no longer under a tutor." Paul is referring to the ceremonial law, not the moral law here, for Christ was the Lamb of God who would be sacrificed for the sins of the world, and the sacrificial system was part of the ceremonial law. When Jesus "Fulfilled the law," *he* was the sacrifice for sin, but he kept the entirety of the moral law too.

Now, some will say that the moral law doesn't apply to us today because we aren't Israel. However, when we read further in the Leviti-

147

cus 18 passage above, starting in verse 24, we see that these moral laws applied to everyone, not just Israel:

> "Do not defile yourselves in any of these ways, because **this is how the nations that I am going to drive out before you became defiled**. Even the land was defiled; so I punished it for its sin, and the land vomited out its inhabitants. But you must keep my decrees and my laws. The native-born and the **foreigners residing among you must not do any of these detestable things**, for all these things were done by the people who lived in the land before you, and the land became defiled. And if you defile the land, it will vomit you out as it vomited out the nations that were before you." (Emphasis added)

God is clear here that these are universally applicable laws. They applied to other nations, for these other nations were defiled by not obeying them, and they applied to foreigners living in Israel too. More than that, this concept of Jesus "fulfilling the law" is grossly misapplied. Matthew 5:17, the verse from which this phrase is taken, actually says "Do not think that I have come to abolish the law or the prophets. I have not come to abolish these things but to fulfill them."

Christ didn't come to get rid of the *moral* law; he came to live under it without sin, and fulfill its requirements. Jesus, existing as both God and man, was the only person who could fulfill the law and be the atoning sacrifice for sin on the cross.

So, the Old Testament prohibitions against homosexuality are extremely clear and still apply today.

Romans 1

While there are those who mistakenly say that the Old Testament doesn't apply anymore, we do see homosexuality addressed multiple times in the New Testament: Romans 1, 1 Corinthians 6, 1 Timothy 1, and indirectly in the words of Jesus.

> 18 For the wrath of God is revealed from heaven against all ungodliness and unrighteousness of people who suppress the truth by their unrighteousness.
>
> 24 Therefore God gave them over in the desires of their hearts to impurity, to dishonor their bodies among themselves. 25 They exchanged the truth of God for a lie and worshiped and served the creation rather than the Creator, who is blessed

> forever! Amen. 26 For this reason God gave them over to dis-
> honorable passions. For their women exchanged the natural
> sexual relations for unnatural ones, 27 and likewise the men
> also abandoned natural relations with women and were in-
> flamed in their passions for one another. Men committed
> shameless acts with men and received in themselves the due
> penalty for their error. 28 And just as they did not see fit to
> acknowledge God, God gave them over to a depraved mind,
> to do what should not be done. (Romans 1:18; 1:24–28)

Paul says that the wrath of God is revealed against all ungodliness and unrighteousness. The example he uses to illustrate this is homosexuality, and he calls it "dishonorable passions" and concludes with saying that it "should not be done." That's pretty clear.

Matthew Vines and others have a few responses to this. First, they try to say that the issue here is lust and that Paul isn't talking about committed, monogamous same-sex relationships. Second, they would say that Paul didn't even understand the concept of same-sex attraction, so he couldn't have been addressing it.

However, Paul grounds his argument in the natural order of things. He says that "women exchanged the natural sexual relations for unnatural ones." This isn't referring to people having sex outside of marriage. What's "unnatural" is that two people of the same sex are having sex. Paul goes on to speak of the "acts" of men, which are wrong *because they are done with other men.*

The claim that Paul didn't understand orientation has two prob-lems. First, orientation is irrelevant; it doesn't matter at all how some-one is orientated in order to make a moral determination about an act. The rightness or wrongness of homosexuality is not based on whether or not people are pointed toward or away from it.

If orientation toward an action makes that action okay, then how could we ever say actions are wrong? For instance, consider murder. Is murder acceptable if someone has had murderous impulses their entire life? "Well, that's just his *orientation,* so it should be accepta-ble." In actuality, the "orientation" argument is saying that some-thing should be allowed simply because someone desired it. This is poor moral reasoning.

The second problem with saying Paul didn't understand orienta-tion is that it seems obvious that he did. Implicit in the Romans 1 passage is an understanding that some people are pointed toward other people of the same sex. Also, through other writings in the first century, we see that it was known that some men were only attracted to other men, and in fact, there were long-term, monogamous same-sex relationships in that time and culture.[3]

As James White points out, "Plato's writings make reference to male homosexuality, lesbianism, the claims of some to be born as a willing mate of a man, the concept of mutuality, permanency, gay pride, pederasty, "homophobia," motive, desire, passion, etc. One would have to assume Paul a very poor student and a very poor observer of the culture around him to be unaware of these things."[4]

"Orientation" just refers to a pattern of attractions and desires, and this is what Paul is referring to when he says, "For this reason God gave them over to degrading passions [desires]." They had a pointing, a set of desires, an *orientation* that Paul is addressing.

So, the claims that Paul wouldn't have understood sexual orientation are both irrelevant and incorrect. Romans 1 is clear about the ungodliness and unrighteousness of homosexuality.

1 Timothy 1:10 & 1 Corinthians 6

After Romans 1, the passages we come to that address homosexuality are 1 Timothy 1:10 and 1 Corinthians 6:9.

"8 But we know that the law is good, if one uses it lawfully, 9 realizing the fact that law is not made for a righteous person, but for those who are lawless and rebellious, for the ungodly and sinners, for the unholy and profane, for those who kill their fathers or mothers, for murderers 10 and immoral men and **homosexuals** and kidnappers and liars and perjurers, and whatever else is contrary to sound teaching, 11 according to the glorious gospel of the blessed God, with which I have been entrusted. (Emphasis added)

Here, in 1 Timothy 1:8–11, Paul describes homosexuals[5] (those who *practice* homosexuality) as: lawless, rebellious, ungodly, and sinners. That's an extremely clear condemnation of them and their behavior. He also doesn't say that the Old Testament law doesn't apply. Instead, like he has done in his other letters, he makes it clear that the law serves to show how sinful we are.

Paul also addresses the issue of homosexuality in 1 Corinthians 6:9–10.

> 9 Do you not know that the unrighteous will not inherit the kingdom of God? Do not be deceived! The sexually immoral, idolaters, adulterers, **passive homosexual partners, practicing homosexuals**, 10 thieves, the greedy, drunkards, the verbally abusive, and swindlers will not inherit the kingdom of God. 11 Some of you once lived this way. But you were washed, you were sanctified, you were justified in the name of the Lord Jesus Christ and by the Spirit of our God. (Emphasis mine)

Paul once again uses homosexuality as an example of unrighteousness. The way Paul sets this up makes it clear that continual participation in homosexuality is directly opposed to how a Christian should act — in other words: it's sinful and wrong. Paul makes no allowance for someone who claims to be a Christian and is engaged in premeditated and habitual sin.

So, what are we to say about *God and the Gay Christian*? Based on this passage, an unrepentant, sexually active, gay Christian is a contradiction in terms in the same way that the unrepentant, heterosexual person who sleeps around would be excluded too, based on this passage.

Interestingly, this paragraph contains both necessary parts of the gospel: 1. a characterization of sin and 2. is the provision of redemption for all, including the adulterer, homosexual, etc., in salvation through Jesus Christ.

Matthew Vines has claimed that there wasn't a word for *homosexuality* in the first century, so Paul certainly couldn't be addressing it in these two passages. This assertion has been around for a long time, and it seems rather embarrassing in light of the evidence.

The word Paul uses that has been translated as "homosexuality" in both passages is the Greek word αρσενοκοίτης [arsenokoitēs]. In the New Testament, this word only appears in these two passages. It looks like Paul made this word up. However, for a Greek speaker, understanding what Paul meant would have been virtually assured. αρσενοκοίτης is actually made up of two other Greek words: ἄρσενος [arsenos] and κοίτην [koiten].

The word ἄρσενος means "man" and the word κοίτην means "bed." Paul is literally referring to "man-bedding" — men going to bed with men, and he most likely chose this wording because the Greek translation of the Old Testament (the Septuagint) uses these exact two words in Leviticus 18:22 that says, "You must not have sexual intercourse with a male as one has sexual intercourse with a woman; it is a detestable act."

Made up word or not, saying that "man-bedding" is forbidden is very clear. An added benefit from understanding that Paul is referencing the Levitical law is that we see he obviously believes that the moral laws it contains still apply to the Christian, under grace, in Christ, today. Moral laws didn't just cease to apply when Christ came. Moreover, Paul cared enough about including and describing homosexuality that he made up a word to describe it in a way that would have been easily understood.

WHAT ABOUT JESUS?

Christians and non-Christians often say, "Jesus never said homosexuality was wrong!" "It's not in the Red Letters."[6] There are several problems with this. First, any argument that treats certain words of the Bible as more authoritative than others, because Jesus spoke them, demonstrates a low view of Scripture.

1 Timothy 3:16 says, "All Scripture is inspired by God ['God Breathed'] and profitable for teaching, for reproof, for correction, for training in righteousness." Since Jesus is God, the words in black are just as authoritative as the words in red. When the Bible speaks, God speaks, regardless of the color the words are written in.

Second, any moral standard built around only what Jesus taught explicitly is doomed to failure, since it will be incomplete. Jesus didn't come to abolish the moral law and institute a new morality; he came to teach that Israel's trust needed to be in a Person (God) to save them, not their own "righteous" acts under the law. Jesus corrected incorrect understanding of the law, but he did negate it and start fresh.

Third, Jesus *does* address sexual sin and homosexuality by direct implicit implication.

Then some Pharisees came to [Jesus] in order to test him. They asked, "Is it lawful to divorce a wife for any cause?" He answered, "Have you not read that from the beginning the Creator made them male and female, and said, 'For this reason a man will leave his father and mother and will be united with his wife, and the two will become one flesh' (Genesis 2:24)? So they are no longer two, but one flesh. Therefore what God has joined together, let no one separate. (Matthew 19:3–6)

When Matthew Vines and others argue *against* differences in gender, they disagree with Jesus, who grounded his answer in how men and women were *designed* by their creator. Being created "male and female" doesn't refer to how we perceive ourselves; it's a description of physical biology and anatomy, at the least. It doesn't take much evaluation to see that certain parts on a man are well suited — dare we say designed — to match with certain parts of a woman, and when these parts are used together in this way, they fulfill a two-fold purpose: Children are created and the bond of the couple is strengthened.

So, when it comes to sex, in the biblical view, there aren't just "people" being considered; there are "men" and "women." God never says, "One person leaves their parents and joins with another person." No. He is explicitly clear that the *design* for sex is for *one man* to leave his parents and join with *one woman*. In the next chapter we'll talk about how there isn't just a generic role of "parent" either; there are *mothers* and *fathers*.

Many people will say that they don't see homosexuality addressed by Jesus' remarks. However, when you look at what he allows — sex between one man and one woman — you must realize that anything outside of that is considered to be against the Creator's design and is excluded as sin.

So, this includes adultery, sleeping around, pornography, incest, homosexuality, prostitution, and the list goes on. When you make a rule by setting a standard, you don't have to go and explicitly condemn every action and case outside of that standard; those are obvious and should be understood as implicit from the standard.

For instance, consider a sign that says the speed limit is 65 miles per hour. Now, if you go 80 mph and get pulled over, the officer isn't going to let you go if you say, "But the sign didn't explicitly say I couldn't go 80 mph." He's going to say, "Your behavior — going 80 mph — was implicitly forbidden by the standard." (Okay, he's probably not going to say it just like that, but you get the point).

WHAT WE LEARNED

- ❖ The Bible condemns and makes no allowance for the act of homosexuality.
- ❖ It is the action, not the attraction, which is the primary concern, just like with all sin.
- ❖ There are three types of OT laws, and the laws dealing with homosexuality did not cease to express God's binding moral standards when Jesus came.
- ❖ Romans 1 offers a clear description and condemnation of homosexuality.
- ❖ 1 Timothy 1:10 & 1 Corinthians 6 use a made-up, but incredibly clear word (*man-bedding*) to describe the act of homosexuality. These passages also say that such an act is an example of unrighteousness, godlessness, and sin.
- ❖ Jesus, by setting the standard of what appropriate sexual behavior looks like, excludes homosexuality and all other sin outside of a one-man, one-woman, exclusive union.

18

HOW SHOULD CHRISTIANS ADDRESS SAME-SEX ATTRACTION?

So far in this book we've established that morality is objective and is rooted in God's nature, and we also have established that God condemns the action of homosexuality. All of this leads to the questions of how Christians should act toward homosexuals (or any sinner for that matter).

LOVE THEM LIKE EVERYONE ELSE!

Just as we confirmed in the chapter on abortion, all people — whether big, small, white, black, heterosexual, or homosexual — are created in the image of God and have innate worth and dignity. All of our interactions with other people need to be rooted in this foundational principle.

In this regard, all people are the same. However, all actions are not the same; a slap to the face is different from a warm embrace. As people, we are used to treating different things differently, and hetero-sexuality and homosexuality are different things, and thus should not, by default, be treated the same.

The Non-Christian

There are two different types of people to consider when we think about the homosexual. The first is the non-Christian. This is the easiest case, at least in theory. A correct understanding of the gospel puts homosexuality into its proper context in the life of a non-Christian: just another sin that the blood of Christ can cover if that person comes to salvation in Christ.

We should treat all non-Christians the same in this area. All of them, regardless of their "major" sin areas, are in need of God's grace and forgiveness, just as we Christians were before salvation. Our love for Christ should compel us to not avoid them, but instead, to be intentional in sharing the gospel with them. As I have grown in Christ, I have learned to see all people as sinners in need of grace just as I am and used to be. Any avoidance of non-Christians on my part is a result of sin, not righteousness.

Once again, we must make this distinction between actions and attraction. When we share the gospel, people need to understand that their deeds are evil, including the act of homosexuality. If they don't accurately see their plight, the "Good News" won't seem very good. Coming to Christ requires everyone to be repentant about their sin, to have a change of mind about it. As Paul made clear in 1 Corinthians 6, you can't come to Christ and continue on in unrepentant, habitual homosexuality.

It also needs to be said that the goal for the homosexual convert isn't heterosexuality. Can the Holy Spirit totally change someone's sexual desires? Absolutely. But there is no guarantee of this. Instead, coming to Christ requires coming to a life of sexual purity, which as Jesus said, requires sex to be between one man and one woman in a committed, permanent, marital union. If the person doesn't wish to get married, then abstinence is required, just as it is for heterosexuals who choose not to marry.

"Where's the love?" you might say. "It's not loving to tell someone that they can't have the sexual or love relationships they desire." However, such a view presupposes that a person's feelings determine what is right and are the most important factors in moral decision making. You may recall from the previous chapters that this is a statement of *subjective morality*.

How Should Christians Address Same-Sex Attraction?

The biblical view of right and wrong is one of *objective morality*, which is the same for everyone, at all times, in the same situation. (For a refresher on this, check out the "Does Truth Exist?" chapter). The moral rightness of a behavior has nothing to do with how someone feels about that behavior. This is why, if homosexuality was wrong 2,000 years ago, it is still wrong today.

More than this, subjective morality elevates a person's *happiness* over their *holiness*. If you know that a high-sugar diet greatly increases the chances that a person will get diabetes, then it isn't loving to feed your child a high-sugar diet, *even if they like that diet the best and reject other options*. In the same way, as Christians, we understand that homosexuality is sin, and sin isn't good for people. Therefore, it isn't loving to support someone in a behavior that God is against, a behavior that isn't good for them.

Many pro-homosexuality advocates such as singer Vicky Beeching try to make their case from the section of the New Testament where Jesus gives the two greatest commandments:

> Love the Lord your God with all your heart, with all your soul, and with all your mind. This is the first and greatest commandment. The second is like it: Love your neighbor as yourself. All the law and the prophets depend on these two commandments. (Matthew 22:36–40)

The second greatest commandment *does* say to love your neighbor, but what does that mean?

The first command is to "love the Lord your God with all your heart, with all your soul, and with all your mind." In John 14:15, Jesus gives us some help on just what this love for God looks like: "If you love me, you will obey my commandments." Showing love for God means obeying him, it means being for the things he is for, and against the things he is against.

If our interpretation of the second greatest command causes us to violate the first, we have made a grave error. We should not, and cannot elevate people's preferences above our devotion to God and what is pure and holy. Many have said that conservative Christians are responsible for the suicides of gays and lesbians because their condemnation of those behaviors causes such great shame that people are moved to end their lives.

So much could be said about this. However, there are a few relevant points. There certainly have been Christians who have attacked homosexuals and have not been motivated by a Christ-like kindness or the gospel. But it is becoming increasingly more common for conservative Christians to be criticized simply for stating that homosexuality is wrong, even if they do it in a kind and loving way.

Neither I, nor anyone I know, want to drive people to kill themselves. However, this does not mean we cease to accurately present what God has to say about this issue. Isaiah 5:20 says, "Woe to those who call evil good, and good evil; who substitute darkness for light and light for darkness; who substitute bitter for sweet and sweet for bitter!"

We cannot take a soft line on important moral issues just because people don't like what the Bible has to say. When we tell people that God is okay with something that he isn't, that puts the person (and us) in a position of opposition to God, a very dangerous place to be.

So, what does it mean to love our neighbor? It cannot mean affirming their sinful behaviors. It cannot mean adopting a revisionist reading of Scripture because the long-standing readings aren't politically correct anymore. Loving your neighbor means that we speak the truth with kindness and conviction. Jesus didn't come to give comfort to sinners so they could continue on their way to hell while feeling good about themselves and their actions. He came so that the world would be changed, so that sins could be forgiven, so that we, through his triumph over sin and death, could be free from sin ourselves, not remain in it.

Lastly, in order to support this incorrect idea of love (telling people only what they want to hear) many people appeal to the Bible. However, they only pick out the parts that they like. How can they claim to be Bible-believing Christians if they just follow the parts that they like?

Moreover, how can you support a claim to follow the Bible, if you reject the parts of Scripture that are no longer politically correct? Wouldn't that imply that culture is your primary authority and moral compass, and the Bible is just a secondary support, only to be used when it agrees with the cultural direction?

In summary, the non-Christian homosexual needs God's grace just as much as anyone, and it is not loving to God, nor to them, to withhold a kind but convictional stand on biblical truth. Coming to

Christ will require them to renounce their sinful actions, just like it does for everyone else.

The Christian

This situation is less clear cut for the Christian who has same-sex attraction, in some ways, than for the non-Christian homosexual. It's not because the Bible is less clear, it's just that terms and definitions aren't always used in consistent ways. Therefore, I will endeavor to be very clear in the terms I use and how I define them.

If you'll recall, when I refer to homosexuality, I'm referring to sexual activity between two people of the same sex, and when I refer to a homosexual, I'm referring to someone who is attracted to someone of the same sex.

Based on the passages we've examined, there certainly is a place for the Christian who is attracted to someone of the same sex. All Christians are attracted to things that they should not act on. The presence of these desires does not disqualify someone from being a Christian.

Remember, though, that being a Christian requires that a person repent of their sin, striving to not commit it anymore, and certainly not to be prideful about it. This is why Paul says in 1 Corinthians 6:9–10, that those who practice homosexuality[1] (people who *participate* in homosexual acts), will "not inherit the kingdom of God." When you look at this passage, and the totality of Paul's teaching under the inspiration of the Holy Spirit, you see no allowance made for consistent, unrepentant sin to exist in the life of a Christian. If it does, one is not a Christian.

So, how should we approach those who claim to be a Christian, and yet participate in homosexual acts? Since, homosexuality is a sin and the person claims to be a Christian, Matthew 18:15–17 is quite relevant.

> If your brother sins, go and show him his fault when the two of you are alone. If he listens to you, you have regained your brother. But if he does not listen, take one or two others with you, so that at the testimony of two or three witnesses every matter may be established. If he refuses to listen to them, tell it to the church. If he refuses to listen to the church, treat him like a Gentile or a tax collector.

In this passage, Jesus instructs us to first confront the person and show them where they have gone astray. If they do not listen, take others with you; if they still do not listen, take them before the church (or the elders), and if they *still* don't listen, "treat him like a Gentile or a tax collector."

In the time of the New Testament, Jews would have had no contact with Gentiles or tax collectors. So, Jesus is telling us to have no contact with a person who, after being confronted with their sin, refuses to repent and goes on sinning. This would certainly apply to the person who participates in homosexuality and claims to be a Christian.

Paul also addresses a situation of habitual, prideful, sexual immorality in 1 Corinthians 5. He says that incest is taking place, and they're prideful about it. They haven't handled the situation. Paul says that, even though he isn't there, he has already judged the person. In other words, there are no possible additional contextual details he could know that would change his perspective on the situation — it's wrong.

He goes on to tell the Corinthians to "remove the evil person from among you... Do not even eat with such a person." Paul also clarifies that he is not prescribing this response for non-Christians, but instead calls for them "not to associate with anyone who calls himself a Christian who is sexually immoral, or greedy, or an idolater, or verbally abusive, or a drunkard, or a swindler."

Jesus and Paul both speak plainly here, and their exhortations to us fit well together. For people who claim to be Christians and yet are involved in habitual, unrepentant sin, we need to call for them to come to repentance (Matthew 18). But ultimately, if they choose to continue to reject God's word, we need to remove them from our social circles, churches, and yes, even shun them (1 Corinthians 5).

You're probably thinking that this sounds very "un-Christian," and due to how Christianity is often presented today, shunning people would likely be considered an un-Christian act. However, no act that Jesus and Paul tell us to follow could possibly be un-Christian. While it might not sit well with us due to our social conditioning, this is what God expects of us.

There are two reasons for this course of action. First, the church needs to look out for its own. It's not loving to leave your brother to flounder in sin, so Jesus tells us to help bring such a person back into right relationship with God. We should be concerned with the resto-ration of the individual (Galatians 6:1).

Second, the purity of the church is extremely important. This is something that is consistently overlooked today, much to our detri-ment as the church. In 1 Corinthians 5, Paul asks, "Don't you know that a little yeast affects the whole batch of dough?" It seems as though many people today have never used yeast, so here's a more current example.

A bunch of our friends got together one night, and one of them, Lis, cooked a large pot of potato soup (actually the largest pot I've seen in my life, outside of a commercial kitchen). Now, we'd all had this soup before, and no one had complained. But this time, people kept commenting on how spicy it was — "My lips are on fire!" one person said.

Lis only did one thing differently that night — she added one tea-spoon of red pepper. One little teaspoon, in the largest pot I've ever seen, made such a difference to many people. For those who have cooked with red pepper, they know that a little affects a lot. Well, Paul is saying the same thing about sin. A little sin, not addressed, will af-fect the whole church. This is the case with most sin. If your church has a gossip problem, it will grow like a cancer and contaminate more and more people and relationships.

So in summary, for the person who claims to be a Christian and is active in a homosexual lifestyle, we need to follow Matthew 18, and appeal to the person, with conviction and kindness, to return to a life of sexual purity. If that doesn't happen, we need to not be around that person, just as 1 Corinthians 5 makes quite clear. In the continuing absence of repentance, the person must be removed from the church. This process and its requirements are the same for any habitual, prideful sin. Homosexuality isn't special in this regard.

SAME-SEX MARRIAGE

One key area where Christians intersect with the issue of homosexuality is same-sex marriage. Right off the bat, I want to encourage you not to call it "gay marriage." This implies that gays have not been able to marry before, as if there were a ban on it.

Gays have always had the same rights as heterosexuals: that is, the right to marry someone of the opposite sex. A government can do three things with regard to any issue: prohibit, permit, or promote. The U.S. Government had never prohibited same-sex marriages; it just hadn't promoted them. Before the 2015 Supreme Court of the United States (SCOTUS) decision, homosexuals were asking for a right that no one had had: the right to marry someone of the same sex.

The government, for the longest time, has promoted long-term, monogamous opposite-sex unions because *as a group* and *by nature* they create and provide for the next generation and stabilize society.

Family and Children

Until 2015, government hadn't *prohibited* homosexuality, it had *permitted* it. However, in order to bestow "dignity" on same-sex couples, SCOTUS redefined marriage to be between any two people, irrespective of their sex. Therefore, the government now *promotes* homosexuality. From a policy perspective, marriage isn't about love, or who you're attracted to. It's about what is best for the common welfare and good. This is the only reason government has been involved in the institution of marriage, historically.

There are certainly families with a mom and a dad that are dysfunctional, and there are functional single-parent homes, but as a group — by and large — children raised in a family with both a mom and a dad consistently lead more wholesome lives than those raised in same-sex parent homes, across a range of markers[2] such as standardized test scores and emotional stability.

Conversely, children raised with homosexual parents are more likely to receive welfare, suffer from depression, be arrested, and attain less education. Specifically, children with lesbian parents are three times more likely to be unemployed, ten times more likely to have been touched sexually by a parent or other adult caregiver, four times as likely to have been physically forced to have sex against their will, and to smoke more frequently than children with heterosexual parents.

These are situations and behaviors correlated with being raised by homosexual parents. Overwhelmingly, the data show that the best thing for children is to be raised by opposite-sex parents. *As a group*, and *by nature*, same-sex parents neither create the next generation, nor best provide for its success and flourishing.

At this time, the three largest statistically representative datasets used to address the question—Regnerus's New Family Structures Survey, with 3,000 cases; the National Health Interview Survey, with 1.6 million cases; and the National Longitudinal Survey of Adolescent Health, with 20,000 cases— have all found that children with same-sex parents fare substantially worse—most measures show at least twice the level of distress—than do children with opposite-sex parents on a range of psychological, developmental and emotional outcomes. The longer social scientists study the question, the more evidence of harm is found.[3]

The whole issue of same-sex marriage has been framed as "marriage equality." A claim of inequality or discrimination is a surefire way to get people on your side today. But all too often people don't realize that discrimination is not always bad. If you put "discriminating" in front of "eater" you've got something good!

To discriminate simply means to treat differently. What makes discrimination good or bad has to do with *why* you're discriminating. We treat 10 year-olds differently than 20 year-olds when considering who to let drive a car. This is discrimination, but it is discrimination for good reasons. In the same way, we should treat opposite-sex and same-sex couples differently when it comes to issues of family and child-rearing because the types of couples are actually different.

As a group and by nature, same-sex couples neither create the next generation nor provide for it nearly as well as opposite-sex couples. Therefore, discrimination, in the areas of marriage and family, makes sense. Please note, however, that I am not for discrimination against homosexuals, simply for the sake of discrimination, nor am I for discriminating against people *simply* because they are homosexuals.

Loss of Rights

The governmental promotion of same-sex marriage is eroding the constitutional right to religious liberty in this country. Moreover, it has led to the redefinition of that religious liberty.

The Roman Catholic Church used to be the largest private provider of adoptions in Massachusetts. When same-sex marriages became legal, they were forced to make a decision: place children into same-sex homes or shut down. The government said that the church couldn't exercise their religion in the area of who they choose to place children with. So, the largest private adoption provider in Massachusetts, after serving over 720 children in the previous 20 years, was forced to close in 2006.

There are cake bakers, florists, photographers, and more who have been sued and punished by the law for refusing to participate in the celebration of same-sex marriages. They weren't discriminating against gay people, since these individuals had baked cakes, arranged flowers, and photographed gays for years. They weren't refusing to serve homosexuals.

They were refusing to be a part of a same-sex wedding celebration, something they believed goes against their Christian convictions. These business owners didn't want to promote the celebration of something that can in no way be pleasing to God and that the Bible condemns.

These Christians have been taken to both criminal and civil courts because of their actions. They have been fined, and some have lost their businesses. In one case the justice said the photographers were "compelled by law to compromise the very religious beliefs that inspire their lives."

Do you see the problem here? The right to religious liberty is in the Constitution, whereas the right to force someone to violate the very convictions that animate their life is not! We are witnessing a redefinition of the freedom of religion in this country. It no longer means that you must be left alone to practice your religion. Now, depending on whom you ask, it either means that you have the freedom to *worship* the way you want in the church (synagogue, or mosque) of your choice, or it means that you have the right to *believe* whichever religious principles and teachings you wish.

The first amendment doesn't simply address the freedom to "worship" or "believe"; it protects us from the government "impeding the free exercise of religion." Refusing to bake, provide flowers, or photograph a wedding is the exercise of religious freedom, and it has been taken away because on June 26, 2015, the Supreme Court ruled same-sex marriage a nationwide right. True Christianity cannot be limited to church on Sunday morning or "personal belief" because it is to be expressed in every aspect of our lives.

The recent ruling eroding religious liberty will not stay in the wedding industry, however. A time is soon coming, and is already here in some pockets of the world, where you will not be able say that homosexuality is wrong without incurring legal and civil charges and penalties.

You need to decide today how you will act when that time comes. If you remain undecided, I fear that you will make the wrong choice. You might ask, "What's the big deal? Why does it matter so much if we can call homosexuality sin?" It isn't just about calling sin, sin. The main issue is one of being able to share the gospel.

As Christians, our primary goal should be the sharing of the gospel — the making of disciples. In 1 Corinthians 6, Paul makes it clear that you can't continually participate in unrepentant sin (of which he lists homosexuality as an example), and be a Christian. The identification of sin is a central part of the gospel, and the battle against sin is a central part of the Christian life. If we lose the ability to point out sin in the lives of the people we witness to, then we lose the ability to show their need for repentance and forgiveness in those areas.

As long as we can speak, we will never have truly lost the ability to speak all parts of the gospel. However, if parts of the gospel are illegal to share, our task becomes more difficult. On the other hand, the church has flourished more while under threat and persecution than at any other time in history. For example, read how Luke documents the initial spread of the gospel in Acts, often as people took it with them as they fled to avoid persecution.

The government's promotion of same sex marriage is bad for children, it celebrates something that God is against, and it continually leads to a loss of our right to the free exercise of religion.

WHAT WE LEARNED

❖ We need to treat the non-Christian homosexual just as any other non-Christian; they don't have the gospel, and we shouldn't expect them to act as if they do. Coming to faith means repentance and a commitment to sexual purity for heterosexuals and homosexuals alike.

❖ For the Christian who participates in homosexuality, we need to follow the pattern of Matthew 18, and try to restore the person to a life of sexual purity. If this process fails, we should cease being around such a person who still claims the name of Christ and remove them from the church.

❖ We should oppose the government's promotion of homosexuality in the form of same-sex marriage or outside of marriage for the sake of children and the protection of religious liberty.

19

HOW DOES IT ALL FIT TOGETHER?

You may have formed some ideas about how all of these seemingly separate concepts fit together. However, please allow me to draw some connections between everything we've covered. I'll also propose some tactics for using this information in practical ways.

This book can be used in at least two ways. The first would be for you to read through and familiarize yourself with the ideas, arguments, and trains of thought. I'm going to assume you have done that if you're reading this chapter.

The second way this book can be useful to you is as a reference. Let's say, for instance, that you're participating in a conversation at work and the Trinity comes up. Perhaps you're a little foggy on the details of how best to describe it. So, you can just pull out this book when you get back to your desk, or home — or if you have it on your phone, that's even easier — and turn to the chapter on the Trinity. Go to the end of the chapter to the bullet point summary and get a quick 30-second refresher. If you need more detail on a section, just go to the relevant heading and read that section.

This book has been laid out to equip you with the knowledge needed to build a compelling case for Christianity and address the majority of issues confronting Christians today. We started with how people view the world and proceeded on to the concept of truth. In many situations, you will need to start by making use of the concepts

in that chapter since relativism and self-defeating statements abound today.

HOW IT ALL FITS

Many people have such a skewed view of truth that it makes any conversation about the Bible, God, or morality a setup for disaster. People need to know that truth is objective, not subjective, before you can meaningfully discuss any other topic.

After discussing truth, we looked at the most compelling argument for God's existence — the universe and its existence. There had to be a first, uncaused, cause of everything. The universe isn't infinitely old, and it couldn't have created itself. God is the best explanation for the existence of the world we live in, considering all of the scientific and philosophical evidence.

If you are able to convince someone that God does exist, this is a huge step! However, just believing that God exists is not enough. We have to be able to demonstrate that the God of the Bible — the Christian God — is that God who created the universe. You have two good options here. The first is to demonstrate that the Bible is a reliable source of truth and is God's revelation to us. The second is to argue from the evidence for the resurrection. In reality, both of these function as two complementary halves that are both necessary.

Once the truthfulness of the resurrection is established, you have built the foundation necessary for the person to trust in Christ. However, most people are going to have more questions than are addressed by the truth, God, Bible, and resurrection chapters. This is where the topics that we covered in the second half of the book come into play.

If you participate in many of these types of conversations, it won't be long before you are called on to address the problem of evil, the age of the earth, evolution, the morality of God, abortion, and homosexuality. Many times, these topics will be brought up by those who are hostile to Christianity, those who aren't actually wanting to dialogue or find answers.

When this happens, keep a couple of things in mind. First, many times the ones who need to and are open to hearing what we have to say are those who are the "spectators" of the conversation — those who are simply watching and listening, but not participating. Our answers and our character in response to those who are hostile can have a large impact on these people. Second, there will be times when you are confronted by a hostile person when it simply doesn't make sense to engage them (a "pearls before swine" [Matthew 7:6] type of situation) and this is okay. Debating for the sake of debating isn't effective.

All of these other secondary topics such as the problem of evil, abortion, homosexuality, etc. are all interconnected. While they can be discussed as separate issues, they all rely on the existence of objective truth — truth that is true for everyone. They also rely on the existence of objective morality, where the rightness or wrongness of an action is a property of the action, and not simply a reflection of how someone feels about it.

Very often, you can take an attack *on* Christianity and turn it around as an affirmative argument *for* Christianity. For example: if someone says, "It isn't loving to oppose equal right for homosexuals" you could ask, "How did you come to the conclusion that we should be loving?" Or, "How did you come to the conclusion that people should be treated equally?" (Another good question would be, "What do you mean by *loving* and *equality*?")

The person has made a moral claim, and all too often, objective morality doesn't even fit in their worldview. You can point this out to them, and then show them that love fits best and is grounded in the Christian worldview. Love makes no sense in a naturalistic worldview, where we are just complex biological machines. Once you learn to see the assumptions behind the other person's question/assertion, making these kinds of connections and pivots will become quite easy.

The more you learn about these topics and the more you participate in discussing them, the more you will see just how incredibly interconnected they are. This is because they are part of a cohesive worldview where everything is linked with and often depends on everything else. In my opinion, the greatest strength and evidence for Christianity is that it has the greatest explanatory power. It answers more questions than all of the other worldviews, and it leaves the least amount of unanswered questions.

All of the other worldviews fail to fully explain reality and our perceptions of it in a compelling way. Christianity stands head and shoulders above the rest for its success in this area where all others fail.

WHERE DO I GO FROM HERE?

More Resources

This book is a starting place, not an ending place. As I said at the very beginning, it is an introduction to these topics because it doesn't go too far in depth into any single topic. My goal has been to present you with the basics to address today's more relevant concerns.

So, if these topics interest you, please make use of the recommended books and resources in the next chapter. These are all from trustworthy sources, and many of them were used in the writing of this book.

Practice

Learning is useless unless you put into practice what you learn. While you should certainly continue learning about these topics, you will fail to be as effective as you could be if you do not practice using these concepts. This is why students are never allowed to just read the chapter in their math book; they have to do many practice problems because this is how they come to master a topic and technique. It is no different for Christianity and its defense.

The time when I started seeing the most improvement in people I taught was when I stopped teaching for 40 minutes and started teaching for 20 minutes followed by 20 minutes of role-play. The practical application and practice of a concept is invaluable. Knowing an argument is one thing; applying it at the proper time is another. Moreover, simply knowing the argument doesn't mean that you can explain it to someone. This is why practice in real or simulated settings is so important.

I would suggest that you find a friend, or group of people, with whom you can discuss these things. Once you've covered a topic, take turns pretending to be the atheist and the Christian. If you're playing the atheist, try to stump the Christian; you do him no favors by going easy on him.

Use this time to practice maintaining a calm demeanor. Often, friends know just what buttons to push to irritate each other, so, use that knowledge to your advantage. If you're the non-Christian, try to irritate the other person! Interrupt them, cut them off, change the topic, be dismissive. In other words, give the person the opportunity to practice behaving in a Christ-like manner, even when the conversation doesn't go perfectly. In his book *Tactics*, Greg Koukl says that it's *your* job to keep the other person calm; if either of you get upset, you lose![1]

As much as is possible, you want to keep the focus on the facts: emotional reactions from either side make this more difficult and will ultimately obscure your message. Use your role-playing time to practice not just your arguments and responses, but *how* you argue and respond to people who are not friendly to your position.

During role-playing, often one of you will come up with a new method of handling an objection that you hadn't read about before. This independent discovery is just one of the many merits of practicing discussing these issues.

Get into the Game

If you've read this book, you have no excuse for not entering into conversations with non-Christians. You now know more than the average Christian, and you certainly have a better handle on your worldview than the average non-Christian. J. C. Ryle said, "The highest form of selfishness is that of the man who is content to go to heaven alone."[2]

You are now equipped to take the truth of the gospel to our dying world in need of its life-giving power. You are equipped to "tear down arguments and every arrogant obstacle that is raised up against the knowledge of God" (2 Corinthians 10:4-5). You are equipped to "give an answer to anyone who asks about the hope you possess" (1 Peter 3:15). In other words, you have no excuse!

You are totally responsible for your part, and God is totally responsible for his. It is through the sharing of his Word that God has chosen to work, so we must be diligent to share that Word and defend it.

It is my prayer that as you act in trust, God will bless your efforts to the furtherance of his Kingdom. Don't let this be an ending place, but a beginning!

WHAT WE LEARNED

❖ This book can make a great on-going reference for you.
❖ To further your study, make use of the recommended resources in the next chapter.

❖ Practice, practice, practice! Get together with friends and take turns role-playing and applying these concepts.

❖ Don't keep what you've learned to yourself. Get out there and enter into conversations with confidence since you are now much more equipped than when you started!

RECOMMENDED RESOURCES

Most of the works below were used in the writing of this book. If you're interested in going into more depth on the topics that *Unapologetic* has covered, I'd recommend starting with the resources below.

BOOKS

Tactics (Greg Koukl)

If you were only going to read one other book, I would read *Tactics*. Now that you've been equipped with information, his book will give you the tools and techniques to use that information persuasively in conversations.

Get it here: http://amzn.to/1GWYMZn

I Don't Have Enough Faith to Be an Atheist (Frank Turek)

Get it here: http://amzn.to/1Chw20S

Did Jesus Rise from the Dead? (William Lane Craig)

Get it here: http://amzn.to/1M1A11w

Does God Exist? (William Lane Craig)

Get it here: http://amzn.to/1GWZdmh

In the Beginning... We Misunderstood (Johnny V. Miller, John M. Soden)

Get it here: http://amzn.to/1JF6Sf7

How to Read the Bible for All It's Worth (Gordon D. Fee, Douglas Stuart)

Get it here: http://amzn.to/1LOKwrY

Reasonable Faith (William Lane Craig)

Get it here: http://amzn.to/1JMRudX

A Reasonable Response (William Lane Craig)

Get it here: http://amzn.to/1GWZ1DC

Darwin's Doubt (Stephen C. Meyer)

Get it here: http://amzn.to/1IBilLn

Philosophy Made Slightly Less Difficult: A Beginner's Guide to Life's Big Questions (Garrett J. DeWeese, J. P. Moreland)

Get it here: http://amzn.to/1Chwah9

The New Tolerance: How a Cultural Movement Threatens to Destroy You, Your Faith, and Your Children (Bob Hostetler, Josh D. McDowell)

Get it here: http://amzn.to/1JMT2EG

PODCASTS

Unapologetic (Brian Seagraves)

http://brianseagraves.com/unapologetic

Stand to Reason (Greg Koukl)

http://www.str.org/podcasts

Defenders (William Lane Craig)

A systematic examination of Christian doctrine and apologetics. http://www.reasonablefaith.org/defenders-2-podc

NOTES

1 Why "Unapologetic?"

[1] The Law of Identity
Things "are" what they "are." "A" is "A." Each thing is the same with itself and different from another. By this it is meant that each thing (be it a universal or a particular) is composed of its own unique set of characteristic qualities or features
The Law of Non-Contradiction
"A" cannot be both "A" and "Non-A" at the same time, in the same way and in the same sense. Contradictory statements cannot both be true in the same sense at the same time.
The Law of Excluded Middle
A statement is either true or false. For any proposition, either that proposition is true, or its negation is true. There is no middle position. For example, the claim that "A statement is either true or false" is either true or false.

2 How Do People View the World?

[1] Dickens, Charles. "Tale of Two Cities." http://literature.org/authors/dickens-charles/two-cities/book-01/chapter-01.html. N.p., n.d. Web. 2 Sept. 2015.
[2] Merriam-Webster Dictionary: http://www.merriam-webster.com/dictionary/truth

3 Does Truth Exist?

[1] Quentin Smith, "The Uncaused Beginning of the Universe," in William Lane Craig and Quentin Smith, *Theism, Atheism, and Big Bang Cosmology* (Oxford: Clarendon, 1993), 135.

4 Is There a God?

[1] Ruse, Michael. "God Is Dead. Long Live Morality." http://www.theguardian.com/commentisfree/belief/2010/mar/15/morality-evolution-philosophy. N.p., n.d. Web. 14 Sept. 2015.
[2] Michael Ruse, "Evolutionary Theory and Christian Ethics," in *The Darwinian Paradigm* (London: Routledge, 1989), pp. 262–269.

5 Is Evil a Problem?

[1] Geisler, Norman L, and Frank Turek. I Don't Have Enough Faith to Be an Atheist. Crossway, 2004. Print.

[2] See Colin J. Hemer, *The Book of Acts in the Setting of Hellenistic History* (Winona Lake, IN.: Eisenbrauns, 1990).

[3] F.F. Bruce, *The New Testament Documents: Are They Reliable?* (Downers Grove, IL: Intervarsity Press, 1981), p. 82.

[4] Geisler, Norman L, and Frank Turek. *"Do We Have Early Testimony About Jesus?"* I Don't Have Enough Faith to Be an Atheist. Crossway, 2004. Print.

6 Can We Trust the Bible?

[1] The belief that there is no moral code that applies to Christians today.

7 Should The Bible Be Taken Literally?

[1] John A. T. Robinson, The Human Face of God (Philadelphia: Westminster, 1973), 131.

[2] Craig, William Lane. Did Jesus Rise From the Dead? 1st ed. Impact 360 Institute. Print.

[3] Jacob Kremer, Die Osterevangelien—Geschichten um Geschichte (Stuttgart: Katholisches Bibelwerk, 1977), 49–50.

[4] Hans Grass, Ostergeschehen und Osterberichte, 4th ed. (Gottingen: Vandenhoeck & Ruprecht, 1974), 80.

8 Did Jesus Physically Rise from the Dead? Part 1

[1] Craig, William Lane. Did Jesus Rise From the Dead? 1st ed. Impact 360 Institute. Print.

[2] Saint John Chrysostom, and Paul William Harkins. *Baptismal Instructions.* Paulist Press, 1963. 61-62. Print.

[3] William D Edwards, MD Wesley J Gabel MDiv Floyd E Hosmer MS AMI. "On the Physical Death of Jesus Christ." *JAMA* (2004): 1–9. Print.

[4] Craig, William Lane. "The Resurrection of Jesus." *Reasonable Faith.* Crossway, 2008. Print.

[5] Baethge, Christopher. "Grief Hallucinations: True or Pseudo? Serious or Not?." *Psychopathology* 35.5 (2002): 296–302. Web.

[6] Psychobiography is a field within the realms of psychology/biography that analyzes the lives of historically significant individuals through the use of psychological theory and research.

[7] Craig, William Lane. "Hallucination Hypothesis." Did Jesus Rise From the Dead? 1st ed. Impact 360 Institute. Print.

[8] Craig, William Lane. "The Resurrection Hypothesis." Did Jesus Rise From the Dead? 1st ed. Impact 360 Institute. Print.

9 Did Jesus Physically Rise from the Dead? Part 2

[1] The Bible never used the word "Bible" either.

[2] This illustrates a good principle: Sometimes, when a question is asked, we don't need to answer the question, but instead, we need to point out how the question is flawed. We don't need to play the hand we're dealt when the deck has been stacked against us. Always be on the lookout for questions that have unfounded assumptions or bad definitions in them.

[3] At a basic level, a "person" is something has intellect and will. It can process and understand information, and it can choose to act on that information. It is the soul (or mind) that makes humans persons. The mind enables us to be not simply deterministic machines, but instead we as people make real choices in a way computers or animals do not.

[4] Tertullian. Against Praxeas. OrthodoxEbooks, 1919. 1097 Print.

10 The Trinity: Three Gods in One?

[1] "Congress shall make no law respecting an establishment of religion, or prohibiting the free exercise thereof; or abridging the freedom of speech, or of the press; or the right of the people peaceably to assemble, and to petition the Government for a redress of grievances."

[2] Calvin, John. "Acts of the Council of Trent with the Antidote." http://www.monergism.com/thethreshold/sdg/calvin_trentantidote.html. N.p., n.d. Web. 2 Sept. 2015.

11 Is Biblical Faith Blind?

[1] Schwarz, Stephen D. The Moral Question of Abortion. Loyola Pr, 1990. Print.

12 Is Abortion a Complicated Issue?

[1] Reardon, David C, Julie Makimaa, and Amy Sobie. Victims and Victors. 2000. 19-22 Print.
[2] Levitt, Steven D, and Stephen J Dubner. "Where Have All the Criminals Gone?" Freakonomics. Harper Collins, 2011. Print.

13 When Is Abortion Justifiable?

[1] "'Love the Lord your God with all your heart, with all your soul, and with all your mind.' This is the first and greatest commandment." Matthew 22:37-38
[2] "If you love me, you will obey my commandments" John 14:15

14 Are Christians Supposed to Be Tolerant?

[1] Miller, Johnny V, and John M Soden. In the Beginning... We Misunderstood. Kregel Publications, 2012. Print.

15 How Old Is the Earth (and Does It Matter)?

[1] Geisler, Norman L, and Frank Turek. I Don't Have Enough Faith to Be an Atheist. Crossway, 2004. Print.
[2] Dawkins, Richard. The Blind Watchmaker. W. W. Norton & Company, 1986. 6 Print.
[3] Gates, Bill. The Road Ahead. Penguin, 1996. 228 Print.
[4] http://www.telegraph.co.uk/news/religion/3512686/Children-are-born-believers-in-God-academic-claims.html

16 Can Evolution Explain the Arrival and Flourishing of Life?

[1] For a summary of his position, see this video: https://www.youtube.com/watch?v=gmp6lLct-fQ accessed September 2nd, 2015
[2] Except for Keeping the Sabbath, which was part of the Ceremonial law.
[3] James B. DeYoung provides a full discussion of this very issue in his work Homosexuality: Contemporary Claims Examined in the Light of the Bible and Other Ancient Literature and Law (Grand Rapids: Kregel, 2000), Excursus Three, 205ff.

[4] White, James, and Jeff Niell. *The Same Sex Controversy*. Baker Books, 2002. Print.

[5] While I am using the word "homosexual" to refer to someone with same-sex attraction who doesn't necessarily act on those attractions, Paul uses the term "homosexual" (literally "man-bedder") to refer to someone who participates in the action of homosexuality, in the same way that he uses the term "drunkard" to refer to someone who participates in the action of getting drunk.

[6] In some Bible translations the words spoken by Jesus are identified by red ink, as opposed to black.

17 What Does the Bible Say about Homosexuality?

[1] While I am using the word "homosexual" to refer to someone with same-sex attraction who doesn't necessarily act on those attractions, Paul uses the term "homosexual" (literally "man-bedder") to refer to someone who participates in the action of homosexuality in the same way that he uses the term "drunkard" to refer to someone who participates in the action of getting drunk.

[2] http://www.frc.org/issuebrief/new-study-on-homosexual-parents-tops-all-previous-research, accessed day, month, year.

[3] Brief of Amicus Curiae American College of Pediatricians, Family Watch International, Loren D. Marks, Mark D. Regnerus and Donald Paul Sullins in Support of Respondents, Obergefell v. Hodges, 3, available online at http://www.supremecourt.gov/ObergefellHodges/AmicusBriefs/14-556_American_College_of_Pediatricians.pdf.

18 How Should Christians Address Same-Sex Attraction?

[1] Koukl, Gregory. *Tactics*. Zondervan, 2009. Print.

[2] Ryle, R.C. Expository Thoughts on the Gospels: Luke volume 1, [Carlisle, PA: Banner of Truth, 1986], 257

MOTHER TONGUE   Gurdeep Loyal

MOTHER

Gurdeep Loyal is a British Indian food writer, columnist and trend consultant, born and raised in Leicester. After studying at Bristol University, he began his career as a marketeer for Innocent Drinks in London, then a pioneering start-up company shaking up how brands interacted with consumers.

After this, Gurdeep travelled the globe on a solo culinary pilgrimage for a year, before returning to London to take up the role of marketing for Harrods Food Halls, where he was one of the instigators of the Taste Revolution re-development of the world-famous halls.

Most recently he headed up the trends division for Marks & Spencer Food, where his chief purpose was to inspire a team of chefs and developers to invent delicious new products that would delight the dinner tables of the nation.

Gurdeep was the winner of the Jane Grigson Trust Award for new food and drink writers in 2021.

His monthly column in *olive* magazine explores culinary ingredients from around the world through recipes, along with the stories of diasporic home cooks and chefs that preserve them. He also curates the online platform MotherTongueTV.com, which celebrates food histories of migration, race and identity.

Gurdeep has written about food and culture for *Courier* magazine, *Suitcase* magazine and *The Food Almanac*, and been a host speaker at the British Library Food Season, Charleston Small Wonder Literary Festival and The Food People Trends Summit.

He lives in Hackney, East London, where his best-loved pastimes are eating out, posting over-filtered selfies and yelling 'play Beyoncé!' at DJs in clubs.

@gurd_loyal.

Gurdeep Loyal

TONGUE

Flavours of a Second Generation

Photography by Jax Walker

4th Estate | London

4th Estate
An imprint of HarperCollins*Publishers*
1 London Bridge Street
London SE1 9GF
www.4thEstate.co.uk

HarperCollins*Publishers*
Macken House
39/40 Mayor Street Upper
Dublin 1, D01 C9W8

First published in Great Britain in 2023 by 4th Estate

1

Text © Gurdeep Loyal 2023
Photographs © Jacqueline Walker 2023

Always follow the manufacturer's instructions when using kitchen appliances.

Designed and typeset by Evi-O.Studio.

Printed and bound by GPS Group.

For mothers, especially my own
ਮਾਂਵਾਂ ਲਈ, ਖਾਸ ਕਰਕੇ ਮੇਰੀ ਮਾਂ ਲਈ

'Tradition is not the worship of ashes,
but the preservation of fire.'

Gustav Mahler

'Excuse me waiter, please can we have some chilli
sauce, black pepper and English mustard?'

Bhupinder Loyal, aka Mum

The irony of writing a book called *Mother Tongue* in a language that my own mum won't be able to fully read is not lost on me. Yet what's missing in her understanding of what these words say is countered by her fluency in the flavours, something that words can barely begin to convey.

Because my culinary palate is rooted to my mother's tongue, and hers to her mother before her; an intergenerational lineage of love that crosses continents, connecting the past to the present through taste.

Nevertheless, the food that has passed along from generation to generation – migrating from India to England and a connecting hyphen-of-places in between – has not remained static along its journey through time and different lands. Far from a fossilised cuisine preserved in aspic, my food inheritance has been an ever-evolving musical score of flavour, a modulating manuscript of taste scribbled over by each new generation, never deleting what came before, but always leaving edible echoes of the past on the plates of the present.

With each era, new chords of flavour have enriched the hereditary palate, as ever more relatives have added a tuneful taste of who they were. Each masala-ed imprint reveals enduring stories of individual loves and losses, toils and travels, follies and fortunes, bestowing new layers of delicious harmony on the generations that follow.

By means of this continual adaptation, the cookery handed down through maternal fingertips has transformed at each fork of the family tree. Today, it is rooted as much to its legacy trail of uprooting as it is to the soil of Punjab: my ancestral motherland and origin of my epicurean mother tongue.

I am a second generation British Indian food writer and home cook, a descendant of Punjabi farmers and Leicester market traders with big appetites, born in the early 1980s right in the very middle of Old Blighty. My paternal grandparents were the pioneers, migrating from the sugarcane fields of Punjab, via Kenya where my dad was born, to England in the late 1960s.

While the history of outward Punjabi migration dates to before the 19th century, the butterfly effects of Indian independence impelled the relocation for my own Mama and Dhadi-Ji. India's emancipation from British rule ripped the state of Punjab in two, through a bloodstained partition that led to the murder of millions and one of the largest mass migrations across borders in recorded human history. Furthermore, the British Nationality Act of 1948 gave all Commonwealth citizens a right to move to a battered post-war Britain. Consequently, it was to Leicester that many displaced Punjabis travelled – a manufacturing hub for textiles, biscuits and crisps – which in decades to follow would become the first British city with a majority non-white population.

My parents married in Leicester in 1981. Mum – a stylish 19-year-old at the time, with kohl-lined eyes and only a handful of English words – arrived from Mehliana in Punjab just a few weeks before the big day. It was her first venture outside India. Meeting for the first time just weeks before their wedding, the pair were bonded for life through a connecting Aunty-Ji who acted as their *bachoolah*, or 'matrimonial fixer'. To be the *bachoolah* for any Punjabi couple is a terrific honour. Indeed, for some in our community it's their fulltime preoccupation, and this brilliant coterie of wedding-mensch really are a force to be reckoned with: their Falstaffian presence always known, their gossiping proudly indiscreet and their elaborate matchmaking the dramatic epicentre of any party worth being seen at. It's the destiny of most Punjabi children to be caught in their cupid-crossfire as soon as adulthood hits. In modern times, this plays out through covert photo albums of unaware nieces and nephews, presented to suitors on phone screens at a moment's notice. In my parents' day, it was done through Polaroid photographs slipped inside blue aerograms, scribbled with a few vital statistics: analog parent-to-parent nuptial Tinder in postal form, if you will.

Their sepia-bleached wedding video, which I still take unparalleled joy in watching, begins with their *Anand Karaj* ceremony in our Leicester gurdwara. My dad, spruced up in a Marks & Spencer suit and wearing a turban for the very first time, sits agitatedly on the floor next to my defiantly composed mum, a firecracker of bridal red with gleaming sequins the size of pennies.

What follows is fragmented footage of their wedding party, which in that archaic era was reserved for the groom and male guests only. This raucous sausage-fest of mostly Punjabi men is a nostalgic window into a past life; the afro haircuts, flared hemlines and retro bhangra dancing preserving a revelry that lies somewhere in the Venn diagram overlap where *Bend It Like Beckham* meets an Abba tribute concert.

But it's the food on the trestle tables of that party – which took place two years before I existed and conjoined my parents in a loving marriage that's still flourishing more than forty years later – that I find myself thinking about at weddings today. Paper plates filled with keema samosas, chilli fish pakoras, spicy cholay with piles of fried puris, tamarind chutney, syrup-swirled jalebi, fudgey cardamom burfi and Johnnie Walker whisky. It's the celebratory feasting of uprooted Punjabi migrants, voyaged from the motherland to their newly adopted home.

This is the flavour-punch of food that I grew up eating and to which my palate is deeply rooted. Yet from an early age my greedy stomach was also seeking out something else; because like all second generationers around the world (and indeed like any first generationers raised away from their native cradle), my British Indian existence, by birth, was the hybrid kind.

Outwardly, my cinnamon-brown skin, almond eyes and aquiline nose mark me out as 'immigrant' in Great Britain, even though I have only ever migrated an hour's train ride from where I was born in Leicester to East London where I now live. Conversely, my broken Punjabi, tattooed wrists and hipster attire mark me out as 'immigrant' in India.

As a result, I grew up being pulled between self-appointed arbiters of both my Britishness and my Indianness, identity jurors who guarded the social rules of what my labels could and could not be. Being born both British and Indian, I qualified for adjudication twice: a perpetual code-switching game of cat and mouse with my own dual-rooted identity.

Never feeling fully on the inside of either culture, I found myself habitually ousted by both: overly 'Foreign-Chutnified-Brit' on the one hand and overly 'White-Washed-Coconut-Indian' on the other.

My cooking today proudly disregards these labels on a plate, reclaiming my whole identity on my terms, through food that inhabits the middle ground in between so-called cultural boundaries. Just as there is no single monolithic way to be 'British Indian', or any other identity label for that matter, my recipes rejoice in the queer-hybridity of who I am and celebrate the uniqueness of the others who share my compounded tick-box.

The preservation of a food culture does not require it to remain static, so my cooking continues the family – and indeed diaspora – tradition of adapting what came before that is the essence of *my* culinary mother tongue.

The hybrid flavours I add to my family's musical score are a taste of my second generation reality: ingredient 'chords' that knowingly cross-pollinate from motherland to adopted land, rooted to uprooted, traditional to remix and back.

This flavourful self-expression – that loudly takes up the centre space – is the essence of third-culture cooking today. Like the plural identities of third-culture cooks themselves, it's food that refuses to be categorised in the binary terms of one nationality or another. Instead, it straddles dotted intercultural lines, simultaneously existing on the inside and the outside of its own blurred borders.

A frequently touted outsider's take on this 'in-between cuisine' is of food that's trapped between worlds, with one hand in the East and the other in the West, while another is to label it as 'fusion'. But both of these reductive slants miss the nuance, because third-culture cooking purposefully sets its own path down the middle, both hands East and West at the same time, neither 'fused' to anything.

Just as the boundaries where seas meet the shore are the most fruitful places for life to flourish, so third-culture cooking thrives in the liminal boundaries where cultures collide. But it also throws out many questions...

Who gets to gatekeep what is and is not permitted as cultures and cuisines migrate, taking on new elements in their travels? As recipes are passed from generation to generation – evolving, morphing and bending across continents through time – at what point is the balance tipped too far? Can anyone ever have 'ownership' of an ingredient or cuisine? In short, what does 'authenticity' in diasporic cooking mean today?

In my view, 'authenticity' should not be absolutely defined, because like food itself, 'authenticity' is ephemeral. Pin-pointing a particular freeze-frame in time as 'authentic' means it must remain there, indefinitely fixed, rigid, impermeable and static.

But the boundaries of a culture's cuisine are in a state of constant flux, not set in stone. Food is a living form of culture that evolves: its boundaries are fluid, blurred, porous and dynamic; arguably none more so than those of Indian food.

Indeed, just as there is no single mother tongue language that's spoken across all of India, so there is no single 'authentic' Indian cuisine. Instead, there is a bountiful spectrum of regional cuisines that stretch from South to North, each equally authentic. And each ever-evolving as they migrate around the world with a global diaspora of home cooks, boundlessly adventurous in their pursuit of new flavours.

Authenticity is an unending reel of culinary snapshots, an evolving spectrum that captures many transformative moments along flavourful journeys in generations of kitchens.

My British Indian cooking may not be deemed 'authentically' Indian or 'authentically' British, but it *is* authentically third-culture. True to my hybrid identity in the middle ground – and dually attached to both my Britishness and my Indianness – its roots are doubled, not split in half.

Yet, just as hybrid British Indianness itself is not a fixed entity but a continuum that's been progressing for as long as migration from my motherland has flavoured the world, the food on my second generation plates tells only my story, and only up to this point in time.

The British Indianness of my parents tells the story from a first generation's perspective; those who came to Britain as children tell it from a 1.5-generation's perspective; those with only one parent of Indian descent tell it from a 2.5-generation's perspective. And then there's my nephew, the third generation, whose identity brings a new layer of nuance to our family's culinary manuscript: his inherited Indianness is not just Punjabi but also Gujarati; he is dual rooted inside his Indian roots, intercultural even within his own Indian culture.

The recipes in this book add my chords of flavour to the living musical score of cookery that is my family's food heritage. Every ingredient adds something of my second generation story to our ever-evolving culinary tale, with hybrid dishes that bridge backwards as they travel forwards, traditions that endure as they morph, flavours that are preserved as they transform.

Some of my flavours connect directly with those cooked on to the pages by my Bibi-Jis decades ago. Others embody the eternal union of my most beloved tastes with those of my own remarkable mum. And some are entirely new flavour chords that tell the story of my life today for future generations to relish. In turn, the chords of their lives will add even more flavours to the music, that in time they can connect back to me.

London, 2022

Recipe notes

- A spice grinder will give you the best result for the spice mixes in this book, although a mortar and pestle, coffee grinder or powerful smoothie-maker would also work. Basically, you need something that can whizz whole spices to powder, or herbs, garlic and onions into paste. Manual choppers also do the trick, though they require a lot more elbow grease.

- I always measure spices before I grind them, so if an ingredients list calls for '1 tablespoon black peppercorns, crushed', for instance, then I have measured out the tablespoon of peppercorns and then crushed them.

- Deep-frying food calls for a few safety rules. Use a sturdy pan and do not overfill it with oil (it should be one-third full, as a general rule). Drop food gently into the hot oil so it doesn't splash, and carefully turn it in the oil with a slotted spoon or a wire mesh 'spider'. And never leave the pan unattended.

- In some recipes, I make sugar syrups as part of the process. I often want to take these syrups to the 'one-string' stage, in the traditional Indian sweet-making terminology. Gently dab your finger in the syrup and press it with your thumb. Don't burn your fingers! The syrup needs to be thick enough to hold in a single thread between your fingers when pulled apart.

- If you are deep-frying and you don't have an oil thermometer, you can still figure out how hot the oil is. Throw in a cube of bread and time how long it takes to turn brown, following this guide:

  160ºC – 45 seconds
  165ºC – 40 seconds
  170ºC – 35 seconds
  175ºC – 30 seconds
  180ºC – 35 seconds
  185ºC – 20 seconds
  190ºC – 15 seconds
  195ºC – 10 seconds

- Buying spices in an Indian or Asian store is the best way to find ingredients that conventional supermarkets don't stock, and is also more cost effective. This also applies to fresh ingredients such as turmeric, lemongrass and coriander. One ingredient for which this is particularly noticeable is fresh curry leaves (which I use in abundance). If you're lucky enough to find them in a supermarket, they'll be in small packets of 15–20 fresh leaves for a couple of pounds, whereas in an Indian or Asian store they're sold in bushy stalks of 150–200 fresh leaves for the same price. For those especially astute, you can try growing your own.

Flavour Chords: how to play with your food

I may not be a trained chef, but I am a very well-seasoned eater. During my twenty-plus years of working in food, a large part of my job has been to determine global benchmarks of taste for two of Britain's most treasured food institutions: Harrods Food Halls and Marks & Spencer.

The 'professional eating' this has entailed has taken me around the world in pursuit of culinary excellence, from fine French patisserie and Hong Kong dim sum to Singaporean hawker rotis and Scottish Highland whiskys. At the same time, I've embarked on countless family excursions into the 'authentic' regional foods of India, alongside an exploration of the cooking of British curry houses that serve up an 'inauthentic' pastiche of that very same Indianness (see page 144).

As you might imagine, the breadth of tasting involved has been extensive. So, now, I am a home cook with a higher-than-average assortment of taste memories to call on, which intermingle with my palate's Punjabi roots, as well as with my third-culture inclinations.

What I lack in classical training as a chef, I can counteract – somewhat synaesthetically – with my years of musical training as a cellist; a parallel education that has infiltrated my cookery and shaped how I play with flavour. You see, in music, you simultaneously hear different notes, just as you simultaneously taste different flavours in food. When I cook, I think about flavours as if they're musical notes, and flavour combinations as if they're chords.

Just as building a chord of musical notes can go in infinite harmonic directions, so 'flavour chords' can be infinitely combined, rearranged and remixed along global keyboards. Ingredients are there to be played with and those from one culture's cuisine can be completely delicious combined with those of another, opening up a spectrum of flavour for us cooks to explore, which can strike thrilling intercultural chords when cleverly combined.

Playing with all the flavour keys

Imagine only ever using the white notes on a piano. Sure, you could plonk away at basic tunes and harmonies fixed within the fence of chords that the white notes can sound...

... but there are also black notes in between the white notes, and even hidden notes in between those. Playing just the black notes rings out a pentatonic scale, a musical foundation for much of Indian classical music, the traditional music of China, Vietnam and Japan, Javanese Gamelan music, and even improvisational jazz, rockabilly and blues. And if you listen to any sitar player, you'll hear them unravel the continuum of notes in between the piano keys, as they bend their strings along the hyphens that connect one-note-to-the-next.

The music I'm most drawn to makes use of the full chromatic spectrum of sound. I'm inspired by composers such as Anoushka Shankar, Maurice Ravel and Nitin Sawhney; singers such as Nusrat Fateh Ali Khan, Billie Holliday and Fiona Apple; musicians such as Yo-Yo Ma, Miles Davis and Yehudi Menuhin; collaborators such as Indialucia, The Silkroad Ensemble and the South Asian underground collective Daytimers. These maestros command the entire harmonic scale of possibilities, blurring borders between melodic scales, syncopating sounds to straddle beats: music that spans the intercultural.

Equivalently, when it comes to cooking, if you only ever shop for ingredients from conventional mainstream supermarkets or online retailers, you'll miss out on all the flavour notes that don't make their way on to edited supermarket shelves, where even 'ethnic aisles' are generally filtered through a white lens and not by the cultures claiming to be represented.

However, if you intermix your pantry with ingredients bought directly from Indian shops, Turkish greengrocers, Vietnamese stores, Ghanaian market stalls, Greek delis and the like, your cooking has the potential to unlock an entire world of flavour possibilities, combining storecupboard staples you know well with ingredients that you've just discovered.

Supporting the diasporic food communities in your neighbourhood is like illuminating every note on a flavour keyboard, not just the white notes. Third-culture inventiveness in the kitchen – cleverly mixing a spectrum of flavours – can lead to delicious combinations that celebrate a diversity of culinary identities in a single bite. This is one of the most exciting ways to expand your cooking repertoire every day, whether for a simple weekday meal or an epic weekend feast.

Appreciation, not appropriation

At this point it's important to make a clear distinction. I don't want you to 'Columbus' the world to fuse 'exotic' ingredients on to a single plate for the sake of it. I don't want you to appropriate a multitude of cultures into one melting pot in a way that erases their distinct identities. Far from it. Third-culture cooking is about celebrating cultural heritage, not deleting it; expanding culinary possibilities by supporting migrating communities, not dominating them. It is food that reflects the evolving plurality of identity through the lens of global diasporas, cooking up stories of migration, diversity and intergenerational connection from their perspectives.

I want you to engage with diasporic shopkeepers in more than a transactional way; ask them to help you to understand the cultural significance of the ingredients they sell. This will help you to trace the journeys told by the products. Take joy in respectfully learning how ingredients used by diverse cultures around the world are shaped by their intertwined histories. No single society can claim sole ownership over an ingredient, but many have deeply rooted cultural connections to it.

Intercultural cooking is filled with syncretic flavour combinations in between porous cultural boundaries. It sings out the harmony that can occur when flavours from different cultures collide into something new. It celebrates unique global narratives born out of unique lived experiences, inviting you in to cook up third-culture food of your own, whoever and wherever in the world you might be.

Turning a world of flavour notes into delicious music

There are many books about the science of flavour, but this is not one of them. Instead, my 'flavour chords' approach is rooted in culinary instincts taught to me through my ancestry of Punjabi mothers. This honed intuition has driven my creativity in the kitchen, culminating in three connected mantras that are my food principles today, that all home cooks, anywhere in the world, of any ability, can also joyfully embrace:

1   **AMPLIFY YOUR PANTRY** with ingredients bought directly from diasporic stores. Go and explore, learn first-hand from them and taste the world from their perspective. The more you immerse yourself, the more you'll discover new flavours aligned with your own personal tastes. If you adore citrussy flavours, investigate what your nearest Chinese or Cypriot supermarkets offer in their citrus section to mix things up in your lemon drizzle cakes. If you're a lover of chillies, explore the range that your closest Turkish or Vietnamese stores have in. Or if you're drawn to heady spices such as cumin and cardamom, check out your nearest Indian grocer and ask the shopkeepers what, in their view, tastes similar, or what is delicious when combined with those flavours. Adding just a handful of new ingredients to your shelves can take your cooking in hundreds of different directions when combined with your staples, while supporting the immigrant communities those ingredients are culturally rooted to.

2   **EMBED GLOBAL INGREDIENTS TO YOUR PALATE THROUGH TASTING**. Before you start cooking, think about the ingredients in your cupboards in terms of the *flavour characteristics* that each could bring to a dish. This means tasting them individually to etch their unique qualities on to your memory and on to your palate. This learning-through-tasting is key when you start to combine ingredients from different cultures. It's a bit like playing out the sound of each note on a piano before you turn those notes into musical chords. As you build your own palate's innate library of tastes, you'll be sharpening your flavour instincts at the same time. Tasting 'flavour notes' in isolation shows how one ingredient can wear many different masks. Take green cardamom pods: when their inner seeds are ground to a powder, they impart a floral-fruity warmth, but if dry-roasted and used whole they give nutty-tropical notes. Similarly, red onion can be chopped into a dish raw to give sharp-pungent bite, or slowly browned to a sweet-sticky caramel. Tasting also reveals how an ingredient is different depending on when and where it is sourced. Fruits and vegetables are always best picked in peak season in their country of origin, which is why a good Indian grocer only ever stocks an abundance of fresh mangos in a small, frenzied window from April to July. But similar principles apply to spices, which were also once fresh produce, their flavours as changeable between seasons as a fine wine and determined by climate, farming methods and the terroir of a place during any harvest.

3 COMBINE FLAVOUR NOTES INTO FLAVOUR CHORDS.

My approach begins by taking established flavour combinations as the base line. With Italian cuisine for example, classic flavour chords include tomato-garlic-basil; fennel sausage-chilli-broccoli; pecorino-black pepper-butter. These timeless triads are innately delicious and proudly Italian. All cultures have their own combinations. My Punjabi upbringing has hard-wired cardamom-almond-rose, tamarind-date-mint and coriander-fennel seed-cumin to my palate. These are cultural markers of my Punjabi identity, the masala base notes of my mother tongue. Likewise, lemongrass-galangal-fish sauce evokes Thailand; oregano-cumin-ancho chilli speaks of Mexico; curry leaf-mustard seed-coconut suggests South India; allspice-Scotch bonnet-thyme takes us to Jamaica; sumac-pomegranate molasses-tahini ushers forth the Middle East. Each of these triads is perfect, but food cultures are not set in stone. Third-culture cooking invites you to remix classic combinations with a spectrum of flavours that reflect the migrating communities living in each of those places today. This is flavour-amplified cooking, combining global ingredients in all their delicious glory. It tells stories of migrating cultures through the flavours you bring together on a plate.

Nevertheless, when adding intercultural flavour notes to a classic flavour triad, bear in mind the *combined characteristics* of the ingredients you're bringing together. A new element can either contrast and counter, or echo and enhance, an overall blend of flavours. The tastiest hybrid combinations do both.

Getting started: flavour chords in action

To think about this approach practically, let's take the classic Italian flavour combination of tomato-garlic-basil in a simple sauce. It is a harmonious combination in itself, almost nothing could be better. But if you wanted to take this flavour chord into a third-culture direction, you could apply the three core principles above to give a hybrid spin on things.

To begin with, consider the base flavours:

GARLIC
sharp
spicy
pungent warmth

TOMATO
sweet
fresh
fruity acidity

BASIL
fresh herbal qualities
anisey-lemon flavour

To third-culture remix this classic sauce, start with what you have available in your pantry and consider how adding new notes could change the combined flavour chord. My own cupboards are filled with Indian ingredients, so I could, for example, add:

I could even add a masala mix or global spice blend; you could think of these as shortcut blocks of stacked flavour chords, playing many notes in the same spoonful:

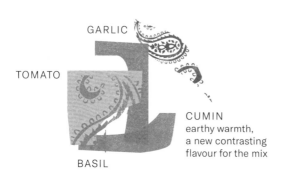

CUMIN
earthy warmth, a new contrasting flavour for the mix

SAMBHAR MASALA
(see page 25)
fragrant South Indian spices bringing new flavour notes as well as some that echo basil

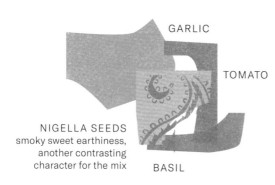

NIGELLA SEEDS
smoky sweet earthiness, another contrasting character for the mix

TOGARASHI
citrussy Japanese chilli spices, a contrasting note to the fruity tomatoes

RAS-EL-HANOUT
rose-scented Middle Eastern warmth to contrast with the herbal basil

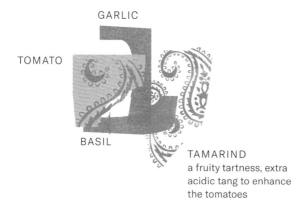

TAMARIND
a fruity tartness, extra acidic tang to enhance the tomatoes

So I could take this classic tomato-garlic-basil sauce into an Italian-Indian direction by:

· Sizzling some toasted cumin and nigella seeds in with the garlic
· Adding a pinch of sambhar masala
· Finishing with a spoonful of tart tamarind

The new notes add something uniquely delicious that changes the classic Italian triad into something Italian with an Indian accent, a blurring of the two worlds that creates something entirely different while celebrating both. Give it a go with what you have in your kitchen cupboards.

Starting with these classic combinations such as tomato-garlic-basil, then bringing in new notes to jazz up the combined flavour chords, is a great place to begin. But with time, as you learn more about different culinary cultures through tasting and become accustomed to combining intercultural ingredients, you can start from a totally blank culinary score and build up hybrid flavour chords from scratch. You can skip straight to the combined flavour characteristics of a dish you want to create, then consider the different ways you can combine global ingredients to get there.

The recipes in this book were developed using this third-culture flavour chords improvisation to some degree. Many amalgamate the flavours of my Punjabi heritage with global ingredients I love. Some take an even more border-free approach, combining ingredients from a wider blend of cuisines that mix up flavour characteristics I love tasting together. You will find these scattered through the pages, in dishes such as Curry Leaf, Lemongrass & Aleppo Pepper Roast Chicken: a mix of South Indian and South East Asian flavours with smoky Middle Eastern peppers. Or Coconut, Za'atar & Maple Chutney: South Asian and tropically Caribbean coconut, with Middle Eastern herby za'atar and Canadian sweet maple. Or even Pistachio & Sumac Madeleines with Rose Milk Jam: Indian and Middle Eastern flavours of pistachio, sumac and rose mixed into French cakes.

Just remember to consider the sum effect of each new note you add to a mix and don't go over the top. While I strongly believe that more is more when it comes to flavour, some ingredients drown out others like a foghorn, so should be used sparingly.

Equally, if you use every intercultural ingredient in your pantry at once, the combined flavour chord will be the culinary equivalent of whacking all the keys on a keyboard at once with a sledgehammer! Third-culture cooking is about letting the different cultures you put into a dish sing out in the mix, not melting everything into an amorphous mass.

Also remember that salt and acid are almost always essential. These two are like the brightness and contrast filters for cooking, vital elements to bring out flavours wherever they're from.

The key to exciting third-culture flavour combinations is what is in your cupboards, so get out to diasporic stores, speak to people from other cultures, learn about cuisines of the world first-hand, explore your own family's culinary heritage, bring your travels into your kitchen, and have a go.

If the worst comes to the worst, you can always order in a curry.

The key to mixing ingredient 'notes' into tasty flavour 'chords' is understanding the combined characteristics of the components you're bringing together. The bubbles over the pages that follow will, I hope, be helpful in introducing this mindset to your cooking.

Each bubble groups together families of ingredients from around the world that share common characteristics – peppery, say, or creamy – at their most basic. The best combinations tend to:

1 CONTRAST ingredients from different bubbles (aim for two or three at a maximum)

2 Ensure NO SINGLE BUBBLE OVERPOWERS the cumulative effect

3 BALANCE any combination with components that ADD SALT to enhance and ADD ACID to brighten the flavours

Each ingredient in a group imparts its character in different ways and at different volumes (a sprinkle of Scotch bonnet delivers more chilli-heat than a sprinkle of sweet paprika; a teaspoon of brown miso delivers more salty-umami than a teaspoon of light soy). The best way to build your knowledge of this is through tasting, embedding each ingredient to your palate as you go.

The bubbles that follow are by no means exhaustive, reflecting my kitchen cupboards as they do, but I hope they will inspire you to explore your local diasporic stores, which can amplify your cooking in delicious new directions.

Flavour chord bubbles

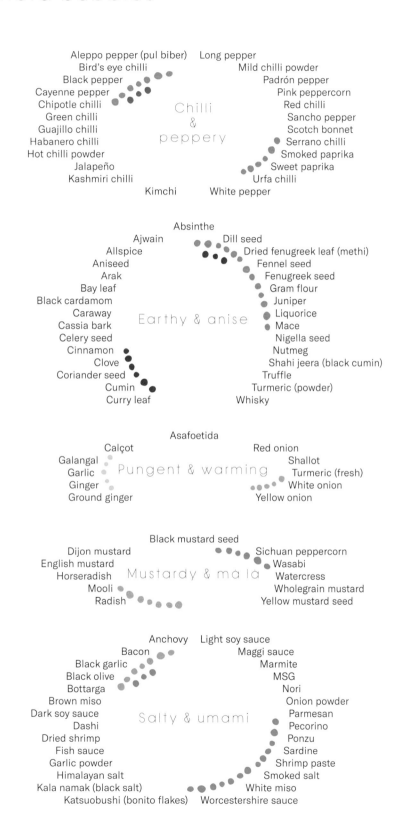

Chilli & peppery

Aleppo pepper (pul biber)
Bird's eye chilli
Black pepper
Cayenne pepper
Chipotle chilli
Green chilli
Guajillo chilli
Habanero chilli
Hot chilli powder
Jalapeño
Kashmiri chilli
Kimchi

Long pepper
Mild chilli powder
Padrón pepper
Pink peppercorn
Red chilli
Sancho pepper
Scotch bonnet
Serrano chilli
Smoked paprika
Sweet paprika
Urfa chilli
White pepper

Earthy & anise

Absinthe
Ajwain
Allspice
Aniseed
Arak
Bay leaf
Black cardamom
Caraway
Cassia bark
Celery seed
Cinnamon
Clove
Coriander seed
Cumin
Curry leaf

Dill seed
Dried fenugreek leaf (methi)
Fennel seed
Fenugreek seed
Gram flour
Juniper
Liquorice
Mace
Nigella seed
Nutmeg
Shahi jeera (black cumin)
Truffle
Turmeric (powder)
Whisky

Pungent & warming

Asafoetida
Calçot
Galangal
Garlic
Ginger
Ground ginger

Red onion
Shallot
Turmeric (fresh)
White onion
Yellow onion

Mustardy & ma la

Black mustard seed
Dijon mustard
English mustard
Horseradish
Mooli
Radish

Sichuan peppercorn
Wasabi
Watercress
Wholegrain mustard
Yellow mustard seed

Salty & umami

Anchovy
Bacon
Black garlic
Black olive
Bottarga
Brown miso
Dark soy sauce
Dashi
Dried shrimp
Fish sauce
Garlic powder
Himalayan salt
Kala namak (black salt)
Katsuobushi (bonito flakes)

Light soy sauce
Maggi sauce
Marmite
MSG
Nori
Onion powder
Parmesan
Pecorino
Ponzu
Sardine
Shrimp paste
Smoked salt
White miso
Worcestershire sauce

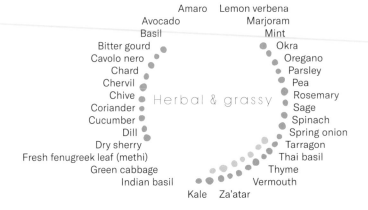

Herbal & grassy

Amaro
Avocado
Basil
Bitter gourd
Cavolo nero
Chard
Chervil
Chive
Coriander
Cucumber
Dill
Dry sherry
Fresh fenugreek leaf (methi)
Green cabbage
Indian basil
Kale
Za'atar

Lemon verbena
Marjoram
Mint
Okra
Oregano
Parsley
Pea
Rosemary
Sage
Spinach
Spring onion
Tarragon
Thai basil
Thyme
Vermouth

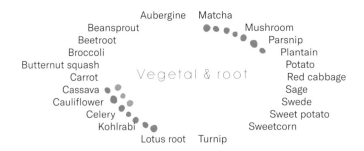

Vegetal & root

Aubergine
Beansprout
Beetroot
Broccoli
Butternut squash
Carrot
Cassava
Cauliflower
Celery
Kohlrabi
Lotus root

Matcha
Mushroom
Parsnip
Plantain
Potato
Red cabbage
Sage
Swede
Sweet potato
Sweetcorn
Turnip

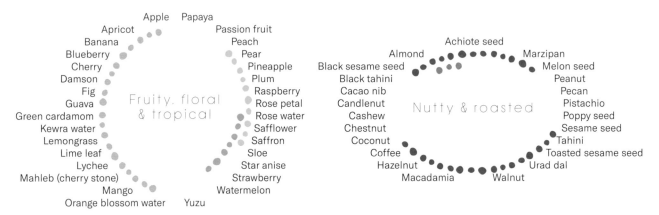

Fruity, floral & tropical

Apple
Apricot
Banana
Blueberry
Cherry
Damson
Fig
Guava
Green cardamom
Kewra water
Lemongrass
Lime leaf
Lychee
Mahleb (cherry stone)
Mango
Orange blossom water

Papaya
Passion fruit
Peach
Pear
Pineapple
Plum
Raspberry
Rose petal
Rose water
Safflower
Saffron
Sloe
Star anise
Strawberry
Watermelon
Yuzu

Nutty & roasted

Achiote seed
Almond
Black sesame seed
Black tahini
Cacao nib
Candlenut
Cashew
Chestnut
Coconut
Coffee
Hazelnut
Macadamia

Marzipan
Melon seed
Peanut
Pecan
Pistachio
Poppy seed
Sesame seed
Tahini
Toasted sesame seed
Urad dal
Walnut

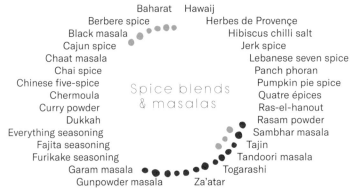

Spice blends & masalas

Baharat
Berbere spice
Black masala
Cajun spice
Chaat masala
Chai spice
Chinese five-spice
Chermoula
Curry powder
Dukkah
Everything seasoning
Fajita seasoning
Furikake seasoning
Garam masala
Gunpowder masala

Hawaij
Herbes de Provençe
Hibiscus chilli salt
Jerk spice
Lebanese seven spice
Panch phoran
Pumpkin pie spice
Quatre épices
Ras-el-hanout
Rasam powder
Sambhar masala
Tajin
Tandoori masala
Togarashi
Za'atar

Creamy & cheesy

Aged hard cheese
Alpine cheese · Kefir
Blue cheese · Labneh
Burrata · Mayonnaise
Buttermilk · Mozzarella
Cheddar · Nut butter
Coconut cream · Paneer
Cream cheese · Processed American cheese
Crème fraîche · Red Leicester
Custard apple · Ricotta
Double cream · Skyr
Feta · Sour cream
Fontina · Washed rind cheese
Greek yogurt · Yogurt
Halloumi

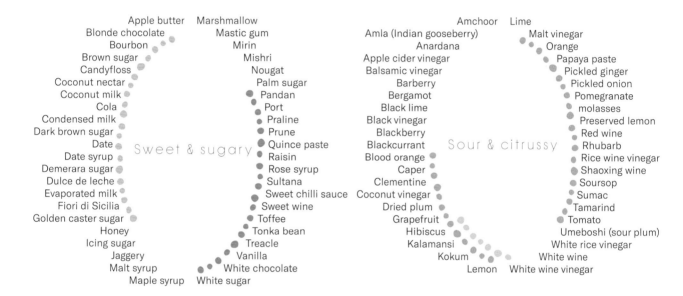

Sweet & sugary

Apple butter · Marshmallow
Blonde chocolate · Mastic gum
Bourbon · Mirin
Brown sugar · Mishri
Candyfloss · Nougat
Coconut nectar · Palm sugar
Coconut milk · Pandan
Cola · Port
Condensed milk · Praline
Dark brown sugar · Prune
Date · Quince paste
Date syrup · Raisin
Demerara sugar · Rose syrup
Dulce de leche · Sultana
Evaporated milk · Sweet chilli sauce
Fiori di Sicilia · Sweet wine
Golden caster sugar · Toffee
Honey · Tonka bean
Icing sugar · Treacle
Jaggery · Vanilla
Malt syrup · White chocolate
Maple syrup · White sugar

Sour & citrussy

Amchoor · Lime
Amla (Indian gooseberry) · Malt vinegar
Anardana · Orange
Apple cider vinegar · Papaya paste
Balsamic vinegar · Pickled ginger
Barberry · Pickled onion
Bergamot · Pomegranate molasses
Black lime · Preserved lemon
Black vinegar · Red wine
Blackberry · Rhubarb
Blackcurrant · Rice wine vinegar
Blood orange · Shaoxing wine
Caper · Soursop
Clementine · Sumac
Coconut vinegar · Tamarind
Dried plum · Tomato
Grapefruit · Umeboshi (sour plum)
Hibiscus · White rice vinegar
Kalamansi · White wine
Kokum · White wine vinegar
Lemon

Sauces, oils & pastes

Chilli crisp oil · Plum sauce
Chipotle paste · Red curry paste
Garlic oil · Rose harissa
Green curry paste · Sambal oelek
Gremolata · Shrimp chilli oil
Harissa · Sriracha
Kecap manis · Sundried tomato paste
Laksa paste · Tapenade
Mango chutney · Tikka paste
Nanami paste · Tabasco
Olive oil · Tomato ketchup
Oyster sauce · Tomato purée
Peanut oil · Walnut oil
Peanut sauce · Yellow curry paste
Pesto · Yuzu kosho
Pistachio oil · Zhoug

Masala Mixes

THIS PAGE, CLOCKWISE FROM LEFT
Minted Baharat, Garam Masala, Black Masala, Gunpowder
Masala, Pistachio-Fenugreek Dukkah, Tandoori Masala

Tip The amount each of these masala mixes makes
will vary depending on the quality of the spices used.
However, as a general guide, each will make 12–14
tablespoons, or about a small jam jar-full.

Garam masala

In essence, any North Indian 'hot spice mix' can be called a garam masala (that being its very literal translation). As a result, no two garam masalas are ever the same; it all depends on what individual home cooks regard as the definition of 'hot', or a desirable 'spice', or a suitable 'mix'! They can be as simple as a trio of cumin seeds, green cardamom and black peppercorns, or they can contain a heady mélange of intoxicating spices such as mace, aniseed, cassia bark and ajwain. My blend is a bit of both: simple to make, but subtly layered. Regardless, this recipe should only be used as a guide, because if you mix your own garam masala, do as us Indians do and really make it your own.

2 tablespoons coriander seeds
2 tablespoons cumin seeds
15 green cardamom pods, split
1 tablespoon black peppercorns
10 cloves
4 dried bay leaves
1 tablespoon fennel seeds
8 allspice berries
1 cinnamon stick
1 tablespoon chilli flakes
1 teaspoon freshly grated nutmeg
1 teaspoon ground ginger

· Dry pan-roast the whole spices for 1–2 minutes until they release their aromas. Let them cool, then transfer to a spice grinder along with the chilli flakes, nutmeg and ginger. Blitz to a fine powder.

To Cheat Garam masala is the most widely available masala blend to buy: you'll find it in small tubs in the spice aisle of most supermarkets, in gigantic bags at Indian shops, or in tiny jars that don't fit a teaspoon at expensive delis. Look for one that has a rounded mix of flavours in the ingredients list: earthy spices such as cumin, caraway or black cardamom; aromatic elements such as cloves, coriander or green cardamom; anisey spices such as fennel seed, aniseed or star anise; warming ingredients such as black pepper, chilli flakes or ground ginger.

Black masala

Kala masala – to use its Marathi name – is a darkly roasted, sweetly nutty and earthy spice blend from the West Indian state of Maharashtra. Slightly mellower than garam masala, it's more aromatically nuanced, with coconut imparting toastiness and black cardamom a slight smokiness. This is a staple in many Maharashtrian vegetable curries, dals and fish dishes, but is also delicious in biryanis, used as a marinade for meats and for sprinkling into yogurt raitas.

65g desiccated coconut
1 tablespoon white sesame seeds
2 tablespoons coriander seeds
2 teaspoons chilli flakes
1 tablespoon cumin seeds
2 teaspoons black peppercorns
6 cloves
2 teaspoons caraway seeds
2 tablespoons fennel seeds
8 green cardamom pods, split
6 black cardamom pods, split
1 cinnamon stick
2 star anise
1 tablespoon black mustard seeds
1 tablespoon black cumin seeds (shahi jeera)
1 tablespoon anardana powder

· Dry pan-roast the desiccated coconut until it just starts to tint in colour, then tip into a bowl. Repeat with the sesame seeds, taking care not to burn them. Next dry pan-roast all the rest of the ingredients together for 1–2 minutes, until they release their aromas.
· Let them cool, then transfer everything to a spice grinder. Blitz to a fine powder.

To Cheat Black masala is also known as kala masala, goda masala or Maharashtrian masala after the Indian state it comes from, so look out for these in Indian shops or online. Any spice blend with a long ingredients list – called something like 'smoky masala' or 'black cardamom masala' – will also be a good approximation. Alternatively, mix shop-bought garam masala with ground desiccated coconut and dark earthy spices such as black cardamom, mustard seeds, black peppercorns and caraway seeds. That should get you pretty close to the real thing.

Chaat masala

Given that chaat means 'to lick', this is a spice blend intended to make you want to do exactly that! Lip-puckeringly tangy, pungently umami and warmingly hot, chaat masala blends can vary, apart from two signature ingredients that are a must: amchoor (dried mango) powder and kala namak: black salt. The volcanic taste of the black salt can take a little getting used to at first, but think of it like the green olive, Marmite or Campari of the spice world: once you develop a taste for it, there's no going back.

2 tablespoons coriander seeds
2 tablespoons fennel seeds
2 tablespoons cumin seeds
1 teaspoon ajwain
1 cinnamon stick
1½ teaspoons black peppercorns
3 tablespoons amchoor
1 tablespoon kala namak (black salt)
1 teaspoon freshly grated nutmeg
1 teaspoon dried mint
2 tablespoons Kashmiri chilli powder
2 teaspoons ground ginger

· Dry pan-roast the first 6 ingredients (the whole spices) for 1–2 minutes until they start to release their aromas. Let them cool, then put them in a spice grinder along with the remaining ingredients. Blitz to a fine powder.

To Cheat Chaat masala is as readily available to buy in stores as garam masala, with amchoor and black salt being the two key components to look for in the ingredients list. You can (sort of) approximate it by mixing garam masala with amchoor and a little fine sea salt; or make a very quick cheat's version by combining Kashmiri chilli powder, amchoor, ground cumin and fine sea salt. Either way, use liberally.

Gunpowder masala

Roasted dals used as spices, and freshly fried curry leaves, are two very South Indian masala traits, and key components of gunpowder masala. Milagai podi in its mother tongue, this traditionally explosive spice mix is used to bring South Indian favourites such as idli, dosa, seafood dishes and coconutty curries to life. The measurement of Kashmiri chilli and chilli flakes here is a baseline minimum: add according to your own palate for heat. This one is meant to have a bang.

1 tablespoon vegetable oil
30–35 fresh curry leaves
2 tablespoons white urad dal
2 tablespoons chana dal
2 tablespoons coriander seeds
2 teaspoons cumin seeds
10 green cardamom pods, split
2 tablespoons white sesame seeds
2 tablespoons amchoor
2 tablespoons Kashmiri chilli powder
½ teaspoon chilli flakes
½ teaspoon asafoetida (hing)

· Heat the oil in a frying pan, add the curry leaves and sizzle for 30–45 seconds. Transfer to a spice grinder, then wipe the pan with some kitchen paper. Next dry pan-roast the urad dal, chana dal, coriander seeds, cumin seeds and cardamom pods for 2–3 minutes until they release their aromas. Finally, add the sesame seeds, roasting just until they start to tint brown. Let cool, then transfer to the spice grinder with the rest of the ingredients. Blitz to a fine powder.

To Cheat Gunpowder spice mixes are relatively easy to find in larger supermarkets and online under their English moniker, but also look out for idli podi, milagai podi or 'chutney masala', which will be very similar, if not the same. Check the ingredients list for roasted dals, curry leaves, sesame seeds and dried chillies in particular. You can use shop-bought sambhar masala (see right) as an alternative, but not garam masala, as it is a North Indian mix: they're distinctively different in their flavour profiles, being from opposite ends of the subcontinent. Essentially, they taste about as similar as piccalilli does to pesto.

Sambhar masala

Tandoori masala

This masala is to South India what garam masala is to the North: a trademark of the region, yet totally different in any two households. Its primary use is in sambhar dals, which are soured with tamarind and eaten alongside rice, idli and dosas. I also like to use it as a marinade for seafood and as the main spicing in quick Indian stir-fries. Curry leaves, mustard seeds, coriander seeds and roasted dals are its key components, with a generous smattering of turmeric for its earthy flavour and South Indian sunshine-yellow vibrancy.

What makes a tandoori masala unique is the addition of one extra ingredient not listed here: fire! This highly aromatic North Indian blend is used most often in a marinade to penetrate flavour deep into meats, paneer and vegetables, right before they are fired, scorched and charred to life. Harmoniously complex in its flavour profile, it takes on a whole new dimension when smoke is added. Don't be intimidated by the number of ingredients: each has its purpose, so just think of it like adding one single spice. Only fourteen times.

1 tablespoon vegetable oil
30 fresh curry leaves
2 tablespoons white urad dal
2 tablespoons coriander seeds
2 teaspoons cumin seeds
1 tablespoon chilli flakes
1 tablespoon black mustard seeds
1 teaspoon nigella seeds
½ teaspoon fenugreek seeds
5 cloves
1 tablespoon black peppercorns
1½ teaspoons ground turmeric
1 teaspoon ground ginger

2 tablespoons cumin seeds
2 tablespoons coriander seeds
1 tablespoon fennel seeds
2 teaspoons black peppercorns
16 green cardamom pods, split
2 black cardamom pods, split
1½ teaspoons aniseed seeds
1 cinnamon stick
4 cloves
1½ teaspoons freshly grated nutmeg
1 teaspoon ground mace
3 tablespoons Kashmiri chilli powder
1½ teaspoons ground turmeric
15–20 saffron strands

· Heat the vegetable oil in a frying pan, add the curry leaves and let them sizzle for 30–45 seconds. Transfer to a spice grinder, then wipe the pan with some kitchen paper. Next dry pan-roast the urad dal, coriander seeds, cumin seeds, chilli flakes, black mustard seeds, nigella seeds, fenugreek seeds, cloves and black peppercorns for 1–2 minutes until they start to release their aromas. Let them cool, then transfer to the grinder along with the curry leaves, turmeric and ginger. Blitz to a fine powder.

· Dry pan-roast the whole spices (the first 9) for 1–2 minutes until they release their aromas. Let them cool, then transfer to a spice grinder along with the nutmeg, mace, chilli powder, turmeric and saffron. Blitz to a fine powder.

To Cheat Sambhar masalas are readily available in Indian shops and bigger supermarkets. Alternatively a 'South Indian masala', 'dosa masala' or 'idli masala' will deliver something similar. Look for one with the defining South Indian flavours of curry leaves, mustard seeds and roasted dals in particular.

To Cheat Tandoori masala mixes are widely available in Indian shops and bigger supermarkets, sometimes sold as 'tikka masala', 'tandoor mix', 'grill masala' or 'Punjabi masala'. You could also use a 'kebab masala', 'sheekh masala' or 'biryani masala' in its place, as these will have a similar deeply aromatic quality. Look for one that has a good rounded mix of spices, not just salt and paprika, which many are based on. Garam masala is a good approximation, just add an extra pinch of the more fragrant components such as clove, cardamom and nutmeg.

Chai masala

We don't actually call it chai in my Punjabi mother tongue, we call it chaah. Either way, it's the most-said word in our household, but then the word 'tea' is arguably the most-said word in the whole of Great Britain across all languages. Slowly boiling chai masala spices with black tea leaves, whole milk, fresh ginger and demerara sugar will give you a truly transportative Indian cuppa. But this is a masala blend that works wonders, too, in cakes, desserts (especially with chocolate), syrups for cocktails, and also as a salted-savoury seasoning.

40 green cardamom pods, split
8 cloves
2 tablespoons fennel seeds
1 star anise
10 allspice berries
1 cinnamon stick
1 teaspoon freshly grated nutmeg
1 tablespoon ground ginger

· Dry pan-roast the green cardamom pods, cloves, fennel seeds, star anise, allspice berries and cinnamon for 1–2 minutes until they start to release their aromas. Let them cool, then transfer to a spice grinder along with the nutmeg and ginger. Blitz to a fine powder.

To Cheat Thanks to the trend for 'chai tea lattes' (which literally translates as 'tea tea lattes'), there is no shortage of chai spice mixes to buy in supermarkets, online, or at those shops in yoga studios where no one seems to ever have to rush back to work and everyone wears Stella McCartney. Look for a good quantity of green cardamom and ginger in the ingredients list as a basic principle, but blends that include aromatics such as clove, star anise and even saffron will give you something extra special.

Tangy chilli-mango sprinkle

This sprinkle stems from my love of Taiwanese fried chicken joints that have a line-up of flavour dusts at the counter, for liberally coating freshly deep-fried morsels of deliciousness. My go-to is crispy chicken strips smothered in a mix of plum sprinkle, numbing má là chilli, nori seaweed, tangy tomato and powdered cheese. This Indian-y take on a flavour dust is salty, sweet, sour and umami all in one. It goes with everything in this book and is intentionally addictive. Don't say I didn't warn you.

3 tablespoons Kashmiri chilli powder
2 teaspoons ground cumin
2 teaspoons ground coriander
2 tablespoons fine sea salt
3 tablespoons caster sugar
4 tablespoons amchoor
2 teaspoons ground white pepper
2 tablespoons onion powder
1½ teaspoons MSG (optional, but infinitely better if added)

· Put all the ingredients in a bowl and whisk together so everything is evenly combined. Transfer to a shaker. Sprinkle liberally. On everything.

To Cheat This is not something you'll find in stores, but lots of things that you *can* buy will give you the intended punchy flavour hit. Try a shop-bought chilli-sea-salt mixed with caster sugar and amchoor; or even a shop-bought chaat masala powder mixed with caster sugar and onion powder. Alternatively, a Japanese shichimi togarashi spice blend mixed with some caster sugar makes for a fantastic flavour sprinkle; a Mexican Tajín or chilli-lime seasoning always delivers; while a Lebanese seven spice mixed with amchoor and caster sugar will also be completely delicious.

Pistachio-fenugreek dukkah

The textures of a dish are just as important as the flavours, making the crunchy Egyptian spice seasoning dukkah something of a double ally in the kitchen. Ajwain, dried fenugreek and pistachios give this version a faintly Punjabi aura, but can be substituted for any roasted nuts or dried herbs that suit your tastes. Try mixing hazelnuts, walnuts or pecans, with dried tarragon, thyme or rosemary. Maybe even all of them together. When it comes to flavour and crunch, more is more after all.

60g shelled unsalted pistachio nuts
2 tablespoons cumin seeds
1 tablespoon coriander seeds
1 tablespoon fennel seeds
¼ teaspoon ajwain
1 tablespoon pink peppercorns
2 tablespoons white sesame seeds
2 tablespoons dried fenugreek leaves
1 teaspoon paprika
1 teaspoon smoked salt
2 tablespoons roasted chickpeas
2 teaspoons onion powder

· Preheat the oven to 150°C fan. Roast the pistachios for 7–8 minutes, then cool completely.
· Dry pan-roast the cumin, coriander and fennel seeds, ajwain and pink peppercorns for 1–2 minutes until they release their aromas. Add the sesame seeds, roasting for 1 more minute. Let them cool, then transfer to a spice grinder – or better still, a mortar and pestle – with the pistachios, dried fenugreek, paprika, smoked salt, roasted chickpeas and onion powder. Grind or pulse to a crumbly rubble, not a fine powder; a coarse sprinkle with some crunch.

To Cheat Standard dukkah mixes are readily available in supermarkets, often using roasted chickpeas and seeds for the crunchy element. Sesame seeds are essential, but look for a blend that includes zesty whole spices such as coriander seeds, fennel seeds or nigella. Or buy a za'atar spice blend, then add your own roasted nuts and toasted whole seeds for extra crunch. Having a little salt in there is essential; smoked salt if you like that extra depth of flavour.

Minted baharat

Given its geographical location, Punjabi food has been greatly shaped by the travelling cuisines of invading Turkish, Persian and Moghul rulers through history. Baharat, the Arabic word for 'spice', also refers to a Middle Eastern blend that imparts its very own sweetly perfumed aromatics to dishes. The addition of dried mint here adds a woody-menthol quality, like capturing the spirited taste of the souk on a teaspoon.

1 tablespoon cumin seeds
2 tablespoons coriander seeds
8 allspice berries
6 cloves
2 teaspoons black peppercorns
1 cinnamon stick
8 green cardamom pods, split
½ teaspoon freshly grated nutmeg
1 tablespoon paprika
1 tablespoon dried mint

· Dry pan-roast the cumin seeds, coriander seeds, allspice berries, cloves, black peppercorns, cinnamon and green cardamom for 1–2 minutes until they release their aromas. Let them cool, then transfer to a spice grinder with the nutmeg, paprika and dried mint. Blitz to a fine powder.

To Cheat Baharat mixes are easy to find in most supermarkets and in Middle Eastern food stores. Look for one that has cumin, cinnamon and cloves as core components in the ingredients list. Versions with mint are a little more difficult to find, but you can add a couple of spoons of dried mint yourself, or even make a paste using shop-bought baharat, fresh mint leaves and a splash of water.

CHAPTER 1

CHAATS,
COCKTAIL BITES &
SAVOURY SNACKS

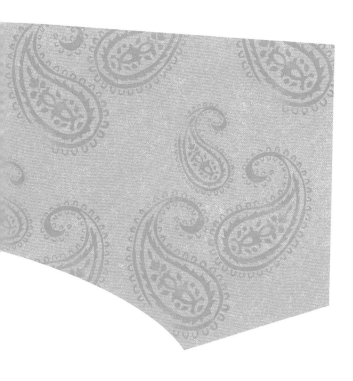

Like many Punjabi families, mine has a somewhat fluid approach to the concept of time, with a marked distinction made between 'English time' (fixed by the laws of physics) and 'Indian time' (flexible to however you happen to feel at any given moment). To us, clocks are general guidelines for life's happenings, within which the acceptable margins of error on either side are limitless. Things occur either later or earlier than planned; they simply happen whenever they happen to happen. This applies whether you're meeting for lunch, catching a train,

or getting married. Precise planning is futile, and, as the timeless Indian aphorism goes, if we are meeting at 7pm and you have arrived at 7pm, then it's your fault.

Likewise, the regimented Western culinary succession of starter to main course to dessert does not strictly exist in the Indian style of eating. It is deemed to be, like English time itself, far too rigid a convention for the boundless gustatory pleasures of food.

In my parents' Leicester household, mealtimes are liberated of any formulaic order or strict rules. We serve dishes simultaneously all at once, dining banquet-style, without any set sequence of courses. Hands and spoons are preferred over forks and knives. Unexpected guests are always expected, fifteen being regularly squeezed around a table constructed for eight. Sweet and savoury go side by side, often in the same dish. Helping yourself is encouraged over pre-plated portioning. Punjabi pickles, condiments and hot sauces are deemed necessities, regardless of the cook's intentions.

And grazing between mealtimes is celebrated as a perpetually revolving meal in its own right. The notion of 'spoiling your appetite' simply does not exist, because, in Punjabi culture, every hour of the day – going by either English time or Indian time – is chaat time!

Chaat are Indian street snacks intentionally designed to be a raucous fiesta of flavour in your mouth, that deliberately hit every single tastebud at the same time. Heralding from the word chaatna, which means 'to lick', they're characterised by their mixed-up mingling of hot, sour, sweet, crunchy, spicy, creamy, umami and tangy sensations all at full volume. Indeed, it's this collective mishmash and sensory overload that distinguishes the zeniths of good chaat.

Chaat o'clock at home (or 'biting' as we like to call it) can kick off at unpredictable hours on any given day. It takes the form of an ever-growing warm-up feast of chutney-loaded samosas, soft cakey dhokla, crispy fried pakoras, masala chips and dips, anisey-savoury biscuits and spicy chilli-ed cocktail nuts. They're served alongside sizzling hot plates of butter-blackened onions crowned with fragrant chicken wings, charred paneer bites or piquant chilli prawns.

Chaat functions just as fittingly for breakfast, afternoon tea or midnight feast, because these are more than just snacks; they are the very spirit of Indian eating itself. The only rule is that, wherever possible, cutlery is left in the drawer: to chaat correctly, your fingers and face must be smothered in chutney by the end. The lip-licking clue is right there in its name.

Bhel puri exudes third-culture energy by design. The whole point of it is to preserve the characteristics of each ingredient as they're mixed into a medley: crunch from sev, fiery-sweet red onion, sour-sharp tamarind, freshness from tomatoes, crispiness from puffed rice, pomegranate juice bombs, cooling yogurt creaminess, tangy chutney bite, earthy-bright coriander, complex intense chaat masala.

It's the antithesis of a culinary melting pot: a jumble of individualism where the collective whole is greater than the sum of its parts. The crispy okra and honey-masala corn I've added here give extra notes of flavour to amplify the overall effect.

More really is more.

Serves 6

For the okra
200g okra, cut into fine strips
1 teaspoon fine sea salt
2 teaspoons Chaat Masala (see page 24),
   plus more for sprinkling
4 tablespoons gram flour
1 tablespoon rice flour
2 tablespoons fine cornmeal
400ml sunflower oil, plus 1 tablespoon

For the corn
40g salted butter, very soft
2 tablespoons runny honey
¼ teaspoon ground cloves
½ teaspoon ground cinnamon
¼ teaspoon cayenne pepper
seeds from 6 green cardamom pods, crushed
1¼ teaspoons fine sea salt
1 teaspoon coarsely ground black pepper
1 teaspoon finely grated lime zest,
   plus 1 tablespoon lime juice
300g (1 large can) canned sweetcorn kernels, drained

For the bhel puri
300g bhel, or Bombay mix
4 tablespoons pomegranate seeds
½ cucumber, deseeded and finely chopped
2 plum tomatoes, deseeded and finely chopped
½ red onion, finely chopped
Tamarind, Date & Mint Sauce and Coriander, Spring Onion
   & Curry Leaf Chutney (see pages 203 and 202)
natural yogurt

· To make the crispy okra, preheat the oven to 150°C fan. Sprinkle the okra strips with the salt and the 2 teaspoons of chaat masala in a small bowl, toss and set aside for 1 minute. Sprinkle in the gram flour, rice flour and cornmeal, then mix in 3–4 tablespoons of water to create a thick, coarse batter for the okra.
· Heat the oil in a saucepan to 160°C (see page 11), then fry the okra for 2–3 minutes (or you can also use half the amount of oil and a small frying pan). Drain on kitchen paper, then spread on to a baking sheet and bake for 15–20 minutes, until crisp but not burnt. Sprinkle liberally with chaat masala.
· Preheat the grill to its maximum setting and line a baking sheet with baking parchment.
· For the corn, in a small bowl, use a fork to mash together the butter, honey, spices, salt, pepper, lime zest and juice. Next add the sweetcorn, mixing well to fully coat the kernels in the honey-spiced butter paste. Spoon on to the prepared baking sheet and cook under the very hot grill for 3–4 minutes until sticky and scorched in places.
· In small bowls or paper cones, layer the bhel or Bombay mix with pomegranate seeds, cucumber, tomatoes, red onion, chutneys and yogurt, leaving enough room to smoosh everything together with a spoon.
· Top with the honey-masala corn and crispy okra, then finish with a final drizzle of chutneys, yogurt and a sprinkle of chaat masala. Eat immediately.

Flaky muthiya with spiced Parmesan

If ever there was a snack to get you hooked on anisey-herbal ajwain seeds, muthiya are it. These salty North Indian butter biscuits are layered with flakiness, like crackling savoury shortbread thins that break with a snap. Crushing the ajwain seeds between your palms before sprinkling them into the flour releases their intoxicating perfume, a botanical mélange of thyme, fennel seed, cumin and black pepper all at once. It's best to make two batches of these, as the moreish combination of baked butter, ajwain and spiced Parmesan strikes chords that keep you going back for another. And then just one more.

Makes 30

For the muthiya
225g plain flour, sifted
1 tablespoon coarse semolina
1 tablespoon gram flour, sifted
¼ teaspoon baking powder
1½ teaspoons fine sea salt
1 teaspoon coriander seeds, crushed
1¼ teaspoons ajwain, crushed
2 tablespoons dried fenugreek leaves, crushed
50g unsalted butter, melted
2 tablespoons rice flour
sunflower oil, to deep-fry

For the Parmesan (optional)
1 teaspoon five-spice powder
4 tablespoons finely grated Parmesan cheese
1½ teaspoons amchoor
1 teaspoon Kashmiri chilli powder

· In a large bowl, whisk together the plain flour, semolina, gram flour, baking powder, salt, crushed coriander seeds, ajwain and dried fenugreek. Drizzle over the melted butter, then rub it into the dry ingredients with your fingerstips until there are no lumps; this will take 3–4 minutes.
· Slowly add 85–100ml warm water, a little at a time, and stir through with your fingers. When the dough starts to come together, knead for 3–4 minutes: it will feel dry at first but will eventually form into a hard pliable ball (add 1–2 extra drops of water if needed). Compress the dough tightly, cover with cling film and rest in the fridge for 30 minutes.
· Divide the rested dough into 6 equal balls. Knead each ball again to remove any air bubbles, then roll into 6 identical discs, 18cm in diameter x 2mm thick.
· Make a thick paste by mixing the rice flour in a small bowl with 4 tablespoons of water, then paint 1 disc with the rice flour paste. Place a second disc on top and paint with rice flour paste again, before topping with a third and final disc. Repeat with the other 3 discs of dough so you have 2 layered stacks.
· Using a rolling pin, separately roll each stack into a 20cm rounded square, then very tightly roll each from top to bottom to form a tightly compacted log. Chop both logs into round cookie slices 1cm thick.
· Take each slice, place flat on a work surface and press down with the palm of your hand. Then flip over and roll into a circle 5cm in diameter x 1.5mm thick; you should be able to faintly see the coiled snail of layers inside each muthi.
· Heat enough sunflower oil to 160°C in a deep saucepan or wok to fill it by one-third (see page 11). Fry the muthiya in batches for 4–6 minutes until golden, crisp and cooked through. Drain on kitchen paper and cool completely.
· Enjoy just as they are, or, for an extra flavour hit, combine the ingredients for the spiced Parmesan sprinkle in a small bowl and smother the muthiya in that before eating.

Tikka-tempura scampi

Our local chippy in Leicester is called Grimsby Fisheries, a family-run institution named after the port where it sources its fish daily. Since 1940 they've won many accolades, most notably in 2011 when they invented a dry salt and vinegar sprinkle for those averse to soggy chips. (Oh those chips! I think about them the second I board a train home from St Pancras Station.) These masala-fied chip shop-style scampi morsels are best eaten within seconds of frying, dipped in fragrant lime leaf–amchoor aioli and then dukkah for extra crunch. A dousing of vinegar is optional, but very much encouraged.

Makes 15–20

For the batter
75g rice flour, plus 2 tablespoons
75g tapioca flour, plus 2 tablespoons
25g plain flour, plus 2 tablespoons
½ teaspoon baking powder
1 egg white
100ml ice-cold India Pale Ale (IPA)
85ml ice-cold sparkling water

For the marinade & scampi
3 tablespoons Tandoori Masala (see page 25)
2 teaspoons amchoor
1 teaspoon ground turmeric
6 tablespoons lemon juice
1 tablespoon finely grated fresh ginger
½ teaspoon fine sea salt, plus more to serve
15–20 large raw prawns, peeled and deveined,
    but with tails left on

To fry & serve
sunflower oil, to deep-fry
malt vinegar, or lime juice
Lime Leaf & Amchoor Aioli (optional, see page 205)
Pistachio-Fenugreek Dukkah (optional, see page 27)

· To prepare the tempura batter, mix the 75g each of rice and tapioca flours, the 25g plain flour and the baking powder in a bowl. In a separate jug, gently stir together the egg white, IPA and sparkling water. Whisk the wet ingredients into the dry to make a smooth, slightly lumpy batter. Cover and chill in the fridge for 30 minutes; it should be really cold for the best results.
· To marinate the prawns, whisk the tandoori masala, amchoor, turmeric, lemon juice, ginger and salt to a paste in a large bowl. Add the prawns and mix well to coat all over. Cover and leave in the fridge for 10 minutes.
· Next prepare a dry flour bowl by mixing the 2 tablespoons each of rice flour, tapioca flour and plain flour.
· Heat enough sunflower oil to 165°C in a deep pan to fill it by one-third (see page 11).
· When ready to fry, toss the marinated prawns one by one in the dry flour mix. Leave for 30 seconds, then toss again so they're completely dry on the surface. Shake off excess flour, then dip into the chilled batter. Gently shake off any excess batter and carefully drop into the hot oil 3–4 at a time: they will sink at first but quickly rise and puff up.
· Cook in batches for 2–3 minutes until fully cooked through and golden on the outside. Drain on kitchen paper, spritz with malt vinegar or lime juice, sprinkle with sea salt and serve immediately, with aioli and dukkah, if you like.

Tip For a vegan option, use tofu instead of prawns, or for a vegetarian 'scampi', try cubes of paneer.

Chaats, Cocktail Bites & Savoury Snacks

Samosas

No emblem of uprooted Indian identity could be more fitting than the samosa: the archetypal Indian chaat that is an immigrant to its adopted motherland.

Originating in the Middle East, this deep-fried pyramid of wonder travelled with merchants and conquerors, morphing along its journey through Northern Africa and Central Asia to the regal courts of India. Over time, it has become the icon of Indianness we know today, ever-evolving as it continues to journey around the world with a diaspora who have made it their own.

Anyone who tells you the filling is the best part of a samosa is lying. The pastry is. A double layer may seem decadent, but icons warrant extravagance.

Makes 16

For Punjabi pea & potato filling (fills 8)
2 tablespoons vegetable oil
1 teaspoon coriander seeds, crushed
1 teaspoon cumin seeds, crushed
2 large potatoes, finely chopped, par-boiled for 5 minutes,
   then drained
100g frozen peas
½ green chilli, finely chopped
1 teaspoon finely grated fresh ginger
1 tablespoon Garam Masala (see page 23)
1 teaspoon fine sea salt
2 tablespoons lemon juice
1 tablespoon finely chopped coriander leaves

For harissa paneer, fennel & pistachio filling (fills 8)
2 tablespoons vegetable oil
1 onion, finely chopped
1 carrot, finely chopped
2 garlic cloves, finely chopped
2 teaspoons fennel seeds
300g paneer cheese, crumbled
2 tablespoons harissa
2 tablespoons pistachio nibs, toasted (see page 40)

For the pastry (enough for 8 double-layered samosas,
   or 16 single-layered samosas)
150g plain flour, sifted, plus more to dust
2 tablespoons coarse semolina
1 teaspoon fine sea salt
½ teaspoon ajwain, crushed
¼ teaspoon nigella seeds, crushed
3 tablespoons unsalted butter, melted
2 litres sunflower oil, plus more to brush

· To make the Punjabi pea and potato filling, heat
the vegetable oil in a pan over a medium-high heat,
then add the crushed coriander and cumin seeds.
Sizzle for 1 minute. Add the potatoes, peas, chilli
and ginger. Cook for 2–3 minutes until the peas are
warmed through. Next add the garam masala, salt
and lemon juice, cooking for another 2–3 minutes,
then finally stir in the coriander and cool to room
temperature.
· For the harissa paneer filling, heat the vegetable
oil in a pan over a medium heat. Add the onion and
carrot, cooking for 5–6 minutes until they begin to
caramelise. Next add the garlic, fennel seeds and
crumbled paneer. Cook for 3–4 minutes until the
paneer just starts to brown. Finally mix through the

harissa and toasted pistachios. Leave to cool to
room temperature.
· To make the pastry, whisk together the flour,
semolina, salt, ajwain and nigella seeds in a large
bowl. Next add the melted butter, rubbing it into
the flour between your fingertips until there are
no lumps. Then add 5–6 tablespoons of ice-cold
water, 1 spoon at a time, using your hands to bring
the dough together. Knead for 4–5 minutes until
smooth and firm. Firmly compact it into a ball,
brush with oil, wrap in cling film and rest in the
fridge for 30 minutes.
· Remove the pastry from the fridge once rested and
knead for 1 minute before dividing into 8 equal balls.
· Lightly flour a work surface and roll a ball of dough
into a circle 18–20cm in diameter and 1–2mm thick;
if like me you can't roll in circles, just cut around a
plate! Use a knife to score a vertical line down the
central diameter of the circle, dividing it into 2 half
moons. You now have two options...
· Classic single layer samosas: use one half-moon of
pastry per samosa. Place a half-moon in front of you
with the flat edge along the top and the round edge
closest to you. Brush the perimeter of the pastry with
water and bring the 2 top corners down to meet in
the middle, forming a cone as you carefully press the
middle seam together. Load with your filling of choice
then seal the rounded edge by pinching the dough
together, or pressing and indenting with a fork. Rest
in the fridge for 15 minutes to let the seams set.
· Stripy double-layer samosas: use 2 half-moons of
pastry per samosa. Leave the half-moon on the left
as it is. With the half-moon on the right, and leaving
a border of 2mm on all sides from the perimeter,
cut straight parallel lines vertically down the pastry
3mm apart. Brush both half-moons with water, then
flip the left-moon on top of the scored right-moon,
pressing the 2 together. Rotate so the flat edge of
the double-layered pastry is at the top and the round
edge closest to you, then continue with the method
as you would for single-layered samosas.
· Bring the sunflower oil to 160°C in a deep
saucepan or wok (see page 11). Fry the samosas, in
batches, for 6–7 minutes, until the pastry is golden
brown and the filling piping hot. Drain on kitchen
paper and serve straight away.

Tip To make 16 double-layered samosas, double the
pastry recipe. Serve smothered in chutneys and Pink
Pickled Onions with Lychee (see pages 200–213 and
209), or go fully loaded with Balti Cholay with Star
Anise & Mint (see page 154) and crunchy sev.
   Other samosa fillings to try include Cauliflower
Cashew Sabji, Turmeric & Black Pepper Larb,
Coconut-Crab and Mukhani Mushy Peas (see
pages 63, 112, 77 and 160).

The broad category of 'dips' is one of the simplest and most crowd-pleasing of all culinary canvases for playing intercultural riffs with flavour. Once you've established the core of a dip – blended pulses in hummus, roasted peppers and nuts in muhummara, or dollops of dairy in a sour cream or yogurt dip – the hybrid diversions you can take are limitless. Whole spices can be infused into oils for aromatic vibrancy, herbs added for verdant zest, chillies for warmth or full-blown fire, pickled and brined elements for piquancy and masala blends for nuanced complexity. And don't stop at the dips, the same applies to the dippers; flavour-on-flavour makes for better dipping.

Pistachio, coriander & green chilli dip

Kashmiri chilli & fennel muhummara

Serves 4

150g shelled unsalted pistachio nuts, plus pistachio nibs (optional), to serve
50g shelled salted peanuts
8 garlic cloves
1 tablespoon finely grated lime zest, plus 8 tablespoons (120ml) lime juice
150ml olive oil, plus more if needed, plus more to serve
1 tablespoon finely grated fresh ginger
1 teaspoon fine sea salt
1½ teaspoons coarsely ground black pepper
1 tablespoon amchoor
2 spring onions, finely chopped, plus more (optional), to serve
1 teaspoon ground cumin
1 green chilli, stalk trimmed off, plus more (optional), to serve
1 tablespoon fennel seeds, crushed
1 tablespoon caster sugar
30g coriander leaves

· Preheat the oven to 160°C fan. Roast the pistachios and peanuts on a baking tray for 6–7 minutes until toasty, then remove from the oven and allow to cool completely.
· Put all the ingredients – including the roasted nuts – in a food processor or blender and whizz to a coarse dip the texture of runny-but-crunchy peanut butter. Add a little extra oil if you prefer a smoother texture. Adjust the salt and pepper to taste, then pulse a few times to finish.
· Empty into a bowl, drizzle with olive oil and garnish with pistachio nibs, spring onions and chillies, if you like.

Serves 4

150g shelled unsalted walnuts, plus more (optional) to serve
8 dried Kashmiri chillies
½ teaspoon ajwain
2 teaspoons cumin seeds
3 teaspoons fennel seeds
1 large fennel bulb, quartered, plus fennel fronds (optional) to serve
65ml olive oil
2 jarred roasted red peppers
4 garlic cloves, very finely chopped
1 tablespoon finely grated fresh ginger
4 tablespoons pomegranate molasses
1 tablespoon finely grated lemon zest, plus 4 tablespoons lemon juice
1 teaspoon sumac, plus more (optional) to serve
1 teaspoon fine sea salt
2 spring onions, finely chopped
barberries, to serve (optional)

· Preheat the oven to 160°C fan. Roast the walnuts on a baking tray for 6–7 minutes until toasty, then remove from the oven and cool completely.
· Dry pan-roast the whole Kashmiri chillies for 3–4 minutes until they just char, then soak in a jug of boiling water for 20 minutes.
· In the same pan, dry-roast the ajwain, cumin and fennel seeds until they release their aromas. Grind to a powder.
· Heat the grill to high. Brush the fennel quarters liberally with olive oil, place on a baking sheet and grill for 15–20 minutes until charred, turning regularly. The quarters should be really soft, fudgey and caramelised, so cook for a little longer if needed.
· Place the very soft fennel, toasted walnuts (reserving some to serve), ground spices, drained chillies and the rest of the ingredients in a blender or food processor, then pulse to a coarse, grainy dip.
· Empty into a bowl, then add a sprinkling of walnuts, barberries and fennel fronds, if you like.

Brown butter, onion & cumin dip

Crunchy pitta chips

Serves 4

5 onions, halved
olive oil
10 garlic cloves, skin on
100g salted butter
1 teaspoon nigella seeds
2 teaspoons cumin seeds, plus more (optional) to serve
1 green chilli, very finely chopped
2 teaspoons ground cumin
4 tablespoons sour cream, plus more (optional) to serve
2 teaspoons white wine vinegar
1 tablespoon caster sugar
1½ teaspoons fine sea salt
1 tablespoon finely grated lemon zest, plus 2 tablespoons lemon juice

· Preheat the oven to 200°C fan. Brush the onion halves liberally with oil and place flat side down on a baking tray. Bake for 20 minutes without touching, then flip over and add the whole garlic cloves to the tray with a drizzle more oil. Cook for another 20 minutes until the onions are blistered and the garlic is fudgey inside, turning if needed so nothing burns. Reserve an onion half for serving, if you like.
· In a saucepan, heat the butter and cook gently for 8–10 minutes until it turns nutty and brown, swirling the pan so it does not burn. Next add the nigella seeds, cumin seeds and chilli, sizzling them all together for 1 minute. Remove from the heat and leave to infuse for 10 minutes.
· In a food processor, blitz the warm cooked onions, squeezed-out garlic cloves, ground cumin, sour cream, vinegar, sugar, salt, lemon zest and juice to a paste. Slowly trickle in the spiced brown butter, pulsing to combine. If the butter cools in clumps, blend into the dip fully, then heat the dip in a pan for 1 minute, stirring well to incorporate it back in.
· Spoon into a bowl and cool completely, then serve with the reserved onion, sour cream and cumin, if you like. For a thicker dip, chill for 15–20 minutes first.

Serves 4

4 pitta breads
olive oil
1 teaspoon fine sea salt
Tangy Chilli-Mango Sprinkle (see page 26), to serve

· Preheat the oven to 165°C fan.
· Split the pitta breads horizontally through the middle so they are 1 layer thick, not 2, then slice into thin triangular shards. Brush with olive oil and sprinkle with the salt, then bake on a baking sheet for 10 minutes until crisp.
· Let them cool completely before coating with Tangy Chilli-Mango Sprinkle. These crunchy chips also make a great salad topping.

In culinary terms, Punjab is a land of tandoor-fired breads, corn smothered in butter, unfiltered sugarcane juice and clotted malai cream. A cuisine that relishes the knowledge that fat is the ultimate carrier of flavour, ghee is an ambrosial dairy-nectar from the gods and carbs are life. Amen.

Malai is also a term used more widely, for the joy of 'thick creaminess' in all its guises.

This indulgent marinade recipe introduces roasted Indian spices to the velvet creaminess of Levantine tahini, with a generous drizzle of double cream for good measure. It should be baked until suitably charred on the outside, as the crème de la crème of Punjabi foods always are.

Makes 10

For the chicken
1 tablespoon coriander seeds
1 tablespoon ajwain
seeds from 15 green cardamom pods
1 teaspoon white sesame seeds
2 tablespoons finely grated fresh ginger
8 garlic cloves, very finely chopped
2 green chillies, finely chopped
1 tablespoon finely grated fresh turmeric
2 teaspoons smoked salt
2 teaspoons coarsely ground black pepper
1 tablespoon finely grated lemon zest, plus 4 tablespoons
    lemon juice
4 tablespoons white wine vinegar
1 tablespoon Garam Masala (see page 23)
4 tablespoons tahini, plus more (optional), to serve
50ml double cream
10 chicken wings
Pink Pickled Onions with Lychee (see page 209),
    to serve (optional)

For the garlic
4 tablespoons vegetable oil
3 garlic cloves, cut into slivers
1 teaspoon coriander seeds, crushed
1 tablespoon white sesame seeds
2 tablespoons finely chopped coriander leaves

· Dry pan-roast the coriander seeds, ajwain and green cardamom seeds for 1–2 minutes until they release their aromas. Next add the sesame seeds and toast for another 45–60 seconds, until they just brown. Take off the heat, tip into a grinder and whizz to a fine powder.
· Next add the ginger, garlic, chillies, fresh turmeric, smoked salt, pepper, lemon zest and juice and white wine vinegar to the same grinder. Blitz to a smooth yellow paste.
· Empty the paste into a large bowl and add the garam masala, tahini and double cream, beating into an indulgently creamy marinade.
· Slash each chicken wing 2–3 times with a sharp knife and smother in the marinade, ensuring it penetrates deep into the flesh. Cover and leave in the fridge for at least 4 hours, ideally overnight.
· Preheat the oven to 180°C fan.
· Place the marinated wings on a baking tray, well spaced apart, and bake for 40–45 minutes, until the skin is crisply charred and they are cooked through.
· For the crispy garlic, heat the vegetable oil in a frying pan, then add the garlic slivers, cooking for 2–3 minutes until they start to crisp, but not burn. Add the crushed coriander and sesame seeds, sizzle for 1 minute, then add the coriander. Spoon over the oven-hot wings and devour with your hands, with Pink Pickled Onions and an extra drizzle of tahini, if you like.
· Cutlery strictly forbidden.

We are a family perpetually primed to put on a party. When there's no occasion, we have one anyway; being together in the same room with fresh-fried pakoras being reason enough. Regional pakora variations across India are a microcosm of the cuisines that make up 'Indian food': garlic-chive pakoras in Manipur, banana blossom pakoras in Bengal, taro leaf patra in Bihar, mutton chop pakoras in Uttar Pradesh, jackfruit bhajis in Kanartaka and fish pakoras in Amritsar, to name but a few. My favourite are bread pakoras, sold on the streets of Jalandhar as deep-fried chutney-paneer sandwiches, and in Mumbai as bhaji-battered potato toasties. After all, nothing says 'party' like carb-on-carb-on-carb.

Serves 4

For the batter (enough for 1 batch of bhajis or pakoras)
2 teaspoons finely grated fresh ginger
185ml sparkling water
125g gram flour, sifted
2 tablespoons rice flour
1 teaspoon amchoor
¾ teaspoon chilli powder
½ teaspoon ground turmeric
2 teaspoons dried fenugreek leaves, crushed
1 teaspoon ground cumin
½ teaspoon ajwain, crushed
1 teaspoon fine sea salt
¾ teaspoon bicarbonate of soda
1 litre sunflower oil
Chaat Masala (see page 24), to serve
chutneys, to serve (see pages 200–213)

For onion bhaji
2 medium onions, sliced into rings

For cauliflower, aubergine, pickled onion & dill pakora
1 medium cauliflower, chopped into florets
1 aubergine, cut into 1cm cubes
1 large pickled onion, chopped
30g dill, chopped

For spring onion, halloumi, pickled walnut & fenugreek pakora
3 spring onions, sliced lengthways into ribbons
225g block of halloumi cheese, coarsely grated
2 tablespoons chopped pickled walnuts
40g fresh fenugreek leaves, chopped

For curried parsnip, kale & peanut pakora
2 large parsnips, cut into thin matchsticks
1 tablespoon medium curry powder
100g kale leaves, chopped, any coarse stalks removed
2 tablespoons shelled dry roasted peanuts

· To make the batter, whisk the ginger in a jug with the sparkling water. Separately whisk together all the dry ingredients and spices in a large bowl. Slowly pour the gingery-water into the dry ingredients, whisking to a smooth medium-thick pancake batter. Let it sit on the work surface for 10 minutes; it will thicken as it rests.
· For onion bhaji, add the onion rings to the batter and coat well.
· Heat the sunflower oil in a deep pan to 165°C (see page 11). Lift out a stack of battered onion rings, form into a loose sphere, shake off the excess and carefully drop into the oil. Cook for 2–3 minutes until golden and cooked through. Drain on kitchen paper, sprinkle with chaat masala and serve with chutneys (or in a sandwich with some good strong Cheddar).
· For all other pakora combinations, mix whatever combination of ingredients you have chosen through the batter, then heat the oil to 165°C (see page 11). Use your hands to bundle, pack and squeeze a small handful of the mix into jumbled nest-like balls, held together by the batter. Give them a final squeeze, then carefully drop the pakora nests into the hot oil. Cook for 3–4 minutes until golden brown and cooked through; don't worry if they fall apart, crispy pakora crumbs are just as delicious!
· Drain on kitchen paper, sprinkle with chaat masala and serve with plenty of chutneys.

Chickpea, togarashi & preserved lemon tikkis

The yearly altercation my parents had with our teachers, for taking us out of school to go to India, always led to the same question: why can't you go in the summer holidays like everyone else? The truth is, for us, the national curriculum came second to the revelries of a Punjabi festivity. Summer holidays, for us, were for escaping who you were, not finding it; our international curriculum, after all, was our identity.

Consequently, I spent much my childhood in the fashion bazaars of Delhi, Phagwara, Ludhiana and Jalandhar, watching flamboyant salesmen drape themselves in sequinned saris to seduce rupees out of my mum and Aunty-Jis. This was a true life lesson: the matriarchs haggling themselves the upper hand, only to lose it when the salesmen sent for banana leaf plates of sizzling tikki hot cakes with spicy tamarind. It worked every time.

These tikkis are speckled with the achaar-like tang of preserved lemon and citrussy Japanese togarashi, but are equally tasty with other intercultural combinations of pickled preserves and spice blends.

· In a food processor, blitz together the spring onions, garlic, coriander, preserved lemon and white wine vinegar until you have a coarse paste; you don't want it to be completely smooth. Add the chickpeas, salt and pepper, then pulse another 5–6 times.
· Next add the plain flour, egg, chaat masala, togarashi and bicarbonate of soda. Pulse until you have a thick batter with flecks of green herbs, lemon and chickpeas speckled through it. Empty into a bowl, mixing again to ensure the flour is fully incorporated with no dry patches. Cover and refrigerate for 30 minutes. When the mix has rested, use 2 heaped tablespoons of it to form each patty, pressing it between your hands.
· Heat the sunflower oil to 160°C in a deep pan or wok (see page 11) and fry the tikkis for 4–5 minutes on each side until they puff up, have a golden-brown crust and are completely cooked through.
· Drain on kitchen paper and enjoy with a squeeze of lemon and chutneys, if you like.

Tip To enjoy these tikkis chaat-style, as in the photo, smother them in chutneys, yogurt, pomegranate seeds, chopped lemon segments, crunchy sev, crushed peanuts and more chaat masala.

Makes 12–14

3 spring onions, chopped
3 garlic cloves, chopped
20g coriander leaves, chopped
65g preserved lemon, chopped
1 tablespoon white wine vinegar
400g can of chickpeas, drained
1 teaspoon fine sea salt
1½ teaspoons coarsely ground black pepper
125g plain flour
1 egg, lightly beaten
1 tablespoon Chaat Masala (see page 24)
2 tablespoons shichimi togarashi (Japanese spice blend)
½ teaspoon bicarbonate of soda
200ml sunflower oil
lemon wedges, to serve (optional)
chutneys, to serve (optional, see pages 200–213)

Sticky treacle & kokum chicken lollipops

A signature of my cooking is combining extremes of sour and sweet with a hint of anise and warming heat, with added textural crunch somewhere in the mix. Subtlety is not a quality revered by Punjabis.

In the sour corner, kokum is my favourite ingredient, a dried Indian fruit similar to mangosteen that has the puckering tartness of tamarind together with the tropical flair of lychee. In the sweet corner, the molasses panache of black treacle has my vote, its burnt syrupy-bitterness adding something that sugar or honey never can. Married together, the two contradictory elements balance each other out and intensify their opposing uniqueness in equal measure. The mind-bending effect on the tongue is very unsubtle and very tasty.

Makes 8 whole wings, or 16 lollipops

For the glaze
50g semi-dried kokum
20g coriander leaves, chopped
1 teaspoon toasted sesame oil
¾ teaspoon fish sauce
2 garlic cloves, chopped
4 tablespoons granulated sugar
2 teaspoons amchoor
½ teaspoon ground star anise
½ teaspoon chilli powder
1 teaspoon coarsely ground black pepper
2 teaspoons smoked salt
3 tablespoons black treacle
4 tablespoons lime juice

For the chicken
8 whole chicken wings, wing tips removed
4 tablespoons rice flour
4 tablespoons baking powder
2 teaspoons fine sea salt
4 teaspoons onion powder
2 teaspoons Garam Masala (see page 23)
sesame seeds, coriander leaves and red chilli, to serve

· To make the glaze, pulse the kokum in a grinder to a coarse crumbly rubble, then pour into a small pan with 200ml of boiling water. Simmer for 5 minutes, take off the heat and leave for 20 minutes.
· Next grind together the coriander, sesame oil, fish sauce and garlic with 50ml water to make a smooth green paste. Leave to one side.
· Strain the sour kokum tea into a pan, pressing the pulp to extract as much flavour as you can. To the strained liquid add the sugar, amchoor, star anise, chilli powder, pepper and smoked salt. Cook over a high heat for 10 minutes, stirring so it does not catch. Next add the treacle, cook for another 2 minutes, then add the green coriander paste. Simmer over a medium heat for a final 12–14 minutes until it resembles a thick honey-like glaze. Squeeze in the lime juice, whisk well and cool.
· To prepare the chicken wings into lollipops, take a whole wing and cut at the centre join to separate the 2 sections: 1 half will have 2 bones and the other will have 1 bone. Taking the half with 1 bone first, use a knife to carefully slit and slide the meat from the top towards the bottom of the bone, tightly twisting the meat into a 'lollipop' at the base. For the half with 2 bones, carefully remove the thin inner bone first, then repeat as before. (You can also ask your butcher to do this, or just use the wings whole!)
· Preheat the oven to 180°C fan. Whisk together the rice flour, baking powder, salt, onion powder and garam masala in a large bowl. Dredge the chicken all over in the dry mix, leave for 30 seconds, then dredge again, coating fully and getting it into the crevices. Tap off the excess, place on a baking sheet, then cover the top of each bone with foil.
· Bake for 40–45 minutes until the chicken is fully cooked through to the middle and has a golden crispy coating. Remove from the oven, brush generously with the sticky kokum glaze, then return to the oven for a final 3–4 minutes.
· Garnish with sesame seeds, coriander leaves and red chilli, and don't forget to have extra glaze on the side for dipping!

Laal mirchi tiger prawns with coriander

My paternal grandfather was very particular about whether he'd choose to bite into a hari mirch (green chilli), or laal mirch (red chilli) to Punjabify what he ate, be it tandoori lamb chop, ham sandwich or Margherita pizza. I never understood his logic for what went with what, but he instinctively knew exactly what a chilli tasted like by simply flashing it in front of his right eye for a split second.

Red chillies were always favoured, because he either liked the flavour or the colour, given that our surname originates in the word laal. (When and how it became 'Loyal' we don't know, being either purposefully Westernised generations back or simply lost in translation as our family migrated.) These fiery scarlet prawns were a favourite of his. Serve with whole red chillies and kachumber on the side, for an untranslated taste of Punjabiness.

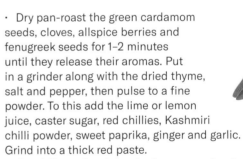

Makes 15–20

seeds from 10 green cardamom pods
6 cloves
10 allspice berries
½ teaspoon fenugreek seeds
1½ teaspoons dried thyme
1½ teaspoons fine sea salt
1 teaspoon coarsely ground black pepper
2 tablespoons lime or lemon juice, plus limes or lemons
  to serve
1 tablespoon caster sugar
2 large red chillies
2 teaspoons Kashmiri chilli powder
2 teaspoons sweet paprika
1 tablespoon finely grated fresh ginger
3 garlic cloves, very finely chopped
15–20 large raw tiger prawns
olive oil
2 tablespoons finely chopped coriander leaves

· Dry pan-roast the green cardamom seeds, cloves, allspice berries and fenugreek seeds for 1–2 minutes until they release their aromas. Put in a grinder along with the dried thyme, salt and pepper, then pulse to a fine powder. To this add the lime or lemon juice, caster sugar, red chillies, Kashmiri chilli powder, sweet paprika, ginger and garlic. Grind into a thick red paste.
· Carefully peel and devein the prawns, leaving the heads on. Thread each prawn on to a skewer from the bottom to the top, stretching it out fully so it cooks evenly. Brush the prawns liberally with the red chilli paste, then cover and leave to marinate for 15 minutes. Preheat the grill to a high setting.
· Arrange the skewers on a baking sheet, drizzle with olive oil and grill on a high heat for 3 minutes per side until charred and cooked through. Halfway through, paint over any chilli paste that has fallen on to the baking sheet.
· Serve straight from the grill with a squeeze of lime or lemon juice and a sprinkling of coriander.

Chaats, Cocktail Bites & Savoury Snacks

For many years, my mum hosted a weekly Punjabi chat show on a multilingual radio station, developing something of a cult following. It was called *Gal Bhaat*, which loosely translates as 'boisterous banter'; her live phone-ins about kitchen mishaps, family cooking secrets and fastidious mothers-in-law really were.

Over the years, she accumulated ancestral recipe wisdom for regional Indian chaats from her listeners. Khaman dhokla – a savoury Gujarati steamed lentil and chickpea cake – was discussed most often, with every caller sharing their family's sworn method for reaching the zenith of light, tangy, sweetly spiced and fluffy all in the same bite.

Mum experimented with every variation, meaning we ate a new dhokla iteration every week. Fermenting the batter is traditional, but this is her go-to method for speed, ease and the joy of feeling the sour yogurty batter foam up as soda is added.

The bacon bits are a relic from my college hangovers, when crispy smoked bacon and something comfortingly Indian combined were the only cures for the after-effects of Malibu and Lilt. The dhokla-bacon sarnie became my restorative mash-up, and still is today.

Serves 4

For the dhokla
5–6 smoked pancetta or bacon rashers, finely
  chopped (optional)
1 teaspoon sweet paprika (optional)
200g gram flour
2 tablespoons coarse semolina
2 tablespoons caster sugar
½ teaspoon ground turmeric
1 teaspoon citric acid
1 teaspoon fine sea salt
1 teaspoon garlic powder
1 teaspoon ground ginger
1 tablespoon vegetable oil (optional), plus more for the tin
2 tablespoons natural yogurt
1¼ teaspoons bicarbonate of soda
coconut chips, to serve
chutneys, to serve (see pages 200–213)

For the tarkha
2 tablespoons vegetable oil
20–25 fresh curry leaves
1 tablespoon black mustard seeds
1 green chilli, finely chopped
1 tablespoon white sesame seeds
1½ tablespoons desiccated coconut
2 tablespoons lemon juice
2 tablespoons caster sugar

· If using pancetta or bacon, gently fry the cubes in a pan for 8–9 minutes. After 2 minutes, when the fat starts to render, sprinkle over the paprika, slowly cooking until crispy all over. Set aside.
· Sift the gram flour into a large mixing bowl, then whisk through the semolina, caster sugar, turmeric, citric acid, salt, garlic powder and ground ginger. In a separate jug, whisk 250ml warm water with the vegetable oil, or 1 tablespoon warm melted bacon fat from the pan, and the yogurt. Slowly pour the wet ingredients into the dry, whisking continuously for 5–7 minutes, until you have a smooth batter. Stir in most of the cooled bacon bits if using, cover and leave to rest for 30 minutes.
· Next, prepare a large steamer and an 18cm round cake tin that fits easily into the steamer basket. Fill the base of the steamer with boiling water and place over the hob to get the steam going steadily. Then brush the inside of the cake tin with vegetable oil.
· Add the bicarbonate of soda to the rested batter and whisk swiftly in one direction for 30–45 seconds. The reaction between the citric acid and soda will cause it to froth up; this is exactly what you want to happen. Quickly pour the foaming batter into the oiled cake tin so it comes three-quarters of the way up and immediately place in the steamer basket. Securely cover with a tight lid; it's important that the steam is fully encased so, if needed, use damp tea towels or foil to seal the lid down, trapping the steam in.
· Steam over a high heat for 35–40 minutes, topping up the steamer base with more hot water if needed.
· Whilst the dhokla is steaming, make the tarkha topping: heat the vegetable oil in a frying pan, then add the curry leaves and mustard seeds, crackling for 45 seconds. Next add the green chilli, sesame seeds and desiccated coconut. Cook for another 1 minute, before adding 75ml water, the lemon juice and sugar. Bring to the boil, then reduce the heat and simmer for 4–5 minutes.
· Remove the dhokla from the steamer, ensuring with a toothpick that it's spongey and cooked all the way through. If still wet in the middle, leave it in the steamer for another 3–4 minutes. Let cool for 10 minutes, then drizzle liberally with the tarkha topping, reserved bacon bits, if using, and coconut chips. Leave for 15–20 minutes for the flavours to soak through, then serve.

Tip You have to have lashings of chutneys with this.

Traditions, like identities, are not fixed. Some persist for years unchanged, while others disappear. New traditions evolve and old traditions resurface generations down the line. I don't remember when 'Friday nachos' became a thing, but it's a tradition that's stuck, instigating many a remix over the years.

Hybrid Punjabi Mexican cuisine has a history dating to the 1800s, when Punjabi immigrant workers arrived in California, only to find their entry rights subsequently outlawed, preventing their Indian partners from joining them. The bigoted laws at the time did however permit marriages between Indians and Mexicans, provided skin tones were deemed equivalently 'brown'. This in turn created an entire generation of marital unions that crossed race, religion and cultural boundaries for the pioneering Mexican women and Punjabi men that entered into them. Through these Mexican Punjabi nuptials the two cuisines conjoined, with restaurants such as El Ranchero in Yuba City serving the newly merged community hybrid creations such as roti quesadillas: shredded beef and cheese in a paratha with curry sauce, rice and beans. Further waves of Punjabi migration to the West Coast in the 1960s brought a new era of culinary crossovers which thrive in home kitchens, food trucks and restaurants to this day.

This recipe celebrates the marriage of Indian and Mexican cuisines. While keema is deemed quintessentially Punjabi today, its origins are actually Turkish, which explains my inspiration for using tomato ezme in place of salsa here. Dishes, like traditions, like identities, are not fixed.

Serves 4

For the baharat keema
2 tablespoons ghee
2 red onions, finely chopped
1 tablespoon fennel seeds, crushed
3 garlic cloves, very finely chopped
2 teaspoons finely grated fresh ginger
1 green chilli, finely chopped
1½ teaspoons fine sea salt
1 teaspoon coarsely ground black pepper
500g minced lamb (20 per cent fat)
1 teaspoon ground turmeric
2 tablespoons Minted Baharat (see page 27)
150g frozen peas
1 tablespoon dark brown sugar
400g can of chopped tomatoes
15g coriander leaves, chopped

For the ezme
65g plum tomatoes, deseeded
2 garlic cloves
1 yellow or red pepper, trimmed and deseeded
1 onion, chopped
15g parsley leaves
1 tablespoon rose harissa
2 tablespoons pomegranate molasses
35ml olive oil
1 teaspoon finely grated lemon zest, plus 3 tablespoons
    lemon juice

For the rest
large bag (about 320g) corn tortilla chips
sliced red onion
Red Leicester cheese, grated
sour cream
1 avocado, chopped

· To make the keema, heat the ghee in a large saucepan. Add the onions and cook for 6–8 minutes until they are translucent and golden. Next add the fennel seeds, garlic, ginger, green chilli, salt and pepper, sizzling for 2 minutes. Crumble in the minced lamb, then brown it in the spiced onions for 5 minutes. Next add the turmeric, minted baharat, peas and sugar. Mix through well, then add the tomatoes before anything has a chance to burn.
· Cover with a lid and cook over a medium heat for 10 minutes, then remove the lid and cook for a final 10 minutes, reducing the sauce to an intensely rich keema. Stir through the coriander to finish.
· For the ezme, blitz all the ingredients together in a food processor until you have a tangy chunky salsa; stop before it becomes soup. Ezme should have some bite!
· Preheat the grill to a high setting, or preheat the oven to 160°C fan, depending on whether you plan to grill or bake the nachos.
· To grill them, put a base layer of corn chips in a flameproof serving dish, then dollop over the keema and sprinkle with sliced red onion and Red Leicester cheese. Grill for 2–3 minutes so the cheese melts. Top with the ezme, dollops of sour cream and the avocado. Or to bake the nachos, layer the chips, onion and cheese in a large cake tin and bake for 15–20 minutes, before adding the ezme, sour cream and avocado.
· Enjoy with friends... or alone with a beer and a Goldie Hawn movie.

Disney's *The Jungle Book* was the first film I ever saw at the cinema. I was five and still remember being enraptured at the adventures of a boy in India (who looked a bit like me), projected on to a megaplex screen, while gorging on toffee-buttered popcorn and 'blue flavour' Slush Puppy. A thrilling sensory overload. But Leicester's Odeon couldn't prepare me for the raucous exhilaration of the Narinder Cinema in Jalandhar, India, a few years later, where the cornucopia of cinema snacks alone was mind-blowing: fresh-fried vada pav, mini samosas with imli (tamarind chutney), salty masala-lime corn, paneer toasties, pista-malai kulfi and glass bottles of mango soda. Street-food celebrities, revered in those Indian movie theatres just as much as the Bollywood stars themselves. The paper cones of sugary-sour masala peanuts, roasted chana and crunchy dal are what I loved most. This moreish take on them is equally terrific with a grown-up cocktail, mango soda or blue slushie.

Makes 350g

1 tablespoon amchoor
½ teaspoon ajwain, crushed
2 teaspoons nigella seeds, crushed
2 teaspoons fennel seeds, crushed
1½ teaspoons ground cumin
½ teaspoon cayenne pepper
1½ teaspoons ground ginger
2 teaspoons coarsely ground black pepper
40 dried curry leaves, crushed to a powder
2 teaspoons ground turmeric
100g caster sugar
1 tablespoon smoked salt
35g unsalted butter
350g mixed shelled unsalted nuts, such as cashews, walnuts, brazils, macadamias, pecans, peanuts...
handful of fresh curry leaves
vegetable oil
1 tablespoon Kashmiri chilli powder

· Preheat the oven to 160°C fan. Prepare a silicon sheet, or line a baking sheet with foil, and keep it close to the hob.
· Mix together the amchoor, ajwain, nigella and fennel seeds, cumin, cayenne pepper, ginger, pepper, crushed dried curry leaves and turmeric in a small bowl, then set aside.
· Next, heat the sugar and smoked salt in a large saucepan with 50ml of water until the sugar and salt dissolve and the syrup thickens to a one-string consistency (see page 11). Add the butter, then whisk continuously for 3–4 minutes over a medium heat until you have a runny honey-like caramel.
· Tip in the spices from the small bowl all at once, mix well, then add the nuts. Stir thoroughly to coat everything in the sticky spiced caramel. Spread on to the silicon mat or prepared baking sheet, scraping the spiced sugar mixture over the nuts. Bake for 15–17 minutes, tossing with a spatula every 5 minutes to coat in the sugar and ensure they don't burn. Remove from the oven, toss one last time and leave to cool completely; the sugar coating will harden around the nuts as they cool.
· Quickly fry the fresh curry leaves in hot vegetable oil for 30–45 seconds, until they crisp up.
· Sprinkle the cooled nuts with the Kashmiri chilli powder and the hot freshly fried curry leaves just before serving.

Tip Serve broken up into clusters and piled high in small bowls, with drinks. It's best to make a double batch, as these can be quite addictive...

CHAPTER 2

NAAN WRAPS,
KATI ROLLS,
TOASTS & SARNIES

events that led to ultimate British rule over India and its subsequent partition along an arbitrary line that went right through the middle of Punjab, the after-effects of which are one reason that an Indian diaspora exists around the world today.

Meanwhile, over in Kent, England, John Montagu, the 4th Earl of Sandwich, was busy honing his gambling skills around a card table. As legend goes, he was so immersed in his twenty-four-hour marathons of play that he paused for nothing, ordering his minions to bring him sustenance that could be eaten single-handed without interrupting his game. Their solution was cuts of roast beef in between two slices of bread, which soon became the most prized vittle among high society's elite. And so a gastronomic superstar was born, all thanks – allegedly – to one British earl's devotion to vice.

In a subtle act of culinary retribution, Indians today are some of the most inventive sandwich makers in the world, playing back the iconic foodstuff of their former coloniser, remodelled through their own culinary lens. Likewise, the Indian diaspora has taken to remixing naan wraps, dosas and kati rolls from the motherland using their own third-culture flair for flavour. Collectively, they are the quickest and easiest way to experiment with intercultural flavour chords, often leading to astonishingly delicious hybrid combinations.

The only rule for this culinary genre is that something crunchy must be added to the mix. Venture into any diasporic supermarket and you'll discover remarkable bags of crunch to rival the walls of crisps found in a British newsagent. Among the temptations on offer in an Indian grocer alone you'll find masala munch, chutney crinkles, chilli-lemon grills, bhaji corn crackers, chaat matchsticks, garam-spiced poppadoms and hot-pepper hoops: carby heroes flavoured at full throttle that can invigorate even the most mundane fridge-cold sarnie eaten at a desk.

But crunch can be stuffed between bread in many other ways: through wasabi peas, toasted nuts, Bombay mix chevda, savoury sev noodles, baked chickpeas, Ritz crackers, crunchy dukkah, lotus root crisps, Twiglets, fried onion sprinkles, dehydrated garlic chips and even roasted whole spices. Think of crunchiness as the essential final seasoning for all sandwiches and wraps, a seasoning that imparts flavour texturally, as well as through sound.

I wonder what the Earl of Sandwich would have made of my go-to chicken tikka, Cheddar and chaat masala toastie with mango pickle and Walkers prawn cocktail crisps? I'd put money on him concurring after just one bite that, when it comes to his namesake snack, hybrid chutnified-Indianness wins the upper hand over plain rosbif-Britishness.

In 1757, over in the motherland, the British East India Company was revelling in their glory over the Nawab of Bengal in the Battle of Plassey. It was a turning point in the history of the British Empire, which saw a foreign private corporation take political control over almost an entire subcontinent. The East India Company had transitioned from a modest trading venture in search of spices, to an imperial military power whose brute force granted them authority to collect taxes from the very people they'd sought to trade with. The victory accelerated

If, as I think of it, flavours are musical notes and flavour combinations musical chords, then this Japanese-Indian fried chicken sando is a Glastonbury megamix serotonin rush in every bite.

Masala-fying the marinade with miso gives the chicken a savoury umami depth that loudly intensifies every other flavour in the mix. The rice flour and potato flour coating fries to a craggy crunch. The chilli-mango sprinkle brings salty tang. There's cooling bite from shredded Iceberg. And the sweet-pepperiness of paprika adds a hint of warmth through the Marie Rose. This isn't an orchestra of taste, it's a full-on third-culture sound system, turned up to eleven.

Makes 4

For the marinade & chicken
1 tablespoon finely grated lemon zest, plus 4 tablespoons lemon juice
4 garlic cloves, finely grated
5 tablespoons red or brown miso
1 tablespoon white wine vinegar
1 teaspoon smoked salt
2 tablespoons Garam Masala (see page 23)
2 teaspoons ground turmeric
seeds from 10 green cardamom pods, crushed
4 boneless, skinless chicken thighs
  (total weight about 500g)

To coat & fry the chicken
50g plain flour
75g rice flour
75g potato flour
2 tablespoons baking powder
1 tablespoon fennel seeds, crushed
2 litres sunflower oil

For the Marie Rose
3 tablespoons Kewpie or other Japanese mayonnaise
3 tablespoons tomato ketchup
¾ teaspoon Worcestershire sauce
1½ teaspoons amchoor
2 teaspoons sweet paprika

To assemble
Tangy Chilli-Mango Sprinkle (see page 26)
1 loaf of brioche or milk bread, thickly sliced and toasted
½ Iceberg lettuce, shredded

· In a large bowl, whisk together the lemon zest and juice, garlic, miso, vinegar and smoked salt, until the salt has dissolved. Next add the garam masala, turmeric and cardamom seeds, mixing well.
· Slash the chicken thighs in their most fleshy parts, then coat them in the marinade and rub it into all the crevices. Cover and leave in the fridge for 4 hours.
· Preheat the oven to 180°C fan. Remove the marinated chicken from the fridge and bring to room temperature; this is important for crispy chicken that is cooked evenly.
· Prepare the coating in a shallow bowl by whisking together the plain flour, rice flour, potato flour, baking powder and crushed fennel seeds.
· In a separate bowl, prepare the Marie Rose sauce by mixing all the ingredients together.
· Heat the sunflower oil in a deep pan or wok to 165°C (see page 11). Lift the chicken pieces out of the marinade one at a time – shaking off any excess – then drop into the dry coating mix. Shake around so the chicken is completely covered, let it sit for 1 minute, then flip over and dredge again. Leave for another 1 minute, then flip and dredge once more. If needed, repeat until the surface is completely powdery and dry.
· Deep-fry the chicken 1–2 pieces at a time for 5–6 minutes, until the coating is lightly browned. Transfer to a wire rack placed over a baking tray and finish in the oven for 5–6 minutes until golden, crisp and cooked through. Smother with Tangy Chilli-Mango Sprinkle the moment they come out.
· To assemble the sandos, from the bottom up: thickly sliced toasted brioche, hot fried chicken covered in tangy sprinkle, shredded Iceberg, a liberal dollop of Marie Rose, toasted brioche... although there are no rules here, except that more is more!
· Serve with matchstick salli fries, if you like.

Turmeric & crispy sage dosas
with cauliflower cashew sabji

There are no written recipes in our family. Anything that is passed on happens by watching, tasting and doing, handed down through the guided movement of fingers, not the marks of a pen. Measurements are instincts to learn, not scientific formulas to follow, beautifully articulated by the Turkish phrase *göz kararı*: 'measure using your eye decision'.

Unlike South Indian friends, the intergenerational fingerprints of dosa-making are not something I've acquired first-hand, though I have a lot of experience at dosa-eating! While traditionally made from fermented rice and lentil batters in states such as Tamil Nadu, Karnataka and Andhra Pradesh, my recipe is instant. Crispy sage and turmeric add herbal-earthy accents here, but are to be used as a mere guide for improvising your own flavours. Just trust your intuition, it's all there in your fingertips.

Makes 8

For the sabji
2 tablespoons vegetable oil
1 tablespoon black mustard seeds
2 teaspoons cumin seeds
6 small shallots, finely sliced
1 tablespoon finely grated fresh ginger
3 garlic cloves, very finely chopped
1 cauliflower, chopped small
50g shelled unsalted cashew nuts, toasted (see page 40) and crushed, plus more to serve
½ teaspoon ground turmeric
2 teaspoons Sambhar Masala (see page 25), plus more to serve
2 tablespoons lime juice
1 tablespoon caster sugar
1 large potato, boiled and crushed
1½ teaspoons fine sea salt
1 teaspoon coarsely ground black pepper
½ x 400g can of chopped tomatoes
2 tablespoons chopped coriander leaves

For the dosas
30g sage leaves, plus more to serve
4 tablespoons vegetable oil, plus 1 tablespoon
100g rice flour
100g gram flour
100g plain flour
2 teaspoons Sambhar Masala (see page 25)
1½ teaspoons ground turmeric
1½ teaspoons fine sea salt
¼ teaspoon baking powder
2 tablespoons natural yogurt
¼ teaspoon bicarbonate of soda
finely chopped red onion, to serve
yogurt raita (see pages 165 and 175), to serve

· To make the sabji, heat the vegetable oil in a saucepan, then add the mustard seeds and cumin seeds. Sizzle for 1 minute, before adding the sliced shallots. Cook for 5–6 minutes, until they soften and caramelise. Next add the ginger, garlic, cauliflower and cashews, along with 100ml water. Cook for 2–3 minutes to soften the cauliflower. Finally add the turmeric, sambhar masala, lime juice, caster sugar, cooked crushed potato, salt and pepper. Mix well, then add the chopped tomatoes.
· Cover with a lid and cook over a medium-low heat for 10–12 minutes, stirring regularly to ensure it does not catch on the bottom and adding a splash of water if it's drying out. Finish with the coriander.
· For the dosas, fry the sage in the 4 tablespoons of vegetable oil until they turn darker green and crisp up, then drain on kitchen paper to crisp up completely. Crisp up extra leaves to serve now, too.
· For the dosa batter, whisk the rice flour, gram flour, plain flour, sambhar masala, turmeric, salt and baking powder together. Add 1 tablespoon of vegetable oil, then use your fingertips to rub the oil into the dry ingredients completely. In a separate jug, whisk together the yogurt with 400ml cold water. Pour into the flour mix slowly and whisk for 1 minute; it should be the texture of loose single cream. Leave the batter to sit on the work surface for 30 minutes, then crumble in the crispy sage leaves and bicarbonate of soda just before cooking.
· Heat a large non-stick frying pan or tawa over a medium heat: you don't want it too hot or the batter won't spread into a circle. Brush the surface with water, then quickly spoon 1 ladleful of batter on to the pan, using the back of the ladle to spread it outwards in concentric circles, spiralling from the middle outwards into a thin pancake. Cook the dosa for 30–45 seconds until it lifts up crisply from the bottom, then brush the top with a little of the sage-infused oil. Flip over and cook the other side for another 30–45 seconds.
· Serve the dosa straight from the pan, filled with cauliflower sabji, more crispy sage leaves, toasted cashews, red onion, sambhar masala and raita.

Shahi lamb kati rolls with pink pickled onions

My daily phone call home follows a ritualistic sequence of sentences: first 'hello', then 'what have you made?', and only then 'how are you?' For a family whose lives revolve around food, the implicit truth about question two lies within the answer to question one. Like clockwork, once a month, my dad will answer with giddy joy: 'Today we didn't make anything, we're getting a takeaway from Shahi Nan.' I salivate immediately, reassured that they really are better than fine.

Three generations of our family have devoured the famous lamb sheekh with tangy red onion chutney from this inconspicuous Leicester institution. And we have also shared a decades-long quest to recreate Shahi Nan's coal-charred kebabs in our own kitchens. The number of iterations we've all attempted over the years goes into the thousands, some coming almost close, but most nowhere near. My pungently spiced homage is not a patch on the original, but is delicious none the less.

Makes 12–14

For the kebabs
3 tablespoons ghee
1 teaspoon ajwain, crushed
1 tablespoon coriander seeds, crushed
2 red onions, finely chopped
500g minced lamb (20 per cent fat)
8 garlic cloves, very finely chopped
4 tablespoons finely grated fresh ginger
4 tablespoons chopped coriander leaves, plus more to serve
4 tablespoons chopped mint leaves
1 green chilli, finely chopped
1 teaspoon ground cinnamon
1 tablespoon ground cumin
2 tablespoons anardana powder
2 teaspoons coarsely ground black pepper
2 teaspoons fine sea salt
2 tablespoons light brown sugar
1 tablespoon finely grated lemon zest, plus 2 tablespoons
    lemon juice
4 tablespoons gram flour

For the minty yogurt & kati rolls
2 tablespoons mint sauce, from a jar
100ml natural yogurt
6–14 rotis, parathas (see pages 184–191), or tortilla wraps
Pink Pickled Onions with Lychee (see page 209), to serve

· Heat the ghee in a large frying pan, then add the crushed ajwain and coriander seeds. Sizzle for 1 minute before adding the red onions.
· Cook for 10–12 minutes over a medium-low heat until really soft and caramelised. Remove from the heat and cool completely.
· Scrape the cooled onions into a large mixing bowl along with the rest of the kebab ingredients. Use your hands to squeeze, pound and combine the mix together evenly; disposable gloves are advised! Cover and refrigerate for 4–6 hours.
· Using either metal or soaked wooden kebab skewers, squeeze the meat around the skewers with your fingers into tightly compacted kebabs.
· Preheat the grill to a high setting. Grill the kebabs on a high heat for 8–10 minutes, turning a couple of times, until they are nicely charred on the outside and cooked through.
· Make a cooling sauce by mixing the jarred mint sauce with the yogurt.
· Take your wrap of choice, fill with 1–2 charred shahi kebabs, drizzle over the minty yogurt, top with pink pickled onions and coriander leaves, roll up and enjoy.

Peanut butter-tandoori mushroom pittas

Mushrooms are the supreme non-binary ingredient, existing somewhere in between plant and animal worlds, with not two but thousands of sexes, each of which can mate with any other. In fact, there could truly be no more fitting a flavour vehicle for the culinary embodiment of 'middleness' that is third-culture cooking.

This recipe brings the ethos of the tandoori clay oven to the home kitchen, with a robust masala paste containing crunchy peanut butter for rich nuttiness along with the crucial ability to burnish the mushrooms to that delicious char synonymous with tandoori cooking. The only binary rule here regards the peanut butter: you simply must use crunchy, smooth just won't do! Load the pittas to bursting point with the scorched masala mushrooms, a good splodge of mango chutney and even more peanuts for extra crunch.

Makes 4

For the peanut butter-tandoori paste
2 tablespoons crunchy roasted peanut butter
   (smooth is unforgivable)
2 tablespoons Tandoori Masala (see page 25)
2 tablespoons finely grated fresh ginger
4 garlic cloves, very finely chopped
½ teaspoon chilli powder
1 teaspoon smoked salt
2 tablespoons gram flour
5 tablespoons natural yogurt, or coconut yogurt
1 teaspoon finely grated lemon zest, plus 4 tablespoons
   lemon juice

For the pittas
150g mixed mushrooms, such as shiitake, chestnut,
   enoki and oyster, halved
4 pitta breads, toasted
mango chutney, to serve
shelled unsalted peanuts, crushed
pickled ginger
coriander leaves
Minty Yogurt (see page 64)

· Whisk together all the peanut butter-tandoori paste ingredients into a thick mass. Smother the raw mushrooms in the mix, cover and leave for 15 minutes. Preheat the oven to 180°C fan.
· Spread the coated mushrooms on a baking sheet and bake for 20–25 minutes until they are cooked through, then switch to a preheated hot grill for 1–2 minutes to burnish them on top.
· Stuff the hot tandoori mushrooms into toasted pitta breads, then load up with mango chutney, crushed peanuts, pickled ginger, coriander leaves and minty yogurt.

Naan Wraps, Kati Rolls, Toasts & Sarnies

Masala-melt quarter pounders with poppadom crumbs

The thrill of embarking on professional taste safaris around the world to cultivate my taste in taste has never wavered. Regardless of where I'm sent, flavour revelations are seldom found in fine dining restaurants, but on market stalls, in home kitchens and on the menu boards of local fast-food joints.

This recipe amalgamates every good burger I've ever encountered on those travels: third-culture Indian in flavour, but global in technique.

A good burger demands a succulent patty. Your butcher will have their own blend of minced cuts, but mine combines beefy brisket, rich marbled short rib and tender sirloin (if you have a taste for offal, I should tell you that the best burger I've ever eaten also had beef heart in the mix). As these cook, the rim of poppadom crumbs sizzles to a crisp, while the blend of masala-fied melty cheeses oozes from the middle. Smother with condiments and have paper napkins to hand. This taste revelation is as far from fine dining as you can get.

Makes 8

For the masala-melt butter
50g unsalted butter, plus 100g very soft unsalted butter
1½ teaspoons coriander seeds, crushed
2 teaspoons fennel seeds, crushed
1 large onion, very finely chopped
drop of vegetable oil (optional)
300g mix of hard melty cheeses, such as mature Cheddar,
   Gruyère and Comté, finely grated
2 teaspoons coarsely ground black pepper
2 green chillies, very finely chopped
2 tablespoons dried fenugreek leaves, crushed
1½ teaspoons ground turmeric
2 teaspoons amchoor
1 tablespoon Garam Masala (see page 23)

For the patties (170–180g each)
3 spring onions, chopped
40g coriander leaves, chopped
6 garlic cloves, very finely chopped
1.1kg minced beef (20 per cent fat)
1 egg, lightly beaten
1 tablespoon English mustard
2 teaspoons fine sea salt
2 teaspoons coarsely ground black pepper
4 tablespoons fresh white breadcrumbs
1 tablespoon finely grated lime zest, plus 4 tablespoons
   lime juice
6 poppadoms, crushed, plus more to layer inside

To serve
8 brioche burger buns, toasted
condiments, chutneys, pickles and gherkins of your choice

· Melt the 50g of butter in a saucepan, then add the crushed coriander and fennel seeds. Sizzle together for 1 minute before adding the finely chopped onion. Cook for 9–10 minutes until the onion is really soft and starting to brown, adding a drop of oil if needed. Take off the heat and cool completely.

· Place the 100g very soft butter in a bowl, along with the rest of the masala butter ingredients and including the cooled onions. Mix well, then spoon on to cling film and form into a round log 4cm in diameter. Twist tightly at the ends to seal, then freeze for 1–2 hours to firm up.

· In a food processor, blitz the spring onions, coriander and garlic until very finely chopped. Add the minced beef, egg, English mustard, salt, pepper, breadcrumbs, lime zest and juice, pulsing until evenly combined. Empty into a bowl, using your hands to fully combine the ingredients if needed.

· Remove the butter log from the freezer and slice into discs about 1.25cm thick.

· Take 170–180g of mince to form each patty. Divide into 2 equal balls, then flatten each into a circle 9cm in diameter and 1cm thick. Place the disc of masala butter in the middle of a patty, then encase with the other. (Pressing the mince into a 9cm cookie cutter or cooking ring makes this easier.) Ensure the top and bottom are completely sealed along the edge, pressing together firmly so they don't break apart as they cook; you want the butter to remain encased. Repeat to form and stuff all the patties.

· Generously roll the sides of each patty in crushed poppadom crumbs, then cover with cling film and leave in the fridge for 1 hour.

· To cook, preheat the oven to 190°C fan. Bake the burgers for 18–20 minutes, carefully turning halfway through. Finish under a very hot grill for 2 minutes to burnish on top.

· Serve in toasted brioche buns with your favourite condiments, gherkins and extra poppadoms stacked inside for even more crunch!

Chaat paneer curry dogs

Currywurst is a German pork sausage, fried, then doused in a curry-spiked ketchup, typically served on a bed of searingly hot French fries. Its invention is credited to post-wartime food kiosk owner Herta Hewer. In 1949, she had acquired ketchup, Worcestershire sauce and the approximation-of-Indianness that is curry powder from British soldiers in Berlin, which she quickly brewed together.

For authenticity, a currywurst must be thickly sliced, served on a paper plate and eaten with a wooden fork like those from a classic British chippy.

Conversely, British chippy curry sauce is more akin to a mild fruit-spiced gravy, tasting nothing like any British or Indian curry, but everything like its unmistakably delicious self. This hotdog merges currywurst and chip shop curry sauce: the sauce squeezed liberally over battered masala paneer with a flourish of chaat garnishes. It is one of the few times I call for generic store-bought curry powder over a 'proper' freshly ground masala blend. It's an ingredient I happen to love that has its own time and place in the kitchen, and this German-British-Indian hybrid is certainly one of those.

Makes 5

For the curry sauce
150ml tomato ketchup
2 teaspoons onion powder
½ teaspoon cayenne pepper
½ teaspoon Worcestershire sauce
2 tablespoons apple cider vinegar
1 tablespoon medium curry powder
½ teaspoon ground turmeric
½ teaspoon ground cumin
2 tablespoons light brown sugar
1 tablespoon tomato purée

For the dogs
3 litres whole milk (organic works best here)
6 tablespoons lemon juice, plus more if needed
1 tablespoon Chaat Masala (see page 24), plus more to serve
1 teaspoon chilli flakes
2 tablespoons finely chopped mint leaves
1 teaspoon fine sea salt
2 tablespoons finely grated lemon zest
500ml sunflower oil
4 tablespoons rice flour
100g gram flour

To serve
5 brioche hotdog rolls
natural yogurt
chaat toppings, such as finely chopped red onion, pomegranate seeds, peanuts, crunchy sev and coriander leaves
cayenne pepper

· Whisk all the sauce ingredients together in a pan with 150ml water. Bring to the boil, then reduce the heat to a gentle simmer for 5–6 minutes, stirring well, until reduced to a thick ketchup. Cool completely.
· To make the paneer dogs, slowly warm the milk in a saucepan to 90°C, just below boiling point. Keep it at this temperature for 2–3 minutes, then remove from the heat.
· Dilute the lemon juice with 2 tablespoons of water. Slowly trickle 1 spoon of the watery lemon into the hot milk at a time, stirring gently and letting it sit for 30 seconds between each spoonful. Eventually the milk will curdle fully with the curds and whey completely separated. If needed, add a little extra lemon juice. Empty the curds into a colander lined with a muslin cloth or cheesecloth, discarding the whey, then run under a cold tap for 30 seconds to cool. Squeeze out as much water as you can, then let it hang to drip in the sink for 30 minutes.
· Crumble the well-drained paneer into a bowl, then add the chaat masala, chilli flakes, mint, salt and lemon zest. Mix vigorously so the paneer is speckled evenly with the spices.
· Spoon the spiced paneer back into its cloth and squeeze into a tight ball, then shape into a rectangular block 15 x 10 x 2cm. Wrap tightly in the cloth, weigh down with a heavy can and leave in the fridge to firm up for 2 hours.
· Heat the sunflower oil to 170°C in a deep frying pan or wok (see page 11). Meanwhile, prepare 2 bowls, 1 with the rice flour, the other with a thick batter made by whisking the gram flour with 100–125ml cold water.
· Cut the firmed-up paneer into 5 paneer 'dogs', each 2cm wide and just a little shorter than your hotdog buns in length. Drop into the rice flour and coat all over, then leave for a minute and roll again so the surface is dry. Shake off the excess, then dip each dog into the gram flour batter.
· Fry for 4–5 minutes, turning, until they are cooked through and crispy on the outside. Drain well on kitchen paper and sprinkle liberally with chaat masala while still hot.
· Sandwich the hot paneer into the hotdog buns, drizzle with the curry sauce and yogurt, then add a generous sprinkle of whatever chaat toppings take your fancy. Finish with a pinch of cayenne pepper for an extra-hot kick!

Hot rhubarb & nigella grilled cheese

Leading up to my parents' nuptials on Indian Independence Day in 1981, my mum lived through a brief period of identity-limbo, suspended in the void between what her life in Punjab was and what her life in Leicester was about to become. When I asked what she recalled most about those weeks before her wedding – in a new country she'd never even been to before – her answer took me by surprise. Cheese.

Her first taste of it was on the plane over: a square of mild Cheddar with a duo of cream crackers which she smothered in the gooseberry pickle that was hidden in her bag. A few days later she had Red Leicester, thickly grated with coleslaw on a white bread sandwich, which she stuffed with Bombay mix and devoured in one. Then just before the wedding was her first encounter with molten mozzarella on a takeaway pizza that she talks about to this day; she drenched it in hot sauce and ate with greedy joy. In all its guises, cheese simultaneously diminished and amplified her longing for Indianness, becoming a way to taste her uprooting, while remaining firmly rooted.

This grilled toastie works with any combination of savoury British or Alpine melty cheese and hotly spiced Indian chutney. (A hot mustardy piccalilli – an amalgamation of the words pickle and chilli – works especially well.) Just be very plentiful with both: generosity on each side of the cultural bridge is what will make it delicious.

· Lightly toast the bread slices, then liberally spread the inside of one slice with chutney. Butter the inside of the other piece and cover with a thick layer of grated cheese or, better still, a mix of cheeses. Press the 2 slices together. Spread butter on the outside of both slices, then sprinkle with chaat masala.
· Place in a frying pan over a medium heat for 3–4 minutes on each side, until the cheese oozes and the outside of the bread forms a spiced crust.
· Serve with fine sev for crunch or – for the full experience – with prawn cocktail crisps slowly pushed into the melted cheese. If you're not a prawn cocktail person, then any other crisps work here apart from ready salted, which is not a real flavour.

Tip I won't specify here how much cheese you need to make this – you know how you like your grilled cheese – but it should be a lot.

Makes 1

2 thick slices of sourdough bread or white crusty loaf
3 tablespoons Hot Rhubarb & Nigella Chutney
  (see page 204)
unsalted butter, softened, for spreading
strong hard melty cheese, such as mature Cheddar,
  Ogleshield, Sparkenhoe Red Leicester, Comté or Gruyère,
  grated (see tip, right)
1 teaspoon Chaat Masala (see page 24)
2 tablespoons fine sev, or Bombay mix (optional)
1 packet of crisps of your choice (optional, though prawn
  cocktail very much advised)

Naan Wraps, Kati Rolls, Toasts & Sarnies

Green chilli & walnut tikka naan wraps

'Jaggi Dhabba' was located on a truck-road (a dirt-track motorway for rural sugarcane and wheat trucks) close to my grandparents' house in Jalandhar, Punjab. Their pink fridge – plastered with posters of the bhangra singer Malkit Singh – was balanced on a pedestal of bricks in the street. From this height, he appeared to be guardian of the tandoor clay ovens below, from which burnished skewers of intensely marinated meats emerged all day and night.

My taste memory of their hariyali tikka chicken – smoky morsels of charred green chicken with flavour penetrating to their cores – is triggered whenever I'm in the presence of open flames. Tikka simply means 'piece', a method of cooking fabled to have been introduced to India by Babur, dynastic father of the Moghul Empire. He insisted his meats were cooked in bite-sized pieces with all bones removed; the Emperor was not for choking in his newly conquered land. The ground walnuts here blacken as they grill, accentuating the fiery green chillies and aromatic whole spices. This paste is also wonderful with thickly cubed tikkas of paneer or tofu.

Makes 4

For the chicken & lemon brine
1 tablespoon finely grated lemon zest, plus 6 tablespoons (90ml) lemon juice
1 teaspoon fine sea salt
seeds from 10 green cardamom pods, crushed
650g boneless, skinless chicken thighs,
   cut into bite-sized pieces

For the tikka paste
50g shelled unsalted walnuts
1 tablespoon fennel seeds
1 teaspoon ajwain
1 tablespoon coriander seeds
8 allspice berries
1 tablespoon white sesame seeds
3 green chillies, stalks trimmed away, plus more (optional) to serve
6 garlic cloves, chopped
2 tablespoons finely grated fresh ginger
1 teaspoon freshly grated nutmeg
25g coriander leaves, finely chopped
1½ teaspoons smoked salt
1½ teaspoons coarsely ground black pepper
1 teaspoon light brown sugar
2 tablespoons apple cider vinegar
2 tablespoons vegetable oil

To serve
4 naans, toasted
yogurt raita or Minty Yogurt (see pages 165, 175 and 64)
hot sauce
Pink Pickled Onions with Lychee (see page 209)
lemon wedges

· In a bowl, whisk together the lemon zest, juice, salt and cardamom. Add the chicken pieces and mix thoroughly, ensuring they are fully coated in lemon brine. Cover and leave in the fridge for 30 minutes.
· Preheat the oven to 165°C fan. Roast the walnuts for 4–5 minutes until they are just starting to toast. Remove from the oven and cool completely. Dry pan-roast the fennel seeds, ajwain, coriander seeds and allspice berries for 2–3 minutes. Next add the sesame seeds, toasting for 1 more minute. Transfer to a grinder and whizz to a fine powder. Add the rest of the tikka paste ingredients to the grinder with the walnuts and a good splash of water. Blitz to a grainy green paste.
· Shake the chicken out of its brine and coat liberally with the green tikka paste in a bowl. Cover and leave to marinate in the fridge for 2–3 hours.
· Preheat the oven to 180°C fan.
· Thread the well-coated chicken tikka pieces on to skewers and place on a baking tray lined with foil, well spaced to allow steam to escape. Cook for 25–30 minutes until fully cooked through, with the juices running clear when pierced. Finish under a hot grill, or on a barbecue, for 1–2 minutes, charring to whatever level of blackened scorch suits your taste.
· Serve in toasted naan breads with plenty of cooling raita or minty yogurt, hot sauce, pickled onions, lemon wedges and green chillies.

The evolution of my Sunday mornings over the years is like a dot-to-dot of my many different selves on a page. As a child, most were spent reciting the alphabet at Punjabi school, then later in cello rehearsals for youth orchestra. My university Sundays were spent sweating out the night before in the gym or mooching around Bristol in search of carbs. In my hedonistic London years, I'd be at the end of a club night in Vauxhall or the beginning of a day rave in Hackney.

Today, they're generally spent lounged on the sofa watching Bollywood anthems while scrolling through my phone, before eventually heading to a pub on Columbia Road for many Sunday pints. Quite what image connecting all those dots will draw I'm not sure, though a feature linking them all is an obligatory big brunch. This is my favourite weekend brunch of all: tropical-spiced Malabar coast meets Harrods tearooms on a plate. The Indian railway cart-style crispy fried egg is optional, but for me that final yolk-yellow dot really completes the picture.

Serves 2

For the crab
10g lemongrass stalks, trimmed and chopped
2 garlic cloves
1 red chilli, stalk trimmed away
2 tablespoons coconut oil
2 spring onions, finely chopped
1 teaspoon coriander seeds, crushed
2 teaspoons black mustard seeds
25g peanuts, roasted and crushed
35g toasted coconut flakes (see page 86), plus more
    to serve
150g white crab meat
1 teaspoon finely grated lime zest, plus 1 tablespoon
    lime juice
1½ teaspoons amchoor
1 teaspoon fine sea salt
2 teaspoons caster sugar
1 tablespoon chopped coriander leaves

For the eggs & crumpets
4 tablespoons olive oil
pinch of ground turmeric
¼ teaspoon Chaat Masala (see page 24)
2 eggs
1 tablespoon finely slivered red onion
2 tablespoons finely chopped plum tomatoes
1 green chilli, finely chopped
4 crumpets, toasted
chives, to serve
fresh green chutney, such as Coriander, Spring Onion
    & Curry Leaf Chutney, to serve (see page 202)

· In a grinder, blitz together the lemongrass, garlic and red chilli with 3 tablespoons of water to a fine paste, then set aside.
· Heat the coconut oil in a frying pan, then add the chopped spring onions, coriander seeds and mustard seeds, frying for 2–3 minutes. Next add the lemongrass paste and fry for 1 minute, before adding the crushed peanuts and coconut flakes. Cook for 2 more minutes. Finally add the crab meat, lime zest and juice, amchoor, salt and sugar. Cook for 3 minutes until the crab is heated through and infused with the spices.
· For the eggs, heat the olive oil in a frying pan until hot, then add the turmeric and chaat masala. Infuse the oil for 30 seconds, before cracking in the eggs. Quickly sprinkle over the red onion, tomatoes and green chilli before the white sets. Use a spoon to baste the yolk with the hot spice-infused oil: you want a softly set yolk and crispy frayed white.
· Stir the coriander into the spiced crab, then pile it high on the toasted crumpets, with crispy eggs on the side and toasted coconut and chives to serve.

Tip I like a layer of fresh green chutney, such as Coriander, Spring Onion and Curry Leaf Chutney, on the crumpets with this.

Stilton & tamarind Mumbai toastie

If frequency of consumption is the deciding factor, then the cheese toastie is arguably even more Indian than 'curry'. It's a culinary canvas adored by diasporic cooks, who have fashioned as many different global variations as there are different ways of being 'Indian'. Chilli-cheese toasts, keema toastie melts, aloo gobi panini, Mumbai bhurta sandwiches, masala chana croque monsieurs, toasted tikka subs, chutney grilled cheese, onion bhaji toasties... what the 4th Earl of Sandwich invented, Indians have adopted and accentuated with the most unapologetically Indian cadence they can.

I've always had a taste for the salty bite of Stilton, particularly those cheeses made in Leicestershire by makers such as Long Clawson Dairy and Tuxford & Tebbutt Creamery, and the masala tamarind potatoes in this recipe bring out the cheese's rich intensity. It's all toasted until everything melts together, revealing a spectrum of spiced savouriness in every bite. This is unapologetic British Indian hybridity at its utmost – multifaceted flavour-on-flavour made in toastie form – and it is sublime!

Makes 2

For the tamarind potatoes
1 tablespoon ghee
1½ teaspoons coriander seeds, crushed
1½ teaspoons fennel seeds, crushed
1 large potato, boiled and mashed
1 small red onion, very finely chopped
1 green chilli, very finely chopped
1 teaspoon fine sea salt
2 tablespoons Gunpowder Masala, or Garam Masala
    (see pages 24 and 23), plus 1 teaspoon
4 tablespoons Tamarind, Date & Mint Sauce (see page 203),
    or bottled tamarind table ketchup, or brown sauce, plus
    more to serve
2 tablespoons chopped coriander leaves

For the toasties
4 thick slices of white bread
2 tablespoons unsalted butter, very soft,
    plus more for spreading
4 tablespoons thick sev, plus more to serve
150g Stilton cheese, crumbled

· To make the tamarind potatoes, gently heat the ghee in a saucepan, then add the crushed coriander and fennel seeds, sizzling for 1 minute. Mix in the mashed potato, red onion, green chilli, salt and gunpowder or garam masala. Turn up the heat to medium, add the tamarind sauce, ketchup or brown sauce and cook for 2–3 minutes. Finish by mixing through the coriander, then leave to cool.
· Heat a toastie maker or sandwich grill so it's hot. (If you don't have one, these can just as easily be made in a griddle or frying pan.)
· Spread the inside of 2 pieces of bread with butter, then spoon over a thick layer of the tamarind potatoes. Sprinkle over the thick sev for some crunch. Butter the other slices of bread then generously crumble over the Stilton. Press the 2 slices together.
· Mix the 2 tablespoons of very soft butter with the 1 teaspoon of gunpowder or garam masala and spread over the outsides of the sandwiches. Grill for 3–4 minutes, until the bread is nicely toasted and the Stilton is oozing out. Serve with extra tamarind sauce for dipping and thick sev for even more crunch.

CHAPTER 3

SPICED SALADS & 'QUICK PANS'

As second generation British Indians, my siblings, cousins and I grew up each having a spectrum of different identities, characterised by a simultaneous longing-for and rejection-of our Indian heritage. Our childhoods played out inside our personal paradoxes, merging our Punjabi cultural inheritance with our ambition to fulfil our birthright Britishness, believing in our entangled minds that progress in life was directly correlated with proximity to 'whiteness'.

Our tolerant parents spoke to us in Punjabi and we'd answer back in English. Sundays were intended for Punjabi school, but our complaining saw this replaced with popcorn-fuelled marathons of *The Goonies*. My granddad even took me to sitar lessons to engrain my performative tendencies within my Indianness, but I insisted on cello. My teens were marked by hours of practising turmeric-stained Bach manuscripts, while the Punjabi anthems that permeated our household played in the background.

But food was where my pursuit for everything that was *not* my Punjabi heritage manifested most. In the playground, I'd trade mooli paratha for stark ham sandwiches, finding their plainness completely thrilling. We begrudgingly ate Mum's home-cooked methi chicken, saag paneer and aloo gobi, but relished pizza, noodles and shawarma. I idolised Julia Child, *The Two Fat Ladies* and Fanny Cradock, strong-spirited women very much like my own Aunty-Jis, yet entirely different at the same time.

My years at the University of Bristol muddled the dilemma further: my life shifted from Leicester, where ethnic minorities were the fabric of the city, to a manor house in overwhelmingly white Clifton Village where my (relatively simple) name proved unpronounceable to many. I'd never felt more 'other', yet never been more proficient at performing whiteness. After all, I'd been practising that for my entire life.

Those four years were truly life-affirming, primarily down to five of the most driven, funny and loving people I've ever met, still among my dearest friends. The universe brought us together in a breeze-block house on Ravenswood Road. As different as we were, we pooled groceries in the shoebox kitchen, our collective palates merging over the years into our signature dish, 'Ravenswood Hot Salad', a hotch-potch that mixed culinary worlds with gusto in the most studenty way.

It started with a tharka-sofrito mash-up of fried onions, garlic and spice. Then came chicken, eggs, salmon or canned tuna, with lentils or chickpeas thrown in. After this was a Jackson Pollock free-hand dollop of every flavour bomb in the kitchen: soy sauce, pesto, curry paste, Tabasco, sweet chilli sauce, ketchup, hummus, Marmite, with a final splodge of Loyd Grossman pasta sauce if you could scrape any out of the jar. This would be smothered over a bed of leaves with a grating of Cheddar, and, for the more cheffy among us, crunched-up cereal as textural contrast. It was a global hybrid salad-sabzi-stir-fry, combining everything – and nothing – of each of our worlds.

I've had a taste for culturally remixed salads and 'quick pans' – a recipe in which all the ingredients can be cooked in the same pan and which does not require long or slow cooking – ever since, that celebrate the freshest seasonal flavours of different places and people around the world I've encountered. To date, my gastronomic wanderlust has sparked voyages around South America, South East Asia, Japan, North America and Europe. Yet what's curious is that, when I get home and recreate the dishes of my travels, what comes out is always infused with Punjabi flavours. My hands unconsciously pull me back to myself as I cook, combining everything new I encounter with my mother tongue.

If recipes are autobiographical, these salads and quick pan recipes tell the story of my journey so far. Which begs the question: where to next?

Jeera-jeera salmon
with pomegranate & chillied sugar snaps

Shahi jeera or black cumin is the sweeter, darker, nuttier relation of conventional cumin. Easy to find in Indian shops, it's easily confused with nigella seeds or caraway. (All is not lost if this happens, as it tastes a little like a combination of the two.) It's often baked into tandoori breads or biscuits, added to 'pilau rice' dishes, or used to bring depth to masala blends through its floral-citrussy notes and hints of flavourful smoke. As the double jeera in the title of this recipe suggests, it uses both types of cumin to create an earthy-sweet crunchy coating for spice-marinated salmon. Combined with tangy pomegranate molasses and chilli-charred sugar snaps, it's a dish that's doubly delicious.

Serves 2

For the salmon
2 tablespoons olive oil, plus 3 tablespoons
1 teaspoon finely grated fresh ginger
3 garlic cloves, very finely chopped
1 teaspoon ground cumin
¾ teaspoon five-spice powder
¼ teaspoon ground turmeric
1 teaspoon fine sea salt, plus 1 teaspoon
500–600g boneless, skin-on salmon side
2 teaspoons cumin seeds
1 teaspoon black cumin seeds (shahi jeera)
1 teaspoon coriander seeds, crushed
2 tablespoons pomegranate molasses
1 teaspoon white sesame seeds
4 tablespoons lemon juice
1 teaspoon coarsely ground black pepper
pomegranate seeds, to serve

For the sugar snaps
200g sugar snap peas
200g okra, cut into stars
3 tablespoons olive oil
1 teaspoon ground cumin
1 teaspoon anardana powder
2 garlic cloves, very finely chopped
2 teaspoons chilli flakes
1 teaspoon fine sea salt

· For the fish, mix the 2 tablespoons of olive oil with the ginger, garlic, cumin, five-spice, turmeric and 1 teaspoon of salt.
· Slash the salmon a few times with a sharp knife, penetrating 2–3mm into the flesh. Smother with the marinade, getting it deep into the grooves, then cover and set aside for 45 minutes.
· For the sugar snaps, mix them with the okra, olive oil, cumin, anardana, garlic, chilli flakes and salt in a bowl. Leave for 10–15 minutes; the okra will release its water in this time.
· Heat a large frying pan or griddle over a high heat, then pour in the sugar snaps with their marinade. Cook for 3 minutes until the garlic just starts to char, then add 30ml water to the pan. Cook in the steam for another 3–4 minutes until the water has evaporated and the vegetables are tenderly cooked through. Spoon out on to a serving dish.
· Add the 3 tablespoons of olive oil to the same pan and bring up to a medium-high heat. Add the cumin seeds, black cumin seeds and crushed coriander seeds, sizzling for 30 seconds. Push the seeds and oil to the sides of the pan, then carefully place the marinated salmon – skin side down – in the middle. Cook for 3–4 minutes until the skin crisps up, carefully basting the top of the salmon with the hot spiced oil and seeds using a spoon.
· Flip the salmon over and cook on the other side for 2–3 minutes, basting the crispy skin with the oil. When brown on the outside and slightly pink in the middle, flip over again, cover with the crunchy spices and lift on to the serving dish with the sugar snaps.
· Add the pomegranate molasses, sesame seeds, lemon juice, pepper and 1 teaspoon salt to the empty pan, whisking well. Reduce for 1 minute until it resembles runny honey, then drizzle over the salmon. Sprinkle with pomegranate seeds to finish.

Tamarind butter skillet chicken with tarragon lentils

Tamarind and butter are two of the defining tastes of my Punjabi upbringing: the former as tangy imli chutney smothered over everything from samosas to saag; the latter as desi white mukhani butter, also interwoven into everything from samosas to saag!

This one-pan skillet chicken dish combines the two into a piquant buttered masala sauce that lusciously coats the seared chicken. The herbal freshness of tarragon lentils adds an anisey note, creating a flavour chord that resonates from Punjabiness to somewhere-elseness.

(Samosas and saag on the side: optional.)

Serves 2

For the chicken & lemon brine
4 tablespoons lemon juice
1½ teaspoons fine sea salt
seeds from 6 cardamom pods, crushed
2 large bone-in, skin-on chicken breasts, legs or thighs

For the glaze
20g salted butter, plus 30g
2 tablespoons olive oil
1 large onion, finely sliced into rings
1 tablespoon finely grated fresh ginger
4 garlic cloves, very finely chopped
10 anchovies in oil, drained and very finely chopped
2 tablespoons tamarind concentrate, or 4 tablespoons tamarind paste or pulp (see page 157)
2 tablespoons caster sugar
2 tablespoons tomato purée
2 teaspoons Garam Masala (see page 23)
1 teaspoon coarsely ground black pepper

For the lentils & to serve
1 tablespoon olive oil
2 teaspoons ground cumin
¾ teaspoon cayenne pepper
2 teaspoons finely chopped tarragon leaves, plus more to serve
1 teaspoon fennel seeds, crushed
400g can of beluga or Puy lentils, drained
½ teaspoon fine sea salt
2 tablespoons lemon juice
dried onion flakes

· To brine the chicken, mix the lemon juice, salt and cardamom in a large bowl, whisking to dissolve the salt. Flatten the chicken a little with a meat tenderiser or rolling pin on a board, then slash each piece 2–3 times with a knife, going through the skin. Place the chicken in the brine, then use your hands to smother the pieces all over, getting the brine deep into the cuts. Cover and leave for 30–45 minutes.
· Start the glaze. Heat the 20g salted butter and the 2 tablespoons olive oil in a large skillet or frying pan set over a medium-high heat. Add the sliced onion and cook for 7–8 minutes until nicely browned. Next add the ginger, garlic and anchovies. Stir well, cook for another 1–2 minutes, then move the onions to the edges of the pan.
· Remove the chicken from the brine, shake off the excess and place in the hot pan skin side down, then spoon the browned onions on top of the chicken. Cook for 6–7 minutes, then turn the chicken over and again spoon the onions over the top. The moisture from the chicken should prevent the onions from burning, but add a little oil if needed.
· Move the chicken pieces to one side of the pan, then add the 30g salted butter, the tamarind, sugar, tomato purée, garam masala and pepper, along with a big splash of water. Whisk the sauce well to combine the ingredients, then spoon over the chicken. Fry, turning, until the chicken is completely cooked through, basting with the sticky buttery-tamarind glaze as it cooks.
· Remove the chicken from the pan on to a plate, spoon over the sauce and let it rest while you heat the lentils.
· In the same skillet, heat the oil and add the cumin, cayenne pepper, tarragon and crushed fennel seeds. Sizzle for 1 minute, then add the lentils and salt. Heat through for 1–2 minutes and finish with the lemon juice.
· Place the rested glazed chicken back into the pan on top of the lentils, then sprinkle with a little more chopped tarragon and some onion flakes. Serve straight away with crusty bread or naan to mop up the tangy sauce.

Spiced Salads & 'Quick Pans'

Juniper-spiced bavette steak with corn ribs & coconut zhoug

My first job in London involved a daily stroll through Smithfield meat market. Daily immersion in the sights and smells of fine butchery, coupled with company-card lunches in nose-to-tail institutions such as St John, nurtured my admiration for the craft. Bavette – 'the butcher's cut' – is a richly flavoured strip from the underbelly, with a loose structure suited to absorbing marinades. The juniper here adds British gin and tonic characteristics that mingle with smoked salt and Indian masala. Corn ribs add sweetness and coconut zhoug a taste of Yemen-via-Kerala.

Serves 2

For the dry rub
1 tablespoon onion powder
2 teaspoons garlic powder
1 teaspoon light brown sugar
1½ teaspoons smoked salt
1 teaspoon coarsely ground black pepper
2 teaspoons Garam Masala (see page 23)
½ teaspoon chilli powder
½ teaspoon ground turmeric
16 juniper berries, crushed, plus more to serve
7 allspice berries, crushed

For the steaks & corn
2 large bavette steaks
1 tablespoon olive oil, plus more to brush and fry the steaks
2 ears of corn on the cob
pea shoots, or mustard cress, to serve

For the zhoug
1 teaspoon cumin seeds
seeds from 6 green cardamom pods, crushed
2 teaspoons fennel seeds
1 teaspoon fine sea salt
4 tablespoons grated fresh coconut
100g jalapeños in brine, plus 2 tablespoons of the brine
4 garlic cloves
30g coriander leaves
30g flat-leaf parsley leaves
1 tablespoon finely grated lemon zest, plus 6 tablespoons lemon juice
2 teaspoons chilli flakes
1 tablespoon caster sugar
100ml olive oil

· Mix the ingredients for the dry rub together in a bowl. Brush the steaks with olive oil, then sprinkle over two-thirds of the dry rub, pressing in well. Cover and leave to marinate for 2–3 hours.
· To make the coconut zhoug, dry-roast the cumin, cardamom and fennel seeds until they release their aromas. Grind to a powder with the salt. Set aside.
· In the same pan, gently toast the grated coconut until it has just hints of brown. Put the toasted coconut and spices in a food processor with all the rest of the zhoug ingredients except the oil. Blitz until the herbs are very finely chopped, then with the blades still going, slowly pour in the olive oil until you have a silky green sauce. Leave the flavours to mingle together for 30 minutes.
· Preheat the oven to 200°C fan.
· Peel away the leaves from the corn, then carefully cut the cobs in half lengthways on a chopping board, going right through the central core; you'll need a big sharp knife and some strength to get through the middle. Be very careful as you do this! Next divide each half cob into 2–3 rib strips, again keeping the central core intact.
· Make a paste with the remaining one-third of the dry rub and the 1 tablespoon olive oil, then brush this mixture over the corn rib strips. Bake in the oven for 20 minutes, until piping hot, charred on the outside and curled up at the edges.
· When the corn is close to ready, flash-fry the marinated steaks in a screaming-hot pan with a little oil for 4 minutes on one side and 2 minutes on the other. I like steak to be charred on the outside and still a little pink in the middle. Plate up with the curled-up corn ribs and a generous drizzle of coconut zhoug. Sprinkle with crushed juniper berries and pea shoots for an extra hit of flavour!

Sambhar sweet potato hasselbacks
with Red Leicester

Kanyakumari on the southern tip of India is the only place on earth where three oceans meet: the Arabian Sea, the Indian Ocean and the Bay of Bengal. Consequently, its shoreline is an optical kaleidoscope of red, black and yellow sands, each saltwater wave reconfiguring the beachfront into an ever-changing chromatic rainbow.

This recipe is a meeting of three culinary cultures: South Indian sambhar masala, South American sweet potatoes – introduced to India by the Portuguese – and Red Leicester cheese from the dairies of my British home county. As with oceans, the boundaries where different cuisines meet often seem to taste the most colourful.

Serves 2

For the hasselbacks
4 medium sweet potatoes
1 tablespoon ghee, melted, plus 2 tablespoons
2 teaspoons amchoor
2 tablespoons Sambhar Masala (see page 25)
1 tablespoon finely grated grapefruit zest, plus
  2 tablespoons grapefruit juice
1 green chilli, finely chopped
3 garlic cloves, finely grated
2 teaspoons finely grated fresh ginger
1½ teaspoons fine sea salt
1 tablespoon finely chopped coriander leaves
4 tablespoons grated vintage Red Leicester cheese
20g hazelnuts, crushed
1 teaspoon coriander seeds, crushed
1 teaspoon coarsely ground black pepper

For the sauce
100g Greek yogurt
1 garlic clove, very finely chopped or finely grated
2 teaspoons anardana powder
3 tablespoons grapefruit juice
¾ teaspoon sea salt flakes

· For the hasselbacks, preheat the oven to 180°C fan.
· Wash and scrub the sweet potatoes, then, using a sharp knife, cut parallel slits three-quarters of the way down, each 2mm apart; an easy hack is to place the sweet potato securely in between 2 chopsticks and slice down until you hit the sticks.
· Place the sweet potatoes on a baking sheet lined with foil (or their juices can spoil the baking sheet). Brush liberally with 1 tablespoon of melted ghee, getting it in between the cuts. Sprinkle with amchoor, cover in foil and bake in the oven for 45–50 minutes.
· Meanwhile, mix together the sambhar masala, 2 tablespoons melted ghee, grapefruit zest and juice, green chilli, garlic, ginger and salt into a thick paste.
· Remove the sweet potatoes from the oven, take off the foil and fan the potatoes out a little: careful, they will be hot! Brush with the spice paste – getting it deep into the slits – then return to the oven without the foil. Bake for 20–25 minutes until cooked through and golden on top. Meanwhile, mix together everything for the sauce in a small bowl.
· For the topping, mix together the coriander leaves, grated cheese, hazelnuts, coriander seeds and pepper. Sprinkle generously over the cooked sweet potatoes, then finish under a hot grill for 2–3 minutes until the cheese has melted. Serve the hasselbacks with the yogurt sauce.

Tip Delicious paired with Mango-Worcestershire Kachumber on the side (see page 176).

The term desi loosely translates as 'from the home or nation'. As there is no singular home for all South Asians, when used as a catch-all term it can be problematic and reductive, erasing the nuances in culture and traditions for people across the subcontinent. The term has also been historically weaponised by the upper classes to demonise anything considered 'backwardly traditional' when compared to their own privileged takes on modernity.

The reclaiming of the word by South Asians today actively untangles all this, empowering the diaspora by outwardly celebrating our differences and the uniqueness of what 'from home' means to each of us. 'Desi' is evolving into a term of collective solidarity, used by those taking up space with their own stories on their own terms: a global community united by our multiplicity, not our sameness.

Mine is a family of Punjabi whisky drinkers with a taste for the sour-sweet, spiced and smoked. This recipe is an expression of my own 'desi-ness' in kofta form. Use it as inspiration to cook up your own.

Serves 2–3

For the meatballs
500g minced pork
4 tablespoons smoky whisky, plus more to serve
1 tablespoon finely grated fresh ginger
6 garlic cloves, very finely chopped or finely grated
10g coriander leaves, chopped
1 tablespoon Garam Masala (see page 23)
2 large shallots, grated
1 teaspoon chilli flakes
1½ teaspoons coarsely ground black pepper
1½ teaspoons smoked salt
2 tablespoons coarse semolina
1 tablespoon ghee
sliced mango, to serve (optional)

For the tomatoes
1 tablespoon finely grated lime zest, plus 4 tablespoons lime juice, plus more to serve
4 tablespoons granulated sugar
2 tablespoons runny honey
3 tablespoons sweet mango chutney
325g baby plum or cherry tomatoes
½ teaspoon smoked salt
2 tablespoons chopped coriander leaves
2 tablespoons chopped mint leaves
2 tablespoons toasted flaked almonds (see page 40)

· To make the meatballs, mix all the ingredients except the ghee together in a bowl using your hands, until everything is evenly combined. Press firmly into 8 large meatballs, compacting each tightly until it is just a little smaller than a tennis ball. Cover and leave in the fridge for 1 hour.
· Next, heat the ghee in a deep ovenproof pan and gently fry the meatballs 2 at a time, browning their outsides. Remove from the pan and set aside on a baking tray or plate.
· Preheat the oven to 180°C fan.
· Using the same pan, heat the lime zest and juice, sugar, honey and mango chutney for 3–4 minutes, whisking until it turns frothy and caramel-like. Add the whole tomatoes and smoked salt, mix well, then cook for 2 minutes until the tomatoes begin to soften. Mix through the chopped coriander and mint, then place the browned meatballs back in the pan, spooning the tomatoes over the top.
· Bake for 45–50 minutes until the tomatoes turn intensely sticky and the meatballs are cooked through and burnished on top. Check in on them regularly to ensure the juices don't dry out, adding a splash of water if needed.
· Finish with toasted flaked almonds, a squeeze of lime juice and an extra drizzle of smoky whisky, with sliced mango on the side, if you like.

Tip Serve with rice, pasta, couscous or good bread. Any starchy carb in fact.

Punjabi fishcakes
with amchoor smacked cucumber

Amchoor is the one ingredient I don't add to my shopping list for my daily jaunts to Taj Stores on Brick Lane. There's no point; I will always be running low. This citrussy, tart seasoning is made from raw unripe mangos, sundried, then finely ground to a sour powder. I use it more than lemon and lime to add that vital acidic halo of brightness to my cooking; it's essentially the Valencia filter of flavour that enhances all it touches.

Smacked cucumbers get their name from the Chinese technique of whacking cucumbers with the flat of a cleaver to break their flesh before soaking them in a piquant pickled dressing. My hybrid remix adds amchoor for a hit of Indian mango sourness, which is fantastic with these Punjabi-spiced fishcakes. Although both the masala-fied fishcakes and smacked cucumbers are equally delicious on their own.

Makes 5 large fishcakes

For the fishcakes

400g mix of poached flaky fish, such as salmon, smoked
   haddock, cod or mackerel
2 shallots, very finely chopped
4 garlic cloves, very finely chopped, or finely grated
2 teaspoons finely grated fresh ginger
1 green chilli, finely chopped
2 tablespoons lemon juice
2 tablespoons Tandoori Masala (see page 25)
15 saffron strands, mixed in a bowl with 2 tablespoons
   hot water
500g potatoes, boiled and mashed
4 tablespoons rice flour, plus more if needed
1¼ teaspoons fine sea salt
2 teaspoons coarsely ground black pepper
1 tablespoon finely grated lemon zest
1 teaspoon fennel seeds, crushed
1 teaspoon anardana powder, plus more to serve
2 tablespoons finely chopped coriander leaves
3 tablespoons white sesame seeds
vegetable oil, for cooking

For the cucumber

1 cucumber
4 garlic cloves, very finely chopped or finely grated
2 tablespoons ponzu, or light soy sauce
2 tablespoons apple cider vinegar
2 teaspoons finely grated fresh ginger
2 tablespoons amchoor
1 teaspoon finely chopped red chilli
1 teaspoon nigella seeds
1 teaspoon toasted sesame oil
2 tablespoons vegetable oil
1 tablespoon caster sugar
2 tablespoons lemon juice

· For the fishcakes, flake the poached fish into a large bowl, keeping some in bigger chunks to bite into. Next add the shallots, garlic, ginger, green chilli, lemon juice, tandoori masala and saffron strands with their water. Mix well and leave for 10 minutes.

· Add the mashed potato, rice flour, salt, pepper, lemon zest, fennel seeds, anardana and coriander to the bowl, then use your hands to combine the mixture together. If it's very sticky, add a little more rice flour. Tightly compact into 5 large cricket ball-sized pieces, then shape each into a tall, round fishcake.

· Roll the outer rim of each fishcake in sesame seeds, then leave in the fridge for 30 minutes.

· When they're firm, brush with vegetable oil and cook under a hot grill for 14–16 minutes, flipping halfway through so they are nicely browned on both sides. (Or shallow-fry in vegetable oil for 4–5 minutes until warmed through with a golden crust.)

· Meanwhile, for the amchoor-smacked cucumber, whack the cucumber with a rolling pin, then ribbon it into long strands using a vegetable peeler, leaving out the very watery seeds in the middle. Whisk together all the remaining ingredients, then toss that dressing through the cucumber ribbons and let it all mingle for 10 minutes.

· Pile the tangy smacked cucumber high on top of the hot fishcakes, then sprinkle with anardana powder to serve.

Ripe fig, burnt onion & guava with cumin & chikki

Those sizzling red-hot plates on which appetisers are served in curry houses around the world – that brand your wrists if you get too close – are, to my mind, the greatest table invention since the Lazy Susan. I think of them as thrones for ghee-fried onions that communicate taste through sound: that smoking-sizzle loudly announces that you're in for a very delicious time before the food even reaches the table. They embedded my taste for charred onions, especially when taken a smidge further into intentionally just-burnt territory, where the flavours that onions impart suddenly multiply exponentially.

This salad pairs just-burnt onions with ripe figs, pear-like guava and a zingy cumin dressing. Scorch the onions as far as your palate has a taste for. The more caramelised the better; brown food really does taste best.

Serves 2

For the dressing
75ml olive oil, plus 2 tablespoons
1 teaspoon ground cumin
1 teaspoon sumac
2 teaspoons cumin seeds
1 garlic clove, very finely chopped
1 teaspoon finely grated lemon zest, plus 2 tablespoons
   lemon juice
1 teaspoon fine sea salt
½ teaspoon Worcestershire sauce
1½ teaspoons dark brown sugar

For the salad
2 onions
3 fresh ripe figs, some halved, some sliced
3 ripe guava, pink or green, sliced into wedges
1 medium mooli, thinly shaved with a vegetable peeler
5 red radishes, thinly shaved with a vegetable peeler
salad greens and mustard cress
Chikki (see page 243)

· For the cumin dressing, gently heat the 75ml olive oil in a pan, then add the ground cumin and sumac, cooking for 1 minute. Increase the temperature slightly, then add the cumin seeds and sizzle for 1 minute until they just start to brown, but not burn. Remove from the heat and pour into a jug to cool. Add the garlic, lemon zest and juice, salt, Worcestershire sauce and sugar. Whisk well and set aside.
· Slice the onions into 1cm-thick discs.
· Bring the 2 tablespoons of olive oil to a high heat in a frying pan and cook the onion discs for 3–4 minutes on each side, until they have softened and nicely blackened.
· Plate up the ripe figs, wedges of guava, shaved mooli and radishes on salad greens along with the charred onions. Drizzle over the cumin dressing and finish with broken shards of crunchy chikki.

Minted baharat tomatoes
with fennel, feta & wasabi pitta chips

On a scale of border-free flavour combinations, this salad is up at the top end of the spectrum: an intermingling of Middle Eastern baharat and pitta bread; Mediterranean tomatoes, pine nuts and fennel; Greek feta; Japanese wasabi and nori... and a good pinch of Indian amchoor! Each component brings something unique that complements and contrasts with the others, and they sing when eaten as one.

In the 1990s this would have been called 'fusion food', a term largely associated with multicultural pick-and-mix box-ticking by restaurant chefs looking to profit from the lure of the 'ethnic exotic'. However, some approached 'fusion' differently, including pioneers such as Peter Gordon, who were more thoughtful, developing a deep understanding of the cultural context and complexity of each ingredient. In his book *Fusion*, Gordon proclaimed that 'any ingredient, from any region of the world, has the potential to be cooked and eaten with any other ingredient from any other part of the world – so long as the result is lip-smackingly delicious... who is to say that we must never experiment with so-called classical dishes?' Third-culture cooks today embrace the essence of this philosophy, although for us, ingredient intermingling is in part an act of culinary self-expression. By decontextualising global ingredients and then mixing them together, our aim is to assert our ethnicity, presenting it back to the world in a new light that reflects the realities of our lives today. You call it 'fusion' if you like, but we just call it really fucking delicious.

Serves 2

For the pitta chips
2 teaspoons wasabi paste
1 teaspoon nori seaweed powder
2 teaspoons runny honey
¾ teaspoon fine sea salt
1 teaspoon olive oil
2 pitta breads

For the tomatoes
5 tablespoons olive oil
2 tablespoons Minted Baharat (see page 27)
1½ teaspoons amchoor
2 garlic cloves, very finely chopped
1 teaspoon fine sea salt
1 teaspoon caster sugar
1 teaspoon finely grated lemon zest, plus 3 tablespoons lemon juice, plus more to serve
250g cherry tomatoes on the vine

For the salad
1 fennel bulb, shaved
80g salad leaves, such as pea shoots, spinach or rocket
leaves from a 25g bunch of mint, finely chopped
100g feta cheese
1 tablespoon shelled unsalted pine nuts, toasted (see page 40)

· To make the wasabi pitta chips, preheat the oven to 175°C fan.
· Make a paste by whisking together the wasabi, seaweed powder, honey, salt and olive oil. Split the pitta breads horizontally through the middle so they are 1 layer thick, not 2, then brush with a thick coating of the wasabi mixture. Bake for 5–7 minutes until they are really crisp, then remove from the oven and let them cool while you prepare the tomatoes.
· To roast the tomatoes, mix together the olive oil, baharat, amchoor, garlic, salt, sugar, lemon zest and juice into a paste. Coat the tomatoes in the mixture, then place in an oven dish and roast for 10–12 minutes, basting with the spiced oil every few minutes. Cook until roasted through and blistered on top, with a pool of spiced juices in the dish.
· Serve the hot roasted tomatoes on a bed of shaved fennel, salad leaves and mint. Crumble over the feta and the pitta chips and scatter with toasted pine nuts. Dress with the spiced tomatoey oils from the oven dish and a squeeze of lemon juice to finish.

Salted cardamom peaches, burrata & saffron

One endearing quirk of my mum's fluently broken English is her constant mixing-up of senses, referring to all that is sensory by how it 'sounds'. The look of a new outfit will always 'sound good', as will the smell of a perfume, the feel of a silk scarf and the taste of a ripe mango. Growing up, we'd correct her, but today we're pretty sure she's synaesthetic so has been correct the whole time. Those things really do sound good to her. That English is not so broken.

'Dynamic contrast' is a scientific term that refers to the phenomenon of encountering multiple sensory elements within the same bite of food; something that I always keep at the forefront of my mind when I'm cooking. This culture-straddling salad combines salty-charred peaches speckled with an Indian hit of cardamom, oozy Italian burrata, the evocative flavour of saffron infused into a vinegary dressing, vibrant herbs and toasty Middle Eastern dukkah for crunch. Trust me, this is a salad that sounds very good indeed.

Serves 2

For the dressing & salad
100ml extra virgin olive oil
30 saffron strands
20ml white wine vinegar
20g mint leaves, chopped
2 burrata, or buffalo mozzarella balls
1 tablespoon Pistachio-Fenugreek Dukkah (see page 27)

For the peaches
seeds from 12 cardamom pods, crushed
1½ teaspoons fine sea salt
1 teaspoon pink peppercorns
2 ripe peaches or nectarines
extra virgin olive oil

· To make the saffron dressing, heat the 100ml olive oil in a pan over a medium heat, then add the saffron and let it infuse for 2–3 minutes. Next add the white wine vinegar and whisk together into a bright yellow dressing. Remove from the heat and let it cool a little.
· Now for the peaches. Preheat the grill to its maximum setting. Grind the cardamom seeds together with the salt and pink peppercorns into a fine powder. Slice the peaches into wedges or halves, brush with olive oil and sprinkle generously with the cardamom salt. Cook under the very hot grill for 8–10 minutes until charred and blistered on top.
· Plate up the hot peaches and fresh herbs and tear over the burrata. Cover generously with the saffron dressing, then sprinkle with dukkah to finish.
· Serve with big chunks of sourdough bread or naan to soak up the oils.

Spiced Salads & 'Quick Pans'

Urfa chilli carrots
with salted chai yogurt & dates

The amount of taste, aroma and flavour that any fruit or vegetable will exude stems from the hardship that it has endured to survive. The most delicious have undergone the most vicissitudes, or devised an ingenious arsenal of defences to procreate. This is the reason that the finest wines are from grapes that can flourish in bone-dry and stony soils; it's why the heat of a chilli is concentrated around its seeds and why the sweetest carrots are those that can organically fend off pests unaided. Flavour is the manifestation of the plant world's tough resilience.

This recipe is an ultimate fighter of flavour: the smoky-sweet urfa chilli adding tobacco-raisiny warmth, the salted chai yogurt an aromatic savoury creaminess and the chopped dates small pockets of toffee caramel. Use the best-quality carrots within your means; after everything they've battled to taste that good, they deserve a winning send-off.

Serves 2

For the carrots
6 large or 12 baby heritage carrots, green tops on
2 teaspoons urfa chilli, plus more to serve
1 teaspoon cumin seeds, crushed
1 teaspoon nigella seeds, crushed
¼ teaspoon ajwain, crushed
2 teaspoons amchoor
1 tablespoon light brown sugar
1 teaspoon fine sea salt
1 teaspoon coarsely ground black pepper
2 tablespoons runny honey
1 teaspoon finely grated lemon zest, plus 2 tablespoons lemon juice
2 tablespoons finely chopped fresh fenugreek leaves (optional)
8 medjool dates, pitted and chopped
4 tablespoons olive oil

For the yogurt & to serve
2 tablespoons olive oil
2 teaspoons Chai Masala (see page 26)
1 teaspoon fine sea salt
200g labneh or Greek yogurt
pomegranate seeds, to serve
finely chopped mint leaves, to serve

· Preheat the oven to 175°C fan.
· Slice large carrots lengthways from top to bottom, leaving the tops intact. If using baby carrots, leave them whole. Place on a baking sheet or oven dish.
· Mix together the spices, sugar, salt, pepper, honey, lemon zest and juice and fenugreek leaves, if using, into a thick sticky coating. Brush over the carrots liberally, then sprinkle over the dates. Drizzle everything with the oil and roast for 30–35 minutes until the carrots are cooked through and charred on the outside, shaking and basting halfway so they cook evenly.
· To make the yogurt, heat the oil in a saucepan, add the chai spice and sizzle for 30 seconds. Remove from the heat, then add the salt and mix well. Let it cool a little before stirring the mixture through the labneh or Greek yogurt.
· Serve the roasted carrots and dates warm, on a generously plated dollop of salted chai yogurt. Finish with a drizzle of urfa chilli oil from the baking tray, pomegranate seeds, mint and more urfa chilli flakes.

Maple-masala chicken Caesar with curry leaf & dhokla croutons

Growing up, certain foods I'd read about in supermarket magazines enthralled me. The pages of those quotidian epics – filled with brands we'd never eaten, 'three-for-two' offers alien to our household and Sunday roast hacks that were of little help to our Indian table – were as thrilling to me as the treasures within the Argos catalogue. What were mundane basics in the pantries of white people were so 'other' to our cumin-scented Punjabi cupboards that they took on a fantastical mysticism.

Close to the top of that list were croutons. From what I could fathom, they were the pinnacle of British sophistication, in part due to not being British at all, but French. With proximity to whiteness being my key to progress in life as a brown boy, I became fixated, slipping them into our shopping trolley concealed under nets of red onions, praying they'd make it to the other side of the till. They rarely did, the pointed *Goodness Gracious Me* catchphrase 'we can make it at home' being the inevitable retort.

Stoic as ever to fulfil my whims for Britishness with Indianness, my mum took to frying cubes of roti dough in ghee, though they little resembled the toasty crusts in those magazines. And so her improvisation pivoted to the Gujarati chickpea-lentil cake dhokla, cut into gigantic cubes, drizzled in oil, then baked to a crusty finish. They may not have tasted the same, but they certainly looked the part.

Many years later, in my early thirties, I went to Zuni Café in San Francisco for the first time and was captivated by Judy Rodgers's infamous Caesar Salad, crowned with gargantuan garlic croutons of wood-fired sourdough on epic stalks of creamy-yet-piquant Romaine. Its taste fixed to my memory immediately, and yet, in that moment, I also found myself hankering for the dhokla croutons of my childhood. The Indian approximation was what I found myself craving, even while tasting the pinnacle of the real thing that I'd revered for so long. If you don't have dhokla for this recipe, use torn sourdough fried in ghee with curry leaves and mustard seeds. It makes a good substitute.

Serves 2–3

For the dressing
200ml olive oil
25–30 fresh curry leaves
1 teaspoon coriander seeds, crushed
¼ teaspoon ajwain, crushed
¼ teaspoon ground turmeric
2 garlic cloves, very finely chopped
6 anchovies in oil, very finely chopped
2 egg yolks
2 teaspoons lemon juice
2 teaspoons white wine vinegar
1 teaspoon coarsely ground black pepper
40g Parmesan cheese, half finely grated, half shaved with
    a vegetable peeler

For the salad
2 large boneless, skinless chicken breasts
4 tablespoons maple syrup
1 tablespoon amchoor
1 tablespoon Garam Masala (see page 23)
4 pieces of dhokla (see page 53), or sourdough bread, cut
    into large squares or croutons
2 heads of Romaine lettuce, leaves separated
2 tablespoons bacon bits, fried until crisp, then drained on
    kitchen paper

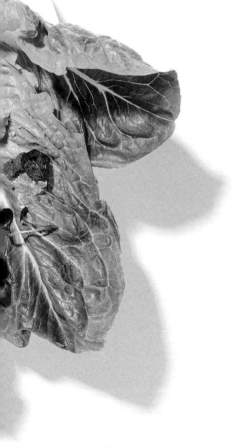

· To make the dressing, heat the olive oil in a saucepan over a medium heat, then add the curry leaves, coriander seeds, ajwain and turmeric. Sizzle the spices for 45 seconds, then remove from the heat. Carefully drain everything into a jug through a sieve, reserving the fried curry leaves and whole spices. Cool the infused oil to room temperature.
· In a separate bowl, mash together the garlic and anchovies to a paste. Next add the egg yolks and whisk well, before slowly mixing in the lemon juice, vinegar and pepper. Drop by drop, add 100ml of the cooled infused oil, whisking continuously so the dressing emulsifies and comes together as one. Add the grated Parmesan, then another 75ml of the infused oil, whisking continuously until you have a thick creamy dressing.
· Flatten the chicken breasts using a meat tenderiser or rolling pin to an even thickness.
· Mix 20ml more of the infused oil with the maple syrup, amchoor and garam masala. Coat the chicken breasts in the maple marinade, cover and leave for 45–60 minutes.
· Cook the chicken breasts in a hot griddle pan for 5–6 minutes until cooked through and charred on the outside, brushing with the maple masala each time you flip it.
· Preheat the oven to 180°C fan. Brush the dhokla or sourdough croutons with the remaining infused oil and roast them on a baking sheet for 10–15 minutes until crunchy.
· Either toss the Romaine lettuce leaves through the dressing, or serve the dressing in a small bowl on the side. Plate up with the maple-masala charred chicken, baked croutons, bacon bits and a sprinkle of the fried curry leaves, coriander and ajwain seeds. Finish with generous shavings of Parmesan.

Tip Fresh dhokla is sold in all Indian sweet shops, and you can buy frozen or instant packet versions in Indian supermarkets.

Gunpowder kale with coconut beets, capers & crunchy chickpeas

The vegetable patch in our Leicester back garden began life 25 years ago as a horticultural recreation of Mum's village in Punjab, an ever-blooming Indian Eden of fenugreek, curry leaves, chickpeas, bitter gourds, mint, coriander, aubergines, saag, ginger, bay leaves, turmeric, peas, tulsi (holy basil) and okra. As she's seen more of the world over the years, that plot has voyaged with her. The soil has never moved, but that pocket of Punjab in Leicester is today intermingled with global saplings of redcurrants, olives, fennel bulbs, courgettes, sage, strawberries, rocket, lemon verbena, aloe vera, pak choi, basil, purple kale, beetroot, avocados, cherries, grapes, walnuts and a giant Bramley apple tree whose shadows guard all that grows beneath. This recipe is the nurturing taste of that garden, rooted to one small patch of earth, that grows new shoots with each journey my mother takes.

Serves 2

For the beets
4 beetroots, total weight 600–700g
1½ tablespoons coconut oil
30 fresh curry leaves
1 teaspoon coriander seeds, crushed
seeds from 10 green cardamom pods, crushed
1 tablespoon capers, finely chopped
2 tablespoons desiccated coconut
1 teaspoon finely grated fresh ginger
2 tablespoons lemon juice
1 teaspoon fine sea salt
1 teaspoon finely grated lemon zest

For the salad
2 tablespoons Gunpowder Masala (see page 24)
2 tablespoons olive oil, plus more to serve
2 teaspoons Worcestershire sauce
½ teaspoon cayenne pepper
1 tablespoon light brown sugar
175g kale, coarse stalks removed, chopped
roasted chickpeas, crushed, to serve
coconut chips, toasted, to serve
coriander leaves, to serve

· Using a mandolin or knife, cut the beetroots into discs 5mm thick.
· Heat the coconut oil in a frying pan, then add the curry leaves and sizzle for 30–45 seconds to infuse the oil. Carefully spoon the crispy leaves out and set aside. Add the coriander and cardamom seeds to the oil, sizzling for 1 minute, before adding the beetroot discs. Cook for 5–6 minutes, until the discs have stopped steaming and have started to char on the outside. Finally add the capers, desiccated coconut, ginger, lemon juice and salt, mixing well to coat the beetroot. Cook for a final 2 minutes until tender.
· Preheat the oven to 200°C fan.
· Mix together the gunpowder masala, olive oil, Worcestershire sauce, cayenne pepper and light brown sugar in a large mixing bowl. Add the roughly chopped kale, then use your hands to massage the kale in the spice mix for 1 minute, ensuring the spicy coating covers everything. Tip into a baking tray.
· Bake in the oven for 7–8 minutes – shaking halfway through – until crisp on the outside, but not burnt.
· To serve, create a bed of the crispy kale and tumble over the hot coconut beets. Top with a good slug of olive oil and a grating of lemon zest, then finish with the fried curry leaves, crunchy roasted chickpeas and a sprinkle of coconut chips and coriander leaves.

Gingery roasted squash
with ajwain-hazelnut chimichurri

I am an archetypal Gen Y Millennial – the Spice Girls Generation – the last to experience the world both before and after the internet. To say I was a fan is an understatement and the assortment of 'Girl Power' paraphernalia collecting dust in my parents' attic includes duvet covers, *Top of the Pops* magazines, Panini stickers, cassette singles of every hit up to 'Viva Forever' and empty Spice edition Walkers Crisp packets. To this day Geri has always been my favourite, not least for being the only one with a moniker at all related to eating.

As with the Spice Girls, ginger takes the spotlight in this recipe, with a double hit of zesty fresh ginger and warming ground ginger combined into an aromatic coating for wedges of roasted squash. The ajwain-hazelnut chimichurri adds herby zestiness, a fitting backing dancer to ginger's centre stage. Don't be put off by the lengthy list of ingredients: remember 'Spice Up Your Life' was not just a song, it was a life mantra.

Serves 2

For the chimichurri
150ml extra virgin olive oil, plus 4 tablespoons
1½ teaspoons ajwain, crushed
30g shelled unsalted roasted hazelnuts (see page 40), crushed, plus more to serve
4 teaspoons dried oregano
50g flat-leaf parsley leaves, finely chopped
20g coriander leaves, finely chopped
1 medium-hot red chilli, finely chopped
3 garlic cloves, very finely chopped
2 shallots, finely chopped
1 tablespoon finely grated lemon zest, plus 3 tablespoons lemon juice, plus more to taste
4 tablespoons red wine vinegar
2 teaspoons fine sea salt, plus more to taste
1 teaspoon coarsely ground black pepper

For the squash
3 tablespoons finely grated fresh ginger
1 teaspoon ground cinnamon
1 teaspoon ground coriander
1 tablespoon amchoor
1 teaspoon finely grated lemon zest, plus 2 tablespoons lemon juice
1 teaspoon Aleppo pepper (pul biber)
1 teaspoon sweet paprika
1 tablespoon ground ginger
2 teaspoons fine sea salt
1 teaspoon coarsely ground black pepper
3 tablespoons olive oil
800g squash, chopped into wedges (ideally Kabocha or Sweet Dumpling variety)
salad leaves, to serve
dollop of sour cream
Muthiya (see page 33), or sev, crushed, to serve

· To make the chimichurri: heat the 4 tablespoons of extra virgin olive oil in a frying pan, then add the ajwain, crushed hazelnuts and dried oregano, sizzling for 1–2 minutes. Scrape into a large mixing bowl, then add the finely chopped parsley, coriander, red chilli, garlic, shallots and lemon zest. Mix together well.
· Whisk the lemon juice, red wine vinegar, the 150ml olive oil, salt and pepper together in a small jug. Gently drizzle the wet ingredients into the mixing bowl, whisking into a slick green sauce. Add extra salt and lemon juice to suit your taste.
· To roast the squash, mix the grated ginger, ground cinnamon and coriander, amchoor, lemon zest and juice, Aleppo pepper, paprika, ground ginger, salt, pepper and olive oil together, to form a thick paste. Coat the squash wedges with the spice paste and leave the flavours to infuse for 1 hour.
· Preheat the oven to 180°C fan. Roast the coated squash on a baking sheet for 30–35 minutes, until tender in the middle and charred on the outside.
· Serve the roasted squash on a bed of green salad leaves, drizzle with the chimichurri and a dollop of sour cream, then scatter with crushed hazelnuts and crushed-up muthiya or sev to finish.

Aloo chaat wedge salad with pink peppercorn ranch

There is something camply retro about a wedge salad that always draws me to it, especially those dolloped with creamy-pink prawn cocktail sauce, dehydrated bacon bits and scissor-snipped chives. They have an ersatz sophistication very much in the 'Fanny Cradock meets breakfast buffet' school of culinary arts, sharing the same splendidly kitsch garnishing principles as Indian street snacks.

This chaat wedge salad recipe marries the two, giving you creative licence to double up on overstated embellishment with gloriously garish toppings. I'm not sure if Fanny Cradock ever wore a sari on Christmas day, but that's the visual moodboard to aim for here.

Serves 2–3

For the ranch
150ml sour cream
1½ tablespoons pink peppercorns, crushed
1 tablespoon onion powder
2 garlic cloves, very finely chopped
1 teaspoon paprika
4 tablespoons very finely chopped mixed dill,
   chives and parsley leaves
2 teaspoons English mustard
3 tablespoons lemon juice, plus more if needed
2 teaspoons amchoor
1 teaspoon fine sea salt

For the potatoes
2 tablespoons Chaat Masala (see page 24)
1 teaspoon dried mint
1 teaspoon ground cumin
1 tablespoon amchoor
1 teaspoon finely grated lemon zest
1 tablespoon caster sugar
1 teaspoon fine sea salt
4 tablespoons vegetable oil
1 large potato, cut into 1cm cubes

To serve
1 Iceberg lettuce
chaat toppings, such as finely chopped cucumber and red
   onion, pomegranate seeds, sev, Tamarind, Date & Mint
   Sauce and Minty Yogurt (see pages 203 and 64)
bacon bits, fried until crisp, then drained on kitchen paper,
   to serve

· To make the ranch dressing, whisk all the ingredients together in a bowl. Cover and refrigerate for at least 1 hour to let the flavours mingle, adding a little extra lemon juice if it becomes very thick. You want it to be dense but still pourable.
· To make the potatoes, whisk together the chaat masala, dried mint, ground cumin, amchoor, lemon zest, sugar, salt and vegetable oil to a paste. Add the cubed potato, mix well to coat and leave to infuse for 15 minutes. Preheat the oven to 175°C fan.
· Roast the spiced potatoes on a baking sheet for 20 minutes, turning regularly and coating with the sticky spices each time you do. They will brown up quickly because of the sugar, just watch that they don't burn!
· Cut the Iceberg into thick quarter wedges and drizzle with pink peppercorn ranch dressing.
· Finish by loading up with the crispy spiced potatoes, your chaat toppings and chutneys of choice and bacon bits.

Spiced Salads & 'Quick Pans'

Rose & ancho chilli baked ricotta
with persimmon & grapefruit

Like all fruits, chillies take on entirely new dimensions when dried, concentrating their complexity and depth of flavours. When rehydrated, their intensity unfurls like a prism of coloured oils marbling in water, swirling into unexpected shapes that can taste extraordinary. The combination of dried ancho chilli and rose petals in a spice paste here has this spiralling effect, a heady mix of spiced fruity liquorice, smoky chocolate and floral berries. The delicious plainness of ricotta is the canvas for this recipe, but you can also use the paste on halloumi, Camembert, feta or paneer.

Serves 2

For the ancho-rose paste
1 large dried ancho chilli
1 teaspoon cumin seeds
1 teaspoon fennel seeds
1 tablespoon dried rose petals, crushed, plus more to serve
½ teaspoon ground turmeric
1 teaspoon fine sea salt
2 garlic cloves, very finely chopped
1 teaspoon sweet paprika
1 tablespoon light brown sugar
1 teaspoon finely grated lemon zest, plus 1 tablespoon lemon juice
1 tablespoon white wine vinegar
2 tablespoons vegetable oil

For the ricotta & salad
500g fresh ricotta cheese
2 eggs, lightly beaten
1½ teaspoons finely grated lemon zest
¼ teaspoon ajwain, finely crushed
½ teaspoon coarsely ground black pepper
1 lettuce
1 ripe persimmon, thinly sliced
1 pink grapefruit, thinly sliced
olive oil, to drizzle
punnet of mixed cress, to serve

· To make the paste, cut open the dried ancho chilli, removing any fibrous veins in the middle. Dry-roast in a pan for 1–2 minutes until it blisters and releases its fruity aromas, then soak in a small bowl of boiling water for 15 minutes.
· Meanwhile, dry pan-roast the cumin and fennel seeds for 1–2 minutes, then put them in a grinder, along with the dried rose petals, turmeric and salt. Whizz to a fine powder. Next add the drained chilli, garlic, sweet paprika, sugar, lemon zest and juice, white wine vinegar and vegetable oil to the grinder, blitzing into a smooth burgundy-red paste.
· Preheat the oven to 180°C fan. Line a ramekin or 8cm round dish with baking parchment.
· Place the ricotta in a muslin cloth or cheesecloth, gather into a ball and squeeze well to remove as much liquid as you can. Let it hang for 5 minutes in the sink (put it in a sieve over a bowl, or tie the cloth to a tap), then squeeze for a final time.
· Mix the drained ricotta, eggs, lemon zest, ajwain and pepper together in a bowl, stirring vigorously until everything is smoothly combined. Spoon a layer of ricotta 1.5cm thick into the prepared ramekin, pressing down with the back of a spoon. Next spoon on a thin layer of the ancho-rose paste, then spoon over another layer of ricotta, pressing down again. Finish with a final 5mm-thick layer of the paste.
· Bake for 25 minutes until the paste is burnished and cracks appear in the top.
· Turn out of the ramekin and serve warm on a bed of lettuce, slices of ripe persimmon and pink grapefruit and a good drizzle of olive oil. Garnish with more dried rose petals and cress.

Tip The ancho paste is also delicious with lamb, salmon and chicken, or swirled into yogurt for an aromatic side dish to eat with parathas.

Turmeric & black pepper larb cups with lime leaf

When haldo dhoodh started to pop up under its newly gentrified guise of 'golden turmeric milk', many of us Indian folk were baffled. The sickness remedy of our childhoods had morphed into a voluptuous hot milkshake with almond milk, honey and cinnamon, and was now the must-have accessory on Abbot Kinney Boulevard, Shoreditch High Street and Wythe Avenue. Our ancestors' mystical wisdom was in, though what had been left out was the one ingredient that, we were taught, unlocked turmeric's mystical superpowers: black pepper. This Indian-accented remix on vibrant Thai larb is plentiful in both earthy fresh turmeric and fiery black peppercorns. Combined with fresh lime leaves, amchoor, soy and fish sauces, it's quite magical.

I like to garnish the dish with very, very paper-thin slivers of fresh turmeric root, as in the photo here, that have a potent earthy kick if bitten into. If you are doing the same, take note: these are not at all delicious if sliced more thickly.

Serves 2–3

For the larb
2 tablespoons whole black peppercorns
8 fresh lime leaves
seeds from 8 green cardamom pods
1 teaspoon coriander seeds
1 teaspoon fine sea salt
2 teaspoons finely grated fresh turmeric
2 teaspoons amchoor
2 teaspoons light soy sauce
¾ teaspoon fish sauce
2 tablespoons rice vinegar
1 onion, finely chopped
2 tablespoons vegetable oil
3 garlic cloves, very finely chopped
½ green chilli, very finely chopped
500g minced chicken thighs, or minced pork
2 tablespoons finely chopped coriander leaves
75g shelled salted peanuts, crushed, plus extra to serve

To serve
1 Gem lettuce, or heads of red or white chicory, or a
   red cabbage, leaves separated
red onion slivers
coarsely ground black pepper
lime wedges

· Using a grinder, blitz the black peppercorns, lime leaves, cardamom seeds, coriander seeds and salt to a fine rubbly powder. Spoon the powdered spices into a jug along with the grated turmeric, amchoor, soy sauce, fish sauce, rice vinegar and 2 tablespoons of water. Whisk well and set aside.
· In a large frying pan, fry the onion in the vegetable oil for 5–6 minutes over a medium heat until it caramelises and turns translucent. Next add the garlic and green chilli, along with the minced meat. Cook for 5–6 minutes until the meat starts to brown.
· Add the spice paste to the pan, cooking for another 2–3 minutes until the meat is fully cooked through and coated in the tangy spices. Finally mix in the chopped coriander and peanuts.
· Spoon the larb into lettuce or cabbage leaf cups, top with red onion, a sprinkle of peanuts and black pepper, spritzing with lime juice to finish.

Spiced Salads & 'Quick Pans'

CHAPTER 4

FEASTING DISHES, CURRIES & THALI BOWLS

There are more than 1.3 billion people in India, which means there are more than 1.3 billion different ways of being Indian in the motherland alone, and more than 1.3 billion different ways of making Indian food, every one of them authentically Indian. But there are also ways of being Indian in Malaysia, Trinidad, Kenya, Mauritius, Guyana, South Africa, Italy and Dubai; as well as metropolis-nuanced ways of being Indian in Sydney, Toronto, Los Angeles, Bangkok, New York, Tokyo, Paris, London and Leicester. Indians are a diaspora with global tastes: rooted to their heritage, but branching out across all borders.

And of course, 1.3 billion is also the number of dishes you're likely to be served at the table should you ever come for dinner at my parents' house, all together at the same time, magically tessellated to fit on to the dinner table like a giant culinary game of Tetris. I may be exaggerating very slightly, but the fact is that, in a Punjabi household, when it comes to the main event of any meal, dishes are only ever served in multiples. This happens regardless of whether you're having an Indian-style banquet or what we refer to as 'English Dinner'; one main course will always be paired with another. At the very least.

Thalis, which are served all over India, are the more elegant way of doing this and have in themselves as much regional variation as there are different facets to Indianness. In essence, thalis are individual metal plates (or large banana leaves), filled to the perimeter with small bowls (or generous dollops) of different sabjis, dals, grilled fish, curries, tandoori meats, raitas, sambhars, kachumbers, saags, spiced grains, breads, rice dishes, chutneys and – of course – pickles. This polychromatic style of eating can feel a little overwhelming, but combining the different rhythms and flavour chords of dishes together on one thali, or indeed at a single dinner table, is to me one of the most wonderful features of my culinary culture.

These third-culture recipes for feasting dishes, curries and thali bowls work as stand-alone centrepieces for a meal, but have also been designed to pair wonderfully with any of the others, if it's more of a banquet you're going for. After all, one can be a bit lonesome, two is great company, but from three-to-1.3 billion is a real party!

Curry leaf, lemongrass & Aleppo pepper roast chicken

The 'edge effect' in nature refers to a phenomenon that occurs where the boundaries of two different habitats meet. Corridors of light that are created in between worlds increase the diversity of plant and animal life. It's in this middle ground that ecosystems are at their most abundant. Third-culture cooking is very much the culinary equivalent.

This chicken is firstly slathered in a North Indian-Chinese-accented lemon brine, then smothered in a masala paste that mixes South Indian-Malaysian curry leaves with Thai-Vietnamese lemongrass and Turkish-Syrian Aleppo pepper. The result shines a light on the space in between cultural borders, where taste is at its most vivid.

Serves 4

For the chicken & lemon brine
8 tablespoons lemon juice
1 tablespoon finely grated fresh ginger
1 tablespoon smoked salt
1 teaspoon five-spice powder
2 teaspoons amchoor
seeds from 12 green cardamom pods, crushed
1.5–1.8kg whole chicken, ideally organic

For the spice paste
4 tablespoons vegetable oil
1 tablespoon coriander seeds, crushed
1 tablespoon fennel seeds, crushed
30–35 fresh curry leaves
40g (2 large stalks) lemongrass, trimmed and finely chopped
4 garlic cloves, very finely chopped
1 tablespoon Aleppo pepper (pul biber), plus more to serve
1 teaspoon finely grated fresh turmeric
1 teaspoon fine sea salt
1 teaspoon coarsely ground black pepper
1 tablespoon light brown sugar
2 tablespoons finely grated lemon zest
2 whole lemons, sliced

To serve
Hot Curry-Crunch Roasties (see page 168)
charred lemon wedges or slices
Pink Pickled Onions with Lychee (see page 209)
chutneys and pickles (see pages 200–213)

· To brine the chicken, whisk together the lemon juice, ginger, smoked salt, five-spice powder, amchoor and cardamom in a large bowl until the salt has dissolved. Take out 2 tablespoons of the brine mix and set aside. Slash the chicken with a sharp knife at the breasts, legs and thighs. Rub over the lemon brine, getting it deep into the cuts, crevices and under the skin. Cover and leave for 60 minutes in the bowl, turning and basting halfway through.
· Remove the chicken from the brine, shake off the excess and place the bird upside-down on a wire rack placed over a roasting tin to dry out, while you make the spice paste. Reserve the brine.
· Heat the oil in a frying pan over a medium heat, then add the coriander and fennel seeds, sizzling for 1 minute. Next add the curry leaves, cooking for another 1 minute until they've infused the oil and crisped up. Transfer the spices, curry leaves and oil to a grinder, along with the lemongrass, garlic, Aleppo pepper, turmeric, salt, pepper, sugar and lemon zest, plus the 2 tablespoons of reserved lemon brine. Grind to a thick smooth paste.
· Smother the dried chicken with the spice paste, getting it deep into the flesh and under the skin. Cover and leave to marinate in the fridge for 2–3 hours.
· Preheat the oven to 180°C fan. Take the marinated chicken out of the fridge and let it come to room temperature. Stuff the cavity of the chicken with the lemon slices, then cover with foil and roast in the oven for 50–60 minutes.
· Remove from the oven and baste with the oily spice paste in the bottom of the pan. Increase the oven temperature to 200°C fan and cook for a final 15–20 minutes without the foil, until the chicken is cooked through and burnished on top. Remove from the oven, cover in foil again and rest for 15 minutes, then sprinkle with Aleppo pepper and serve with the roasties, charred lemon, pickled onions, chutneys and pickles.

Lamb shank biryani with black masala
& figs

The pomp and ceremony that a lovingly made biryani warrants is equal to that of a Royal wedding, in my opinion. It calls for the full English: BBC televised horse and carriage through Trafalgar Square, frou-frou taffeta from The Emmanuels, Pimm's and lemonade for breakfast, Elton John in a top hat and vintage Harrods silver from the vaults. A biryani makes a meal an occasion by its sheer presence, transforming an otherwise unremarkable table into a momentous feast.

This slow-cooked take on biryani is majestically complex, layered with lamb shanks on the bone for their marrowed richness, ripe figs for vanilla-honeyed sweetness, saffron rice for its regal fragrance and heady Maharashtrian black masala for smoked cardamom spice. Flamboyant theatrics, when revealing the jewels hidden beneath the foil-covered dish, are greatly encouraged here.

Serves 4

For the rice
500g basmati rice
1 tablespoon ghee
2 teaspoons fennel seeds
40 saffron strands
1 teaspoon fine sea salt

For the lamb
1.5kg (4–5 large) lamb shanks
fine sea salt
2 tablespoons ghee, plus 1 tablespoon
10 green cardamom pods, split
3 green chillies, split
2 large onions, sliced into rings
8 garlic cloves, very finely chopped
2 tablespoons finely grated fresh ginger
8 tablespoons (yes 8!) Black Masala (see page 23), plus more to serve
6 tablespoons apple cider vinegar
6 tablespoons tomato purée
8 ripe figs, halved, plus more to serve
100g Greek yogurt
2 tablespoons dark brown sugar
1 tablespoon smoked salt
2 teaspoons coarsely ground black pepper
500ml lamb stock, or beef stock, plus more if needed
mint leaves, chopped, to serve
pomegranate seeds, to serve
edible unsprayed rose petals (optional), to serve

· Wash the rice in a sieve under a cold running tap until the water runs clear, then leave in a large bowl of cold water for 2–3 hours.
· Meanwhile, use a sharp knife to slash the lamb shanks 3–4 times in their most fleshy parts. Season generously with salt, using ¼ teaspoon for each shank, and leave for 10 minutes. Heat 2 tablespoons of ghee in a large pan, then brown the shanks on all sides for 6–7 minutes each, turning to sear all over. Remove from the pan and set aside.
· To make the sauce, in the same pan, add the 1 tablespoon of ghee along with the cardamom pods and green chillies, sizzling for 2 minutes. Next add the onions and cook gently for 10–12 minutes until soft, then add the garlic and ginger. In a separate jug, mix all 8 tablespoons of the black masala with 75ml cold water, the cider vinegar and tomato purée to make a paste. Pour over the onions and cook over a medium heat for 2 minutes.
· Return the browned lamb shanks to the pot and add the figs. Mix well so the shanks are well coated in the spiced liquid.
· Finally add the yogurt, sugar, salt and pepper, mixing well, before pouring in the stock. Bring to the boil, then reduce the heat to a medium simmer. Cover with a lid and slow-cook for 2½–3 hours until the lamb is tender and the sauce has reduced by half. Stir regularly to stop it catching on the bottom, topping up with a little more stock if needed.
· To prepare the rice, in a separate pan, heat the ghee, then add the fennel seeds and saffron, sizzling for 1 minute, before adding the drained rice. Mix well to coat the grains all over in the spiced yellow ghee. Next add enough boiling water to cover the rice plus 1cm extra, along with the salt. Bring to the boil for 4–5 minutes, then remove from the heat and let it steam, without a lid, for 5 minutes.
· Preheat the oven to 175°C fan.
· Remove the lamb shanks from their sauce, then simmer the sauce over a high heat for 2–3 minutes, reducing it to a thick but still runny gravy.
· Take a large deep ovenproof pot or casserole dish and spoon a thick layer of sauce into the base, then spoon over half the cooked rice. Carefully place the lamb on top with the bones meeting together, then spoon over the last of the sauce. Finally add the rest of the rice, encasing the lamb shanks completely.
· Cover with 4–5 layers of foil to create a sealed lid, with the tops of the bones sticking out in the middle. Bake in the oven for 45 minutes.
· Take to the table with the foil lid still on, then lift it off very carefully for that Bisto-advert 'ahhh' moment. Sprinkle with mint, pomegranate seeds, figs, a little more black masala and rose petals, if you like, then dive in, getting your serving spoon right to the very bottom of the pot as you dish the biryani out.

Hariyali-coconut fish pie

I can speak my Punjabi mother tongue, but I can't write it, and my reading is somewhere in between things that I can and can't do. The only place I have fluency is the very first line of the alphabet: *oora, aira, erre, susaa, hahaa*. It's indelibly tattooed in my mind thanks to the cartoon posters my mum plastered on our bedroom walls. I can still picture the image paired with every letter: *oot* – camel, *anar* – pomegranate, *ela* – eagle, *santra* – orange and *hari* – green.

That last letter was illustrated with a metallic plate overspilling with jade-green chillies, verdant herbs and bulbous green coconuts, the collective inspiration behind the ingredients in this pistachio-tinted fish pie. Use whatever green herbs you have available and don't hold back on the double cream; if there is a Punjabi word for diet, I've never learned it.

Serves 6

For the sauce
70g cashew nuts, toasted
1 tablespoon finely grated lemon zest, plus 4 tablespoons lemon juice
2 tablespoons finely grated fresh ginger
8 garlic cloves
4 tablespoons white wine vinegar
2 tablespoons Garam Masala (see page 23)
100g freshly grated coconut
100g mixed green herbs, such as mint, coriander, dill and parsley leaves, plus more coriander leaves to serve
2 green chillies, stalks trimmed away, plus more to serve
3 tablespoons vegetable oil
30–35 fresh curry leaves, chopped
1 tablespoon coriander seeds, crushed
2 teaspoons fennel seeds, crushed
6 small shallots, finely chopped
1 teaspoon fine sea salt
125ml double cream
1 teaspoon coconut chips (optional), to serve

For the fish and marinade
1 tablespoon finely grated lime zest, plus 8 tablespoons lime juice
seeds from 15 green cardamom pods, crushed
2 teaspoons fine sea salt
850g fish pie mix (cod, haddock, salmon, raw prawns), in big chunks

For the mash
850g potatoes, peeled and chopped
2 egg yolks
4 garlic cloves, very finely chopped or finely grated
1 teaspoon freshly grated nutmeg
2 teaspoons amchoor
35g salted butter
2 teaspoons coarsely ground black pepper

· To make the hariyali sauce, in a grinder, blitz together the toasted cashew nuts, lemon zest and juice, ginger, garlic, white wine vinegar and garam masala, adding a splash of water to form a thick paste. Empty into a bowl and mix in the grated coconut.
· Next, pulse the mixed green herbs and green chillies in a blender with 75ml water, to get a coarse paste that is not completely smooth.
· Heat the vegetable oil in a large pan, then add the curry leaves, coriander seeds and fennel seeds, sizzling for 1 minute. Add the chopped shallots and salt and cook for 7–8 minutes over a medium heat until they are golden and translucent. Next add the cashew-coconut paste to the mix and cook for 5 minutes, then add the blended herbs. Finally add the double cream, cook down for 1–2 minutes over a medium heat, then set aside.
· For the fish, whisk the lime zest and juice, cardamom and salt together in a bowl until the salt has dissolved. Add the chunky fish mix, mix well to ensure it's fully coated, then cover and set aside for 10 minutes.
· Boil the potatoes in salted water for 10–12 minutes until tender. Carefully spoon into a food processor with the egg yolks, garlic, nutmeg, amchoor, butter and pepper. Blitz to a fine purée.
· Preheat the oven to 175°C fan.
· Using a deep pie dish, first ladle in a base layer of the green sauce. Spoon over all the fish along with its citrussy marinade, then top with the rest of the green sauce. Top with the mashed potato, either using a spoon or piping it on Duchess-style if feeling fancy.
· Bake for 40–45 minutes until bubbling on the inside and crisp on top. Serve piping hot, scattered with coconut chips, if you like, with a green salad, coriander leaves, green chillies to bite into, crusty bread and cold Vinho Verde.

Fenugreek, pecan & black lime halibut with turmeric malai

Ice-cream tubs rarely contain ice cream in a diasporic Indian freezer. Instead, they're filled with frozen chopped coriander, grated ginger or minced garlic, a culinary deception that has scarred second generationers around the world for more than a century. Our minds are hard-wired to expect it, but that doesn't stop our hearts leaping with joy when a new ice-cream tub manifests in the freezer. Maybe this luxurious carton is a rogue exception to the rule, placed there by Bacchus for our ecstatic enjoyment? Maybe for once, just once, this tub really is filled with the Double Chocolate Swirl seductively pictured on its label? Or maybe it's frozen fenugreek.

Unlike ice cream, we're not programmed to enjoy the taste of bitterness, but when the innate software of your instincts is overwritten and you develop a taste for it, the flavour possibilities are limitless. This recipe combines earthy bitter fenugreek with the buttery tannins of pecan nuts and sour bite of black limes in an aromatic crust that pairs perfectly with flaky halibut. Try it once and you'll be filling ice-cream tubs with fenugreek yourself.

Serves 4

For the fish & marinade
2 teaspoons finely grated fresh ginger
3 garlic cloves, finely grated
1 teaspoon finely grated fresh turmeric
2 teaspoons powdered dried black lime, plus more to serve
1 teaspoon olive oil
550–600g halibut fillet, or other chunky white fish fillet

For the crust
50g fresh fenugreek leaves
1 tablespoon Greek yogurt
1 medium shallot, chopped
1 green chilli, stalk trimmed away
1 teaspoon fine sea salt
1 teaspoon coarsely ground black pepper
1½ teaspoons coriander seeds, crushed
40g roasted chickpeas, crushed
60g shelled unsalted toasted pecan nuts (see page 40), crushed, plus more toasted pecans to serve

For the malai
3 tablespoons olive oil
4 garlic cloves, cut into slivers
1 teaspoon cornflour
½ teaspoon fine sea salt
200ml double cream
1½ teaspoons finely grated fresh turmeric
1 teaspoon finely grated lime zest, plus 2 tablespoons lime juice

· Mix the marinade ingredients together into a thick paste. Smear over the halibut fillets, then leave for 15 minutes.
· For the crust, using a grinder, blitz together the fenugreek leaves, yogurt, shallot, chilli, salt and pepper to a coarse paste. Empty into a bowl, then mix through the crushed coriander seeds, chickpeas and pecans. Spoon a thick layer of the crust on to the marinated fish.
· Preheat the oven to 200°C fan.
· Heat the oil for the malai in a frying pan, then gently fry the garlic for 1–2 minutes until the slivers just start to brown.
· Next make a paste out of the cornflour, sea salt and 1 tablespoon of water. Add to the pan and whisk well, before adding the cream, grated turmeric and lime zest. Bring to just below boiling point, whisking continuously, until you have a creamy, thick, fragrant yellow sauce. Whisk in the lime juice.
· Bake the crusted halibut in the oven for 12–14 minutes until cooked through, then finish for a final 1 minute under a hot grill to crisp up the top crust.
· Serve alongside the turmeric malai sauce, then finish with a sprinkle of toasted pecans and black lime powder.

It was the daytime clubbing scene where the boundaries of bhangra and Asian underground were pushed, blending Punjabi folk music, classical Indian melodies and Bollywood anthems with hip hop, R'n'B, soul, dance and garage. I remember South Asian friends bunking off college on Wednesday afternoons, heels in their bags, to get to afternoon raves. Created by and for the diaspora, they served a generation of young adults, united by a need to party coupled with a need to be at home in time to make roti. I encountered offshoots of the scene much later, through the queer-desi night Club Kali and sporadic bhangra DJs that played Popstarz at the Apollo. Those 2am moments on the dance floor were rare times I could be every layer of my identity at once, illuminating with lasers what was often concealed by the code-switching of my life by daylight. Identity is like lasagne: each layer unique, but transformed when brought together as a whole.

Serves 4

For the kasundi keema
2 tablespoons ghee
2 large onions, finely chopped
1 tablespoon coriander seeds, crushed
1 tablespoon black mustard seeds
1 tablespoon cumin seeds
8 garlic cloves, very finely chopped
2 tablespoons finely grated fresh ginger
2 teaspoons chilli flakes
500g minced lamb (20 per cent fat)
2 tablespoons Garam Masala (see page 23)
2 teaspoons fine sea salt
5 tablespoons tomato purée
2 tablespoons dark brown sugar
3 tablespoons apple cider vinegar
½ x 400g can of chopped tomatoes

For the cheese paste
200g mature Cheddar cheese, grated
2 teaspoons cumin seeds, crushed
3 tablespoons coarse semolina
1 teaspoon coarsely ground black pepper
1 egg, lightly beaten

For the greens
200g cavolo nero, coarse stalks removed
1 tablespoon English mustard
4 garlic cloves, very finely chopped or grated
4 tablespoons lemon juice

For the lasagne rolls & tarkha
10–12 lasagne sheets
500g jar of tomato pasta sauce
2 tablespoons vegetable oil
30–35 fresh curry leaves
1½ tablespoons black mustard seeds
1 teaspoon chilli flakes

· To make the keema, heat the ghee in a large pan, add the onions and cook for 7–8 minutes until golden.
· Next add the coriander, mustard and cumin seeds, cooking for another 2–3 minutes, before adding the garlic, ginger and chilli flakes. Now add the lamb, browning for 4–6 minutes before mixing through the garam masala and salt. Finally add the tomato purée, sugar and vinegar, along with the tomatoes. Simmer and reduce for 5–7 minutes, then set aside.
· To make the cheese paste, mix all the ingredients together into a crumbly mixture.
· For the greens, boil the cavolo nero in salted water for 5–6 minutes until tender, then blend with the mustard, garlic and lemon juice into a thick smooth paste. Add a little water if needed, then let it cool.
· Preheat the oven to 200°C fan.
· Cover the lasagne sheets with boiling water and leave for 4–5 minutes to soften a little. Slice each lasagne sheet down the middle lengthways, making 2 strips ready for rolling.
· Take one pasta strip, spread with 1 tablespoon of the mustard greens, sprinkle over some cheese paste and finally add a spoon of keema. Roll up tightly into a snail. Repeat to form all the lasagne rolls.
· Pour the jarred tomato pasta sauce into an ovenproof dish and tightly pack in the lasagne rolls.
· Cover with foil and bake for 25 minutes, then remove the foil and bake for a final 10–15 minutes until piping hot and crusty on top.
· Meanwhile, for the tarkha, heat the vegetable oil in a pan, then add the curry leaves, mustard seeds and chilli flakes. Sizzle for 1 minute, then drizzle over the baked lasagne rolls just before serving.

Masala brisket pie

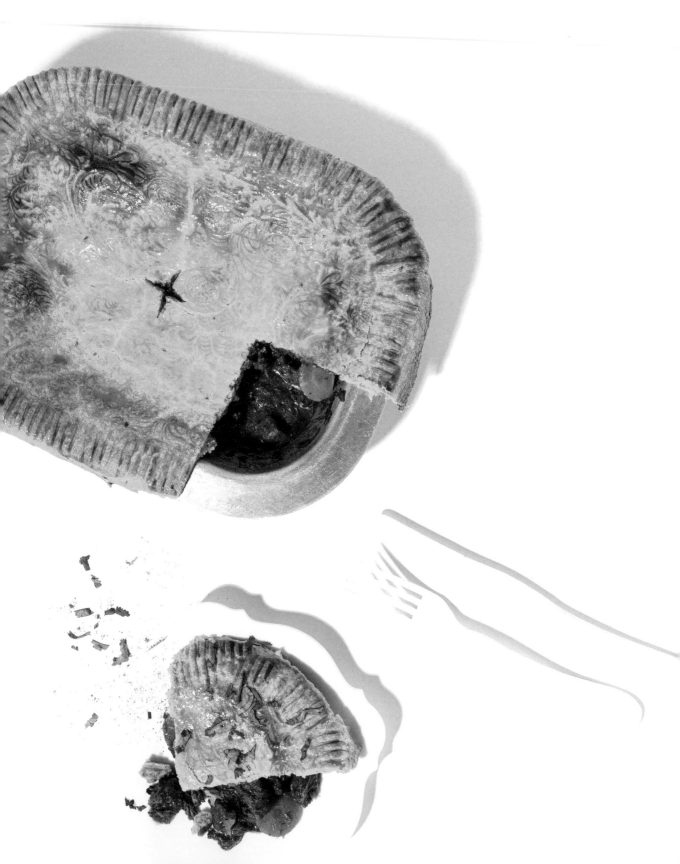

The Chicken Balti Pukka Pie has a lot going for it. I was ten the first time I ate one. It was a frosty Saturday afternoon in the middle terraces at Leicester City Football Stadium. I had little interest in the game but a lot of interest in that steamy, mildly curried pie, a not-so-guilty pleasure I still hanker for whenever I see that orange Pukka sign.

The Storer family started making their iconic pies in Leicester in 1963, the earliest being sold in chip shops and sports stadiums around the Midlands. As their popularity grew, they added their homage to the great British curry houses on Leicester's Golden Mile and changed their name to 'Pukka': a Hindi-Urdu word meaning 'genuinely authentically solid'. The filling in this intricately spiced, tangy and smoky masala brisket pie is as far from their mild Balti pie as you can get. Neither claim a line of authenticity back to India, but both are solidly pukka in their celebration of our beloved city.

Serves 6

For the pastry
275g plain flour, plus more to dust
125g unsalted butter, chilled and chopped
½ teaspoon ajwain, crushed
1 teaspoon ground turmeric
½ teaspoon fine sea salt
1 egg yolk

For the filling
4 black cardamom pods, split
2 cassia bark sticks, or cinnamon sticks
2 star anise
2 onions, sliced
2 tablespoons vegetable oil, plus more if needed
1 tablespoon finely grated fresh ginger
4 garlic cloves, very finely chopped
30g can of anchovies in oil, drained and chopped
625g beef brisket, cut into cubes
1 tablespoon Garam Masala (see page 23)
2 teaspoons chilli flakes
2 teaspoons fine sea salt
1 teaspoon coarsely ground black pepper
175g carrots, chopped
8 large Medjool dates, pitted and chopped
500ml beef stock
4 tablespoons malt vinegar
2 tablespoons chopped coriander leaves

· First make the pastry: pulse the flour, cold butter, ajwain, turmeric and salt in a food processor into fine crumbs. Next add 5–6 tablespoons of ice-cold water, one at a time, pulsing between each spoon until it just starts to form a dough; you may not need all the water. Press together into a tight ball, wrap in cling film and chill for 1 hour.
· For the filling, dry pan-roast the black cardamom, cassia or cinnamon and star anise for 1–2 minutes until they release their various aromas, then grind to a fine powder.
· Next take a large pan and fry the onions in the oil for 5–6 minutes until golden. Add the ginger, garlic and anchovies, then cook for another 3–4 minutes. Add the brisket to the pan and brown the meat for 4–5 minutes, with a drop more oil if needed, then add the freshly ground spices, garam masala, chilli flakes, salt, pepper, carrots and dates. Mix thoroughly to prevent it from burning, then pour in the beef stock and malt vinegar.
· Cover with a tight lid and simmer over a medium-low heat for 90 minutes until the meat sauce has reduced by one-quarter. Stir in the coriander, pour into a deep pie dish and leave to cool.
· Preheat the oven to 190°C fan.
· Roll the chilled pastry on a floured surface into a pie lid 3–4mm thick and just a little bigger than the dish. Brush the edges of the pie dish with egg yolk, drape over the rolled pastry and press down the edges, crimping and pinching tightly to encase the filling. Make a small cross in the middle of the pastry to let steam escape and fork down around the edges.
· Brush with egg yolk and bake for 25–30 minutes until golden on top and succulent inside. Serve hot with mashed potatoes and greens, or just on its own alongside some good crusty bread and a spicy red Malbec or richly tobaccoed Chianti.

Tamarind, miso & date short ribs with Kashmiri chilli

There's a lot to be said for subtle flavours that allow fresh ingredients to shine through. There's also a lot to be said about extremely loud flavours that shine through fresh ingredients. When everything is loud, then, relatively, nothing is loud; it's all just normalised to higher decibels of taste. More is more, as my mantra goes. This recipe very much embodies the maximalist approach to playing with flavour, where parallel forces of sour, sweet, umami, fragrant, meaty, hot, spicy and salty each magnetically pull towards and repel against each other in equal force. This is a time to use jarred tamarind concentrate rather than fresh pulp, as its intense sourness lends itself well to the robust meatiness of short ribs. Use the most savoury miso you can find, ideally brown and red pastes which are fermented for longer and have deeper flavour. Balanced with the caramel sweetness of dates, what shines through is quite extraordinary.

Serves 4

For the beef & salt rub
2 tablespoons vegetable oil
3 tablespoons smoked salt
3 tablespoons Chaat Masala (see page 24)
1 tablespoon amchoor
2kg (about 6 large) beef short ribs
3 tablespoons finely chopped coriander leaves, to serve
Kashmiri chilli powder, to serve

For the marinade
4 tablespoons date syrup
6 tablespoons red or brown miso
4 tablespoons tamarind concentrate, or 8 tablespoons
  fresh tamarind pulp or paste (see page 157)
6 garlic cloves, very finely chopped, or finely grated
2 tablespoons finely grated fresh ginger

For the sauce
4 tablespoons apple cider vinegar
2 large onions, sliced
a little vegetable oil, if needed
6 dried Kashmiri chillies
8 cloves
2 cassia bark sticks, or cinnamon sticks
10 green cardamom pods, split
8 large Medjool dates, pitted
1 lemon, deseeded and chopped into segments,
  with rind left on
8 garlic cloves, peeled
4 tablespoons tomato purée
1 tablespoon coarsely ground black pepper
2 teaspoons smoked salt

· For the salt rub, mix the oil, smoked salt, chaat masala and amchoor into a paste. Smother over the short ribs and leave to salt for 2–3 hours.
· Using a large pan with a tight lid, brown the salted ribs for 6–7 minutes each, one at a time, turning to render the fat on all sides. Remove to a baking tray, leaving the fat in the pan.
· Make a thick marinade paste by mixing the date syrup, miso, tamarind, garlic and ginger. Smother the browned ribs all over in this paste, cover with cling film and leave for 2–3 hours, or ideally overnight.
· Preheat the oven to 175°C fan.
· Add a splash of the cider vinegar to deglaze any charred meaty bits from the bottom of the pan, then add the onions to the beef fat and fry them for 10–12 minutes until caramelised. If needed, add a spoon of oil. Next add the whole Kashmiri chillies, cloves, cassia or cinnamon, cardamom pods, dates, chopped lemon, garlic, the rest of the vinegar and the tomato purée. Cook for 4–5 minutes before returning the ribs along with all the sticky marinade.
· Cover with 500ml of water, add the pepper and salt, then place a lid tightly over the pan and slow-cook in the oven for 3½–4 hours until the meat is tender. Every hour, turn the ribs and carefully skim off any excess fat that has separated on top (save this for making parathas, see pages 189–191). When fully cooked, carefully remove the ribs from the pan and place on a serving dish: the meat will be falling off the bones.
· Spoon away any excess fat from the top of the juices, then heat them over the hob for 10–12 minutes into a thickened sweet-tangy glaze. Smother the ribs in the thick sauce, then sprinkle with chopped coriander and Kashmiri chilli powder to finish.

Tip Serve with warm rice, hot naans or anything else starch-based and carby. These ribs are not an occasion for salad.

The British Empire gave very few things back to partitioned India in return for what it pillaged to fund London's gentrified elite. But of those few, cricket and cauliflowers are arguably the two most embraced to this day; it's not a long list. Either way, these imports are now so integrally Indian that Indians beat Brits in their skilful mastery over both. This whole roasted cauliflower makes for a vibrant vegetarian centrepiece (vegan if you make a coconut- or oat-based minty yogurt) that both looks and tastes delectable on any feasting table. The cauliflower is poached in a liquor with saffron, cardamom and turmeric, imparting a sunshine yellow colour and subtle kiss of flavour. It's then coated in a spice paste that travels from South India to Thailand, blending fiery gunpowder masala with sweet chilli sauce. When slow-roasted, the core of the cauliflower turns tender and succulent, while its top scorches to a satisfying char. Adorn liberally with sauces, herbs and spiced crunchy bits.

Serves 4

For the cauliflower
10 green cardamom pods, split
6 cloves
20 saffron strands
10 allspice berries, crushed
½ teaspoon ground turmeric
1 teaspoon fine sea salt
1 large cauliflower, with leaves

For the glaze
4 tablespoons Gunpowder Masala (see page 24)
4 tablespoons sweet chilli sauce
1 tablespoon finely grated fresh ginger
4 garlic cloves, very finely chopped
1 teaspoon finely grated lime zest, plus 4 tablespoons lime juice
1 teaspoon coarsely ground black pepper
2 tablespoons olive oil

To serve
Minty Yogurt (see page 64)
Pistachio-Fenugreek Dukkah (see page 27)
pomegranate seeds
finely chopped mint leaves
crunchy fried dal, crushed (optional)
roasted chickpeas, crushed (optional)
sev (optional)

· For the cauliflower, put the cardamom, cloves, saffron, allspice, turmeric and salt in a large pan big enough to hold the whole cauliflower, then half-fill the pan with boiling water. Simmer for 3 minutes until the spices have infused the liquor and the salt has dissolved completely.
· Carefully drop the cauliflower in upside down, ensuring the florets are fully covered and with the green stem poking out. Boil for 10 minutes, turning if needed, to ensure it cooks evenly. Carefully remove the cauliflower from the yellow liquor (this makes a delicious stock for dal, soup or risotto) and place upside down in a colander or on a wire rack. Leave for 10 minutes to let the liquid drain away and all the steam escape.
· Preheat the oven to 200°C fan.
· Mix all the ingredients for the glaze together into a thick paste. Place the drained cauliflower on a baking tray and brush liberally with the sticky glaze.
· Bake in the oven for 20 minutes until golden and burnished on top, but tender all the way through.
· Serve with dollops of minty yogurt, dukkah, pomegranate, mint and generous sprinklings of any crunchy toppings that take your fancy.

Baby aubergines
with coconut, aniseed & pistachios

Recordings of the late cellist Jacqueline du Pré are easily identified by her stylistic use of portamento. Instead of precisely stepping from one note to the next, she liked to slide, revealing the hyphen-of-notes in between those written on the page. It divides opinion to this day, critics deploring her as overly sentimental and decadent. To me, her ethereal flair has no match.

In the kitchen, some ingredient combinations can also somehow reveal flavours that seem to exist in between the actual flavours you've put into a dish. A scientist could tell you precisely why; all I know is that when it does happen, your dinner guests will swoon in puzzled intrigue, interrogating 'but how exactly did you make this?' The flavour alchemy of this recipe always gets that reaction. I can't tell you why, but here's how.

Serves 2–3

1 tablespoon coriander seeds
2 teaspoons fennel seeds
seeds from 6 green cardamom pods
1 teaspoon cumin seeds
1 tablespoon aniseed seeds
2 tablespoons chana dal
1 teaspoon fine sea salt
1 teaspoon coarsely ground black pepper
50g almonds, toasted
75g shelled unsalted pistachios, toasted (see page 40), plus pistachio nibs, to serve
1 tablespoon Kashmiri chilli powder
2 teaspoons anardana powder
1 teaspoon ground turmeric
4 tablespoons desiccated coconut, toasted, plus more to serve
1 tablespoon finely grated fresh ginger
1 teaspoon finely grated lemon zest, plus 3 tablespoons lemon juice
4 tablespoons vegetable oil, plus 2 tablespoons
500g (about 10) baby aubergines
5 large red chillies
Rotis and Coriander, Spring Onion & Curry Leaf Chutney (see pages 187–188 and 202), to serve

· Dry pan-roast the coriander, fennel, cardamom, cumin and aniseed seeds and chana dal for 2 minutes until toasty and releasing their aromas. Spoon into a grinder with the salt and pepper, then blitz to a powder and empty into a mixing bowl.
· Next grind the toasted almonds and pistachios to a coarse powder and add to the bowl with the Kashmiri chilli powder, anardana powder, turmeric, toasted coconut, ginger, lemon zest and juice and 4 tablespoons vegetable oil. Mix well until everything is fully combined into a crumbly damp rubble.
· Slit the baby aubergines from the bases in a cross three-quarters of the way up. Using your fingers, stuff the filling down into the cross, pressing it in and compacting the sides of the aubergines inwards as you do. You want the surface to be smooth, with a clear cross of the stuffing showing at the base.
· For the large chillies, slit them down the middle, remove the seeds and fill with the stuffing, compacting the sides inwards firmly as you do.
· Heat the 2 tablespoons of vegetable oil in a deep frying pan until hot, then drop in the stuffed aubergines and red chillies. Char for 2–3 minutes, then pour in 100ml of water and cook in the steam for 5 minutes, turning carefully so they cook evenly on all sides. Add another 100ml of water, cover with a lid and cook for 12–15 minutes until cooked and tender all the way through. Remove the lid and finish by cooking over a high heat for a final 5 minutes.
· Serve straight from the pan, sprinkled with pistachio nibs and coconut, with rotis and coriander chutney on the side.

Tip This filling is also delicious stuffed into bitter gourds, potatoes, squash, samosas or parathas.

Achaari mango pulled pork

Mango pickle adorns most of what I eat, both the sweetly sticky chutney version from British supermarkets that comes in paisley-patterned jars from the 'ethnic foods' aisle and 'proper' cuttingly sour bitingly spiced achaar from Indian shops that comes in thick, tightly lidded screwtop pots with an extra plastic bag inside to protect the pot from the pickle. Yes, it really is that potent. This mango achaari-marinated pulled pork combines elements of both the 'real' thing and the British approximation. Freshly blitzed in-season mangos are best, but Alphonso mango pulp from a can has its own delicious charm that works just as well. The pork is slow-cooked in three different stages, which creates layers of flavour that you didn't even realise you'd put into the pot, much like the sympathetic strings on a sitar that sing out sumptuous notes on top of the notes actually plucked. Serve with extra mango pickle on the side, either the sweet version or the proper stuff. It's all good.

Serves 6

For the marinade
4 teaspoons fennel seeds
1 tablespoon cumin seeds
2 teaspoons nigella seeds
1 tablespoon aniseed seeds
2 tablespoons smoked salt
2 teaspoons black pepper
150ml canned Alphonso mango pulp
1 tablespoon smoked paprika
3 tablespoons amchoor
1 tablespoon English mustard powder
2 teaspoons ground turmeric
1 teaspoon ground cinnamon
8 garlic cloves, very finely chopped or finely grated
3 tablespoons finely grated fresh ginger
3 tablespoons apple cider vinegar
2 tablespoons light brown sugar
4 teaspoons chilli flakes

For the pork
1.3–1.5kg pork shoulder, off the bone
500ml dry cider, plus more if needed
1 tablespoon Worcestershire sauce
250ml canned Alphonso mango pulp

· Dry pan-roast the fennel, cumin, nigella and aniseed seeds for 2–3 minutes until they release their aromas. Spoon into a grinder with the smoked salt and pepper, then blitz to a coarse powder, with some seeds still left whole for texture. Add the coarse spices to a large bowl along with all the rest of the marinade ingredients. Mix well.
· Carefully remove the rind from the outside of the pork, leaving behind a little of the fat for flavour. Score with a criss-cross of slashes and rub the mango paste over the entire pork shoulder, getting it deep into the cuts and crevices. Cover and leave in the fridge for at least 8 hours, ideally overnight, turning and basting halfway through.
· Remove the pork from the fridge, place in a deep roasting tin – covering with all of the marinade – and let it come up to room temperature. Preheat the oven to 180°C fan.
· Pour the cider, Worcestershire sauce and mango pulp into the tin, covering the bottom of the pork, then give it a quick whisk.
· Cover with foil and cook for 2½ hours. Remove from the oven, siphon away the excess fat and spoon the thick juices over the meat. Cover with foil once more.
· Reduce the oven temperature to 160°C fan and cook for another 1½–2 hours. Check in regularly to ensure it doesn't dry out, topping up with cider if needed.
· Finally, drain away the excess fat again, baste over the thick glaze from the tin and remove the foil. Increase the oven temperature to 200°C fan and cook uncovered for 10 minutes to burnish the top.
· Remove the pork from the oven, spoon away any excess fat from the juices for a final time and let it rest for 15 minutes. Shred the meat with 2 forks – it will pull apart easily – then spoon over the achaari mango glaze from the tin.

Tip Serve with warm naan, Kokum Mooli Slaw with Cashews and Lime Leaf & Amchoor Aioli (see pages 177 and 205). Or stuff the pulled pork into burger buns with shredded lettuce, slivers of ripe mango and a spritz of lime juice.

Feasting Dishes, Curries & Thali Bowls

Cinnamon tandoori chicken traybake with pickled ginger & pineapple

Cinnamon, and its cousin cassia bark, are two of the underlying cornerstones of Indian cooking. Unlike attention-hungry cardamom, cumin and curry leaves, they happily hang out in the shadows, the cool understated backbone of all good masala mixes, curries and slow braises. When brought into the foreground and deliberately given a lead role, their warming sweet earthiness imparts a unique complexity. This spiced traybake combines cinnamon's woody clove-like aromas with zingy pickled ginger, sharp juicy pineapple and fresh peppery oregano. Cinnamon is first infused into the lemon brine, which gets its mellow citrussy notes deep into the chicken, then layered into the pungent spice paste which bakes to a charred tandoori finish. The impact of the cinnamon double hit is deliciously distinct and anything but understated.

Serves 4

For the chicken & lemon brine
4 large bone-in, skinless chicken legs
4 tablespoons lemon juice
1½ teaspoons ground cinnamon
seeds from 8 green cardamom pods, crushed
2 teaspoons fine sea salt

For the tandoori paste
3 shallots, grated or blitzed to a paste
1 tablespoon finely grated lemon zest
2 tablespoons finely grated fresh ginger
6 garlic cloves, very finely chopped or finely grated
1 teaspoon English mustard
2 tablespoons vegetable oil
1 teaspoon aniseed seeds, crushed
1 teaspoon coriander seeds, crushed
½ teaspoon ground mace
1 teaspoon coarsely ground black pepper
1 tablespoon Kashmiri chilli powder
2 tablespoons white wine vinegar
2 teaspoons ground cinnamon
1 tablespoon caster sugar

For the traybake
250g canned pineapple rings
2 tablespoons pickled ginger, plus more, finely sliced, to serve
1 tablespoon finely chopped oregano leaves
400g can of chickpeas, drained
rice and chutneys (see pages 199–213), to serve

· Slash the chicken legs 3–4 times in parallel diagonal lines so the flavours really penetrate the meat. Whisk together the lemon juice, cinnamon, cardamom and salt, then coat the chicken all over, getting it deep into the grooves. Cover and leave for 30 minutes.
· Next mix together all the ingredients for the tandoori paste. Remove the chicken from its brine and spoon a thick layer of the spice paste over it, getting it into the cuts. Cover and leave to marinate for 1 hour.
· Preheat the oven to 200°C fan.
· Arrange the pineapple rings in a shallow oven tray, then place the chicken on top. Sprinkle over the pickled ginger and oregano, cover with foil and bake in the oven for 30 minutes.
· Remove from the oven, take off the foil, then pour the chickpeas into the juices at the base of the tray. Return to the oven, uncovered, to finish cooking for 20–25 minutes, until the chicken is cooked through with the juices running clear.
· Remove from the oven, cover with foil and let it rest for 5 minutes. Enjoy with rice, chutneys and more pickled ginger on top!

Feasting Dishes, Curries & Thali Bowls

Hazelnut & black pepper lamb korma

Black pepper is often relegated to 'best supporting background seasoning'. Historically, however, it was so prized by the West that the quest for it sparked the legacies of empire we live with today. When assigned its rightful place as headline act, black pepper is one of the most complex, distinctive spices in existence. Similarly, korma is often consigned to the role of 'mild introductory beginner' in the British hierarchy of curries, when nothing could be further from the truth. The intricate qormas of the Moghul courts were slowly braised with velvety cream, ground nuts and aromatic spices, with a base of deep caramelised onion. My take has sharp, complex black pepper centre stage, exactly where it should be.

Serves 4

For the lamb & marinade
1 tablespoon coarsely ground black pepper
10 garlic cloves
2 tablespoons finely grated fresh ginger
2 green chillies, stalks trimmed away
6 tablespoons (90ml) lemon juice
2 teaspoons smoked salt
seeds from 12 green cardamom pods, crushed
2 teaspoons ground coriander
2 teaspoons ground cumin
1 teaspoon ground turmeric
800g lamb neck fillet, chopped into bite-sized chunks

For the spice paste
400ml vegetable oil
30 fresh curry leaves
2 large onions, sliced
75g shelled unsalted roasted hazelnuts (see page 40),
   plus more to serve
25g shelled unsalted roasted almonds (see page 40)
2 tablespoons Tandoori Masala (see page 25)
2 tablespoons coarsely ground black pepper, more to serve

For the curry
200ml coconut milk
4 tablespoons lemon juice
2 tablespoons caster sugar
2 teaspoons fine sea salt
2 tablespoons finely chopped coriander leaves

· Blitz all the marinade ingredients together in a grinder to make a thick, smooth yellow paste, then scrape into a large bowl. Add the lamb, coating it with the marinade. Cover and chill for at least 4 hours, ideally overnight.
· To make the spice paste, heat the oil in a deep saucepan or wok to 160°C (see page 11). Add the curry leaves, let them pop for 30 seconds, then carefully remove from the oil, drain on kitchen paper and set aside.
· Next add the onions and fry for 13–15 minutes until they are deeply golden but not burned; these will form the base of the curry. Remove from the oil and drain well on kitchen paper. Reserve the oil.
· Using a grinder, blend the roasted nuts, tandoori masala, pepper, fried onions and fried curry leaves with 200ml water into a thick nutty paste.
· Heat 3 tablespoons of the onion-frying oil in a large pan with a lid, then add the lamb with all the marinade. Cook for 12–14 minutes; it will steam at first, but eventually sizzle and brown. Add the spice paste, cook for 2 minutes, then pour in 500ml water. Cover with a lid and simmer over a low heat for 45 minutes, stirring every 10 minutes. Add a little more water if it's drying out.
· Next stir in the coconut milk, lemon juice, sugar, salt and coriander. Cover again and cook for a final 45–60 minutes until the lamb is tender and the oils are separating in the sauce.
· Garnish with a sprinkling of black pepper and roasted hazelnuts and serve.

Tip Delicious eaten on the day it's made, with rice and naan. Even better the day after.

Chilli paneer & pepper fry

This Indian-Chinese hybrid dish is unquestionably the most-featured on the menus of Punjabi weddings around the world, certainly in my lifetime. It's been served at every Loyal wedding of my generation to date and, should I ever tie the knot myself, this will be the first dish out. There's something remarkable about the rich bite of fried paneer with the crunch of chilli crisp and masala-fied soy, a combination with the power to make even green peppers taste good.

The history of Indo-Chinese cuisine can be traced back to the Chinese diaspora who settled in Kolkata in the 1700s, many opening restaurants serving a blended cuisine adapted to Indian tastes, using Chinese ingredients such as soy sauce, vinegar, Szechuan peppercorns and sesame seeds, but in an Indian style, which created something totally new. Today, Indo-Chinese food is a celebrated cuisine in itself; proudly third-culture to its delicious core.

Serves 4

For the paneer
2 tablespoons light soy sauce
2 garlic cloves, finely grated
2 teaspoons finely grated fresh ginger
1 tablespoon lime juice
2 teaspoons Chaat Masala (see page 24)
½ teaspoon toasted sesame oil
1½ teaspoons ground turmeric
450g paneer
2 tablespoons baking powder
4 tablespoons tapioca flour
4 tablespoons plain flour
200ml sunflower oil

For the sauce
2 spring onions, chopped lengthways into ribbons
2 red onions, sliced
2 teaspoons finely grated fresh ginger
4 garlic cloves, cut into slivers
1 green pepper, sliced into strips
2 tablespoons soy sauce
4 tablespoons tomato ketchup
2 tablespoons apple cider vinegar
2 tablespoons Chinese chilli crisp (Lao Gan Ma)
1 teaspoon Worcestershire sauce
1 tablespoon amchoor
1 teaspoon coarsely ground black pepper
2 teaspoons white sesame seeds, plus more (optional)
  to serve
1 tablespoon cornflour

· To make the crispy paneer, mix the soy sauce, garlic, ginger, lime juice, chaat masala, sesame oil and turmeric together into a thick paste.
· Cut the paneer into chunky bite-sized squares, then coat it in the marinade and leave for 30 minutes.
· Whisk together the baking powder, tapioca flour and plain flour in a separate bowl. Toss the marinated paneer into the dry mix, leave for 1 minute, then toss again so it's coated all over.
· Heat the sunflower oil in a deep pan or wok to 160°C (see page 11) and fry the paneer for 3–4 minutes until golden and crisp all over. Drain on kitchen paper.
· Now heat 2 tablespoons of the sunflower oil in a wok, then stir-fry the spring onions and red onions for 4–5 minutes. Next add the ginger, garlic slivers and green pepper, cooking for another 2 minutes.
· Make a thick paste by mixing the soy sauce, ketchup, vinegar, Chinese chilli crisp, Worcestershire sauce, amchoor and pepper together. Pour into the wok and stir-fry for 2 minutes, before adding the fried paneer and sesame seeds.
· Finally make a paste by mixing the cornflour with 2 tablespoons of water. Add to the wok and mix through, cooking until the sauce begins to thicken.
· Serve, sprinkled with sesame seeds, if you like, with rice or stuffed into pittas.

Yellow chana-moong dal
with chorizo tarkha

Does your house smell of curry? That is the question. Maybe not the one Hamlet was asking, but the one that connects the Indian diaspora around the world. I used to disregard it as another micro-aggression to absorb under my cultural chameleon-cloak of 'ethnic' (in)visibility, but now my answer is more resolute: no, it doesn't smell of curry, it smells of tarkha.

Tarkhas – also known as oggarane, thamlimpu, bagharis, vagharni or chaownks – are the key vehicle through which flavour is manifested in Indian cooking. The process involves sizzling, tempering and blooming whole spices, ground spices, onions, shallots, garlic, ginger, chillies, dried fruits and herbs in fat to extract their aromatics. When amply infused, the hot fat, be that vegetable oil, coconut oil, mustard oil or ghee, is incorporated into a dish, either in the beginning, middle or end – sometimes all three – creating the multi-layered depth of deliciousness that is Indian food.

Playing with tarkhas is an exciting way to remix cross-culturally in the kitchen, as I do here, where chorizo sausage adds a meaty paprika-ed slick of Spanish heat to the oily mix. Does my house smell of tarkha, you ask? Abso-fucking-lutely!

Serves 4

For the dal
200g chana dal
100g yellow moong dal
5 cloves
2 dried bay leaves
1 cinnamon stick
1½ teaspoons fine sea salt
1 teaspoon ground turmeric
1 tablespoon Garam Masala (see page 23)
1 tablespoon finely grated lemon zest
coriander leaves, to serve
rice or Rotis (see pages 187–188), to serve

For the tarkha
3 tablespoons ghee
1 teaspoon coriander seeds, crushed
1½ teaspoons cumin seeds, crushed
1 teaspoon fennel seeds, crushed
2 medium shallots, very finely chopped
125g raw chorizo sausage, casing removed, finely chopped
4 garlic cloves, very finely chopped
1 tablespoon finely grated fresh ginger
2 medium plum tomatoes, finely chopped
1 teaspoon fine sea salt
1 teaspoon Kashmiri chilli powder
2 tablespoons lemon juice

· Wash both dals in a sieve under a cold tap, then soak in a bowl of cold water for 45 minutes.
· Drain away the water, pour into a saucepan, then cover with 900ml boiling water and add the cloves, bay leaves, cinnamon stick, salt, turmeric, garam masala and lemon zest. Bring to the boil for 1 minute, then reduce the heat to a low simmer, cover with a lid and cook for 45–50 minutes, stirring regularly to ensure it doesn't catch on the bottom.
· Cook until the moong dal disintegrates and the chana dal is cooked through with a very slight bite; top up with water if it's drying out and skim off any foam that gathers on top.
· For the tarkha, heat the ghee in a frying pan, then add the crushed coriander, cumin and fennel seeds. Sizzle for 1 minute before adding the shallots. Cook for 8–10 minutes, until translucent and caramelised. Reduce the heat to medium-low, then crumble in the chorizo and add the garlic and ginger. Cook the mixture gently for 5–6 minutes: the chorizo will render out its red paprika oils as it cooks.
· Add the chopped tomatoes, salt and Kashmiri chilli powder. Cook for 4–5 minutes until the tomatoes have broken down, the chorizo is cooked through and the tarkha is an intense reddish colour. Finish by mixing through the lemon juice.
· Ripple the cooked dal with the intense chorizo tarkha, swirling it through with all of the flavourful bits, then scatter with coriander. Enjoy with rice or rotis... or just on its own in a big bowl with a spoon.

On going for an 'Indian' as a British Indian

Feasting Dishes, Curries & Thali Bowls

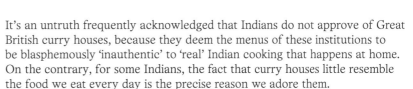

It's an untruth frequently acknowledged that Indians do not approve of Great British curry houses, because they deem the menus of these institutions to be blasphemously 'inauthentic' to 'real' Indian cooking that happens at home. On the contrary, for some Indians, the fact that curry houses little resemble the food we eat every day is the precise reason we adore them.

Growing up in 'multicultural' Leicester, devouring a diverse spectrum of regional cuisines from across South Asia was a routine part of my upbringing. Along with the Punjabi food of my family table, I was immersed in the heritage cooking of households whose origins stretched from Lahore, Gujarat, Maharashtra, Delhi and Goa, across to Uttar Pradesh, Bengal, Tamil Nadu, Sri Lanka and Bangladesh.

Weeks rarely went by without an inter-diaspora dinner party, cultural festival or religious celebration, a rolling cornucopia of sharing feasts, where flavourful abundance and communal joy were the principal goals. Over the course of these bountiful shindigs, Tupperware boxes filled with Mum's Punjabi cooking would be endlessly swapped for others in a revolving constellation of masala-stained containers, orbiting between households like little home-cooked planets. Their bursting lids would be sealed tightly with a sari-pleat of foil, then tiffin-stacked into paper bags and taped with mostly indecipherable hand-written recipes, sketchily scribbled in collectively understood pidgin English.

While dishes from fellow Punjabis often led to heavy critique: ('So little butter in that saag! Don't think much of this achaar! The dal is too watery!'), the cooking of families from other South Asian provinces was infinitely exhilarating: ('What is in that chutney? Toasted cashew, coconut and mustard seed masala, wow! It's so savoury-sweet and tangy, we must try to cook this!'). Every tub revealed an unique culinary manuscript completely different to the next, filled with flavours that sang the chords of each family's migratory journey to Leicester, uprooted from disparate places across the subcontinent, but now affiliated through one British city. By means of this kitchen-to-kitchen exchange of mother tongues, I grew up tasting the multiplicity of intertwined cuisines that in the West are often merged under the collective label of 'Indian food'. And there's another genre of food in Britain that comes under this moniker: something called 'curry'.

It's another untruth frequently acknowledged that whichever of the languages or dialects of India – more than 100 of them – you take (Marathi, Telegu, Bengali, Malayalam, Hindi, Kannada and my own Punjabi, to name a few), not one contains anything that can be directly attributed to 'curry' as we know it today. This line of enquiry often cites words that come phonetically close as curry's subverted root, such as khadhi, a turmeric-yellow yogurt dish with an assortment of regional variants, thuuri, which means 'gravy' in many languages of Northern India and Pakistan, or karil, which refers to spice blends and sautéed dishes.

Yet the word curry – pronounced as such – does in fact exist in Tamil, referring to spicy braised dishes with a wet sauce. Nevertheless, use of the word 'curry' as a blanket shorthand for all South Asian food collectively is quintessentially British, melting the rich cultural and regional complexity of the subcontinent into one monolithic mass. 'Curry' used as such is troublingly reductive, containing within its etymology the entire chronicle of colonial rule over formerly undivided India, in abridged form. Yet it's a word that also represents the domino-run of events that led to many Indians being in Britain today, who, along with a wider global diaspora, in time came to reclaim 'curry' as their own.

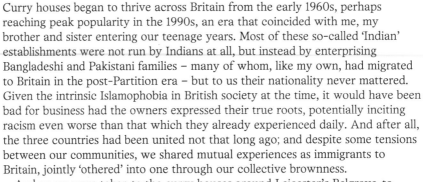

Curry houses began to thrive across Britain from the early 1960s, perhaps reaching peak popularity in the 1990s, an era that coincided with me, my brother and sister entering our teenage years. Most of these so-called 'Indian' establishments were not run by Indians at all, but instead by enterprising Bangladeshi and Pakistani families – many of whom, like my own, had migrated to Britain in the post-Partition era – but to us their nationality never mattered. Given the intrinsic Islamophobia in British society at the time, it would have been bad for business had the owners expressed their true roots, potentially inciting racism even worse than that which they already experienced daily. And after all, the three countries had been united not that long ago; and despite some tensions between our communities, we shared mutual experiences as immigrants to Britain, jointly 'othered' into one through our collective brownness.

And so we were taken to the curry houses around Leicester's Belgrave-to-Melton Road 'Golden Mile' almost weekly, eating at institutions such as Indian Queen, Curry Fever, The Tiffin, Curry Pot, Mirch Masala, Shimla Pinks, Rise of the Raj and Flamingo Grill as often as any other garlic naan-loving family in 1990s Britain. After all, we were British; going for an 'Indian' was part of our culture.

The food these restaurants served up on broadly identical menus was unashamedly adapted to suit the British palate: a spice-laden merging of North Indian, Bengali and Pakistani flavours, forming an unique cuisine that uninformed customers stoically believed to be 'authentically Indian'. In this respect, curry-house menus were a form of third-culture cooking, purposefully cross-pollinating between cultural boundaries. Only these menus were not a means of culinary self-expression, but the exact opposite: they held up a mirror to the reductive way in which many Britons perceived all South Asians collectively as one, plated it up and sold it back to them.

Most Brits were none the wiser, so the same idiosyncratic dishes popped up again and again, typically made using base mother sauces that could be tweaked into hundreds of 'hot-medium-or-mild' variants at the flick of a masala. Their extravagant names – like nothing we'd ever encountered in any South Asian's home – evoked exotic palaces and regal Indian dynasties.

Rogan josh was medium-spicy with tomatoes, while balti came in a little steel wok. Dhansak was with lentils, while dopiaza was full of onions. Jalfrezi had green chillies in a thick sauce, while saag was leafy-green and earthy. Vindaloo was one of the hottest, korma the mildest. Poppadoms and chutneys kicked things into play. Tandoori dishes came wood oven-charred. Naan or roti was the edible scoop for everything and Cobra or Kingfisher beer washed it all down, with a pyramid of pistachio kulfi for those with room after all this.

It was a gloriously self-exoticised pantomime of food that knowingly served up a parody of its own culinary self. Yet this canon of performatively 'Indian' curries – filled with amalgamated flavour chords that purposefully took away the intricacies of 'authentic' home-cooking – formed a pan-British cuisine, in a way that no single cuisine of India has ever become truly pan-Indian.

To label it as subservient or invalid misses the subtlety of the dynamics at play, because the resourceful owners of those curry houses knew exactly what they were doing. As Indian customers regularly eating there, we were jointly in on the charade. As it wasn't the restaurateurs' job to educate the citizens of their former coloniser, they purposefully played into orientalist sentimentalities for economic gain. And besides, regardless of the food's spurious connection to 'real' Indian home cooking, the curries they served were completely and utterly delicious!

My undisputed favourite of all Leicester curry houses was Nila Palace, a kitsch wonderland of domed turquoise arches, peacock feather chairs, glitzy paisley motifs, shiny mosaic elephants, brilliantly vulgar water features and an azure mirrored ceiling for maximum kaleidoscopic effect. Taking the definition of 'camp' as 'to do something as if you're doing it', this was an Indian restaurant,

being an Indian restaurant, as if it was an Indian restaurant. Like Liberace impersonating a Maharajah on the set of a Bollywood musical.

For brown families like my own, who regularly ate at restaurants like this, there was a clandestine scale of 'authenticity', reserved solely for us diasporic insiders. If we wanted, our food could be finely tailored in the kitchen to be as true to our particular, infinitely complex motherland cuisine as we desired. All we had to do was ask... something that caused an inter-generational tussle every time. My parents on one side, able to converse with the waiters in fluent Punjabi, conversational Urdu or broken Bengali, forged a fraternal bond in the few steps from door to table, signalling that ours was an order for the chefs to prepare 'home-style'. On the other side were me, my brother and sister, perpetually intrigued by the caricature Indian curries so revered by the white people sitting at tables just across from ours. In the stand-off, both generations compromised; as every notch along the authenticity scale came from the same kitchen, we'd settle on half the order being prepared home-style and the other half British-style.

Only one dish was never disputed – a curry that ambiguously resembled murgh makhani or butter chicken, but was so much more a British than an Indian invention that there was no truly 'authentic' version anyway – the supreme superstar of the curry house that is our national dish: chicken tikka masala.

CTM, as it's known to aficionados, is an institution with even more spurious origins than the collective label of 'curry' under whose umbrella it falls. Tales of its inception stretch from Glasgow to Delhi: some trace its legacy to the culinary courts of the Moghuls; others to a can of Heinz tomato soup.

Whatever its true roots, it's a dish that represents the resilience of the South Asian diaspora: a symbol of enterprising immigrants twisting a cuisine, not to delete their identity or tradition, but to financially benefit the next generation of South Asians.

The more we ate in British curry houses growing up, the more I developed a taste for these pastiche versions of my culture's 'authentic' cuisine. Cyclically, recreating curry-house food became as much a part of our home cooking as those dishes passed down through generations from the motherland. So CTM now *is* real Indian home cooking to me: a dish filled with delicious contradictions that mirror my own second generation experience of the world.

It's a dish invented by entrepreneurial Pakistani and Bangladeshi immigrants that is now an integral part of my own British Indian identity. It's a dish that symbolises India on supermarket aisles and takeaway apps around the world, but which includes ingredients such as tomatoes and chillies that are themselves immigrants to India. Most gratifyingly, it's a dish that – like the Indian diaspora itself – has travelled from Britain across the globe and back to India. It embodies the transformational quality of Indian cuisine, its ability to be warped and contorted into any direction that the world twists it, yet always be lovingly welcomed back home.

Melton Road chicken tikka masala

CTM. A single dish layered with flavourful contradictions that - like identities - span histories, continents and generations. Over my career, I've been entwined into the creation of countless versions of it: a luxury Michelin-starred take, frozen ready meal versions, the dish as a sandwich, as a pasta bake, as crinkle-cut crisps. None, however, have beaten my memory of CTM from the curry houses of Melton Road in Leicester. This recipe is my ode to them. Proudly British *and* Indian in equal measure, and authentic in its delicious inauthenticity.

Serves 4

For the chicken & lemon brine
650g boneless, skinless chicken thighs
6 tablespoons (90ml) lemon juice
1 tablespoon smoked salt
¾ teaspoon ground cloves
1 tablespoon amchoor

For the tikka paste
4 tablespoons Tandoori Masala (see page 25)
6 garlic cloves, finely grated
2 tablespoons finely grated fresh ginger
3 tablespoons natural yogurt
1 tablespoon vegetable oil

For the sauce
6 tablespoons (90ml) ghee
1½ tablespoons fennel seeds
10 green cardamom pods, split
2 medium onions, finely chopped
3 tablespoons finely grated fresh ginger
6 garlic cloves, very finely chopped
4 tablespoons Tandoori Masala (see page 25)
2 tablespoons Kashmiri chilli powder
2½ teaspoons fine sea salt
2 tablespoons granulated sugar
3 tablespoons dried fenugreek leaves, plus more to serve
4 tablespoons tomato purée
400g can of chopped tomatoes
75g unsalted toasted almonds (see page 40), ground
85g freshly grated coconut
150ml double cream, plus more to serve
4 tablespoons lemon juice
2 tablespoons finely chopped coriander leaves

· Cut the chicken thighs into equal bite-sized pieces. Whisk together the lemon juice, smoked salt, cloves and amchoor in a bowl, then add the chicken and mix thoroughly, ensuring the pieces are fully coated in the brine. Cover and leave for 30–45 minutes, tossing halfway.
· Next, combine the ingredients for the tikka paste together in a bowl and mix well. Drain the chicken from the brine, smother in the tikka paste, then cover and leave in the fridge for at least 4 hours, or preferably overnight.
· To make the sauce, heat the ghee in a large saucepan until it just begins to smoke, then add the fennel seeds and bashed green cardamom pods. Cook for 2 minutes until the cardamom turns pale. Add the onions and cook over a medium heat for 5–7 minutes until they become translucent. Next add the ginger and garlic, cooking for another 2–3 minutes until golden but not burnt. Now add the tandoori masala, Kashmiri chilli powder, salt, sugar and dried fenugreek. Cook with the onions for 2 minutes, then add the tomato purée, canned tomatoes and 250ml water.
· Cook over a high heat for 5 minutes, then reduce the heat to low, give it a good stir and add the toasted ground almonds and grated coconut. Cover with a lid and simmer for 20–30 minutes. Add a splash of water if it gets too dry. Add the double cream, then cook over a medium heat for a final 5 minutes until luscious and creamy. Stir through the lemon juice to finish.
· Preheat the grill to the highest it will go. Place the coated chicken pieces on a baking tray lined with foil, spaced well apart. Cook for 12–15 minutes, turning occasionally, until fully cooked through and charred on the outside. Drop the charred tikka chicken into the masala sauce and finish with a drizzle of cream, a sprinkle of dried fenugreek and the chopped coriander.

Tip Serve with rice, yogurt, chillies, naan and an ice-cold beer. Cobra, Kingfisher, Singha, Tiger or Red Stripe are best suited, although I also adore this curry with a heavier Hoegaarden or Leffe Blonde.

The Grand Trunk Road stretches from Chittagong in Bangladesh to Kabul in Afghanistan, one of the oldest and longest highways on the Asian continent. It passes through Indian Punjab like a sixth river, connecting Ludhiana, Phagwara, Jalandhar and Amritsar, the Punjabi cities that are the soul of my family's heritage. The smell of truck diesel runs through my veins as much as the sweetness of sugarcane, the char of tandoori roti and the butter-slick of dal makhani.

The curb-side dhabba eateries along the GT Road's route serve some of the most delicious food in the whole of India; they are especially famed for their black dals, which are like no other. This is my take on the many dhabba dals I've eaten over the years, unapologetically rich with a base of smoky ghee, made richer with creamy malai and finished with a punchy garlic tarkha. This is a dal whose flavours drive at full speed, just like the road it's named after, on which there is no slow lane.

Serves 4

For the dal
250g black urad dal
8 cloves
2 dried bay leaves

For the spice paste
4 small shallots, finely chopped
2 tablespoons finely grated fresh ginger
6 garlic cloves, very finely chopped or finely grated
3 tablespoons ghee
2 green chillies, pierced
½ teaspoon ajwain
2 teaspoons cumin seeds
2 teaspoons anardana powder
6 black cardamom pods, split
2 teaspoons smoked salt
1 teaspoon coarsely ground black pepper
2 teaspoons Garam Masala (see page 23)
3 tablespoons tomato purée
100ml double cream, plus 2 tablespoons

For the tarkha
4 tablespoons ghee
1 teaspoon cumin seeds
1 teaspoon coriander seeds
1 tablespoon Kashmiri chilli powder
2 garlic cloves, cut into slivers

· Rinse the black dal in a sieve under a cold tap until the water runs clear. Empty into a pan of cold water and soak for 4 hours, ideally overnight. Drain away the water and bring to a boil in 1.5 litres of fresh water along with the cloves and bay leaves. Simmer over a high heat for 40–45 minutes, removing any frothy bubbles that form on the surface. Keep boiling until the dal is cooked through and starting to fall apart; top up with water if needed and stir regularly so it doesn't catch on the bottom.
· To make the spice paste, grind the shallots, ginger and garlic to a smooth paste with a splash of water.
· Heat the ghee in a saucepan, then add the green chillies, ajwain, cumin seeds, anardana powder and black cardamom. Sizzle for 2 minutes, but make sure they don't burn! Add the shallot paste and cook for 2–3 minutes until the water has evaporated and the paste takes on a little colour. Next add the smoked salt, pepper and garam masala, with the tomato purée. Cook for another 3 minutes until the oil starts to separate.
· Tip in the cooked black dal along with its poaching liquid, cloves, bay leaves and 400ml of water. Bring the saucepan to the boil, cover with a lid and gently simmer for 30–40 minutes, stirring regularly and topping up with water if needed.
· Use a potato masher to squash some of the dal, stir in the cream and cook for a final 10 minutes.
· Prepare the tarkha by heating the ghee in a frying pan, then add the cumin seeds, coriander seeds, Kashmiri chilli powder and garlic slivers. Sizzle for 2 minutes until the garlic just starts to brown, then pour the tarkha slick over the dal, either stirring it in completely or leaving it in a rippled pool on the surface. Drizzle with the remaining 2 tablespoons of double cream to finish.

Tip Enjoy hot with rotis, rice and whole green chillies to bite into.

Cavolo nero & watercress saag
with anardana paneer

My mum's mum, Swaran Kaur, was an only child. Her own mother died when she was just one year old, following complications giving birth to a second child, a boy. He didn't make it either.

Swaran was subsequently raised by her blind grandmother, Ma-Ji, and two aunts, Sewa Kaur and Kartar Kaur, a trio of exceptional cooks whose mastery was notorious. What Ma-Ji lacked in vision was countered by her acuteness of feeling: she could cut saag on a dhatti foot-blade with more precision than any fully sighted person in the village. Sewa and Kartar were meticulous with their flavours: the first to greet the sabjiwala at dawn, the fussiest with the masalawala at midday, and the last ones awake at night, pressing freshly curdled buffalo milk into paneer for the next day.

My culinary mother tongue is bound not just to my ancestry of mothers, but to the Aunty-Jis whose familial love nurtured the roots next to their own. I'm not sure what they would have made of my take on saag paneer, but this one's for them.

Serves 4

For the paneer
2 tablespoons anardana powder
1 tablespoon Kashmiri chilli powder
2 teaspoons ground coriander
2 teaspoons fine sea salt
1 teaspoon coarsely ground black pepper
1 tablespoon granulated sugar
1 teaspoon ground turmeric
2 tablespoons lemon juice
1 tablespoon melted ghee
250g paneer, cut into cubes or triangles

For the saag
4 tablespoons ghee
2 teaspoons cumin seeds
4 cloves
1 teaspoon caraway seeds
1 teaspoon nigella seeds
1 large onion, finely chopped
2 tablespoons finely grated fresh ginger
4 garlic cloves, very finely chopped
2 green chillies, finely chopped
300g cavolo nero, coarse stalks removed
100g watercress
200g baby spinach
75g fresh fenugreek leaves
2 teaspoons fine sea salt
1 tablespoon lemon juice
drizzle of double cream, to serve

· For the paneer, make a thick paste in a bowl by mixing the anardana powder, Kashmiri chilli powder, ground coriander, salt, pepper, sugar, turmeric, lemon juice and melted ghee together. Coat the cubed paneer pieces with the marinade all over and leave for 30 minutes.
· Meanwhile, to make the saag, heat the ghee in a saucepan, then add the cumin seeds, cloves, caraway seeds and nigella seeds. Sizzle for 1 minute, then add the chopped onion. Cook for 8–10 minutes until it starts to soften and turn translucent. Next add the ginger, garlic and green chillies, cooking for another 2 minutes.
· Preheat the oven to 200°C fan.
· Tip the paneer pieces with their tangy coating on to a foil-lined baking tray. Bake for 12–15 minutes until the paneer is cooked through and starting to char.
· In a separate saucepan, blanch the cavolo nero, watercress and spinach in boiling water for 2 minutes. Drain, then put in a blender along with the fenugreek leaves. Blend to a chunky paste (how I like it), or a smoother saag if you prefer. Pour the blended greens into the pan of spiced onion, season with the salt and mix well. Add 50ml water with the lemon juice, cover and simmer for 8 minutes.
· Dot the warm paneer on top of the hot saag and finish with a drizzle of double cream.

Balti cholay with star anise & mint

A bucket and spade are not the first things that come to mind when thinking about Indian food in Britain, but they are players in the tale. The first recipe for curry 'the Indian way' appears in Hannah Glasse's 1747 *The Art of Cookery Made Plain and Easy*: she calls for browning peppercorns, rice and coriander seeds 'over the fire in a clean shovel', adding rabbit, onion, butter, salt and water. She wasn't kidding when she called it 'plain'. Fast forward 250 years, and that spade meets its bucket. Restaurateurs in Birmingham began serving dishes in the steel karahi 'bucket' woks they were cooked in, with 'pillow naans' the size of the table. They took off in a big way, giving rise to the City's 'Balti triangle'. This dish celebrates their spirit: serve it with big naans.

Serves 4

For the spice paste
2 teaspoons cumin seeds
3 star anise
2 teaspoons coriander seeds
½ teaspoon aniseed seeds
2 black cardamom pods, split
6 cloves
½ teaspoon asafoetida powder (hing)
1 tablespoon chilli flakes
1 tablespoon dried fenugreek leaves
1 tablespoon amchoor
1 teaspoon ground mace
1 teaspoon ground turmeric
4 tablespoons tomato purée

For the balti
4 tablespoons vegetable oil
6 small shallots, finely chopped
2 tablespoons finely grated fresh ginger
8 garlic cloves, very finely chopped
2 x 400g cans of chickpeas, drained
400g can of chopped tomatoes
2 teaspoons fine sea salt
4 tablespoons dark brown sugar
30g mint leaves, finely chopped, plus more to serve
3 tablespoons fresh tamarind pulp or paste (see page 157)
1 tablespoon lemon juice
sliced red onion, to serve

· To make the spice paste, dry pan-roast the cumin seeds, star anise, coriander seeds, aniseeds, black cardamom and cloves for 1–2 minutes until they release their aromas, then grind to a fine powder. Spoon the ground spices into a mixing bowl along with the asafoetida, chilli flakes, dried fenugreek, amchoor, mace and turmeric. Next add the tomato purée and 100ml of cold water. Mix into a thick paste.
· To cook the cholay, heat the vegetable oil in a large wok or pan, then add the chopped shallots. Cook for 3–4 minutes until cooked through and just turning translucent. Next add the ginger and garlic, cooking for another minute before adding the spice paste. Stir well, then add the drained chickpeas, coating in the spices completely.
· Cook for 2 minutes over a high heat, before adding the chopped tomatoes, salt, dark brown sugar and another 100ml of water. Cover with a lid and simmer for 15 minutes.
· Grind the fresh mint with 50ml of water and the tamarind pulp to make a minty purée. Stir into the wok and simmer for a final 15 minutes, adding a splash of water if it's drying out.
· Remove from the heat, mix through the lemon juice and scatter with mint and chopped red onion.

Tip Enjoy with puris (see page 196) or poured over any chaat: samosas (see page 36) especially!

Feasting Dishes, Curries & Thali Bowls

Singapore's Little India houses a microcosm of Indian dishes that have absorbed influences from the Chinese, Malay, Indonesian and Peranakan cuisines among which they have settled, dishes that have modulated along many intercultural routes at once. Tekka hawker market is its bustling heart, where traditional dum biryanis, idlis, samosas, parathas and tandoori chicken are interspersed with hybrids such as masala roti john omelette baguettes with chilli ketchup, Indian prawn fritter rojak salads with spiced peanut-palm sugar dressing, and Indian mee goreng fried noodles with tofu and soy. Fish head curry is Little India's most famous invention, an extraordinary Chinese-Singaporean-inflected South Indian-style curry, soured with tamarind and cooked with okra, aubergines and – in some versions – pineapple. This recipe is my take on it, a remembrance of my own time spent in Singapore, with a touch of Punjab-via-East London added to the mix.

Serves 4

For the marinade
1 teaspoon ground coriander
1 teaspoon amchoor
1 teaspoon ground cumin
2 teaspoons finely grated lemon zest
500g mixed fleshy fish fillets with skin, such as cod, haddock or hake, cut into large cubes
220g raw prawns

For the spice paste
6 small shallots
6 garlic cloves
1 tablespoon finely grated fresh ginger
30g (2 medium-small stalks) lemongrass, trimmed and finely chopped
10 fresh lime leaves
2 green chillies, stalks trimmed away

For the curry
4 tablespoons vegetable oil, plus more if needed
2 teaspoons fennel seeds, crushed
2 teaspoons coriander seeds, crushed
½ teaspoon aniseed seeds, crushed
30–35 fresh curry leaves
1½ teaspoons fine sea salt
1 teaspoon coarsely ground black pepper
1½ tablespoons medium curry powder
1 teaspoon ground turmeric
400ml can of coconut milk, plus more to serve
2 tablespoons fresh tamarind pulp or paste (not concentrate, see tip, right)
1 tablespoon dark brown sugar
chopped coriander leaves, to serve
toasted coconut, to serve

· To make the marinade, mix the ground coriander, amchoor, ground cumin and lemon zest together. Sprinkle over the raw fish and seafood in a bowl, then cover and set aside for 10 minutes.
· Next make a paste by blitzing the shallots, garlic, ginger, lemongrass, lime leaves and green chillies in a grinder, with a splash of water.
· Using a large pan or wok, heat the oil, then add the crushed fennel, coriander and aniseed seeds. Sizzle for 2 minutes before adding the curry leaves. Let them crackle for 45 seconds to infuse the oil.
· Next add the fragrant spice paste, salt and pepper. Cook for 3–4 minutes over a medium heat, adding a little more oil if needed. Next add the fish skin-side down, along with the prawns, frying for 2 minutes.
· Whisk together the curry powder, turmeric, coconut milk and 100ml water in a jug. Add to the pan, cover with a lid and simmer for 10 minutes.
· Remove the lid and mix through the tamarind and sugar, cooking for a final 6–8 minutes until the sauce has thickened and the seafood is cooked through.
· Sprinkle with chopped coriander, toasted coconut and a drizzle of coconut milk to serve.

Tip Fresh tamarind pulp is made by boiling down dried tamarind blocks with water into a tangy-fruity sour purée; it's the best thing for this recipe. A brown and zingy tamarind paste – found in jars at Indian or Asian stores and larger supermarkets – could also be used. Black treacly tamarind concentrate is extremely sharp and intensely tart: it has its place in other recipes but is not advised for this delicate curry.

CHAPTER 5

The *Kama Sutra* is frequently sensationalised in the West as some sort of salacious soft porn of courtly Indian sex positions and lusty bedroom manoeuvres. It does indeed get quite sexy in one part, but only one very small part. The Sanskrit text is in fact a much broader treatise on the pleasures of all the senses, written as a thread of aphoristic guidelines in which the realm of food can offer nourishment for the soul as well as the body. Among the advice it offers is a host of aphrodisiac recipes and libido-boosting supplements, including saffron, sugary milk, nutmeg and the slightly more unlikely (and pungent) suggestion of raw garlic.

Two things have always fascinated me about the *Kama Sutra*. First, how it joyfully discusses homosexuality as a 'third sex' to be enjoyed freely, as if it's one of the arts. Second, how it portrays courtesans as learned custodians of pleasure, culturally proficient in sixty-four specifically identified arts, including dancing, poetry, architecture, writing, chemistry, imitating natural sounds, perfumery, magic, gambling, teaching parrots to talk, carpentry, making a tune by hitting differently filled glasses of water, tattooing, coded languages, cocktail-making and cooking. Evidently, there is ancient heritage in both homosexuality and in being an accomplished bit on the side.

Each of these culinary bits on the side plays with third-culture flavour chords for pure pleasure. They are a collective of hybrid accompaniments that can be relied on to bring titillation to any meal, however unsexy the main event.

Makhani mushy peas

Punjabi beans on toast goes something like this: start by masala-fying Heinz baked beans with a spice tarkha of fried onions, cumin, fennel seeds and garam masala; next add anything from one-to-fifty cracks of black pepper and a ludicrously generous desi-dollop of butter; spoon over slightly burnt thickly buttered toast; top with Cheddar cheese and then finish with flecks of green chilli. It's about as British and Punjabi as you can get on the same plate.

This hybrid makhani (literally 'buttery') remix on another British classic, mushy peas, makes a great side dish and also works well on toast. Don't be shy with the butter, or it's just not makhani.

Serves 4 as a side dish

2 tablespoons vegetable oil
1 teaspoon coriander seeds, crushed
1 teaspoon fennel seeds, crushed
seeds from 10 green cardamom pods, crushed
1 tablespoon finely grated fresh ginger
2 garlic cloves, very finely chopped
1 green chilli, minced to a paste
60g unsalted butter, cut into cubes
400g frozen peas, defrosted
1 teaspoon fine sea salt
1 teaspoon coarsely ground black pepper
1 tablespoon dried fenugreek leaves, crushed
1 teaspoon finely grated lemon zest, plus 1 tablespoon lemon juice
double cream, to serve

· Heat the oil in a large saucepan, then add the crushed coriander, fennel and cardamom seeds. Sizzle for 1 minute before stirring through the ginger, garlic and green chilli.
· Next add the cubes of butter. Let them melt completely, then leave to infuse with the spices over a low heat for 2–3 minutes, stirring to ensure they don't burn. Finally stir through the peas, salt, pepper and dried fenugreek.
· Cook for 2 more minutes, then blitz in a food processor with the lemon zest and juice into either a smooth or a chunky pea mash as you prefer. Drizzle with double cream to finish.

Dopiaza dauphinoise with za'atar

The dopiaza, an Indian restaurant favourite, is a fragrantly sweet curry with Persian origins that translates to 'double onion'. It refers to the two different ways in which onions are flavourfully layered into the dish: some fried alongside the marinated meat, then more added as the blended body of the sauce itself.

This decadently creamy potato dauphinoise also puts double onions at its heart, with two different types in two layers, together with floral za'atar, generous gratings of strong cheese and aromatic spices from its curry-house namesake. The two dishes are absolutely nothing alike, but equally delicious nonetheless.

Serves 4 as a side dish

1kg Maris Piper potatoes, scrubbed
3 tablespoons ghee
2 teaspoons coriander seeds, crushed
2 teaspoons fennel seeds, crushed
4 medium onions, finely sliced
4 medium shallots, finely sliced
1 tablespoon finely grated lemon zest, plus 2 tablespoons
 lemon juice
butter, for the dish
2 tablespoons za'atar
175g mixed strong hard cheeses, such as Cheddar, Comté,
 Gruyère, vintage Red Leicester or Ogleshield, grated
600ml double cream
seeds from 6 green cardamom pods, crushed
4 cloves
2 teaspoons Garam Masala (see page 23)
6 garlic cloves, very finely chopped
2 teaspoons fine sea salt

· Use a mandolin or the slicing attachment on a food processor to cut the potatoes into very thin (2mm thick) discs; there is no need to peel them. Cover with a damp cloth and set aside.
· Heat the ghee in a large saucepan, then add the coriander and fennel seeds, sizzling for 1 minute. Next add the sliced onions and shallots. Cook for 13–15 minutes over a medium heat until they have turned golden brown, then stir through the lemon zest and juice.
· Butter a deep 22cm round or oval ovenproof dish. Spoon two-thirds of the cooked onion mixture into the dish, setting aside the remaining one-third for scattering over later, then sprinkle over 1 tablespoon of the za'atar plus half the grated cheese.
· Preheat the oven to 180°C fan.
· In the same large pan used to fry the onions, heat the cream with the cardamom, cloves, garam masala, garlic and salt. Bring to the boil, then reduce the heat to medium and add the sliced potatoes, submerging them as much as possible in the cream. Cover with a lid and cook for 4–5 minutes until they are just tender, then spoon the potatoes out into the prepared dish, fanning the slices out in overlapping layers on top of the cheesy onions.
· Pour the spice-infused cream over the potatoes – shaking the dish so it sinks right to the bottom – then sprinkle over another 1 tablespoon of za'atar.
· Place the pie dish on a baking tray – to capture any overspill – then bake for 45–50 minutes.
· Preheat the grill to its highest setting.
· When bubbling and cooked all the way through, remove from the oven and sprinkle over the last of the grated cheese and fried onions. Finish under the hot grill for 2–3 minutes until the cheese has melted and nicely scorched on top.

Tip Serve as a decadent side dish, or as a main with a peppery green salad.

Panch phoran broccolini with chard & piquant yogurt

The Bengali five-spice blend panch phoran is a mixture of cumin, nigella, fenugreek, fennel and mustard seeds; the word *panch* literally means 'five'. This quintuple combination is generally left whole and seldom ground to a powder; instead, each seed imparts its own earthy, nutty, bitter, anisey and peppery characteristics to a dish or pickle.

I like to use it for roasting vegetables, where it adds a spiky crunch of flavours that are different with each bite. Try this garlicky-spiced panch phoran treatment with whatever vegetables are in peak season, or just with potatoes, which are in season year-round.

Serves 4 as a side dish

For the greens
250g broccolini (Tenderstem broccoli)
200g rainbow chard, or green chard, stalks trimmed
3 garlic cloves, very finely chopped
1 teaspoon finely grated lemon zest, plus 1 tablespoon lemon juice
3 tablespoons olive oil
1 teaspoon Kashmiri chilli powder, plus more to serve
1 teaspoon finely chopped oregano leaves
1 tablespoon panch phoran, plus more to serve
1 teaspoon fine sea salt

For the yogurt
5 tablespoons natural yogurt
1 teaspoon finely grated lemon zest, plus 2 tablespoons lemon juice
1 tablespoon sriracha
2 teaspoons amchoor
½ teaspoon fine sea salt
finely chopped mint leaves, to serve
fried garlic slivers, to serve

· Preheat the oven to 180°C fan.
· Blanch the broccolini and the chard stalks in boiling water for 1 minute (don't separate the chard leaves from the stalks, just make sure as far as possible that it's only the stems in the water). Drain in a colander and leave to dry out so that the steam can escape.
· Mix the garlic, lemon zest and juice, olive oil, Kashmiri chilli powder, oregano, panch phoran and salt together in a bowl to form a paste. Smother the broccolini and chard with the paste, tossing to coat all over, then spread out on a baking sheet. Roast in the hot oven for 12–14 minutes until the vegetables are cooked through and are just starting to crisp up at the edges.
· For the piquant yogurt, whisk together the yogurt, lemon zest and juice, sriracha, amchoor and salt. Drizzle over the hot greens just before serving, then sprinkle with mint, fried garlic slivers, Kashmiri chilli powder and panch phoran to finish.

Fennel confit with lime leaf & cumin

Fennel is my favourite of all vegetables, its grassy anise-like flavours capable of extraordinary transformation in countless different directions. This is a feather-trimmed culinary prima donna with real range, the Shirley Bassey of the vegetable kingdom, that takes to chilli and spice like Liberace took to a rhinestone. Eaten raw, fennel's lemony-liquorice vibes pair deliciously with zingy amchoor, sumac or anardana. Slowly braised in stews, it marries with ginger, nigella and juniper berries. But my favourite method is to confit-roast fennel slowly in liberal sloshes of olive oil infused with fragrant lime leaves, earthy cumin and dried chillies. As it roasts, fennel's inner diva manifests, transforming the bulbs into caramelised fudge while the spiced oils become a fiery ingénue of their own.

Serves 4 as a side dish

200ml olive oil

10 fresh lime leaves, torn

1 tablespoon cumin seeds

4 cloves

1 teaspoon chilli flakes

2 teaspoons fine sea salt

1 tablespoon finely grated fresh ginger

1 tablespoon finely grated lemon zest, plus 2 tablespoons lemon juice

3 large fennel bulbs

· Preheat the oven to 175°C fan.
· Pour the olive oil into a small roasting tin; it should lie at least 1cm deep along the bottom. Toss in the torn lime leaves, cumin seeds, cloves, chilli flakes, salt, ginger, lemon zest and juice, submerging everything in the oil.
· Stand the fennel bulbs up on a chopping board and halve them vertically (if any are very large, they might need to be quartered). Place the fennel in the tin, spooning over the oil and spices. It may not be fully submerged in the oil at first, but this will happen as it cooks.
· Roast in the oven for 50–55 minutes until the fennel is fudgey-soft and tender all the way through, turning and basting every 15 minutes.

Tip Enjoy with fish, roast chicken or on its own with hunks of sourdough and a dollop of sour cream.

Hot curry-crunch roasties

The perfect roast potato is always on the culinary cusp where roasting meets frying, combining what's best about both cooking techniques to reach a satisfactory level of crunch. These roasties do just that, with a spice-infused olive oil, a curry-salted coating, and a rather long roasting time where the potatoes are left untouched.

This method works with any combination of dried herbs and spice blends, just replace the curry powder with your preferred masala mix. They will elevate any Sunday roast, but I also like them midweek, piping hot from the oven, smothered in mint chutney, yogurt and tamarind. 'Crunchy Roastie Chaat' is an entire meal in itself!

Serves 4 as a side dish

For the potatoes
1.5kg Maris Piper or King Edward potatoes
100ml olive oil
6 garlic cloves, cut into slivers
3 small shallots, very finely chopped
20 fresh curry leaves, cut into strips
1 teaspoon fennel seeds, crushed
2 teaspoons chilli flakes
1 tablespoon dried tarragon
fine sea salt

For the curry-crunch sprinkle
2 tablespoons amchoor
1 tablespoon medium curry powder
2 teaspoons smoked salt
2 teaspoons coarsely ground black pepper
1 tablespoon Kashmiri chilli powder
1½ teaspoons ground cumin
4 tablespoons polenta
2 tablespoons coarse semolina

· Peel the potatoes and chop into chunky angular pieces, creating 3–4 flat sides and corners on each. Parcook in a saucepan of boiling salted water for 5 minutes, then drain the water away, cover the pan with a lid and shake vigorously for a few seconds to create lots of crags on the surface of the potatoes. Set aside, uncovered, to let the steam escape.
· Heat the olive oil in a frying pan, then add the garlic slivers and shallots. Gently fry for 2–3 minutes before adding the curry leaves, fennel seeds, chilli flakes and dried tarragon. Fry the spices for another 2–3 minutes until the oil is well infused and the garlic just starting to brown. Drain the infused oil into a jug through a sieve, setting the crispy curry leaves, spices and garlic aside for now.
· In a separate bowl, mix all the ingredients for the curry-crunch sprinkle together.
· Preheat the oven to 190°C fan.
· Pour the infused oil all over the potatoes, then liberally cover with the curry-crunch sprinkle. Place the potatoes on an oven tray, well spaced apart, and bake untouched for 30 minutes, then flip them over and bake for another 20–25 minutes until each roastie is crunchy all over. Remove the potatoes from the oven and scatter over the crispy garlic, curry leaves and spices to finish.

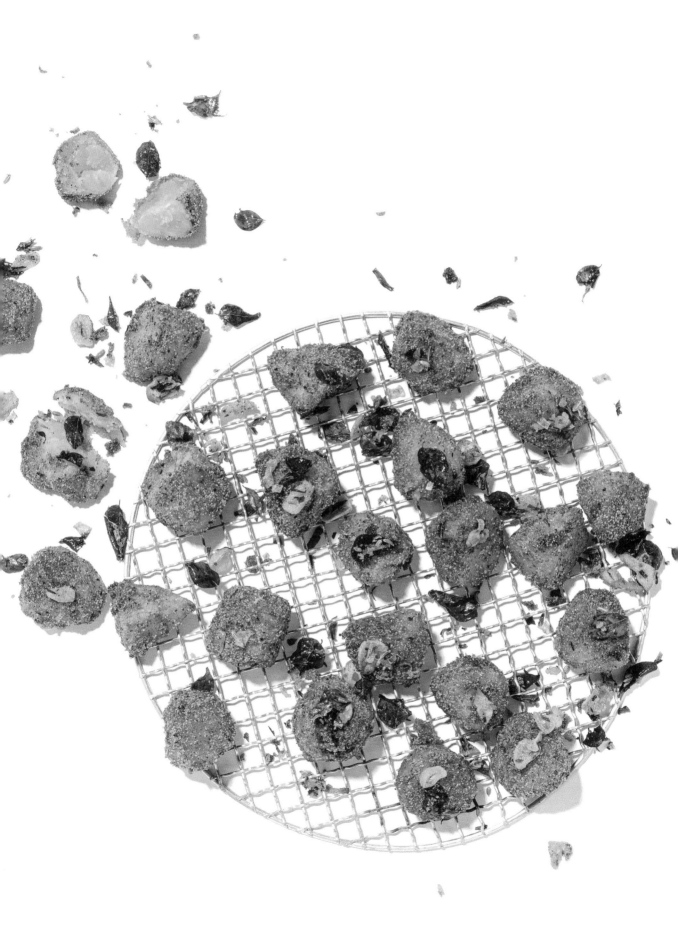

Mogo cassava chips with hot hoisin

In the seminal 1993 diasporic movie *Bhaji on the Beach*, there's a moment when two of the Aunty-Jis sit on a bench by Blackpool beach eating chips. Not looking entirely content, one of them pulls out a salt shaker of chilli from her handbag. The lid is removed and they both freehand sprinkle the bright red powder all over the hot blandness in their paper bags. The British seaside is transformed into something deliciously hybrid-Indian, in fried potato form. Cassava chips were my favourite treat growing up, always sprinkled with lime juice or malt vinegar, then with generous dustings of salt, chilli, cumin and amchoor. We'd dip them into anything saucy to hand, be that baked beans, lamb curry or pasta sauce. Nothing, however, beat hot fried mogo dipped in takeaway leftovers from our local Chinese restaurant Yum Sing, an institution that has shaped my culinary palate just as much as my mum's home cooking. This recipe evokes my memories of that, but feel free to take it in whatever direction you like.

Serves 4 as a side dish

For the hoisin
6 tablespoons hoisin sauce
2 tablespoons malt vinegar, plus more to serve
½ teaspoon cayenne pepper
1 teaspoon chilli powder (regular, not milder Kashmiri)
1 teaspoon ground cumin
1 teaspoon English mustard

For the chips
650g cassava
1 litre sunflower oil

To serve
lime juice
malt vinegar
smoked salt
Kashmiri chilli powder
amchoor
MSG (optional)

· For the hot hoisin, whisk the ingredients together until you have an intense ketchup, then leave the flavours to mingle for 15 minutes.
· For the mogo chips, peel the cassava, then very carefully slice into long thick chips in triangular finger shapes. You'll need a big sharp knife for this.
· Heat the sunflower oil to 170°C in a wok or large pan (see page 11), then fry the cassava chips in batches for 6–7 minutes until crispy on the outside and cooked through. Drain on kitchen paper, then sprinkle with the following (in this very specific order): lime juice, then malt vinegar, then smoked salt, then Kashmiri chilli powder, then amchoor and then MSG, if using.
· Toss, then serve with hot hoisin sauce for dipping.

Tip The order in which I sprinkle these chips with condiments is the order in which I was always told to do things when we ate these: the Loyal family way. It gets the acid into the chips deeper and the salt and spices hit your mouth straight away. It's not essential to follow suit, but I was raised never to question the wisdom of elders!

Crispy vindaloo aubergines with anchovy-chilli yogurt

Despite vindaloo's reputation as one of the hottest and therefore 'most authentically Indian' of dishes in the British curry-house canon, it is in fact a hybrid dish of Portuguese origin, regionally specific to the Catholic communities of Goa. The word vindaloo itself is an amalgamation of *de vinha d'alhos* which means 'in wine vinegar and garlic'. After the British came to Goa in the early 1800s, the dish was brought back to England, morphing centuries later into the patriotic anthem of Englishness that's sung in football stadiums today. What could be more English than Portuguese-Goan vinegar and garlic?

These crispy aubergines are vinegary, garlicky and hot in equal measure, using a South Indian sambhar masala that typifies vindaloo's Goan roots. The creamy umami hit of the anchovy yogurt quells its heat a little, but the aubergines are just as delicious on their own if it's full fire you're after.

Serves 4 as a side dish

For the yogurt
50g anchovies in olive oil, drained
2 garlic cloves
2 red chillies, stalks trimmed away, plus finely sliced chillies, to serve
1½ tablespoons amchoor
3 tablespoons vegetable oil
1 tablespoon coriander seeds, crushed
1 tablespoon black mustard seeds
2 tablespoons lemon juice
175g thick natural yogurt
pinch of fine sea salt, if needed

For the aubergines
8 garlic cloves, very finely chopped
6 tablespoons white wine vinegar
2 teaspoons English mustard
3 tablespoons Sambhar Masala (see page 25)
1 teaspoon cayenne pepper
2 teaspoons fine sea salt
2 tablespoons tomato purée
1 tablespoon caster sugar
2 large aubergines, cut into finger-sized strips
6 tablespoons polenta
4 tablespoons coarse semolina
2 tablespoons cornflour
500ml sunflower oil

· For the yogurt, grind the anchovies, garlic, red chillies and amchoor together into a thick paste.
· Heat the oil in a frying pan, then add the crushed coriander seeds and mustard seeds, sizzling for 1 minute. Next add the anchovy chilli paste and cook through for 1 minute, before adding the lemon juice.
· Tip the mixture into the yogurt in a bowl, stirring well. If needed, add a pinch of salt, then let cool.
· For the aubergines, whisk together the garlic, vinegar, English mustard, sambhar masala, cayenne pepper, salt, tomato purée and caster sugar into a thick paste. Toss in the aubergine strips, coat them all over, then leave for 20 minutes.
· Make the crispy coating by mixing the polenta, semolina and cornflour together in a shallow bowl.
· Toss the marinated aubergine into the crispy coating mix, leave for 30 seconds, then toss through again so they are dry on the surface.
· Heat the sunflower oil in a deep frying pan to 160°C (see page 11).
· Fry the aubergines for 4–5 minutes – turning carefully – until they are cooked through and crispy on the outside. Drain well on kitchen paper and serve hot with a good dollop of the anchovy yogurt and a sprinkling of chilli slices.

Raitas

A raita is nothing more than a cooling thick yogurt with 'stuff' added to it, making it completely open to the spectrum of 'stuff' you happen to have in your cupboards. I like to add elements of citrussy sourness to sharpen the yogurt, pockets of juiciness or salady crunch, a sizzled smattering of whole and ground spices for complexity, chopped herbs for freshness and generous amounts of garlic and salt to amp up the volume. These are two of my favourite raita combinations, but do play around. Intercultural improvisation is a fun way to find delicious happy accidents, and every so often you'll uncover something special that becomes a new favourite at your table.

Pomegranate pachadi

Serves 4

3 tablespoons vegetable oil
4 small shallots, finely chopped
1 teaspoon cumin seeds, crushed
1 teaspoon fennel seeds, crushed
1 tablespoon black mustard seeds
2 teaspoons anardana powder, plus more to serve
1 teaspoon chilli flakes
4 tablespoons freshly grated coconut
½ teaspoon fine sea salt
1 teaspoon coarsely ground black pepper
2 garlic cloves, very finely chopped
1 tablespoon finely grated fresh ginger
2 tablespoons pomegranate juice
1 tablespoon finely grated lime zest, plus 2 tablespoons lime juice
300g natural yogurt
2 tablespoons chopped mint leaves, plus more to serve
2 tablespoons pomegranate seeds

·   Heat the oil in a deep frying pan. Add the shallots and cook for 5–6 minutes until soft and translucent. Next add the cumin, fennel and mustard seeds, anardana powder and chilli flakes. Cook for 1 minute, then add the grated coconut, salt and pepper, mixing all the ingredients well.
·   Finally add the garlic, ginger, pomegranate juice, lime zest and juice. Sizzle for 1–2 minutes, then finish by swirling through the yogurt and mint. Enjoy warm or chilled, sprinkled with the pomegranate seeds, mint leaves and a pinch of anardana powder.

Cucumber, black lime & jalapeño raita

Serves 4

1 cucumber
40g jalapeños in brine, drained and chopped, plus more to serve
1 large garlic clove, finely grated
1 dried black lime, plus more to serve
1 teaspoon cumin seeds
3 cloves
1½ teaspoons fine sea salt
1 teaspoon granulated sugar
300g Greek yogurt
20g chopped mint leaves
20g chopped coriander leaves
1 tablespoon finely grated lime zest, plus 3 tablespoons lime juice, plus more lime zest to serve

·   Ribbon the cucumber into long strands using a vegetable peeler, leaving out the very watery seeds in the middle. Spoon into a mixing bowl with the chopped jalapeños and garlic. Mix well.
·   In a grinder, blitz the dried black lime, cumin seeds, cloves, salt and sugar to a fine powder. Sprinkle into the mixing bowl, toss well and leave for 5 minutes.
·   Drain away any excess liquid that has seeped out of the cucumbers, then mix through the yogurt, mint and coriander leaves, lime zest and juice.
·   Serve chilled, with lime zest, jalapeños and crushed black lime on top for an extra flavour hit!

Mango-Worcestershire kachumber

It's a cliché for an Indian person to write about mangos, but that isn't going to stop me. Mangos have such an ubiquitous presence in my life that leaving them out – for fear of affirming a stereotype – would be siding with those who lazily accept the stereotypes, and not with my truth. In India, there is not one singular mango season but a rolling cycle of seasons for each unique variety, which separately ripen when their time is right, each inundating the markets in turn, with names such as Rajapuri, Neelam, Benishan, Amrapali, Totapuri, Manohar, Chaunsa, Mulgoba and Gullab Khas (along with the Alphonso and Kesar that make their way to Southall, Brick Lane and Leicester). Mango and Worcestershire sauce may seem a peculiar flavour hybrid, but the iconic British condiment is in essence a matured concoction of tamarind, molasses, onion, garlic and spices. These two were meant to be.

Serves 4 as a side dish

1 large ripe mango, peeled
½ cucumber, halved and deseeded with a teaspoon
½ red onion, very finely chopped
2 tablespoons shelled salted peanuts, crushed
1 red chilli, finely chopped
½ teaspoon cumin seeds
½ teaspoon fennel seeds
¾ teaspoon fine sea salt
2 teaspoons light brown sugar
1 teaspoon amchoor
1 teaspoon finely grated lemon zest, plus 1 tablespoon lemon juice
1½ teaspoons Worcestershire sauce
1 tablespoon finely chopped mint leaves

· Chop the mango and cucumber into small (3mm) cubes, then place in a bowl with the red onion, crushed peanuts and red chilli.
· Dry pan-roast the cumin and fennel seeds for 2 minutes, then spoon into a grinder along with the salt and blitz to a fine powder. Sprinkle the spices into the mango bowl and mix well.
· Next add the light brown sugar, amchoor, lemon zest and juice and Worcestershire Sauce. Finally toss through the mint and mix one last time to finish. Serve immediately.

Kokum mooli slaw with cashews

More than any other food, mooli – or daikon radish – is hailed as the salve for all of life's troubles in our Punjabi household. Woken up with an upset stomach? Eat some mooli. Failed an exam? Eat some mooli. Lost your wallet? Eat some mooli. Although turmeric hogs the Indian remedy limelight in the mainstream, it's actually mooli's mystical powers that heal all ailments: physical, spiritual or emotional. And it's mighty tasty to boot.

This juicy slaw combines the sharp crispness of shredded mooli with the tropical sourness of kokum and toasted cashews for crunch. It's delicious as a side dish with any main course, or piled high in sandwiches and burgers. When the catch-all cure for life's plights is this tasty, there really is nothing to worry about.

Serves 4 as a side dish

70g semi-dried kokum, or 2 tablespoons fresh tamarind pulp
  (not concentrate, see page 157)
2 tablespoons vegetable oil
¾ teaspoon ajwain, crushed
1 tablespoon coriander seeds, crushed
6 tablespoons light brown sugar
1 teaspoon fine sea salt
½ large red cabbage, shredded
½ large mooli, shredded
2 large carrots, shredded with a julienne cutter
1 spring onion, finely chopped
1 garlic clove, very finely chopped
1 red chilli, finely chopped
2 tablespoons finely chopped dill
2 tablespoons shelled unsalted toasted (see page 40)
  and crushed cashew nuts

· Using a grinder, blitz the semi-dried kokum, if using, to a crumbly powder. Spoon into a saucepan with 250ml of water, then bring to the boil for 5 minutes. Remove from the heat and leave it to steep for 20 minutes into a strong, sour tea. If using tamarind pulp, mix it with 100ml water.
· In a separate pan, heat the vegetable oil to a medium-high heat, then add the ajwain and coriander seeds, sizzling for 1 minute. Strain the kokum tea into the pan of spices through a sieve, pressing to extract as much of the flavourful pulp as possible, or just add the diluted tamarind pulp. Reduce the heat to medium, then add the brown sugar and salt. Simmer for 13–15 minutes until about two-thirds of the water has evaporated and the mixture thickens to a loose syrup.
· Put the red cabbage, mooli and carrots in a mixing bowl with the spring onion, garlic and red chilli, mixing well.
· Pour the sweet-sour dressing over the slaw and toss well to coat all over. Leave the flavours to mingle for 10 minutes, then finish with a sprinkling of dill and crushed toasted cashews.

'Pilau rice'

I came across Dr Amber Spry when a tweet of hers went viral. It read: 'Every year when I teach identity politics I ask the same question on the first day of class. Rather than the usual icebreakers, I ask: "How does your family/your culture cook rice?"' It's a beautifully insightful question, structured to explore perspectives not only between cultures, but also within them. Indian food is often crudely divided between South Indian rice-based food and North Indian wheat-based cookery, a binary distinction that overlooks a spectrum of nuance which Dr Spry's question can unravel. Both South and North India have culinary customs around rice, just very different ones. Northern Indian rice dishes are influenced by Moghul legacies, where separated basmati grains are favoured for biryanis and pilaus to be served alongside wheat breads. In Southern India, they tend to favour stickier rice to complement sambhars and lentil dishes, and for grinding into idli, dosa and uttapams. But today, even this distinction is blurry, as there's a cornucopia of Southern Indian biryanis, and you're as likely to find idli and dosa in a North Indian dhabba as you are naans and roti. What's more, my own upbringing, frequenting the British Indian curry houses of Leicester, has planted the grammatically incorrect menu moniker of 'pilau rice' – which broadly translates as 'rice rice' – in my lexicon. Dr Spry's question, therefore, has answers that are as endlessly changeable as there are facets to Indianness. With that in mind, this is how I cook rice. How do you cook yours?

Raitas, Rice & Sides

Lemony fennel seed pilau

Serves 4 as a side dish

225g basmati rice
3 tablespoons ghee
3 teaspoons fennel seeds, crushed
½ teaspoon ajwain, crushed
1 teaspoon coriander seeds, crushed
1 cinnamon stick
1 red onion, finely chopped
2 tablespoons finely grated lemon zest, plus 3 tablespoons
   lemon juice
1 tablespoon finely grated fresh ginger
½ teaspoon ground turmeric
2 teaspoons fine sea salt
20 saffron strands, mixed in a cup
   with 1 tablespoon boiling water
20g coriander leaves

· Wash the rice under a cold tap until the water runs clear, then soak in a bowl of cold water for 1 hour.
· Heat the ghee in a saucepan, then add the fennel seeds, ajwain, coriander seeds and cinnamon stick. Sizzle for 1 minute before adding the red onion. Cook for 4–5 minutes until the onion starts to brown, then add the lemon zest, ginger, turmeric, salt, saffron threads with their water and the drained rice. Mix well so the rice grains are fully coated in the spiced ghee.
· Finally add the lemon juice with 500ml boiling water (or enough to cover the rice plus 1cm). Bring to the boil, then reduce the heat to a low simmer and cover with a lid. Cook for 20–25 minutes until the water has been absorbed, then take off the heat and leave covered for a final 5 minutes.
· Take off the lid, stir through the coriander, fluff up with a fork and enjoy.

Charred red pepper & mustard seed pilau

Serves 4 as a side dish

225g basmati rice
3 tablespoons ghee
1 tablespoon black mustard seeds, plus more to serve
1 teaspoon cumin seeds, crushed
1 teaspoon aniseed seeds, crushed
1 teaspoon coarsely ground black pepper
2 star anise
5 small shallots, finely chopped
2 garlic cloves, very finely chopped
75g jarred roasted red peppers, chopped, plus 75g jarred
   roasted red peppers, puréed, plus a few roasted peppers
   from the jar (optional), sliced, to serve
2 teaspoons Kashmiri chilli powder
2 teaspoons fine sea salt

· Wash the rice under a cold tap until the water runs clear, then soak in a bowl of cold water for 1 hour.
· Heat the ghee in a saucepan, then add the mustard seeds, cumin seeds, aniseed, pepper and star anise, sizzling for 1 minute. Next add the chopped shallots, browning for 4–5 minutes, before adding the garlic and drained rice. Mix well so the rice grains are coated in the spiced garlicky ghee.
· Finally add both the chopped and puréed red peppers, Kashmiri chilli powder and salt, along with 500ml boiling water (or enough to cover the rice plus 1cm). Bring to the boil, then reduce the heat to a low simmer and cover with a lid.
· Cook for 20–25 minutes until the water has been absorbed, then take off the heat and leave covered for a final 5 minutes. Take off the lid, fluff up with a fork, scatter with sliced red peppers, if you like, and mustard seeds and enjoy.

CHAPTER 6

ROTIS, NAAN, PARATHAS & PURI

Given that Punjab is the 'breadbasket of India', it's somewhat fitting that my studio flat is effectively the 'breadbasket of East London'. My weekly local circuit regularly takes in: fresh pillowy bacon naan from Dishoom in Shoreditch, sourdough from Jolene Bakery, char siu buns from Ong Ong, challah bread from Rinkoffs, spinach gözleme from Saray Broadway Café, custard-filled brioche from Yeast Bakery, garlic-coriander flatbreads from Ararat Bread, Dalston, focaccia from Dusty Knuckle, bacon croissant from Pophams, beigels (not bagels) from Brick Lane, and, my favourite of all, filled flaky parathas from The Kati Roll Company.

If it's a hand-kneaded baked or pan-griddled dough of any sort that's liberally enriched with butter, ghee, olive oil or another form of fatty dripping, filled or topped with something lusciously sweet, savoury or both, then toasted, charred or browned in some way, then you can count me in!

This assortment of roti, paratha, naan, stuffed kulcha and puri recipes epitomises my third-culture approach to flavour, made unapologetically carbohydrate. Each of these Indiany breads can serve as either edible scoops for curries, soups and dals; as tasty wraps to fill with whatever leftovers you have (provided an obligatory layer of chutney is included); or even serve as meals in themselves when loaded abundantly with spiced fillings that bulge from their middles right to their edges.

A good heavy rolling pin, cast-iron tawa griddle pan and gas hob are regarded as essentials to guarantee success with these types of bread. I possess none of these things, so please rest assured that using a bottle of wine to roll and a large frying pan on an induction stove also works just as well. Enjoy to your belly's content. After all, there's no such thing as bad carbs.

Making round rotis is not a skill I have mastered. My mum has gone through it with me step by step, hand-in-hand, moment-by-moment thousands of times, yet while I've inherited my mother tongue for flavour, my mother's touch for round rotis slapped to circular perfection between her hands I certainly have not. Whatever shape yours come out, the joy of mopping up a flavoursome dal, buttery saag or spicy curry with piping-hot roti straight from the pan is like no other. The brightly coloured variations on classic rotis or chapatis you'll find overleaf bring an additional facet of flavour to any meal. Though ask any Punjabi and they'll tell you that a traditional plain roti, such as this, freshly buttered by the hands of your mother, will always be flavour enough.

· Put the atta flour in a bowl along with the salt and sugar, mixing well. Add the vegetable oil, then use your fingers to rub the oil into the flour completely.
· Slowly pour the hot water into the middle of the flour a little at a time, stirring with a spoon until you can handle the dough. Different flours take different amounts of water: you want a soft, slightly tacky dough, so add as much as you need to achieve that. Knead the dough in the bowl for 7–8 minutes with your hands, dipping your knuckles into cold water a couple of times to get more water into the dough. Soft dough means it's well hydrated, will puff up and make soft rotis! Keep kneading until it has a smooth firm texture; don't be tempted to add more flour if you can avoid it. After 7–8 minutes it will turn from sticky to smooth as the gluten is activated. Brush with oil, cover with cling film and rest for 20 minutes.
· When ready to use, knead the rested dough for 1 minute. Take a ball of dough (about 50g), press slightly between your hands, then, as if making a dumpling, pull the sides of the circle into the middle. Pinch together where they meet, then press down on a work surface into a disc.
· Dip the dough disc in flour, then roll it out (as roundly as you can get it) using small, short rolls in one direction, spinning the roti each time. Alternatively, cheat by rolling it into whatever shape you can manage and cutting around a plate. It should be 16–18cm in diameter and 2mm thick.
· Heat a tawa or large frying pan to the hottest it will go. Slap the rolled chapati on to the hot tawa or pan and cook for 45 seconds until you see that the wetness has evaporated.
· Flip over and cook until bubbles appear on the surface, then flip again and use a damp cloth to press down along the perimeter of the roti, which helps it to puff up.
· Cook until very slightly charred but softly cooked through. Smother in butter and eat immediately.

Makes 10

275g wholewheat atta flour, plus more to dust
½ teaspoon fine sea salt
¼ teaspoon caster sugar
2 tablespoons vegetable oil, plus more for brushing
160–175ml hot water
salted butter, for smearing over

Turmeric, tarragon & ginger

2 teaspoons dried tarragon, crushed
1 tablespoon amchoor
2 teaspoons finely grated fresh turmeric
2 teaspoons finely grated fresh ginger

· Follow the recipe for plain chapatis, but add the tarragon and amchoor to the flour at the beginning and whisk the turmeric and ginger into the hot water.

Spinach, basil & ajwain

125g spinach
3 tablespoons lemon juice
25g basil leaves
2 garlic cloves, very finely chopped
2 teaspoons finely grated fresh ginger
½ teaspoon ajwain, crushed

· Heat the spinach in a saucepan with a splash of water and the lemon juice until completely wilted. Spoon into a blender along with the basil, garlic, ginger, ajwain and a splash of water. Blitz to a fine green paste.
· Follow the recipe for plain chapatis, reducing the amount of hot water to 110–120ml and whisking the spinach paste into the water. If needed, add an extra 4–5 tablespoons of atta flour to stop the dough being overly sticky.

Beetroot, cumin & dill

1 tablespoon vegetable oil
2 teaspoons cumin seeds
1 teaspoon ajwain seeds
150g beetroot, grated
2 garlic cloves
1 tablespoon amchoor
2 teaspoons finely grated fresh ginger
1 teaspoon black pepper
15g dill, finely chopped

· Heat the oil in a frying pan, then add the cumin seeds and ajwain. Sizzle for 1 minute before adding the grated beetroot. Cook for 2–3 minutes until soft with a little bite. Blitz in a blender with a splash of water to a fine red paste, along with the garlic, amchoor, ginger and pepper.
· Follow the recipe for plain chapatis, reducing the amount of hot water to 110–120ml, whisk the beetroot paste into the water and add the chopped dill. If needed, add an extra 4–5 tablespoons of atta flour to stop the dough being overly sticky.

Parathas

We are not entirely sure how old my paternal great-grandfather Payaah-Ji was when he died. There were such creative versions of his date of birth across various migratory documents over his lifetime – each telling a different truth – that we've never got to the bottom of it. We know he was over 100, possibly 105, but perhaps even older, although you wouldn't have thought it to look at him. In his final years, he had a daily routine of eating two parathas with mango pickle for breakfast, then going to the Coach and Horses Pub in Evington for half a pint of Guinness. Savoury breakfasts are a defining feature of Eastern cultures, correlated in some way I'm sure with living a long and happy life. As with baking croissants, the key to flaky parathas is interspersing stacked layers of dough with butter, oil or ghee, the fat causing the layers to puff apart as they are cooked. Here, you can either use the 'brush-then-Swiss-roll' technique, or the slightly more elegant 'brush-then-concertina-fold' method to achieve this textural result. Just ensure you eat them straight away, and always serve in plurals; a single paratha without at least a second is just not the done thing.

Plain

Mooli & coriander seed stuffing

Makes 8

150g wholewheat atta flour, plus more to dust
100g plain flour
1 teaspoon fine sea salt
½ teaspoon caster sugar
4 tablespoons ghee, melted, plus more to brush
175–200ml warm water

· Whisk together the atta flour, plain flour, salt and sugar. Next add half the melted ghee, along with the warm water, stirring well and only adding the water a little at a time to bring together into a dough; you may not need it all. Knead for 6–7 minutes until it's smooth and springy: you want a pliable soft dough. Brush with melted ghee, wrap in cling film and rest for 20 minutes. When rested, knead for a final 1 minute. It's now ready to use.
· Divide the dough into 8 equal balls. Take 1 and roll into a circle 18–20cm in diameter and 3mm thick. Brush generously with ghee all over, then sprinkle with a little flour; this helps to create the flaky layers.
· Use your fingers to either concertina fold the dough, or tightly roll it from top to bottom into a Swiss roll log. Brush with ghee, then twist inwards into a tightly compacted snail shape, tucking the end into the middle.
· Dip the coiled dough in flour, place flat on a floured work surface, then press down with your hand. Carefully roll out the paratha into a circle 18cm in diameter.
· Cook in a hot frying pan or tava for 2–3 minutes on each side, brushing with ghee each time you flip it. Serve immediately with pickles and salted yogurt while you form and fry the rest.

Makes 6

½ mooli, finely grated, water squeezed out
1 teaspoon coriander seeds, crushed
1 green chilli, finely chopped
1 teaspoon finely grated fresh ginger
2 teaspoons Chaat Masala (see page 24)
¾ teaspoon fine sea salt

Taleggio, sage & onion stuffing

Makes 6

150g Taleggio cheese, chilled and finely chopped
2 teaspoons finely chopped sage leaves
1 garlic clove, very finely chopped
1 small onion, very finely chopped
1 teaspoon amchoor

Schmaltzy potato, bacon & nigella stuffing

Makes 6

2 large potatoes, boiled and mashed
2 tablespoons schmaltz (chicken fat)
2 tablespoons fried bacon bits
½ small red onion, very finely chopped
1 teaspoon coarsely ground black pepper
1 teaspoon nigella seeds

· Whichever stuffing you prefer, just mix all the ingredients together in a bowl.
· Divide the paratha dough into 6 equal balls; you'll use slightly more dough than with plain parathas, in order to contain the filling.
· Roll a ball into a circle 20cm wide and 3mm thick. Brush generously with ghee all over, then press a thin layer of your chosen stuffing mix all over the surface.
· Use your fingers to either concertina fold the dough, or tightly roll it from top to bottom into a Swiss roll log, ensuring the stuffing is fully enclosed. Brush with ghee, then twist inwards into a tightly compacted snail shape, again ensuring the stuffing is enclosed, then tuck the end into the middle.
· Dip the coiled dough in flour, place flat on a floured work surface, then press down with your hand. Use the flat of your hand to press the paratha and filling out a little, then carefully roll it out into a circle 15cm in diameter; you'll need to be delicate to keep the stuffing contained, but don't worry if it spills out as those bits will crisp up deliciously.
· Cook in a hot frying pan or tava for 3 minutes on each side, brushing with ghee each time you flip it. Serve immediately with pickles and salted yogurt while you form and fry the rest.

Plain naan

The difference between naan and kulcha (see overleaf) is hotly contested, though I've always used the terms interchangeably. The debate centres on differences in refined flour vs wholewheat flour, yeasted leavening vs baking powder leavening, pan-fry baking vs tandoor-grill baking, stuffed vs not, high heat vs low heat. A debate of binaries that I take joy in meddling with.

My take borrows and intermixes from all sides to give a pillowy-soft texture, complex yeasty flavour, satisfying chew and rewarding puff. These are delicious plain; smothered in ghee, coriander and nigella seeds; or stuffed with whatever your imagination fancies. Call them naans or kulchas, but just don't call them 'Indian flatbreads'. There's nothing flat about these.

Makes 10

125–135ml whole milk
2 teaspoons caster sugar
1¾ teaspoons dried active yeast (I use Allinson's)
1 egg, plus 1 egg yolk
80g natural yogurt
2 tablespoons unsalted butter, melted,
  plus more to knead and brush
275g strong white bread flour
200g plain flour
1½ teaspoons fine sea salt, plus more to serve
1 teaspoon cornflour
½ teaspoon baking powder
1½ teaspoons nigella seeds
a little vegetable oil
chopped coriander leaves

· Gently heat the 125ml milk until lukewarm. Pour into a jug along with the caster sugar and yeast. Whisk well and leave in a warm place for 10 minutes to foam up.
· Add the egg and egg yolk, yogurt and 2 tablespoons of melted butter to the frothy wet mix. Whisk well and set aside.
· Sift the bread flour, plain flour, salt, cornflour and baking powder into the bowl of a stand mixer fitted with the dough hook. Add the nigella seeds and mix well so the dry ingredients are evenly dispersed. Set to a medium speed. Slowly pour the wet ingredients into the flour mix in a steady stream. When it begins to form a single lump of dough, increase the mixer speed to medium-high for 1–2 minutes. Depending on your flour, you may need to add the extra 1–2 teaspoons of milk.
· Spoon a little melted butter on to a work surface, empty out the dough and knead for 7–8 minutes, pressing and stretching heavily with your fists to develop the gluten and slapping it down from a height a few times. Eventually it will become a smooth, elastic and slightly tacky dough. Form the dough into a ball, brush with melted butter and place in a bowl. Cover with cling film, then leave in a warm place for 3–4 hours until doubled in size.
· Punch the dough down in the bowl, then knead for a final minute. Divide into 10 equal balls, brush with melted butter and cover with a damp cloth until ready to use.
· Preheat the grill to the highest it will go.
· Roll out a ball of dough on an oiled surface into a teardrop shape about 15cm long and 3mm thick; this will take a little effort but the elasticity of the dough is what gives it a chewy-crispy texture.
· Heat a large heavy-based tawa or frying pan to a high temperature over the hob. Brush the top of the rolled-out dough with cold water, then carefully lift and slap it on to the hot pan, water-side down. Cook for 45 seconds until the underside has started to colour and it begins to bubble up, then quickly place under the hot grill, as close to the bars as you can get. Cook for 1–2 minutes until bubbly and burnished.
· Remove from the grill, brush with melted butter, then sprinkle with a little salt and the chopped coriander. Serve, while you form and cook the rest.

Rotis, Naan, Parathas & Puri

Stuffed kulcha

Amritsar potato & cauliflower stuffing

Makes 8

1 quantity Naan dough (see page 192)
vegetable oil
1 quantity of your chosen filling
unsalted butter, melted

· Divide the dough into 8 equal balls and cover them with a damp cloth until ready to use. Roll 1 piece out on a well-oiled surface into a circle 20cm in diameter x 4mm thick. Spread a thick layer of filling in the middle, leaving a broad border clear, then pull the sides of the dough inwards all around, encasing the filling completely, with pleats meeting in the middle to seal the circle.
· Flip so it's seam side down, then use your hands to gently press from the middle outwards a little with your fingers. Next use a rolling pin to roll into a circle 15cm in diameter x 5mm thick. Be careful not to overstretch, to avoid the stuffing breaking out.
· Flip over again and brush the sealed seam side of the stuffed kulcha with water.
· Preheat a tawa or frying pan over a medium heat and carefully place the kulcha, wet seam side down, in the pan. Cook for 2–3 minutes until the bottom is starting to colour. Carefully flip over and cook for another 3–4 minutes until the edges have turned pale.
· Continue to cook and flip for another 1–2 minutes until both top and bottom are crisp and the inside is fluffy, not doughy. Finish by brushing with melted butter and enjoy.

Makes 8

1 tablespoon vegetable oil
1 onion, finely chopped
2 teaspoons coriander seeds
1 teaspoon cumin seeds
½ teaspoon ajwain seeds
2 teaspoons finely grated fresh ginger
3 garlic cloves, very finely chopped
1 green chilli, finely chopped
2 potatoes, chopped, boiled and drained
½ cauliflower, finely chopped
2 teaspoons Garam Masala (see page 23)
½ teaspoon ground turmeric
1 teaspoon fine sea salt

· Put the oil in a pan, then fry the chopped onion for 3–4 minutes before adding the coriander seeds, cumin seeds and ajwain. Sizzle for 1 minute, then add the ginger, garlic and green chilli. Next add the potatoes and cauliflower to the pan, coating in the spices. Finally add the garam masala, turmeric, salt and 100ml water. Cook for 4–5 minutes until the cauliflower is cooked through and you have a thick spiced mash. Allow to cool.

Saffron, pea & paneer stuffing

Makes 8

1 onion, finely chopped
1 tablespoon vegetable oil
1 teaspoon fennel seeds
1 teaspoon coriander seeds
150g paneer, grated
20 saffron strands
2 teaspoons Sambhar Masala (see page 25)
1 teaspoon fine sea salt
200g frozen peas, defrosted

· Fry the onion in the oil for 4–5 minutes until it is translucent, then add the fennel seeds and coriander seeds, sizzling for 1 minute. Next add the grated paneer, saffron, sambhar masala and salt. Cook for 2–3 minutes until cooked through, then add the peas. Keep cooking for another 1–2 minutes. Allow to cool.

'Nduja-mooli stuffing

Makes 8

400g mooli
½ teaspoon fine sea salt
100g soft 'nduja
2 tablespoons chopped coriander leaves

· Grate the mooli into a bowl and sprinkle with the salt. Leave to stand for 10 minutes, then squeeze out the liquid over a sink. Return to the bowl, add the 'nduja and coriander and mix well.

Tip You can also choose to stuff kulcha with a keema stuffing in the same way: make Baharat Keema or Kasundi Keema (see pages 55 and 125) and allow to cool before you use it to stuff the kulcha.

Puris or bhaturas

'Shall we make puris?' means 'I've made puris.' As with doughnuts, fries and pakoras, there's something just a smidgen naughty about deep-fried crispy puris, which seems lessened if you phrase what's already happened as a question. Sort of.

Chickpea curry with tamarind and a swirl of yogurt are the classic pairing for puris, but I also love them with drier dishes such as chutney-sizzled paneer, for scooping up Chinese stir-fries, with Thai and Malaysian curries, or even with leftover bolognese sauce. As with many occasions in Indian cooking, the secret ingredient to crunchy-fluffy puris that don't absorb too much oil, that puff up in the middle and stay dry-yet-soft, is semolina and a pinch of sugar. Enjoy with full gusto; their deep-fried wickedness is why they're such a joy.

Makes 10–12

225g wholewheat atta flour, plus more to dust
¾ teaspoon fine sea salt
1 teaspoon caster sugar
1 tablespoon coarse semolina
3 tablespoons sunflower oil, plus 500ml more for frying
150–175ml warm water

· Put the atta flour, salt, sugar and semolina in a large bowl and mix until combined. Next add the 3 tablespoons of oil and rub through completely with your fingertips. Add the warm water very gradually, bringing everything together into a pliable dough.
· Knead for 8–10 minutes until smooth, then cover with a damp cloth and leave to rest for 15 minutes.
· When ready to use, knead the dough once more for 2 minutes, then divide into 10–12 equal balls.
· Heat the 500ml of oil in a wok or deep pan to 185°C (see page 11); it needs to be hot to get the puris to puff!
· On a floured surface, flatten the dough balls, then roll them out into even circles 10cm in diameter x 2cm thick. Carefully drop a puri into the hot oil, using a wire mesh 'spider' or slotted spoon to keep it submerged under the hot oil. After 20–30 seconds, the steam in the dough will puff the puri up from the middle, either in small pockets of bubbles or a big balloon. Carefully turn over and fry for another 30–45 seconds until golden brown, but not burnt.
· Drain on kitchen paper and repeat the process for the rest of the puris, always ensuring the oil is hot! Eat straight away.

CHAPTER 7

CHUTNEYS, SAUCES, PICKLES & ACHAAR

Watching guests smother their plates in chutneys, sauces, pickles and achaars is a sight that Punjabi home cooks enjoy above all others. Far from being optional flourishes or side-saddle extras, condiments are considered integral elements of a meal, each given as much consideration by cooks as the main event itself.

In our house, they're placed on an actual pedestal in the middle of the table, to be freely slathered over whatever is being served at a guest's own discretion. Some will carefully place a small teaspoon of mango-lime achaar on to mooli parathas, while others dollop out an entire jar. Some trickle a thimble of tamarind chutney on to samosas, while others drown them in an ocean. Some just kiss their kati rolls with a whisper of spiced ketchup, while others go in for a full-on snog. There really is no impolite way of doing it, apart from not doing it at all.

The mark of a good chutney or pickle is how khararah it's considered to be – one of my favourite Punjabi words of all – which refers to a very specific form of highly spiced, cuttingly flavoured potency. Something adorned with the khararah label is both admired for its undiluted hot-sour taste extremity, and also slightly feared for its addictive palate-hogging qualities.

This assortment of third-culture chutney, sauce, pickle and achaar creations is on the more approachable side of khararah, to be used as a starting point for flexing to your own taste. The recipes are designed to be played with, so do dial up the spices, chilli or sourness to suit your palate. You not following the recipes precisely is my exact intention.

OUTSIDE THE HOLDER, CLOCKWISE FROM TOP
Hot Rhubarb & Nigella Chutney;
Tamarind, Date & Mint Sauce;
Coriander, Spring Onion & Curry Leaf Chutney

IN THE HOLDER, CLOCKWISE FROM TOP
Coconut, Za'atar & Maple Chutney; Black Garlic,
Tamarind & Kokum Ketchup; Sour Cherry & Caraway
Chutney; Cherry Tomato, Chilli & Dill Chutney;
Lime Leaf & Amchoor Aioli

Coriander, spring onion & curry leaf chutney

There is no 'correct' way to make a green chutney, because every home cook is adamant that theirs is it. Subsequently, there are billions of correct ways, every one of them perfect... as well as primed for critique. You can add mint and green apple if you like, though some will see that as sacrilege. You can opt for raw yellow onions, though to some only shallots will do. And you can stick to simple fresh herbs with citrus, though others will insist on adding a sizzling tarkha of spices.

My take has evolved over the years, freely ricocheting in a new direction whenever I encounter a superior green chutney whose secrets I have no shame in borrowing. This is a snapshot of how I make it at the time of writing: with both coriander and mint blitzed into the mix, spring onions for mild bite and a tarkha of curry leaves, cumin and coriander seeds for extra depth. Adapt according to your own tastes and change it up if your tastes change: the dynamic ping-pong sensibilities of Indian chutneys are part of their joy.

Makes 1 small jam jar/Serves 6

3 tablespoons vegetable oil
1 teaspoon coriander seeds, crushed
1 teaspoon cumin seeds, crushed
30–35 fresh curry leaves
50g coriander
2 spring onions, chopped
20g mint leaves
1 green chilli, stalk trimmed away
1 tablespoon finely grated lime zest, plus 4 tablespoons lime juice
1 large garlic clove, very finely chopped
1 teaspoon finely grated fresh ginger
5 tablespoons natural yogurt
1 teaspoon amchoor
¾ teaspoon fine sea salt
2 tablespoons light brown sugar

· Heat the oil in a frying pan, then add the coriander and cumin seeds. Sizzle for 1–2 minutes until they release their aromas, then add the curry leaves. Cook for 1 more minute, then remove from the heat.
· Using a blender, whizz together the coriander, spring onions, mint, green chilli, lime zest and juice, garlic, ginger, yogurt, amchoor, salt and sugar with a splash of water.
· Add the infused oil with its spices and curry leaves and blend once more into a smooth green chutney. Refrigerate to cool before serving.

Tamarind, date & mint sauce

HP sauce is iconic Britishness in both name and flavour: its initials standing for 'Houses of Parliament' and its taste standing for 'bacon sarnie'. Curiously, a glance through its ingredients list reads like a classic imli chutney – tamarind, tomatoes, dates, molasses, spices, malt vinegar – the very makings of Indianness! Just as every Brit has their unique way of making Yorkshire puddings (add extra egg whites, use sizzling dripping or bacon fat, never open the oven door!) so every Indian has their own signature imli. Mine is very liberally spiced, layered with different types of sourness, twice sweetened by means of date syrup and dark brown sugar, then brightened with mint at the very end. It goes with everything, bacon sarnies especially.

Makes 1 small jam jar/Serves 6

1 teaspoon ground cinnamon
¼ teaspoon ground cloves
1 teaspoon amchoor
1 teaspoon fine sea salt
2 tablespoons vegetable oil
1½ teaspoons cumin seeds, crushed
1 teaspoon fennel seeds, crushed
3 tablespoons tamarind concentrate, or 6 tablespoons
　(90ml) fresh tamarind pulp (see page 157)
6 tablespoons (90ml) date syrup
1 teaspoon finely grated lime zest, plus 5 tablespoons
　lime juice
4 tablespoons dark brown sugar
2 teaspoons finely grated fresh ginger
15g mint leaves, very finely chopped

· Mix the ground cinnamon and cloves, amchoor and salt with 2 tablespoons of water into a paste.
· Heat the vegetable oil in a frying pan, then add the cumin and fennel seeds. Sizzle for 1 minute, then stir in the spice paste and cook for 30 seconds. Next add the tamarind concentrate, date syrup, lime zest and juice, sugar and ginger, along with 50ml cold water. Bring to the boil, then reduce the heat to low and simmer for 3–4 minutes, whisking well. Remove from the heat and cool to room temperature.
· Finally, stir through the mint and dilute to whatever level of intensity suits your taste. I only add a splash of water to keep it syrupy, sharp and tangy, although a gentler, looser sauce is just as good.

Coconut, za'atar & maple chutney · Hot rhubarb & nigella chutney

Although my non-scientific approach to playing with intercultural flavours is driven by instinct over science, this chutney is a precise textbook illustration of my loose method in practice. Borrowing za'atar from the Middle East, maple syrup from Canada and coconuts from every place in the world that lays claim to them, the chords these flavours strike in combination are chromatically divine. Don't be shy with the sourness and salt here; balancing the elements is what makes it sing.

Makes 1 small jam jar/Serves 6

50g desiccated coconut
4 tablespoons vegetable oil
2 teaspoons black mustard seeds
1 teaspoon coriander seeds, crushed
1 teaspoon fennel seeds
1 tablespoon za'atar
2 garlic cloves, chopped
2 teaspoons finely grated fresh ginger
2 green chillies, stalks trimmed away
1½ teaspoons fine sea salt
1 teaspoon finely grated lime zest, plus 6 tablespoons
   (90ml) lime juice
2 tablespoons white wine vinegar
4 tablespoons maple syrup
30g mint leaves, chopped
30g coriander leaves, chopped

· Dry pan-roast the desiccated coconut in a frying pan until it just starts to brown. Empty into a bowl and leave to cool.
· Heat the oil in the same pan, then add the mustard, coriander and fennel seeds, sizzling for 1 minute. Next add the za'atar and toasted coconut. Cook for 1–2 minutes, mixing well, then take off the heat and set aside.
· In a blender, blitz the garlic, ginger, green chillies, salt, lime zest and juice, vinegar and maple syrup to a smooth paste. Add the mint and coriander with 75ml water. Blend again into a verdant green pulp.
· Finally stir through the za'atar-spiced coconut mix, pulsing to finish. Refrigerate to cool before serving.

I'm as hysterically obsessive about rhubarb season as I am about mango season; a quick glance through my technicolour Instagram will affirm this. But then this combination of sharp appley-rhubarb with thymey burnt onion-like nigella seeds is one that more than warrants fanaticism in my view. This chutney is mouth-puckeringly sour and moreish, with specks of toasted whole spices that add textural crunch. It is best made with fresh, neon-pink, sherbety rhubarb at the height of its late winter-early spring season, but frozen rhubarb works just fine if, like me, you need your fix year round.

Makes 1 small jam jar/Serves 6

2 tablespoons vegetable oil
1 medium onion, very finely chopped
1 tablespoon nigella seeds
½ teaspoon ajwain
2 tablespoons finely grated fresh ginger
1½ teaspoons fine sea salt
2 teaspoons chilli flakes
325g rhubarb, fresh or frozen, chopped
100g granulated sugar
90ml white wine vinegar
2 teaspoons anardana powder
1 teaspoon beetroot juice (optional)

· Heat the vegetable oil in a large saucepan, then add the onion, nigella seeds and ajwain. Cook for 4–5 minutes until translucent. Next add the ginger, salt, chilli flakes and rhubarb along with a splash of water. Cook for 4–5 minutes until the rhubarb fibres begin to untangle.
· Finally add the sugar, vinegar and anardana powder along with 50ml water. Simmer over a medium heat for 25–30 minutes, stirring occasionally, until the rhubarb has broken down. When it reaches a runny jam-like consistency, stir through the beetroot juice, if using, for a blush-pink colour.
· Cool completely and enjoy inside toasties (see pages 72 and 78), with cheese, or dolloped on to any chaat.

Lime leaf & amchoor aïoli

Fresh lime leaves always come connected in pairs, paisley teardrops bonded by a stalk, like a fragrant artery conjoining two hearts. Their aromas are at once herbal, citrussy, tropical and zingy, dancing along the flavour spectrum from lemongrass to basil to sharp lime. Infused into garlicky Japanese mayonnaise, with a little amchoor for zest, the flavour chords this aioli strikes are divine.

Makes 1 small jam jar/Serves 6

2 tablespoons vegetable oil, plus 1 tablespoon more
  if needed
12 fresh lime leaves
1 teaspoon fennel seeds
½ teaspoon fine sea salt
1 fat garlic clove
1 teaspoon caster sugar
2 teaspoons amchoor
100g Kewpie, Thomy or other egg yolk-based mayonnaise

· Heat the oil in a frying pan, then gently sizzle the lime leaves and fennel seeds for 1–2 minutes to release their aromas. Spoon into a spice grinder along with the salt, garlic, caster sugar and amchoor, then blitz to a grainy paste. Add an extra tablespoon of oil if needed to get it going.
· Mix or ripple the fragrant green paste into the mayonnaise in a bowl and let the flavours mingle for 15 minutes before serving.

Cherry tomato, chilli & dill chutney

This piquant tomato chutney is my take on a Bengali kasundi, a sweetly sour East Indian condiment that's spiked with mustard seeds, cumin and chilli. Cherry tomatoes add concentrated brightness, while dill brings an anisey nuance to the blend. Swirl into dals, smear over burgers or simply spread on buttery toasted bread for tomatoes on toast with a distinct Indian twist.

Makes 1 small jam jar/Serves 6

2 tablespoons vegetable oil
1 tablespoon black mustard seeds
1 teaspoon cumin seeds, crushed
2 garlic cloves, very finely chopped
1 teaspoon finely grated fresh ginger
2 teaspoons chilli flakes
¼ teaspoon ground cloves
1 teaspoon amchoor
300g cherry tomatoes, halved
1 teaspoon fine sea salt
2 tablespoons dark brown sugar
1 tablespoon apple cider vinegar
1 teaspoon finely grated lime zest, plus 1 tablespoon
  lime juice
2 tablespoons finely chopped dill

· Heat the oil in a saucepan, then add the mustard and cumin seeds, sizzling for 1 minute. Next add the garlic, ginger and chilli flakes, stirring for 30 seconds, before adding the ground cloves and amchoor.
· Next add the halved cherry tomatoes. Cook over a high heat until the tomatoes blister and pop, then reduce the heat to medium and simmer for 2–3 minutes.
· Add the salt, dark brown sugar, vinegar and lime zest, simmering for another 5–6 minutes until the tomatoes have broken down fully. Mix through the dill and lime juice to finish. Let it cool completely and enjoy.

Sour cherry & caraway chutney

Sour cherries have a lipstick-red colour and tart lemony-rose flavour that marry superbly with the toasted-pepperiness of caraway. This chutney crosses continents when it comes to pairing with food, working well with everything from French cheeses to Louisiana fried chicken, or Thai spring rolls to Cornish pasties. Dollop it generously, wherever in the world you take it.

Makes 1 small jam jar/Serves 6

1½ tablespoons caraway seeds
½ cinnamon stick
1½ tablespoons coriander seeds
1 teaspoon black peppercorns
1½ teaspoons fine sea salt
3 tablespoons vegetable oil
2 shallots, blitzed to a paste
2 garlic cloves, finely grated
300g frozen sour cherries, defrosted
3 tablespoons apple cider vinegar
2 tablespoons tomato purée
2 tablespoons very finely chopped mint leaves
3 tablespoons light brown sugar

· Dry pan-roast the caraway seeds, cinnamon stick, coriander seeds and peppercorns for 1–2 minutes until they release their aromas. Pour into a grinder and blitz to a powder with the salt.
· Heat the oil in a frying pan, then add the shallot and garlic pastes. Cook for 4–5 minutes until they take on a little colour, then add the powdered spices and cook for another 1 minute.
· Next add the sour cherries and continue to sauté for 4–5 minutes until they blister in the pan. Add the vinegar, tomato purée, chopped mint and brown sugar along with 100ml water. Simmer gently for 10–15 minutes until you have a thick runny jam. Cool completely, then blend to a smooth or chunky chutney, depending how you like it.
· This is great straight away, or even better after the flavours have mingled for 5 days in a sterilised jar.

Tip To sterilise a jar, wash it with hot soapy water and rinse. Plunge into a pot of boiling water for 10 minutes, then very carefully remove and allow to dry. Use as soon as possible.

Chutneys, Sauces, Pickles & Achaar

Black garlic, tamarind & kokum ketchup

Like practising scales on a cello or rehearsing lyrics for a Madonna karaoke-off, repetition is the best way to make something stick in your mind. I've said it many times but I'll say it once more: subtle flavours that let ingredients shine are wonderful, but more-is-more flavours that all shine together can be equally so! This ketchup is very much the latter, with flavour bombs of umami-rich black garlic, tangy tamarind and sour kokum each beaming their lustre on to the next. Use in place of, or in addition to, tomato ketchup. More really is more.

Makes 1 small jam jar/Serves 6

50g semi-dried kokum
12 black garlic cloves
1 small onion, chopped
2 tablespoons vegetable oil
1 tablespoon finely grated fresh ginger
1 teaspoon ground cinnamon
115g dark brown sugar
3 tablespoons tamarind concentrate, or 6 tablespoons fresh tamarind pulp or paste (see page 157)
2 tablespoons tomato purée
2 tablespoons dark soy sauce
2 tablespoons lime juice
2 tablespoons apple cider vinegar
2 garlic cloves, very finely chopped
1 teaspoon toasted sesame oil

· Grind the kokum to a crumbly rubble, then empty into a saucepan with 150ml water. Bring to the boil, then take off the heat and let it steep for 20 minutes, to make a strong sour kokum tea. When cool, pour through a sieve, squeezing out the tart juices from the pulp.
· Next grind the black garlic and onion to a paste with 50ml cold water. Leave to one side.
· Heat the oil in a frying pan, then add the black garlic paste and ginger, cooking for 3–4 minutes until it just starts to caramelise. Add the cinnamon, dark brown sugar, sieved kokum tea, tamarind, tomato purée, dark soy, lime juice and vinegar. Simmer for 20 minutes over a low heat until you have a runny ketchup, whisking throughout.
· Finish by adding the garlic and sesame oil. Simmer for a final 2–3 minutes to thicken a little more, then cool completely.

Pink pickled onions with lychee

Mango hot sauce

There's something mesmerising about the giant jars of pickled onions found on the neon-lit shelves of fish and chip shops across the land. They're almost comical to look at, preserving what looks like translucent space-alien heads in mysteriously murky brine. These pink-pickled onions with lychees are more My Little Pony than *Dr Who* at first glance, but don't be fooled by their cutesy blushed appearance: their otherworldly flavours pack a real flavour punch!

When Beyoncé sang, 'I got hot sauce in my bag, swag,' the Punjabi diaspora around the world collectively nodded. Tabasco, Encona and Cholula Original hot sauce are always guaranteed centre-stage at our tables, a triad of flavour as familiar to our plates as tamarind, coriander chutney or lemon achaar. This hot sauce marries elements of all three, mixed with the tropical velvet-sweetness of puréed mango. In food, as in life, it's always good to ask: what would Beyoncé do?

Makes 1 large jar/Serves 10

Makes 1 large jar/Serves 10

100ml lychee syrup from a can, plus 15–20 canned lychees in syrup, halved
100ml clear distilled malt vinegar
4 tablespoons lime juice
1 tablespoon fine sea salt
2 tablespoons caster sugar
1 teaspoon coriander seeds, crushed
½ teaspoon nigella seeds
1 teaspoon chilli flakes
4 cloves
2 medium red onions

400g ripe fresh mango purée, or canned Alphonso mango pulp
4 tablespoons light brown sugar
2 tablespoons apple cider vinegar
3 tablespoons lime juice
2 teaspoons finely grated fresh ginger
1 garlic clove, very finely chopped
1 tablespoon amchoor
2 teaspoons fine sea salt
4 tablespoons vegetable oil
¼ teaspoon ajwain
seeds from 6 green cardamom pods, crushed
½ Scotch bonnet pepper, finely chopped
1 teaspoon ground turmeric

· For the pickling liquor, whisk together the canned lychee syrup, vinegar, lime juice, salt and caster sugar with 100ml hot water. Whisk until the sugar and salt have dissolved.
· Next add the crushed coriander seeds, nigella seeds, chilli flakes and cloves to the liquor.
· Slice the red onions into thin 5mm rings, then layer into a sterilised glass jar (see page 206) with the lychees. Pour over the pickling liquor, including the whole spices. Seal with an airtight lid and leave to pickle in a cool dark place for 3 days.

· Mix together the mango purée or pulp, sugar, vinegar, lime juice, ginger, garlic, amchoor and salt into a thick paste, adding a splash of water.
· Next, heat the oil in a frying pan. Add the ajwain, cardamom seeds, Scotch bonnet and turmeric. Sizzle for 2 minutes, then remove from the heat to let the oil infuse for 3–4 minutes. Pour in the mango mixture and mix well. Slowly bring to the boil, then reduce the heat to low and cook for 10 minutes until you have a jammy sauce.
· Cool completely, then refrigerate for at least 1 hour to let the flavours mingle before serving.

Punjabi pickle party

Achaari-lemon chilli crisp

Stories surrounding the lengths the Punjabi diaspora will go to in order to transport pickles across borders, from pind (motherland village) to adopted-land pantry, are worthy of a three-volume novel each mango season. *Ulysses* has nothing on the tales that those pots of pickle have to tell: some arriving intact safely inside their gaffer-taped containers; others bursting open in suitcases to be salvaged by spooning out from inside jacket sleeves at the other end; still others pinched along their voyages by snaffling security, on the proviso that they could be explosives. Which, in taste, they most certainly are.

Pickles, achaars, masala preserves, whatever you want to call them, these are the soul of Punjabi cooking itself, the halo that hovers over the cuisine and people, connecting them through flavourful bhangra on the tongue. These recipes give you basic guidelines, but achaars are meant to be personal, a way to share your own tale through fermented flavour in as epic a manner as you see fit.

Punjabi lemon pickle and Chinese chilli crisp smothered over hot mooli parathas are my secret breakfast of choice: a combined chord of deliciousness so good that, to date, I've kept it to myself. This is a merging of flavour bombs that explodes everything you put it on and saves a step in the process. Patience may be a virtue, but blissful greed calls for speed.

Makes 1 large jar/Serves 10

65ml vegetable oil
2 teaspoons coriander seeds, crushed
1 teaspoon black mustard seeds
1 teaspoon cumin seeds
2 teaspoons fennel seeds
¼ teaspoon ajwain
5 allspice berries, crushed
1 tablespoon finely grated lemon zest
1 tablespoon finely grated fresh ginger
125g preserved lemons, deseeded and finely chopped,
    plus 2 tablespoons preserved lemon brine
6 tablespoons Chinese chilli crisp (Lao Gan Ma)

· Heat the oil in a frying pan, then add the coriander, mustard, cumin and fennel seeds, the ajwain and allspice berries. Sizzle for 1–2 minutes until they release their aromas.
· Next add the lemon zest, ginger, preserved lemons and their brine and the chilli crisp. Cook for 2 minutes, stirring well, then spoon into a large sterilised jar (see page 206).
· Cool completely, then let the flavours mingle for at least 1 hour.

Chutneys, Sauces, Pickles & Achaar

Punjabi vegetable pickle

The combination of anisey whole spices, zesty sliced lemon, ginger and sugar provide the alchemy that can transform any mix of crunchy vegetables into the most Punjabi of pickles. In India, at the beginning of the process the vegetables are scattered over large tea towels, then air-dried on rooftops to intensify their flavours. If you are graced with a suitable rooftop and abundant sunshine, it's worth giving it a go.

Makes 1 large jar/Serves 10

3 tablespoons vegetable oil
2 green chillies, split
2 tablespoons fennel seeds
2 teaspoons aniseed seeds
1 tablespoon cumin seeds
2 tablespoons black mustard seeds
250g mooli, chopped
200g carrots, chopped
200g cauliflower florets
2 tablespoons finely grated fresh ginger
1 teaspoon finely grated fresh turmeric
½ lemon, sliced, slices deseeded
2 tablespoons fine sea salt
3 tablespoons caster sugar
2 tablespoons clear distilled malt vinegar

· Heat the vegetable oil in a deep frying pan, then add the chillies and let them sizzle away for 1 minute. Next add the fennel, aniseed, cumin and mustard seeds, sizzling for another minute, but watch that they don't burn.
· Now add the vegetables to the pan, along with the ginger, fresh turmeric and sliced lemon. Mix well, before adding the salt, sugar and vinegar. Cook for a final 2 minutes, let it cool completely and then spoon into a large sterilised jar (see page 206). Leave in a cool dry place to pickle for at least 7 days, then enjoy.

Tip The method is the same whatever combination of vegetables you use, so get experimental. Try turnips, whole garlic cloves, beetroot, cooking apples or even pineapple!

Punjabi mango pickle

Sharp, unripe mangos being sizzled in peppery spiced mustard oil is one of the most distinctive smells of my childhood. As mangos pickle in their jars they very gradually soften in texture, releasing their juices into the oils and developing their flavours on an hourly basis. Be sure to dive in with a spoon at regular intervals: tasting the voyage of their evolution from spiky-bitterness to tangy-sweetness is quite a ride.

Makes 1 large jar/Serves 10

5 tablespoons (75ml) mustard oil
1 tablespoon black mustard seeds
2 tablespoons fennel seeds
2 teaspoons nigella seeds
½ teaspoon ajwain seeds
¾ teaspoon fenugreek seeds, crushed
500g green mango, chopped into small wedges, skin on
1 teaspoon chilli powder (regular chilli powder, not Kashmiri)
1 teaspoon ground turmeric
2 tablespoons fine sea salt
3 tablespoons light brown sugar
4 tablespoons clear distilled malt vinegar

· Heat the mustard oil in a large, deep frying pan over a high heat for 2 minutes until it gives off a faint smell of mustard. Remove from the heat and let it cool slightly.
· With the hot oil off the heat, add the mustard, fennel, nigella, ajwain and crushed fenugreek seeds; mix well as it froths up, so the spices do not burn. Next add the green mango and chilli powder, mix well, then finally mix through the turmeric, salt, sugar and vinegar.
· Cook over a gentle heat for 1 minute so the salt and sugar dissolve. Cool completely, then spoon into a large sterilised jar (see page 206). Close firmly and shake to mix everything together well.
· Leave to pickle in a cool dry place for at least 7 days, then enjoy.

CLOCKWISE FROM TOP LEFT
Achaari-Lemon Chilli Crisp; Punjabi Vegetable Pickle,
Punjabi Mango Pickle

CHAPTER 8

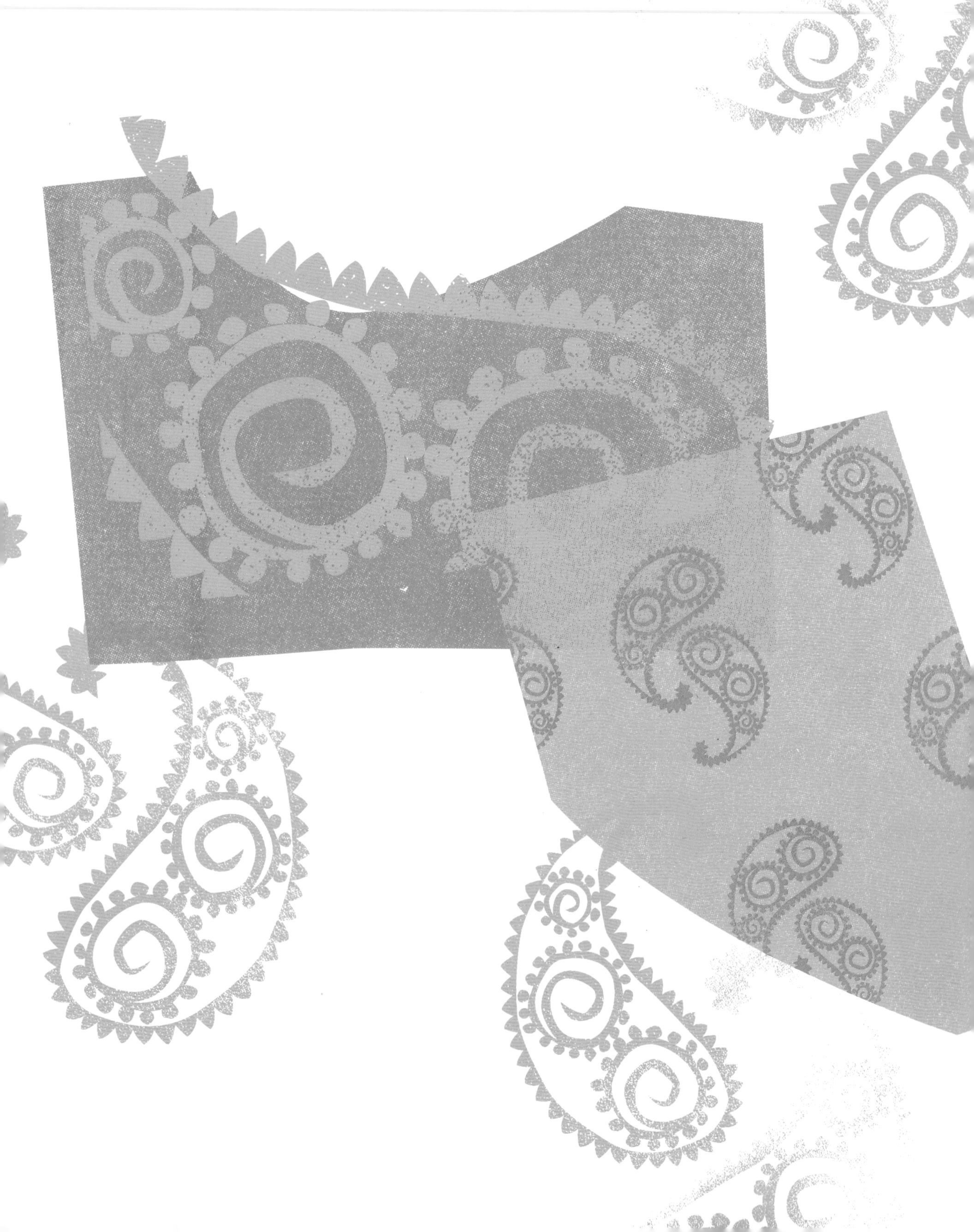

SWEET THINGS,
BURFIS & DESSERTS

I was six the first time I went to Mehliana, my mum's village in Punjab. We'd landed in Delhi a week before and were travelling across in a convoy of minivans, acclimatising with each sweltering mile to the disorientating mishmash of senses that was India in 1988. This brilliant disorganised chaos of a country was a collision of technicolour sights my eyes had never seen, smells I'd never encountered and a car-horn cacophony of sounds I'd never heard. It was an all-encompassing sensory overload, even for someone genetically wired to overload their senses. It was a homecoming to somewhere I didn't realise was home. It was, and is, my motherland.

I distinctly remember the intrigue of cows in the road being trumped by my first glimpse of a painted elephant during the journey. I remember buses filled with people inside and out, on top, and on every side. I remember Aviator-wearing women in kurtha pyjamas side-saddling indifferently on scooters that snaked in between trucks. I remember crowds of worshippers gathering outside neon-lit gurdwaras, marble mandirs and metallic-domed mosques. I remember roadside chaat vendors acrobatically frying tikkis on hot plates of oil, just millimetres away from whooshing traffic. I remember the landscape changing from densely urban to serenely pastoral, the haze of metropolitan smog replaced by the verdant lucidity of agrarian fields. I remember a sharp left turning from a tarmacked road on to a dirt track, pastures of emerald sugarcane suddenly dominating the horizon on both sides.

I remember my mum's composure switching from quiet nervousness to emotional frenzy as we passed her primary school along the lane: classes of uniformed children sat under a tree, each attentively clutching an abacus. I remember parking as far as the suitcase-filled minivans could reach

before Mehliana turned into a narrow maze of cobbled alleyways... with loud cries from a rooftop somewhere above, 'Baby ghar arghay! Baby ghar arghay!' 'Baby is home.' I remember my mum crying with a hysterical joy that I didn't know humans could feel as she ran through a silver gate into the arms of my Nani-Ji; the first time she'd seen her mum since leaving to marry eight years before. I remember being swamped by aunts and uncles, cheeks pulled, clothes tugged, rupees stuffed into our pockets, glass bottles of fizzy mango Mirinda thrust into our hands and orange ladoos force-fed into our mouths.

But most of all I remember seeing a top-knotted boy and ribbon-braided girl, the same age as me and my brother, staring from behind a wicker chair as we stared back; all four of us startled by what appeared to be our exact almond-brown eyes on the faces of foreign strangers. Here were two people that looked more like me than even I looked like me. Unnerving at first, the longer the stand-off prevailed the more it felt as though a hidden part of my life had just revealed itself. Like finding the missing piece of a jigsaw I didn't know I was trying to complete, in which I myself was also one of the missing pieces.

The boy, my cousin Jeevan, was the first to approach. 'Thusi toffee khanthee?' he asked inquisitively, to see if we understood. We understood perfectly and the answer was yes, we did eat toffees. They grabbed our hands and together we ran through the village to an inconspicuous green door which the younger girl, my cousin Satnam, knocked on aggressively. 'Khuuloo! Khuuloo! Englaaind-walleh nooh khelana!' 'Open up! Open up! We want to feed the English ones!'

A plump lady with one eye and a nasal twang of a voice opened the gate, behind which was a fantasia of sweet jars the like of which we'd never seen. We handed over the rupees acquired minutes before and filled paper bags with rose milk toffees, fennel seed butter candies, cardamom eclairs, liquorice jelly beans, clove bonbons, lychee honey drops, nutty jaggery brittle, pineapple pastels and tamarind caramels, before meandering home silently, chewing sticky sugar between our teeth. We'd never met before, but the hereditary sweet tooth of our family's mother tongue cemented our cousinly bond for life. Even now, almost in our forties, every time I see Jeevan he still has a foil-wrapped toffee in his pocket for me.

Like my mum, and her mum before her, I savour the joy of eating something sweet every day; honouring an intergenerational sugar-trail of treats, a blood-line of pudding eaters, an ancestry of rejoicing in the Punjabi mantra of moo mitha karo: 'sweeten your mouth'.

Chocolate-orange jalebi

Jalebi batter being piped into hot oil, in a freehand Cy Twombly spiral of concentric coils, is one of the most mesmerising sights in all of food. Whether in a giant wood-fired wok outside Jalandhar's bustling markets, on a gas-fired stall garlanded with marigolds in Southall, or in my Leicester Aunty-Ji's stove-top frying pan, the swirling randomness of sizzling jalebis will always be a thrill.

I don't remember the first time I combined crisp saffron-soaked jalebi with a segment of Terry's Chocolate Orange in the same bite, but it was something of an epiphany. Since then, I've thought about jalebis as a sticky blank canvas, for projecting any sweet flavours I adore both into and on to. Once you've nailed the basic batter, infuse the delicate shells with whatever cocktail of syrups and toppings suits your mood, though they're just as enjoyable soaked in a plain sugar syrup. When the canvas is this remarkable, leaving it blank is mood enough.

Makes 25–30

For the batter
180g plain flour, plus 1 tablespoon more if needed
1 tablespoon cornflour
2 tablespoons rice flour
1 tablespoon fine cornmeal
2 tablespoons natural yogurt
1 litre sunflower oil, plus 1 teaspoon
1 tablespoon lemon juice
¼ teaspoon bicarbonate of soda

For the syrup
400g granulated sugar
2 tablespoons finely grated orange zest
10 green cardamom pods, split
2–3 drops orange extract
15 saffron strands
2 tablespoons orange juice
1 tablespoon lemon juice

To serve
200g milk or dark chocolate, melted
pistachio nibs
thin orange segments, or finely grated orange zest
sea salt flakes
silver leaf (optional, see page 224)

· To make the batter, whisk the 180g of plain flour, the cornflour, rice flour and fine cornmeal together in a mixing bowl. In a separate jug, whisk together the yogurt, the 1 teaspoon of sunflower oil, the lemon juice and 185ml cold water.
· Slowly pour the wet ingredients into the dry, whisking for 2–3 minutes until you have a smooth dense pancake batter; if needed, add another 25–50ml water. It should be pourable, but also thick enough to drop in smooth ribbons so the coiled spirals keep their shape when fried; you don't want it too runny or too thick.
· Cover and rest for 10 minutes.
· Meanwhile, to prepare the syrup, put the sugar, orange zest, bashed cardamom pods, orange extract and saffron in a deep frying pan, along with 275ml water. Bring to the boil, then reduce the heat to a simmer for 3–4 minutes, until the syrup reaches a one-string consistency (see page 11). Finally add the orange and lemon juices, whisking well. Keep warm over a low heat to one side; warm syrup will soak into the fried jalebi shells more easily.
· Heat the 1 litre of oil to 160°C in a deep frying pan or wok (see page 11). Keep it at this temperature, not too high, or the jalebis will cook too quickly.
· Add the bicarbonate of soda to the rested batter and whisk thoroughly, then pour into a squeezy bottle with a small (3mm) nozzle, or a plastic piping bag snipped at the end. When the oil is ready, swiftly pipe the batter into the hot oil in spiralling snail shapes, pressing the bottle hard as you coil from the inside out, then coil back from the outside in. The swifter you are, the better the shapes will be! Only fry 2–3 at a time; the batter will sink at first, then quickly rise and puff up. If the batter is scattering in the oil, thicken it with the extra 1 tablespoon of flour.
· Fry for 2–3 minutes on each side until golden and crispy. Use tongs to remove the hot jalebi shells from the oil. Drain on kitchen paper, then immediately drop into the warm syrup. Leave for 3–4 minutes to fully absorb the sugary liquid, flipping over halfway. Pile on to a plate and cool to room temperature.
· Dip the cooled jalebis into the melted chocolate, then sprinkle with pistachio nibs, orange segments, orange zest and sea salt flakes. You could even add some silver leaf, if you want. Let the chocolate set hard if you like, although that's not essential.

Tip Delicious eaten on their own, dunked into a milkshake, or used as an ineffective-but-delicious spoon for ice cream.

The 'Drama Triangle' is a pattern of social interaction that occurs among people entangled in some form of salacious conflict; a soap-operatic power game that's deeply dysfunctional by definition. The recurrent pyramid of characters – 'persecutor', say, or 'victim' – which individuals tend to adopt in the throes of their altercation does little to defuse any situation, instead creating a destructive gridlock that accentuates the melodrama. As the unashamed gossip among my friends, I find nothing more thrilling than being at the gooey centre of such a triangle, stirring every corner of it with a chutney-stained spoon. After all, getting involved in other people's business is a big part of my culture: it's simply my Aunty-Ji genetics shining through.

These shorties merge the flavour trinity of a Bakewell tart, crumbly Walker's shortbread from Aberlour and the Indian almond drink 'milk badam'. They're a triangle of taste with a cherry jam centre, whose very entanglement is what makes them delicious. Serve them with chai and a large helping of good gossip, adorning the cherries with silver leaf (see page 224), if you want to be fancy.

Makes 12

For the shorties
250g unsalted butter, softened
200g caster sugar
1 egg yolk
½ teaspoon almond extract
1 teaspoon rose water
325g plain flour
1 teaspoon fine sea salt
seeds from 12 green cardamom pods, crushed
1 tablespoon dried rose petals, crushed, plus 1 tablespoon uncrushed dried rose petals for the caramel
12 teaspoons morello or sour cherry jam
a little vegetable oil
25g pistachio nibs, toasted (see page 40)
75g flaked almonds, toasted (see page 40)
sea salt flakes, to serve
12 fresh cherries, or maraschino cherries

For the caramel
395g can of condensed milk
75g unsalted butter
50g caster sugar
25 saffron strands, crushed
1 teaspoon kewra water
½ teaspoon fine sea salt

· In a stand mixer fitted with the paddle attachment, cream the soft butter and sugar for 3–4 minutes until light and fluffy, scraping down the sides every minute. Next add the egg yolk, almond extract and rose water, beating for another minute.
· In a separate bowl, whisk together the flour, salt, cardamom and rose petal powder. Tip into the stand mixer all at once, then, with the speed as slow as it goes, mix for 45–60 seconds until it just comes together as one. Refrigerate for 15 minutes.
· Line a muffin tray with 12 cases (silicon are best) and divide the dough into 12 balls, each 60g. Press two-thirds of each dough ball into a muffin case, then make a jam indent in the middle by pushing the dough into the sides of each case. Spoon a generous dollop of cherry jam into each.
· Make 'lids' with the final one-third of each dough ball, then top the shortie with its cap, enclosing the jam in a small bump. Press firmly along the rim of each shortie, connecting the lid to the sides, then refrigerate for 15 minutes.
· Preheat the oven to 150°C fan with a baking sheet on the middle shelf.
· Bake the shorties – with the muffin tray placed on the hot baking sheet – for 35–40 minutes until golden on top. Remove from the oven and cool completely in the muffin tin. Once the shorties are cooled, take them out of the muffin tin and carefully remove the muffin cases.
· Brush the inside of each compartment of the muffin tray with vegetable oil, then sprinkle each with most of the pistachio nibs, flaked almonds and uncrushed dried rose petals.
· For the caramel, heat the condensed milk, butter, sugar, saffron, kewra water and salt in a pan. Bring to the boil, whisking continuously, then reduce the heat to medium and cook for a further 8–10 minutes until it starts to thicken.
· Carefully spoon the warm caramel into the muffin tray compartments on top of the nuts and rose petals, filling each at least one-third of the way up, or even higher if you like a thicker caramel layer. Cool for 10–15 minutes, then carefully loosen the caramel discs with a knife and flip out of the muffin tin.
· Press a caramel disc down on to each of the cooled cherry shorties while the caramel is still warm and pliable, sprinkle with more flaked almonds, pistachios and rose petals, then chill for 30 minutes to set.
· Finish with a sprinkle of sea salt flakes and (of course) a cherry on top.

Passion fruit & raspberry-rose
Victoria sponge

Through its rapid awakening into a global powerhouse, India has transformed not only physically but also culturally, especially in the realm of food where the porous culinary boundaries of 'Indianness' are more fluid than ever. One consequence has been India's baking revolution, which has seen cities such as Mumbai, Delhi and Kolkata now producing some of the most exceptional cakes, breads and patisserie on the continent; no small feat for a country whose historic cuisine seldom calls for an oven and in which few homes even have one!

Indian artisans especially excel at classic British sponge cakes, baked to perfection and stamped with assertions of modern India within their creamy layers. This take on a Victoria sponge combines the citrussy tang of passion fruit with hints of rose and cardamom; the most quintessential British bake intertwined with the most classic Indian flavours.

Serves 8 greedy people, with very large tall slices

For the sponge
175g unsalted butter, softened
450g caster sugar
140ml olive oil
6 eggs, at room temperature
150g Greek yogurt
3 tablespoons finely grated lemon zest
350g plain flour
2 teaspoons baking powder
¼ teaspoon bicarbonate of soda
seeds from 20 green cardamom pods, crushed
2 tablespoons dried rose petals, crushed
¾ teaspoon fine sea salt
6 tablespoons (90ml) lemon juice
edible unsprayed rose petals or silver leaf (see page 224), to serve (optional)

For the fillings
225g passion fruit pulp, with seeds
1 tablespoon finely grated orange zest, plus 2 tablespoons orange juice
80g icing sugar
fine sea salt
250g raspberries, fresh or frozen
1½ teaspoons rose water
1 tablespoon finely grated lime zest, plus 2 tablespoons lime juice

For the frosting
100g unsalted butter, very soft
200g mascarpone, at room temperature
1 teaspoon vanilla extract
125g icing sugar
300ml double cream

· Preheat the oven to 170°C fan and line 3 x 18cm springform cake tins with baking parchment. If you don't have those, you can use 20cm cake tins and bake the cakes for 3–4 minutes less (as they will be thinner), which will make a slightly less tall tower.
· In a stand mixer fitted with the paddle attachment, beat the butter, sugar and oil for 5–6 minutes on a medium-high speed until velvety and frothy, scraping the sides if needed to incorporate the butter fully. In a separate jug, whisk together the eggs, yogurt and lemon zest. Pour into the butter mix and beat for 2–3 minutes, until evenly combined. In a separate bowl, whisk the flour, baking powder, bicarbonate of soda, cardamom, rose petal powder and salt.
· Add one-third of the dry ingredients to the mixer and beat slowly until just combined. Now tip in the rest of the flour mix and the lemon juice, beating slowly until there are no dry patches. Divide the batter between the prepared tins, using about 500g in each. Smooth the tops with a spatula, then sharply tap each tin on the work surface.
· Bake for 30–35 minutes until a skewer comes out clean. Cool a little in the tins, then carefully turn out on to a wire rack, top-side down. Remove the baking parchment and cool completely.
· To make the fillings, heat the passion fruit pulp with seeds, orange zest and juice and 40g of the icing sugar in a saucepan with a pinch of salt. Bring to the boil, then reduce the heat and simmer for 10–12 minutes until you have a thick jam. Pour into a bowl and refrigerate until cool. Repeat the process with the raspberries, rose water, the remaining icing sugar, lime zest and juice and another pinch of salt.
· To make the frosting, in a stand mixer fitted with the paddle attachment, whisk the very soft butter, mascarpone, vanilla extract and icing sugar with a pinch of salt until well combined. If the butter and mascarpone are not the same temperature, they will clump, not blend! In a bowl, whip the cream to medium peaks. Carefully fold the cream into the buttery mascarpone until fully combined.
· Place a sponge layer on a plate or stand. Mix two-thirds of the passion fruit jam with one-third of the frosting and pipe or spread it over. Spoon the rest of the passion fruit jam over the cream. Sandwich on the middle sponge, then repeat with the raspberry-rose jam and another one-third of the frosting.
· Sandwich on the final sponge layer and top with the final one-third of frosting, using a palette knife to smooth the top. Scatter with the rose petals, or drape with silver leaf, if you like.

Tip Use fresh passion fruit here, or some larger supermarkets sometimes sell the pulp and seeds in pouches, if you're feeling lazy.

Classic vanilla, cardamom & saffron burfi

My madeleine; my childhood in taste. If I was Dorothy escaping from Oz, my ruby-slippers picture of home would unquestionably be the red box of Milan's Sweets that lives on top of the bread bin in our Leicester kitchen. Perpetually replenished, it's filled with a malai-crumbled burfi patchwork of coconut-pink rectangles, almond-speckled spheres, terracotta oblongs, pistachio orbs, chocolatey squares, mango-yellow ovals and silver-crackled diamonds. That box is the first thing I reach for when I arrive home, and the last thing I snaffle before leaving to get back to London.

Burfi comes from the Urdu word barf, meaning 'snow', echoing the soft powdery texture you're aiming for with this creamy fudge-like treat. Shortening the milk powder with melted butter, incorporating fresh curd and adding a squeeze of lemon juice helps, but do be patient with it: the rewards are infinitely greater than the time it takes. As with ice-cream bases, once you've cracked classic plain burfi the variations (such as those overleaf) are limitless. There really is no taste like home.

Makes 16–18 pieces

For the curds & milk powder
6 tablespoons (90ml) lemon juice
750ml whole milk (organic works best here)
225g whole milk powder
20g unsalted butter, melted

For the burfi
125ml whole milk
50g unsalted butter
100g granulated sugar
½ teaspoon fine sea salt
1½ teaspoons vanilla bean paste
seeds from 10 green cardamom pods, crushed
10 saffron strands, crushed
1 tablespoon lemon juice
a little vegetable oil, for the tin
silver leaf, to serve (optional, see overleaf for instructions)

· Put the 6 tablespoons of lemon juice in a small bowl and dilute it with a splash of water.
· Slowly heat the 750ml whole milk in a saucepan to just below boiling. Keep steady at this temperature for 2–3 minutes, then remove from the heat. Leave to rest for 1 minute, before adding 1 tablespoon of diluted lemon juice. Mix well, leave for 1 minute, then add another 1 tablespoon of diluted lemon. The curds and whey will eventually start to separate. Add more lemon until the curds have fully formed and completely separated, with the liquid turning translucent. Leave for 10 minutes.
· Drain the curds into a sieve lined with a muslin cloth or cheesecloth, discarding the whey, then wash under a cold tap for 1 minute to remove the lemon juice taste. Squeeze into a ball and hang-drip over the sink for 15 minutes.
· Put the milk powder in a large mixing bowl and pour over the melted butter. Using your hands, rub the butter into the milk powder fully. Next add 100g of the fresh curd and again rub it into the milk powder until you have a fine sandy rubble. Set aside.
· For the burfi, in a large wide non-stick saucepan or wok, heat the milk and butter over a low heat until fully melted. Next add the sugar and salt, stirring until dissolved. Next tip in the shortened milk powder. You now need to stir continuously in a circular motion for 14–16 minutes over a medium-low heat, constantly smearing the mixture into the bottom of the pan with a spatula, then scraping it up and turning it over so it doesn't catch on the bottom.
· After 10 minutes, add the vanilla, cardamom and saffron, mixing well. Cook for another 3–4 minutes until it comes away easily from the sides and starts to form together as a single mass. At this stage, add the lemon juice, mixing it in thoroughly.
· Spoon the hot mixture into a well-oiled cake or loaf tin lined with cling film (I use a standard 450g capacity loaf tin measuring 20 x 9.5cm), pressing firmly into a single layer 3–4cm deep. Let it cool to room temperature, then set in the fridge for at least 2–3 hours until you have a densely crumbly fudge. Slice into diamonds, cover in silver leaf, if you like, and enjoy!

Strawberry, salted almond & rose

Mocha-marzipan

· After 10 minutes of stirring the burfi mixture, stir in 25g crushed freeze-dried strawberries, 75g toasted flaked almonds (see page 40), 1 tablespoon rose syrup and ¾ teaspoon fine sea salt. Sprinkle the warm burfi with sea salt flakes, freeze-dried strawberries and dried rose petals, then leave to cool.

· After 10 minutes of stirring the burfi mixture, stir through 2 teaspoons instant coffee powder. When it's cooled to room temperature, roll out 100g marzipan and use to cover the burfi, then coat with 100g melted chocolate and leave to set in the fridge.

Tip If you want to use silver leaf here, take a sheet of silver leaf paper in its wrapper and remove the top layer of paper. Carefully place it flat, silver-side down, on the top of the burfi, then use a paintbrush to carefully brush the silver into the surface, away from the paper.

Banoffee crunch

· After 10 minutes of stirring the burfi mixture, stir through 2 tablespoons banana milkshake powder and 2 tablespoons crushed butterscotch candies. Sprinkle 2 tablespoons crushed banana chips over the warm burfi, then leave to cool.

Pandan, honeycomb & pistachio

· After 10 minutes of stirring the burfi mixture, stir through 50g shelled unsalted roasted (see page 40) and crushed pistachios, ½ teaspoon pandan paste and ¼ teaspoon kewra water. Crumble 75g crushed chocolate honeycomb over the warm burfi, then leave to cool.

Lychee, coconut & dark chocolate muffins

When George Michael was caught cruising on Hampstead Heath, his sharp-witted retort to the photographer who confronted him are six of the greatest words in all queer culture, and arguably in the history of identity itself. He stood his ground, made no apology and is reported to have shouted, as bluntly as he could: 'Fuck Off, This Is My Culture!'

Canned fruit is my culture, and I make no apology for that. Canned peaches, canned pears, canned pineapple rings, canned mangos, canned cherries, canned mandarins, an entire subgenre of foods, the economy for which must be largely driven by the wallets of Punjabis. Indeed, one of the most common desserts you're likely to have in a Punjabi household is canned fruit cocktail with cold double cream, sometimes drizzled with canned condensed milk for an extra kick of saccharine sweetness.

These muffins celebrate my favourite canned fruit of all: lychees. The plump orbs are cooked down to a jammy pulp which enlivens the cakey batter, while a lychee-infused sugar syrup adds tropical flair to the glaze. This recipe is equally (if not more) delicious made with in-season freshly peeled lychees, but I tend to stick with canned. It's my culture.

Makes 12

For the muffins
100g desiccated coconut
2 x 400g cans of lychees in syrup, plus lychees
  to serve (optional)
2 tablespoons finely grated orange zest, plus
  75ml orange juice
1 teaspoon vanilla bean paste
50g unsalted butter, very soft
250g caster sugar
110ml extra virgin olive oil
3 eggs, at room temperature, lightly beaten
50ml double cream
225g plain flour
100g polenta
1¼ teaspoons baking powder
¼ teaspoon bicarbonate of soda
1 teaspoon fine sea salt
180g dark chocolate, finely chopped, plus chocolate curls
  to serve (optional)
coconut flakes, to serve (optional)
silver leaf, to serve (optional, see page 224)

For the glaze
200g icing sugar
4 tablespoons lychee syrup from the can
2 tablespoons orange juice
2 tablespoons olive oil
dash of natural pink food colouring

· Dry pan-roast the desiccated coconut until it's toasty and just tints brown. Remove from the heat.
· Drain the lychees from the cans, reserving their syrup for the glaze. Pulse the drained lychees in a blender until coarse, then empty into a large saucepan and bring to the boil. Simmer over a medium heat for 20–25 minutes, stirring continuously so it doesn't catch on the bottom. You want the water to evaporate fully and the sugars to caramelise, leaving a thick jammy lychee pulp. When thickened and just beginning to caramelise on the bottom, add the orange juice, mixing well. Remove from the heat, then stir through the orange zest, toasted coconut and vanilla. Cool to room temperature.
· Preheat the oven to 175°C fan and line a muffin tray with muffin cases (silicon cases are best). Place a baking sheet in the centre of the oven.
· In a stand mixer fitted with the paddle attachment, cream the very soft butter and sugar for 3–4 minutes, then, with the paddle still going, slowly pour in the olive oil. Beat vigorously for another 3–4 minutes until you have a smooth frothy batter with no lumps. Scrape down the sides if needed. Add the eggs and cream, then beat for another 3 minutes until velvety and aerated. Next spoon in the lychee-coconut mix, beating for a final minute.
· In a separate bowl, whisk together the plain flour, polenta, baking powder, bicarbonate of soda, salt and chopped chocolate. Tip these into the mixer all at once, then beat on a low speed for 45–60 seconds until just combined. If needed, use a spatula to slowly mix in any dry patches of flour that remain.
· Fill each muffin case to the top with the batter, then place the muffin tray on the hot baking sheet and bake for 30–35 minutes until golden on top and cooked through. Remove from the oven and cool in the tray.
· Whisk together the icing sugar, lychee syrup, orange juice, olive oil and colouring into a syrupy glaze. Dip the tops of the cooled muffins in the icing.
· Sprinkle with coconut flakes, chocolate curls, lychee segments and silver leaf, if you like.

Tip Enjoy with hot cardamom coffee.

Mango & mandarin granita-golas

On our arrival in India for what were usually month-long jaunts throughout my childhood, my Aunty-Jis would fill their pantries floor-to-ceiling with crates of glass soda bottles. There was always more soda than any person could drink in a lifetime, my aunties having followed the Punjabi method of forecasting where you round up to the nearest hundred regardless. To get through it, we resorted to simultaneously popping two lids of iconic drinks – such as Thumbs Up, Frooti or Limca – at a time. The cocktail I liked was an orange Mirinda in one straw with a mango Maaza in the other; pure carbonated bliss. These tropical frozen ices are a grown-up take on that flavour mélange, in the un-grown-up form of a gola lolly as found in technicolour street carts around Chowpatty Beach and all over India. Double-park at your own discretion.

Makes 8

850g can of Alphonso mango pulp, or the same amount of
  ripe fresh mango purée
250g granulated sugar
2 tablespoons finely grated mandarin zest, plus
  125ml mandarin juice
2 tablespoons finely grated pink grapefruit zest, plus
  125ml pink grapefruit juice
60ml lime juice
1 tablespoon orange blossom water
¼ teaspoon fine sea salt
1¼ teaspoons citric acid
2 tablespoons yuzu juice (optional)
½ teaspoon orange bitters (optional)
375ml crémant, champagne or other dry sparkling
  white wine

To serve
condensed milk
Kashmiri chilli powder
1 ripe mango, finely chopped

· Pour the mango pulp into a large mixing bowl.
· Next heat 150ml of water and the granulated sugar in a saucepan until boiling. Simmer for 2 minutes until it thickens to a one-string consistency (see page 11), then pour it over the mango pulp. To this add the mandarin and grapefruit zests and juices, the lime juice, orange blossom water, salt and citric acid. If using, also add the yuzu juice and orange bitters at this point. Whisk well, then very slowly pour in the sparkling wine, mixing through carefully to combine.
· Now you have two options...
· To make granita, pour the yellow mixture into a shallow freezer container, cover with a lid and freeze for 4 hours. Take out of the freezer, then use a fork to break the semi-frozen ice into smaller crystals. Freeze for another 2–3 hours, breaking up the crystals with a fork again, before serving in glasses.
· To make gola lollies, pour the mixture into ice lolly or kulfi moulds and pop in wooden sticks. Freeze for 4–6 hours until frozen solid.
· Serve with a drizzle of condensed milk, a sprinkle of Kashmiri chilli powder and chunks of mango.

Tip Look for firm mandarins here, which will be easier to zest than softer fruits.

Saffron custard tart with candied fennel seeds & roasted strawberries

Even if you deem everything else about a British curry house to be 'inauthentic', the 'authenticity' of the after-dinner palate cleanser is undisputedly Indian. Typically served in faux-gilded bowls with ornate spoons, or small square sachets printed with peacock feathers, mukhwas is a jumbled mix of rock sugar crystals, aniseed balls, sesame seeds, menthol candies, toasted flaxseeds, dried coconut, ajwain, green cardamom pods and candied fennel seeds.

Such is my love for that final component in the mix that I have glass jars filled with them: troves of sugar-coated fennel sprinkles with an anisey chew, that I delve into throughout the day.

Mukhwas are easy to find in Indian shops, but combining coloured sprinkles with fennel seeds gives a similar kaleidoscopic effect and taste. Or try asking nicely at your local curry house; they're bound to have a stash somewhere out the back.

Serves 8

For the crust
150g unsalted butter, melted, plus more for the tin
125g Nice coconut biscuits
175g digestive biscuits
2 tablespoons fennel seeds, crushed
1 teaspoon freshly grated nutmeg
4 tablespoons good-quality confetti sprinkles,
    non-colour-bleeding (I use Rainbow Jimmies)
1 tablespoon finely grated orange zest
¾ teaspoon fine sea salt

For the filling
12 egg yolks
85g caster sugar
1 teaspoon vanilla bean paste
600ml double cream
40 saffron strands, crushed

For the strawberries
12 strawberries, sliced into discs
2 tablespoons caster sugar
1 teaspoon coarsely ground black pepper
1½ teaspoons fennel seeds, coarsely crushed
candied fennel seeds, to serve

· Butter and line a deep 18cm springform cake tin with baking parchment along the base and sides.
· In a food processor, blitz the coconut biscuits and digestives to a fine powder. Add the crushed fennel, nutmeg, sprinkles, orange zest and salt, blitzing to evenly distribute. Pour in the melted butter in a slow stream, pulsing until you have a damp sandy rubble that holds its shape when pressed together.
· Tip the buttery crumbs into the prepared tin, reserving a few. Using the bottom of a sharp-sided cup, use circular movements from the middle to gently push the crumbs into the sides of the tin so there is a thick even layer along the base and sides, all the way up. Then use your fingers to compact the crust into the sides and base very firmly, ensuring there are no gaps, as you don't want the custard to leak out! Finally, use the cup again to press tightly into the circumference of the tin along the bottom corner edge. Freeze for 1–2 hours to set hard.
· For the filling, whisk the yolks, sugar and vanilla in a large jug (keep the egg whites to make meringues). In a saucepan, slowly bring the cream to a boil with the saffron, then remove from the heat. Whisk a little of the cream into the egg yolks, then pour the tempered egg yolks into the pan of cream. Whisk well, then remove from the heat and decant into the jug. Cover with cling film, pressing it on to the surface to prevent a skin forming. Cool for 15 minutes.
· Preheat the oven to 145°C fan and place a baking sheet in the centre of the oven. Remove the biscuit crust from the freezer, checking there are no cracks or holes. If there are, patch up with the reserved buttery biscuit crumbs. Give the slightly cooled custard a quick whisk, then carefully pour into the crust, ensuring there are no big bubbles.
· Bake in the oven, on the hot baking sheet, for 65–70 minutes until the custard is just set. If the top of the tart looks like it's burnishing too quickly during cooking time, cover loosely with foil.
· Meanwhile, mix the sliced strawberries with the caster sugar, black pepper and fennel seeds. Spoon on to a lined baking sheet and bake in the bottom of the oven for 25–30 minutes, with the custard tart.
· Remove from the oven. Cool, then refrigerate the tart for 3–4 hours to set completely.
· Serve generous slices of custard tart garnished with spiced strawberries and candied fennel seeds.

Carrot halwa & damson galette

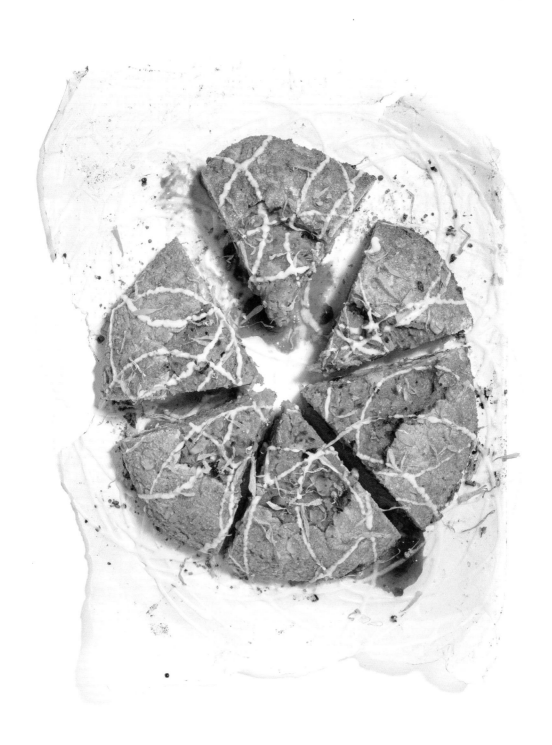

Three sets of fruit trees distinguish the three successive houses I grew up in, each dwelling's era marked by its own corresponding pickles and jams. Pear trees dominated our first home, a fruit that would be salted with cumin and chilli, or poached to a confit with jaggery and cloves. A majestic Bramley apple tree overshadows our current, third home. Its annual fruits are fermented into achaars or stewed into crumbles, customarily drowned in Bird's Custard from a packet.

But it's the preserves of our second home that my memory tastes the most, from a resplendent trio of plum, greengage and damson trees. This stone fruit trinity that lined our back fence were an alliance of nature's jesters, unpredictably switching from bitter to sour to sweet each season, and taking it in turns to play dead, too. Eating their fruits was orchard roulette, so they were usually simmered to a sweetly tart pinky-green jam, for dolloping over everything from buttery toast to carrot halwa. This recipe is exactly that in galette form. Everything's just better in pastry, including memories.

Serves 8

For the crust
250g plain flour, plus more to dust
35g caster sugar
¾ teaspoon fine sea salt
50g ground almonds
1 tablespoon finely grated orange zest
2 tablespoons coarse semolina
100g unsalted butter, chilled and chopped
1 egg, lightly beaten, plus 1 more, also lightly beaten, to glaze
5 teaspoons milk

For the halwa
800g carrots, grated
2 tablespoons ghee
500ml whole milk
20 saffron strands
200g caster sugar
50g flaked almonds, toasted (see page 40)
50g coconut flakes, toasted (see page 86)
50g whole milk powder
seeds from 10 green cardamom pods, crushed
1 teaspoon fine sea salt
1 tablespoon cornflour
2 tablespoons lemon juice

To fill & serve
4 tablespoons damson or plum jam
2 tablespoons flaked almonds
2 tablespoons demerara sugar

· To make the crust, in a food processor, blitz the plain flour, sugar, salt, ground almonds, orange zest and 1 tablespoon of the semolina until well combined. Next add the cold butter cubes, pulsing the ingredients to a fine crumb texture. Add 1 beaten egg – pulsing until fully incorporated – then add the milk 1 teaspoon at a time. The dough will eventually come together, so only add as much milk as needed to make a rough hard dough.

· Tip the rubble out on to a work surface and press together very firmly into a ball. Cover in cling film and chill for 1 hour.

· For the carrot halwa, tip the grated carrots on to a clean tea towel, then cover with another clean tea towel. Press down to squeeze out and absorb as much water as you can.

· Melt the ghee in a large saucepan, then add the squeezed grated carrots. Cook over a high heat, mixing continuously for 10 minutes until most of the water has evaporated and they turn bright orange. Next add the milk and saffron, then cook over a medium-high heat for 20–25 minutes until the milk solids are coating the carrots, stirring continuously. At this stage add the caster sugar, flaked almonds, coconut flakes, milk powder, cardamom powder, salt and cornflour. Cook for another 8–10 minutes until it starts to thicken. Stir through the lemon juice and leave to cool.

· Preheat the oven to 180°C fan.

· Roll out the pastry on a floured surface into a circle 28cm in diameter, then sprinkle with the remaining 1 tablespoon of semolina, pressing it into the pastry; this prevents a soggy bottom! Spoon a thick layer of jam into the middle of the pastry, leaving 4–5cm of empty border.

· Next spoon over a very thick layer of the cooled carrot halwa, before folding the edges of the pastry up and inwards in pleats, all around the halwa. Press the 2 tablespoons flaked almonds into the pastry edge, brush it with beaten egg and sprinkle with demerara sugar.

· Bake for 35–40 minutes until golden on top, covering the pastry edges with foil if they are starting to catch and burn. Remove from the oven and cool for 10 minutes before serving.

Tip Delicious warm or cold, with a generous drizzle of double cream either way.

Salted besan butterscotch tarts

Every August on Rakhi day, brothers across the world have ornate threads tied on to their wrists by female siblings, while being fed vast quantities of ladoos and burfi. In exchange, sisters get envelopes of hard cash: a symbolic swap to strengthen sibling bonds (until next year at least). I used to think men got the hard side of the bargain, but these days I'm inclined to think it's the other way round.

Besan burfi is what we make at home to see in Rakhi day's annual get-together, made by very slowly heating and stirring gram flour in melted ghee until it becomes golden, caramelised and nutty. These delectable tarts have besan burfi as their toasty crumbling base, filled with salty butterscotch fudge and crushed butter candies for nostalgic crunch. Given a choice between cash and these tarts, I'll take the besan.

Makes 8 small tarts

For the base
160g ghee
225g gram flour, sifted
20g coarse semolina
50g icing sugar
50g caster sugar
seeds from 15 green cardamom pods, crushed
1 teaspoon ground cinnamon
1 teaspoon fennel seeds, ground
1 tablespoon white poppy seeds
1 teaspoon fine sea salt
a little vegetable oil

For the filling
175g unsalted butter
200g light brown sugar
75ml single cream, plus 65ml
1 teaspoon vanilla extract
1½ teaspoons fine sea salt
35g plain flour

To serve
icing sugar
8 hard butterscotch candies, crushed
1 teaspoon fennel seeds, crushed
1 teaspoon ground cinnamon
1 teaspoon sea salt flakes

· For the base, melt the ghee in a saucepan over a medium-low heat, then add the gram flour. Mix well and cook over a medium-low heat for 20–25 minutes, stirring continuously to ensure it doesn't catch on the bottom. The gram flour will start very thick and hard but will soon soften, eventually turning a dark shade of mustard yellow and giving off a nutty aroma.
· In a separate bowl, mix together the semolina, icing sugar, caster sugar, cardamom, cinnamon, fennel, poppy seeds and salt. Tip the dry ingredients into the hot pan all at once, increase the heat to medium and cook for 4–5 minutes, stirring the whole time. The mixture will again harden up at first, but just keep stirring! It's ready when it resembles a thick grainy yellowy-brown porridge; the amount of time this takes will vary depending on your brand of gram flour.
· Leave to cool in the pan for 2–3 hours until it's easy to handle and has the texture of pliable putty that keeps an indentation when pressed.
· Brush 8 individual tart cases with vegetable oil (mine are 7.5cm in diameter) along the bases and sides, then press 1 heaped tablespoon of the base into each case, leaving a dip in the middle for the filling. Refrigerate for 1 hour to set hard.
· For the filling, melt the butter in a saucepan over a medium heat. Add the light brown sugar, whisking well. When fully dissolved, whisk in the 75ml of cream, the vanilla and salt, stirring the whole time. In a separate jug, whisk together the 65ml of cream with the plain flour to make a smooth paste. Slowly whisk this paste into the hot sauce, then reduce the heat and cook for 2–3 minutes until it stiffens to a thick-but-still-pourable caramel.
· Pour the butterscotch filling into the chilled tart bases, then return to the fridge for 4 hours.
· To serve, dust the tarts with icing sugar. Mix the butterscotch candies with the crushed fennel seeds, cinnamon and salt. Sprinkle over the tarts and enjoy.

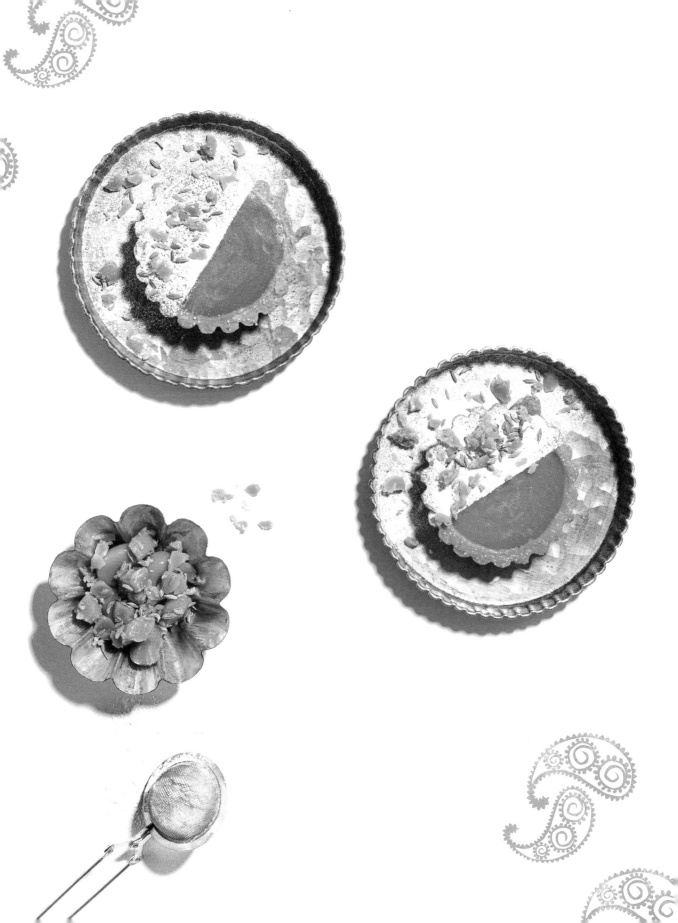

Pistachio & sumac madeleines with rose milk jam

Although we holidayed in India growing up, I was always somewhat jealous of white friends who went to France: the land of hot chocolate in bowls for breakfast, a thousand delectable cheeses and something magical called a 'soufflé'. Now, the roles have reversed: I go to France every year to gorge on patisserie and drink crémant in French drag bars, while my white friends fly off to silent ashrams in Rishikesh to do yoga and eat dal.

Lyon has garnered my most treasured Gallic taste memory to date: oven-warm pistachio madeleines with vanilla crème anglaise. This is my spice-scented take, true to my memory of the Lyonnaise *bouchon* where I ate them, but masala-fied just *un petit peu*. The flavours of baked cardamom, nutmeg, clove, saffron and sumac create fragrant undertones that complement the cakey core of roasted pistachios and the sweet rose milk jam. *Bon appétit!*

Makes 16

For the madeleines
100g shelled unsalted pistachio nuts, plus pistachio nibs, to serve
150g plain flour, plus more to dust
1 tablespoon baking powder
2 tablespoons finely grated lemon zest
150g unsalted butter
¾ teaspoon fine sea salt
2 teaspoons Chai Masala (see page 26)
2 tablespoons (yes, tablespoons) sumac
25 saffron strands, crushed
3 eggs, plus 1 egg yolk, at room temperature
100g caster sugar
25g light brown sugar
1 teaspoon vanilla extract
1 tablespoon runny honey
vegetable oil, for the tray
icing sugar and silver leaf (optional, see page 224), to serve

For the jam
120ml whole milk
1 tablespoon rose water
dash of natural pink food colouring
1 tablespoon caster sugar
¼ teaspoon fine sea salt

· Preheat the oven to 165°C fan, then bake the pistachios for 5–6 minutes until golden and toasty. Cool completely, then grind to a fine powder.
· In a large bowl, whisk together the plain flour, baking powder, lemon zest and ground pistachios.
· Next, heat the unsalted butter, salt, chai masala, sumac and saffron in a saucepan until melted and starting to froth. Remove from the heat and leave to infuse for 5 minutes.
· Using a stand mixture fitted with the whisk attachment, whisk together the eggs and egg yolk, caster sugar, light brown sugar, vanilla and honey for 8–10 minutes on a medium-high speed. It should be light in colour, frothy and aerated. Reduce the speed slightly, then slowly pour in the slightly cooled melted butter – 1 tablespoon at a time – speckling the mix with all its spices. Remove the mixer bowl from the stand and tip in the dry ingredients all at once. Use a spatula to cut and fold them into the wet ingredients until there are no dry patches, keeping in as much air as possible.
· Spoon into a piping bag and refrigerate for at least 4 hours, or ideally overnight.
· Slowly bring all the ingredients for the jam to the boil in a saucepan. Reduce the heat to medium, then simmer for 35–45 minutes, stirring continuously until you have a lusciously thick runny caramel. Alternatively, you can cheat by mixing condensed milk with rose water, a pinch of salt and some natural pink colouring. Cover and chill until ready to serve.
· Preheat the oven to 185°C fan and place a baking sheet on the middle shelf. Brush each scallop shell of a madeleine tray with vegetable oil and dust lightly with flour. Pipe the batter in a thick line down the middle of each shell, filling the moulds to the top.
· Place the filled madeleine tray on the hot baking sheet, then bake for 10–12 minutes, until each has a nice hump in the middle. Remove from the oven, cool for a few minutes, then carefully slide the madeleines out of their shells.
· Serve warm, dusted with icing sugar or adorned with silver leaf, if you like, with pistachio nibs and cool rose milk jam for dipping.

Pear & panjiri trifle

Polari was a secret-speke adopted by gay men in England up until the late 1960s, when homosexuality was legalised. Not quite a full 'language', it was more a cross-pollinated third-culture mash-up of dialects compounded together, notably Yiddish, Romany, Paltry Slang, Parlyaree, East End Slang, Theatre Slang and 20th-century radio jargon. This encoded tongue was added to by its covert keepers over centuries, their very survival depending on its hidden meanings remaining so. The legacy of Polari still infiltrates the campest corners of the English vernacular today through words such as dolly, bijou, naff, butch and clobber; while lesser-used Polari often conjures up lingo from the many branches of languages in India. Vada, which in Polari means 'to see', is also a South Indian fried street food; nishta meaning 'nothing' in Polari is the word for 'devotion' in Punjabi; while the Polari word manjaree meaning 'to eat' is also a word for 'mango flower' in India.

Panjiri – the Sanskrit word for a crumbly Punjabi dessert made from wheat flour cooked in ghee, jaggery, ground nuts and spices – would lend itself to Polari well, both phonetically and in taste. This zhuzhed-up 'fifty shades of brown' trifle combines panjiri with spiced cardamom pears, sponge and custard. Manjareed together, the mix is quite fabulosa!

Makes 1 large or 6 individual trifles

For the panjiri
200g mixed shelled unsalted nuts (walnuts, almonds,
   pistachios, hazelnuts, pecans)
75g linseeds (flaxseeds)
35g white sesame seeds
65g ghee
250g coarse semolina
1 tablespoon fennel seeds, crushed
1 tablespoon ground ginger
75g toasted coconut flakes (see page 86)
½ teaspoon fine sea salt
30g jaggery, or dark brown sugar
100g icing sugar

For the pears
500g Conference pears, chopped
1 tablespoon finely grated fresh ginger
4 tablespoons dark brown sugar
seeds from 8 green cardamom pods, crushed
75g sultanas
1 tablespoon finely grated lemon zest, plus 4 tablespoons
   lemon juice
½ teaspoon fine sea salt

To assemble
300ml double cream
1¼ teaspoons kewra water
450g fresh custard (go for the fancy stuff)
1 shop-bought Madeira loaf cake, cubed
fresh or dried pear slices, to serve

· Start with the panjiri. Preheat the oven to 165°C fan then roast all the mixed nuts on a baking sheet for 7–8 minutes. Remove from the oven and allow to cool completely.
· Next toast the linseeds in a large frying pan for 3–4 minutes. When they start to pop, cover with a lid and shake on the hob for 1 minute, then empty into a food processor. Now toast the sesame seeds in the pan for 1–2 minutes until they just tint brown. Spoon into the food processor also, then blitz the 2 seeds together to a very fine powder.
· In the same pan, melt the ghee, then add the semolina, fennel and ginger. Cook for 10–15 minutes – mixing constantly with a spatula – until the semolina turns golden and crunchy. Cool completely, then add to the food processor. Blitz the toasted nuts, semolina, flaxseed-sesame powder, toasted coconut flakes, salt, jaggery or dark brown sugar and icing sugar for 1–2 minutes. You want a crumbly rubble that still has some bite. Empty into an airtight container.
· For the pears, preheat the oven to 180°C fan.
· In a deep roasting tin, toss together the pears, grated ginger, dark brown sugar, crushed cardamom, sultanas, lemon zest and juice and salt. Bake for 30–40 minutes, mixing every 15 minutes, until the fruit is tenderly softened but not mushy. Remove from the oven and cool completely.
· Whip the double cream to a medium thickness, then stir through the kewra water.
· Layer the panjiri, spiced pears, kewra cream, fresh custard and Madeira cake in martini glasses or a big trifle dish. Finish with fresh or dried pear slices and a generous sprinkling of panjiri.

Tip Panjiri is also delicious on its own with a cup of tea, or sprinkled over thick Greek yogurt with honey.

Fiery gingersnap s'mores with pink peppercorn bark

My mum was twenty-one when she became pregnant with me in the winter of 1982. She'd been in England for two years, had developed a good grasp of spoken English and recently begun working in a biscuit factory. Far from putting her off, the permeating smell of baked sugar and butter that seeped into her hair gave her a permanent craving for biscuits in the last months of pregnancy. Shortbread, malted milks, Bourbons, custard creams and – most of all – gingersnaps were in effect my first mother tongue, the in-utero communication of my mum's appetite before I was even born.

These crunchy-chewy gingersnaps combine ginger in three different ways: ground for warmth, stem for candy sweetness and fresh for vibrant zing, with cayenne for a gentle-fiery burn. They're delicious on their own, or sandwiched into s'mores with marshmallow fluff or ice cream and peppery white chocolate bark, even decorated with silver leaf (see page 224), if you like. Enjoy them as you wish; biscuits are an international language for all.

Makes 16 cookies (8 s'mores)

For the bark
150g white chocolate
a little vegetable oil (optional)
1 tablespoon pink peppercorns, crushed
1 tablespoon black peppercorns, crushed

For the gingersnaps
200g unsalted butter, very soft
250g caster sugar, plus 4 tablespoons
3 tablespoons finely grated fresh ginger
85g drained stem ginger in syrup, finely chopped, plus
   2 tablespoons of the syrup, plus more to serve
4 tablespoons black treacle
1 egg, at room temperature, lightly beaten
325g plain flour
1¾ teaspoons bicarbonate of soda
2 tablespoons ground ginger
1 tablespoon ground cloves
½ teaspoon cayenne pepper, plus ¼ teaspoon
½ teaspoon fine sea salt
4 tablespoons icing sugar
marshmallows, or ice cream, for the filling

· To make the bark, melt the white chocolate in a heatproof bowl over a pan of simmering water, making sure the bowl does not touch the water, or in a microwave. Spread in a thin layer on a silicon sheet, or a sheet of oiled baking parchment. Sprinkle over both types of crushed peppercorns, chill or freeze until solid, then break into shards.
· In a stand mixer fitted with the paddle attachment, beat the softened butter and the 250g of caster sugar for 3–4 minutes until fluffy, scraping the bottom and sides to ensure everything is fully incorporated. Next add the grated ginger, stem ginger, ginger syrup and black treacle, beating for another minute, before finally mixing in the beaten egg.
· In a separate bowl, whisk the flour, bicarbonate of soda, ground ginger and cloves, ½ teaspoon of cayenne and salt together. Tip the dry ingredients into the mixer all at once, then beat on a very slow speed for 1–2 minutes, just to the point where the flour is fully incorporated with no dry patches. Scrape the wet dough into a tight ball in the bowl, then cover and refrigerate for at least 2 hours to firm up.
· Preheat the oven to 180°C fan.
· Set up 2 bowls in front of you, one with the 4 tablespoons of caster sugar, the other with the icing sugar mixed with the ¼ teaspoon of cayenne.
· Form a tight 40g ball of chilled dough for each gingersnap, then roll in the caster sugar before rolling in the cayenne-icing sugar. Place on a silicon mat or a baking tray lined with baking parchment. Repeat to form all the gingersnaps, spacing each well apart. Bake on the middle shelf of the oven for 14–15 minutes until golden on the edges and crinkled on top. Remove from the oven and cool completely on the tray; they'll become crunchy as they cool.
· Sandwich the gingersnaps with either marshmallows toasted under a grill, or ice cream, chopped stem ginger, and generous shards of the pink peppercorn bark.

Any food lover will have a goodies cupboard in their kitchen, and intuitively know where the goodies cupboard is in other food lovers' kitchens. My own is filled not only with chocolate but with salty spiced chevda, known commonly in the West as Bombay mix. To Indians, chevda is an entire genre of food in itself, with as much regional variation, inter-family nuance and gourmet adaptability as a Sunday roast. There are entire stores devoted to it in Tooting, Southall and Leicester, and entire aisles given to it in any Indian supermarket worth its weight in masala. Munching on chevda and chocolate buttons with rose milkshake is one of my earliest memories of Mehliana, my mum's pind in Punjab. The jumbled collision of flavours here evokes that memory in ice-cream sundae form: the chevda morphed into chocolatey 'chow', the rose syrup muddled with berries and moreish chikki brittle crowning the top. If in doubt, simply empty your goodies cupboard into an ice-cream glass and enjoy.

Makes 4

For the chevda chow
200g icing sugar
2 tablespoons fennel seeds, crushed to powder
250g dark chocolate
1 teaspoon vanilla extract
seeds from 12 green cardamom pods, crushed
100g crunchy peanut butter
50g salted butter
200g bite-sized wheat cereal
80g peanut M&Ms
125g chevda, or cornflake Bombay mix

For the chikki
a little vegetable oil (optional)
150g light brown sugar
50g shelled unsalted roasted pistachios (see page 40)
25g shelled unsalted roasted hazelnuts (see page 40)
1 tablespoon fennel seeds
1 tablespoon white sesame seeds
20g mini salted pretzels
1 teaspoon fine sea salt

For the sundaes
150g raspberries or blackberries
2 tablespoons rose syrup, or rose cordial
1 tablespoon lemon juice
2 large scoops of ice cream for each person
4 meringue nests

· For the chevda chow, whisk together 150g of the icing sugar and the powdered fennel in a large bowl.
· Put the dark chocolate, vanilla extract and cardamom powder in a heatproof bowl and place over a saucepan of simmering water, making sure the bowl does not touch the water. When completely melted, add the peanut butter and salted butter, mixing well. Take off the heat and add the wheat cereal, carefully tossing to coat every piece in chocolate. Empty on to a tray and cool for 2 minutes.
· Spoon the chocolatey cereal into the fennel-icing sugar, turning in a circular motion so everything gets fully coated. Empty on to a baking tray in a single layer, then sprinkle over the remaining 50g of icing sugar so everything is powdery white. Chill in the refrigerator for 1–2 hours until completely set, then jumble together with the M&Ms and chevda.
· To make the chikki, get a silicon sheet or a sheet of oiled baking parchment close to the hob. In a saucepan and using a sugar thermometer, slowly bring the light brown sugar up to 150°C – don't mix it too much – swirl gently until it's frothing and has reached temperature. Remove from the heat and carefully pour on to the prepared sheet. Immediately sprinkle over the pistachios, hazelnuts, fennel seeds, sesame seeds, pretzels and salt, very carefully pressing them into the hot molten sugar. Cool until hard, then break into shards.
· When ready to serve, mash the berries in a bowl, then add the rose syrup or cordial and lemon juice, mixing well. Let the flavours mingle for 10 minutes.
· After this there are no rules: layer up scoops of ice cream, crushed meringue, chevda chow, berries, chikki... go wild! Think 'Punjabi Aunty-Ji style': generous portions of each component, so you get a bit of everything in each spoonful.

Tip The best ice creams to choose here are vanilla, pistachio or raspberry ripple.

Vanilla kheer with pink pralines

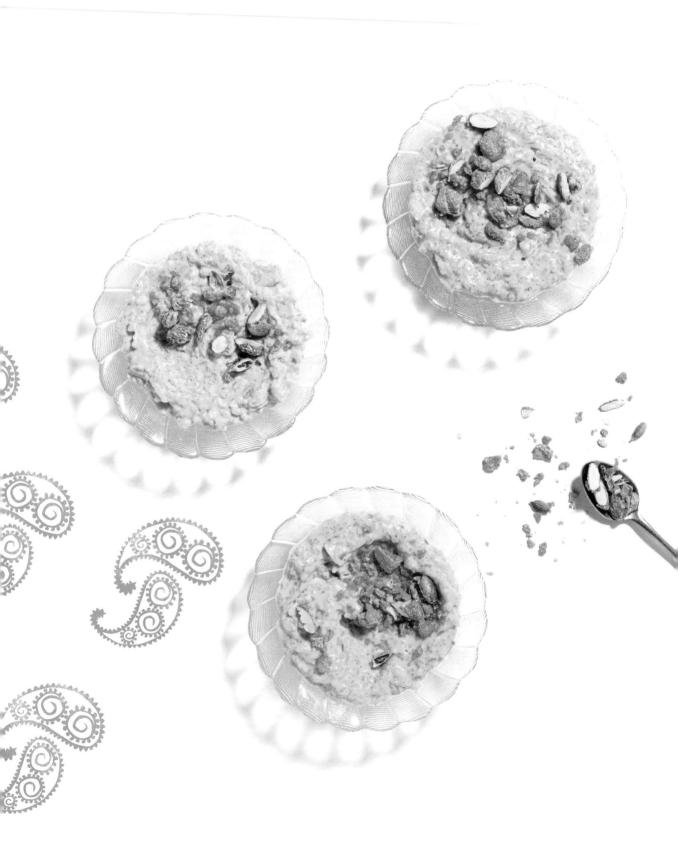

The singer Farrokh Bulsara was born in 1946 to Parsi-Indian parents in Zanzibar. In the aftermath of Zanzibar's Revolution, his parents fled for Middlesex, in England, where Farrokh was raised. He later changed his name to Freddie Mercury after 'Mother Mercury', as a tribute to his mother. As with his sexuality, Freddie had a conflicted relationship with his Indianness, whitewashing his heritage in public to avoid British society's misconceptions about his roots. It's an identity dilemma still faced by the Indian diaspora, a perpetual negotiation regarding what to reveal about ourselves, fearful of rejection if we outwardly show who we really are. Acceptance does come, but often at the price of self-concealment and assimilation.

Parsi-Indians originated in Persia, ancestors of the followers of Zoroaster, forced to flee modern-day Iraq and Iran in the seventh century to avoid religious persecution. The exiles landed in Gujarat on the North Western coast of India, where they met with the state's Hindu king. Sharing no common language, the King asserted his message through a symbolically filled bowl of milk: Gujarat's capacity was full to the brim, there was no room for others. A Zoroastrian priest responded by adding a spoon of sugar to the bowl, sweetening the milk as it dissolved, just as the Parsis would sweeten society without tipping the balance. The King was charmed, offering asylum, but only if the Parsis adopted the local language; their religious freedom granted through assimilation to a foreign mother tongue.

Add as much sugar to this creamy rice pudding as your taste desires and be liberal with the crushed pink praline. Milk seldom spills over when lovingly shared by all, no matter how much sugar you add.

Serves 6

For the pralines
200g caster sugar
dash of natural red food colouring
150g unsalted shelled skin-on almonds
2 teaspoons orange blossom water

For the kheer
150g basmati rice
2 tablespoons ghee
10 green cardamom pods, split
700ml whole milk
300ml double cream
2 teaspoons vanilla bean paste
85g dark brown sugar
1 teaspoon kewra water
3 tablespoons toasted flaked almonds (see page 40)
¼ teaspoon fine sea salt

· First make the pink pralines; you will need a sugar thermometer. Preheat the oven to 140°C fan.
· Gently heat 150g of the sugar with 40ml water in a saucepan. Dissolve the sugar, then increase the temperature to a simmer, swirling occasionally, until it reaches 135°C. Remove from the heat, add the food colouring and almonds, then mix vigorously for 2–3 minutes. As the sugar cools it will start to crystallise around the almonds. Just keep mixing hard right to the bottom of the pan! Carefully remove the sugar-coated almonds from the pan, leaving behind as much of the loose pink sugar as you can.
· Add another 40ml water to the pan of pink sugar, the remaining 50g of caster sugar and the orange blossom water. Bring up to 135°C again, scraping down any sugar stuck to the sides of the pan. Remove from the heat, add more food colouring and then drop in the sugar-coated almonds. Mix vigorously again for 2–3 minutes until the sugar crystallises another pink layer around the almonds. (If you like them really sugary, repeat the process for a third or fouth time.)
· Bake in the preheated oven for 15–20 minutes to dry out and roast the nuts internally, but be careful not to burn them or they will be bitter.
· To make the kheer, rinse the rice under a cold running tap until the water runs clear, then soak in cold water for 1 hour. Drain the rice well, then take 2 tablespoons of it and pound in a mortar and pestle into a coarse rice paste.
· Heat the ghee in a large saucepan along with the bashed cardamom pods, cooking until the pods have turned pale. Next add the drained rice, mix well and cook for 1 minute, coating fully in ghee. Add the milk, cream and vanilla to the pan. Bring to the boil, then reduce the heat to medium-low and simmer for 20–25 minutes, stirring often so it doesn't catch. Finally add the dark brown sugar, kewra water, ground rice paste, flaked almonds and salt. Cook for a final 10–12 minutes until thick and luscious.
· Enjoy hot or cold, topped with a generous sprinkle of the crushed pink pralines.

Chocolate chai pie

Of all the TV cooks I grew up obsessing over, none held my affection quite like the *Two Fat Ladies*. These were loud boisterous women with Punjabi Aunty-Ji bravado, who existed in a real-life musical where anyone could burst into song at any moment. In one episode, Jennifer Paterson spontaneously erupts into a solo rendition of 'Shoofly Pie and Apple Pan Dowdy' by Dinah Shore. I've had the song repeating in my head for the more than 20 years that has passed since I saw that episode.

Out of curiosity, I made a shoofly pie recently and was struck by how the gooey American molasses crumb pie with a flaky crust transported me to Punjab. To me, it tasted just like fresh molten jaggery eaten lava-hot from the back of a wooden spoon out of a wood-fired thali. My rendition of the Pennsylvania Dutch classic adds chai spices and chocolate to the mix, for a touch of masala-fied decadence. A pie worth singing about.

Serves 8

For the pie
1 large sheet (375g) ready-rolled shortcrust pastry
unsalted butter, for the dish
2 tablespoons coarse semolina
335g golden syrup
2 tablespoons black treacle
250g dark chocolate (at least 65 per cent cocoa solids),
  90g of it grated, plus more to serve
2 Earl Grey tea bags
1 egg, plus 1 egg white, lightly beaten together
1 teaspoon bicarbonate of soda
300ml double cream, whipped to soft peaks
1 teaspoon cornflower tea petals, to serve (optional)

For the chocolate crumbs
175g plain flour
75g good-quality cocoa powder
100g dark brown sugar
75g demerara sugar
1 tablespoon Chai Masala (see page 26),
  plus more to serve
¾ teaspoon fine sea salt
1½ teaspoons instant coffee powder
150g unsalted butter, chilled and chopped

- Roll the shortcrust pastry over a well-buttered 22cm deep pie dish, rolling it out a little more thinly first, if needed. Use your hands to mould the pastry into the corner edges, pushing out any air bubbles; it should sit tightly in the dish and hang over the edges to make up for shrinkage. Sprinkle the base with the semolina, gently pressing it into the pastry, then chill in the fridge.
- Next make the chocolate crumbs: in a large mixing bowl, whisk together the flour, cocoa powder, dark brown sugar, demerara sugar, chai masala, salt and coffee powder. Using your hands, rub in the cold butter until you have chocolate crumbs. Leave in the fridge until you're ready to bake the pie.
- Take a large bowl and pour in the golden syrup and black treacle, then sprinkle the grated dark chocolate over the top of the syrups.
- Boil 300ml of water in a saucepan with the Earl Grey tea bags to make a piping-hot strong tea. Remove the bags, then pour the tea over the grated chocolate, mixing well and scraping the syrups from the bottom to fully incorporate into an emulsified mixture. Let it cool for 2 minutes, then add the beaten whole egg and extra egg white. Mix thoroughly, add the bicarbonate of soda and stir one last time.
- Preheat the oven to 215°C fan.
- Remove the pie crust and chocolate crumbs from the fridge, placing the pie dish on a baking sheet. Pour two-thirds of the chocolate crumbs into the pie crust, pressing them down into the pastry. Next pour the pie filling over the crumbs, shaking it a little so it soaks down to the bottom. Let it sit for 1 minute, then sprinkle over the final one-third of the crumbs.
- Place the baking sheet with the pie dish on top of it in the oven, then bake for 10 minutes.
- Reduce the oven temperature to 165°C fan and bake for a further 50 minutes, covering with foil if it's burning on top.
- When ready it will be puffed up like a soufflé with a slight wobble in the middle. Remove from the oven and let it cool to room temperature; it will sink right down as it cools.
- Melt the remaining 160g of dark chocolate, spread it over the cooled pie, then leave to set fully in the fridge for at least 2 hours.
- Generously dollop on whipped cream to fill the dip in the middle, grate over chocolate and sprinkle on chai masala and cornflower petals, if you like.

Cardamom crumble scones
with kewra & cassis

I can recite the 1964 *Mary Poppins* film from start to finish. Something about Julie Andrews as a matronly nomad comforted me: the placeless visitor forever drifting in between worlds, never fully home but never quite away. The scene that enchanted me most was the floating tea party, sparking a lifelong fascination with British afternoon tea, something entirely other to afternoon chai in our house. I'd dream about ornate porcelain stands filled with dainty pastries, jam tarts and crustless cucumber sandwiches, wishing them real each time I turned on the VHS.

The manifesting worked: in my Bristol years, I was commis chef at a tearoom in Clifton Village, where baking scones became my forte; then in my time at Harrods, re-imagining one of the world's most prestigious afternoon teas with the pastry chefs became my actual job. Clotted cream dreams can come true. These cardamom and kewra scones with blackcurrants are what I'd bake if Mary Poppins ever came to visit. Serve with tea or chai, whichever makes you feel most at home.

Makes 10

For the crumble
75g plain flour
seeds from 20 green cardamom pods, crushed
50g caster sugar
½ teaspoon fine sea salt
2 teaspoons kewra water
50g unsalted butter, chilled and chopped

For the scones
325g plain flour, plus more to dust
1 tablespoon baking powder
¼ teaspoon bicarbonate of soda
seeds from 20 green cardamom pods, crushed
75g light brown sugar
1 tablespoon finely grated lemon zest
1 teaspoon fine sea salt
100g unsalted butter, chilled and chopped
75ml double cream
5 tablespoons buttermilk
1 egg, separated
1½ teaspoons vanilla extract
85g frozen blackcurrants, or berries

To serve
6 tablespoons blackcurrant jam
2 tablespoons blackcurrant liqueur
1 teaspoon kewra water
75g clotted cream

· First make the crumble. Whisk the plain flour, cardamom, caster sugar and salt together in a bowl. Add the kewra water and cold butter, rubbing them in using your fingers until you have a rough crumble consistency. Cover and chill in the fridge.
· For the scones, in a large mixing bowl, whisk together the plain flour, baking powder, bicarbonate of soda, cardamom, light brown sugar, lemon zest and salt. Next add the cold cubed butter, rubbing with your fingertips to work the butter completely into the mix. You want a consistent fine crumb texture. Cover and chill in the fridge for 30 minutes.
· Whisk the cream, 4 tablespoons of the buttermilk, the egg white and vanilla together in a small jug. Take the scone mix out of the fridge, then slowly trickle in the wet ingredients, stirring until the liquid is absorbed. Use your hands to bring together loosely into a plump dough. Empty out on to a lightly floured surface and knead for 1–2 minutes until smooth on the outside; you want to develop the gluten a little, to the point where it just begins to spring back. Tightly compact the dough into a ball, squeezing out any air, then roll into a circle 3cm thick. Cover with cling film and refrigerate for 30 minutes.
· Remove the cold dough from the fridge and roll out a little wider. Next, lightly press the frozen blackcurrants or berries into the surface, then gently fold and knead from the outside in until the fruit is speckled throughout. The berries will burst a little as you do this, bleeding into the dough. Compact into a tight ball again to push out any air, then roll into a circle 3cm thick that is completely flat on top.
· Dip a 5cm round biscuit cutter into flour, then press slowly-but-firmly straight down to punch out each scone, pulling the cutter straight back up each time; don't twist it or the scones will be wonky! Flip each scone upside down on to a baking tray so the sharp bottom edge is on top, then chill for 1 hour.
· Preheat the oven to 190°C fan and remove the chilled scones from the fridge.
· Make a glaze by whisking the egg yolk with the remaining 1 tablespoon of buttermilk, brush the scones on top with glaze, then sprinkle over a generous layer of cardamom crumble.
· Bake in the middle of the oven for 15–16 minutes until golden on top and cooked through. Transfer to a wire rack to cool completely.
· To serve, mix the jam with the liqueur and kewra water, then dollop on to the warm split scones, topping them with clotted cream. Alternatively, you can go clotted cream first and then jam if you're that way inclined, just be generous with both.

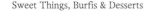

Acknowledgements

With loving thanks...

· To **Michelle Kane** my Publishing Director at 4th Estate for believing in this book from the very beginning, for backing the vision so resolutely, for never compromising with *almost there*, for encouraging me that *shy bairns get nowt* at every step, and for your brilliant friendship along the way. I love you very dearly.

· To **Mia Colleran** for your impeccable coordination, seamless organisation, and patient calm in pulling every strand of this book together – it couldn't have happened without you – and thanks also to the rest of **the team at 4th Estate**. It's been a special privilege to be commissioned by such a distinguished publisher and supported by such an exceptional team.

· To **Lucy Bannell** my Editor for your meticulous work sharpening, refining and illuminating the words that grace these pages. I loved every moment of working in partnership with you – especially over pots of tea in Soho – and learnt so much from your generous wisdom.

· To **Jax Walker** whose photography is beyond what I'd ever imagined it could be. Your creative talent, exacting eye and mastery with a camera have captured the spirit of this book with such brilliance. I can't imagine having done this with anyone else. Those weeks you, me and Lucy had together in our creative Brixton-bubble will always be a very special memory for me. Thank you eternally.

· To **Lucy McCormick** who I have so much to thank for that I don't know where to begin! Planning the shoots, management of all our diaries, prop sourcing, food styling, cheffing, heavy lifting, ingredient sourcing and production management of every kind were completely invaluable. Thank you for your joyful energy at every moment. And of course to **Brioche** for bringing you and Jax into my world.

· To **Evi O** and **all at Evi O Studio** for bringing the creative design to life with such artistic genius, imaginative flair and panache! This festival of paisley brings me so much joy on every single page – I love it so much. Thank you for making the vision shine so brightly.

· To all at the **Jane Grigson Trust** for their support and backing, without which this book would not be what it has become.

· To **Ravneet Gill, Anna Jones, Chetna Makan, Cynthia Shanmugalingam** and **Emily Sweet** who all offered me fantastic advice along the way. And to all the **food writers who endorsed my proposal** back when this was all just a hazy idea and title in my head.

· To **Lulu Grimes, Christine Hayes, Janine Ratcliffe** and the rest of the team at *olive* magazine for giving me such a wonderful platform to share my culinary passions with the world. It makes me smile uncontrollably to see my words and recipes in print every single month.

· To **Richard** and **Sue Mason** for their immense generosity with the apartment in Nice where much of this book was written. And of course, to **Oli Mason** – my chilled crémant-, smoked almond- and praline chocolate bar-sharing balcony muse.

· To **April Preston** for your unwavering support professionally and raucously loving friendship personally.

· To **Jenny Lau** for our enlightening lockdown walks that helped form the narrative of this book more than you'll ever realise.

· To **my dearest friends** and **cousins** who've endured my only chat being book-related for the last two years: Babaajj, Sis, Val, Sam, Ben, Sarah Penji, Louie Penji, Ravenswood (Willcocks, Dudley, Tom, Frank), Cerence, Ailana, Emily S, Olly, Fourelly, Stuey, Joel, Mark, Eddy, Phil K, Blackers, Frog, Roy and everyone I've forgotten.

· To **Ali Mitchell** because I drunkenly promised I'd mention her in the book whilst dancing to Donna Summer at The Glory... and I never go back on my word.

· To **all my neighbours** and **local home-cooking experts** that tested recipes along the way – sometimes multiple times and often with methods that didn't make literal or logistical sense. Especially to **Barbara** and **Ernie** for tolerating the pots and pans that crash around my studio apartment from five am on a daily basis.

· To everyone I've had the pleasure of working with over the last twenty-plus years at **innocent drinks, Harrods** and **Marks & Spencer.** My culinary education has been strengthened by your collective passion for food, enlightening knowledge, and wine-fuelled conversations.

· To the **first generation shop owners and staff** of the diasporic stores around Brick Lane, Broadway Market, Drummond Street, Tooting Broadway, Southall and Bethnal Green for everything they do. It's your produce that shines in the photographs on these pages.

· To **Sunny, Jasmin, Kully** and **Shreya** for standing by me always. And to **Nayan, Anaiya, Reeva** and our soon-to-arrive **Miss Loyal** – this book is for you to add the chords of your own remarkable lives to. Do it loudly, I can't wait to have a taste.

· To **Dad.** I am the luckiest son in the world to be cherished and loved like no other person in the world ever could be by a father.

· And to **Mum.**
ਮੈਂ ਤੁਹਾਨੂੰ ਲਿਖ ਕੇ ਦਸ ਨਹੀਂ ਸਕਦਾ, ਤੁਹਾਨੂੰ ਕਿੰਨਾ ਪਿਆਰ ਕਰਦਾ ਹਾਂ

Inspirational reading, viewing & listening

Books
- *Curried Cultures: Globalization, Food and South Asia*, edited by Krishnendu Ray and Tulasi Srinivas (University of California Press)
- *Curry: Eating, Reading and Race*, by Naben Ruthnum (Coach House Books)
- *Curry: A Tale of Cooks and Conquerors*, by Lizzie Collingham (Vintage)
- *Curry – The Story of the Nation's Favourite Dish*, by Shrabani Basu (Sutton Publishing)
- *Rambutan*, by Cynthia Shanmugalingam (Bloomsbury)
- *The Migrant's Table*, by Krishnendu Ray (Temple University Press)
- *Fusion*, by Peter Gordon (Jacqui Small)
- *Masala Lab: The Science of Indian Cooking*, by Krish Ashok (Penguin)
- *Sameen Rushdie's Indian Cooking*, by Sameen Rushdie (Picador)
- *You and I Eat The Same*, edited by Chris Ying (Artisan)
- *The Lies That Bind*, by Kwame Anthony Appiah (Profile Books)
- *Authenticity In The Kitchen – Proceedings of the Oxford Symposium on Food and Cookery 2005*, edited by Richard Hoskings (Prospect Books)
- *Identity and the Second Generation*, edited by Faith G Nibbs and Caroline B Brettell (Vanderbilt University Press)
- *The Settler's Cookbook*, by Yasmin Alibhai-Brown (Granta Books)
- *Brit(ish)*, by Afua Hirsch (Vintage)
- *The Good Immigrant*, edited by Nikesh Shukla (Unbound)
- *Empireland*, by Sathnam Sanghera (Penguin)
- *Making Ethnic Choices: California's Punjabi Mexican Americans*, by Karen Isaksen Leonard (Temple University Press)
- *Fabulosa!: The Story of Polari, Britain's Secret Gay Language*, by Paul Baker (Reaktion Books)
- *The Anarchy: The Relentless Rise of the East India Company*, by William Dalrymple (Bloomsbury)

Online Articles
- Four Pounds Flour http://www.fourpoundsflour.com/eight-flavors-punjabi-mexican-cuisine-and-the-roti-quesadilla/
- Eater https://www.eater.com/2019/4/23/18305011/punjabi-mexican-migration-roti-quesadilla-el-ranchero
- Quartz India https://qz.com/india/994082/the-ancient-indian-aphrodisiacs-from-the-kamasutra-lurking-in-your-cupboard/
- Literary Hub https://lithub.com/when-my-authentic-is-your-exotic/
- LA Times https://www.latimes.com/entertainment/movies/la-et-mn-freddie-mercury-race-religion-name-change-20181102-story.html
- Mic https://www.mic.com/impact/i-am-asian-american-no-hyphen-required-81037228

YouTube
- *Punjabi Mexicans of California Roots in the Sand* https://www.youtube.com/watch?v=236AWbnDtBc

Radio
- Radio: 'In Our Time', BBC Radio 4: *The Kama Sutra* https://www.bbc.co.uk/programmes/b01bb9c9

Twitter
- Twitter: tweet by Dr Amber Spry: https://twitter.com/amber_spry/status/1285229622091751424?s=20&t=7tsuJ---En53udrTDGSM

Podcasts
- Sikh Archives *Karen Leonard Podcast* https://podtail.com/en/podcast/sikharchive/punjabi-mexicans-with-professor-karen-leonard/
- Gastropod *The Curry Chronicles* https://gastropod.com/the-curry-chronicles/
- The Seasoned Migrant *Curry: The Social History of a Globalized Dish* https://podcasts.apple.com/us/podcast/curry-the-social-history-of-a-globalized-dish/id1511532006?i=1000487875401
- The Seen and the Unseen *episode 95: The Indianness of Indian Food*, hosted by Amit Varma https://seenunseen.in/episodes/2018/11/19/episode-95-the-indianness-of-indian-food/

Index